PSCC
0 2079

MW01292745

DEEP THINGS OUT OF DARKNESS

John G. T. Anderson

DEEP THINGS OUT OF DARKNESS

A History of Natural History

University of California Press
Berkeley Los Angeles London

University of California Press, one of the most distinguished university presses in the United States, enriches lives around the world by advancing scholarship in the humanities, social sciences, and natural sciences. Its activities are supported by the UC Press Foundation and by philanthropic contributions from individuals and institutions. For more information, visit www.ucpress.edu.

University of California Press
Berkeley and Los Angeles, California

University of California Press, Ltd.
London, England

Library of Congress Cataloging-in-Publication Data
Anderson, John G. T., 1957–
Deep things out of darkness : a history of natural history / John G. T. Anderson.
p. cm.
Includes bibliographical references and index.
ISBN 978-0-520-27376-4 (cloth : alk. paper)
1. Natural history—History. 2. Naturalists—History. I. Title.
QH15.A72 2012 2013
508—dc23 2012017404

Manufactured in the United States of America
21 20 19 18 17 16 15 14 13
10 9 8 7 6 5 4 3 2 1

The paper used in this publication meets the minimum requirements of ANSI/NISO Z39.48–1992 (R 2002) *(Permanence of Paper)*.

Cover image: Elephant and dragon from the *Aberdeen Bestiary*.
Cover design: Glynnis Koike.

For Karen, Clare, and David
For things that grow . . .

He discovereth deep things out of darkness.

JOB 12:22

CONTENTS

ILLUSTRATIONS

FIGURES

MAPS

PREFACE

We are all born natural historians. What happens next is up to chance, environment, and the circumstances of our particular narrative. I was lucky enough to be born of two serious amateur naturalists. My mother had been a lab scientist "before children" and my father was a classical archaeologist, but both had a deep and abiding passion for wild things, wild places, and careful observation of their surroundings. I grew up in the California of the 1960s and 1970s, when it was still assumed that children could and should spend as much time on their own outdoors as possible. I was a Scout in the last generation for whom camping skills were considered fundamental. Every summer of my teens, I spent up to a month in the Sierra, hiking, camping, swimming in cold lakes, and drinking unfiltered water from snow-fed streams.

After I had had a couple of summers to establish myself at camp, my father made it a habit to visit for a week every summer to be the resident adult and to offer training for the nature merit badge. The badge required us to identify a variety of plants and animals and to gain a good overall sense of where things could be found, what they were likely to be doing, and what else could be expected around them. I remember the fun of sneaking up on marmots sunning themselves on a rocky ledge above camp, and the relief of finding a snowplant in the nick of time to complete my list of plants identified. Nature was regarded as a "difficult" merit badge, not one to be taken lightly, especially when Professor Anderson was doing the testing.

Later I attended the University of California. I was *not* a good student. I wish

I could blame it on too many afternoons lying on my back watching vultures tip and rock above the golden hillsides of the Bay Area, or too much time on my knees, watching garter snakes slither across dusty trails, but I am afraid that I was just lazy and self-satisfied, and by the time I woke up and realized that my grades weren't going to get me into medical school, it was too late.

For some reason that I still cannot fathom, the pre-med major at Berkeley then required all students to take either Vertebrate Natural History or Invertebrate Natural History. This was a class that had been founded by Joseph Grinnell, the pioneering ornithologist responsible for setting Berkeley on a par with East Coast institutions in field biology. I went to the bookstore and found my first copy of Joel Welty's *The Life of Birds*. I was lost from the moment I opened the text. The course was team-taught by three remarkable naturalists: Ned Johnson (ornithology), Robert Stebbins (herpetology), and Bill Lidicker (mammalogy). Besides the usual lecture/lab format, the class required half-day weekend field trips to regional parks and wildlife refuges. We were responsible for memorizing a subset of California vertebrates for later examination, and also had to keep field notebooks using the highly formalized Grinnell System (I still remember coming upon two of my erstwhile pre-med friends in the bathroom of the Life Sciences Building busily shaking water on their notes before turning them in. When I asked them what they were up to, they replied that they had rewritten their notes—strictly forbidden under the system—and had then remembered that it had rained heavily on the day of the field trip. The teaching assistants would immediately have cried foul had they received unblemished notes lacking clear evidence of raindrops!).

To my eternal gratitude, Ned Johnson allowed me to both take his ornithology class and to work at the Museum of Vertebrate Zoology as an unpaid, extremely junior assistant to the assistant curator. Both experiences put me into direct contact with the lineage of California natural history, extending back to the museum's founders: Joseph Grinnell and Annie Alexander. I remember the museum as a dim, cavernous place entered through an undistinguished door firmly marked "No Public Displays." It contained endless stacks of containers of study skins, each carefully labeled, and each label traceable to a field notebook similar to those that I had tried to emulate in class. Sometimes the notes were full of detail about locations and behaviors. Others were less informative about natural history, but contained hints about natural historians. All suggested a remarkable world of adventure and understanding that extended far beyond the endless rows of seats in lecture halls.

Best of all was the Grinnell-Miller Library, a small room at one side of the collections, filled with light and housing the very books that Grinnell had worked with, each bearing his personal bookplate with its motto, *Inter folia, Aves:* "There are birds between the leaves." Oddly, I cannot remember any single book in the library, but the *idea* of a library containing books filled with birds caught my attention. The idea stays with me yet.

The next autumn, I managed to slip into Bill Lidicker and Jim Patton's mammalogy course as the only undergraduate, and the die was cast. Besides giving me a lifelong appreciation for taxidermy and fieldwork, Patton made it clear that natural history was, above all, *fun*. Natural historians got to go to interesting places, see beautiful things, meet unusual people, and ask endless questions. Natural history was science at its living, breathing best. I sat in on the museum lunches, listening to professors and graduate students fight it out over questions of ecology and biogeography, and realized that much of what was being presented to me in lectures as "fact" was actually at best a set of preliminary hypotheses, and that it would be our job to challenge, check, and refute these facts if we could.

All of this was enormously exciting. I was still not a very good student, but at least I knew what I wanted to do, which was to somehow join the remarkable company of people whose origins stretched back ever farther the more I looked: Ned Johnson was a student of Alden Miller, Miller was a student of Grinnell, Grinnell read Darwin, Darwin read Humboldt. . . . They went on voyages of discovery, they laughed, they swore, they ate bad food in dreadful conditions, they fought with friends, and they made friends of enemies, and each had a story that became part of a larger story that is history. Over time, I have been lucky enough to do many of the same things, visit some of the same places, and meet some of the people involved in natural history.

Eventually I became a professor. I have students. Some of them are not very good—at least at first. Some are far cleverer than I will ever be. Some require care and patience; others just need an opportunity to get out and shine. I try to find the things that will be useful to all of them; I try to let them learn from my mistakes. All too often these days, I encounter people who, when I ask them what they think or know about history, they reply, "Essentially nothing; only that it is boring." This is both enormously sad and also troubling, for with a loss of history there is also an inevitable loss of connection with one's culture and indeed with much of oneself—we are, after all, the product of a personal history that ties back into more broadly defined ideas of a greater history of places, peoples, and civilizations.

I confess that I have never found history boring. It is *stories*—accounts of real people who did real things that had consequences for themselves and for us. It is hard to imagine truly understanding an event if you had no idea of the context in which the event occurred, and it is much easier to understand why someone did or thought something if you have some idea of the world that she or he took for granted. What makes history so fascinating is that history is *us*. History is gossip. History is savage, tender, inspiring, depressing, funny, and ironic, but never, ever boring. We came out of an infinitely long chain of events and people, and we are also links in a chain that extends toward an infinite future. My hope is that this book will introduce you to some of the people and stories that have helped me make sense of the science that I do and the culture that I do it in. We are going on a journey together; I hope you will find the company enjoyable.

ACKNOWLEDGMENTS

Few books are solo enterprises, and this one certainly is not. I would like to thank Tom Fleischner and the other organizers of the Organized Paper Session on Natural History at the Ecological Society of America meetings in 2009 for inviting me to give the presentation that started this off. Tom and I met across a conference table and have killed many a bottle since in discussing natural history, naturalists, and the species and places we love. I would also like to thank Blake Edgar of UC Press for seeing something in my rather harried presentation that he felt worth following up on. Laura Harger has been everything one could ask for in a copyeditor, saving me endless embarrassment from foolish mistakes, and patiently correcting the grammar that would have been the despair of my teachers. I would also like to express my gratitude to Sarah McDaniel for her encouragement, editing suggestions, and periodic swift kicks in the behind when my whining got past bearing. No teacher is any good at all without great students, and I have been blessed with some of the best. As the most recent iteration of the New Lunar Society, Franklin Jacoby, Kaija Klauder, Hale Morrell, Luka Negoita, and Robin Van Dyke have been more helpful than I can express with proofing early drafts, typing bibliographies, criticizing silly ideas, suggesting good reads, and just by being. Thank you, every one. Robin Owings was a patient consultant on illustrations, as well as serving as cartographer. Kate Shlepr poured cup after cup of chai and shared wonderful insights into books, birds, and nature. I would also like to acknowledge my debt to the Selborne Society and the Linnean Society of London for access to Gilbert

White's sermons and letters, and to Tricia Cantwell-Keene and the staff of the Thorndike Library for endless interlibrary loans. Petronella and David Natrass provided shelter and suggestions while I explored White's Selborne and Darwin's Down. My son David was a wonderful navigator and companion during journeys from the Natural History Museum to the winding lanes of rural Kent and back. Jim Patton, naturalist extraordinaire, was incredibly generous with his time and enthusiasm to a very ignorant would-be ecologist thirty years ago and to a somewhat more seasoned one more recently. Finally, I would like to thank my family for putting up with a grouchy husband and father who would regularly slide off into soliloquies about people long dead and ideas always new. Without magical cups of tea and tolerance, this book would never have happened. Funding for research and writing the book was provided by the W. H. Drury Fund of the College of the Atlantic. Additional support came from the College of the Atlantic Professional Development Fund.

Introduction

Adam's Task, Job's Challenge

This book is neither by nor intended for a professional historian. I am advancing no overarching thesis about the development of science or culture. Instead, I aim to resurrect the people and the stories that set the stage for modern ecological understanding. I am writing, first of all, for the advanced undergraduates and beginning graduate students who have so enriched my own teaching and research experience. Second, but of equal importance, I am writing for the serious amateur naturalist—the sort of person who has played such an important part in the development and recognition of natural history across time, and who may feel a little shut out of the rise of increasingly theoretical and technologically driven brands of science. I hope that both groups may benefit from the book and enjoy some insights into the history of their discipline.

Reading an early draft of this book, some of my students asked me why I had selected biblical themes for the title and introduction. They were concerned that some readers might be turned off by a religious motif, or might form an odd picture of the author and his intent. My choices are deliberate and have very little to do with anything I may or may not believe about any religion. But in evaluating history and historical personages, I think it is important to consider context and background. For better or for worse, for over seventeen hundred years western culture has had a biblical backdrop. Whether you were Frederick von Hohenstaufen, the Holy Roman emperor; Gilbert White, curate of Selborne; or Charles Darwin, discoverer of natural selection, you would have been familiar with biblical stories of creation, order, history, and purpose. Much that was thought and much that was written played out within the framework of this cultural commonality, and a strand of this book deals with how this commonality affected the development of natural history and what has happened as we moved away from it. Religion and science have always been uneasy bedfellows, but both of them are parts of the stories that we live by.

In the second book of Genesis, God brings every beast of the field and every fowl of the air to Adam so that they can be named. Adam names the creation, and that seems to be sufficient as far as both he and God are concerned. By contrast, in chapters 38 to 41 of the Book of Job, God lays out what amounts to an ambitious research program lying at the heart of natural history. As God taunts Job, he points out that Job is supremely ignorant of everything from astronomy to zoology. Job has not "perceived the breadth of the earth" (Job 38:18) and does not know "the time when the wild goats of the rock bring forth" or "mark when the hinds do calve" (Job 39:1), among many other puzzles, and therefore he is in no position to demand explanations from God.

By naming things, humans established a common currency for a social structure that permitted increasingly complex hunting patterns and land use. Naming also provides a framework for a variety of taxonomies that can include comparative details of ecology and behavior. In a metaphorical sense, Adam starts a process that Job's predecessors have built on and his successors will build on. Sadly, as an increasing proportion of humans live in cities, there is real danger that we will lose much of our understanding of undomesticated nature. The loss may be more than one of knowledge—it is much easier to get rid of things that one does not even recognize as being there, and, conversely, it is much harder *not* to care about things that one has spent time in understanding.

Humans evolved in an extremely complex world, both in terms of biological diversity and of experience. Much of the deliberate effort of civilization has been to eliminate or replace this diversity and to make our world a much more predictable and stable place. We invest enormous amounts of energy into ensuring that the temperature we encounter never varies by more than a few degrees in a day; our food intake generally stays within set bounds; our chance of a genuinely hazardous encounter is slim; and our patterns of movement, whether around the block or around the world, fit within orderly and predictable frameworks. There are enormous advantages to this world control, of course, but one has to wonder whether its downside may include even more than the effects of our energy consumption on global climate. If our humanity is a product of selection for life in a diverse world, and we lose that diversity through either ignorance or extinction, might we not expect dire consequences for ourselves? In this context, natural history serves as a basis for the appreciation and conservation of wild things, of wild places, and, ultimately, of ourselves.

In trying to read history, we must keep in mind the similarities and differences that time and culture create in the ways that we understand what we read. I remember a world without the Internet, but my students cannot. I cannot remember a world without the direct-dial telephone, yet when I was young I talked to people who could describe needing to go through an operator. They in turn had known people who could remember the first postage stamp. We all had and have a similar need to communicate with one another, but the methods available in a given era make for profound differences in both the form and the substance of communication, and these differences in turn both affect and are affected by the culture of our time. When Darwin on the *Beagle* wanted to communicate with his teachers in Cambridge, he wrote a letter and left it at a consulate or with a merchant in the next port, hoping that a passing ship might take it back to England. There might be a gap of six months to a year between his writing of the letter and his receipt of an answer. Today, in contrast, I can talk to a student in New Zealand as easily (and sometimes more cheaply) than I can to one a few hours' drive away.

We can *talk* about Darwin and the gaps and lag time in his correspondence, but can we really *understand* what these were like for him? We take certain things so much for granted that we may miss how they have shaped our world. Darwin didn't take a camera with him on the *Beagle*, as there were no cameras to take. Instead he took a painter and a gun, and he shot and stuffed or pickled as many specimens as he could. A nineteenth- or even early-to-mid-twentieth-century vertebrate zoologist was seldom without a gun, but a twenty-first-century zoologist might have never fired one. These differences lead to confusion. A very bright student said to me, speaking of Aldo Leopold, "Well, he sure didn't like nature." I was shocked and asked what she meant. She replied, "He always seemed to be shooting something." The idea that Leopold could have a deep love and respect for a goose, the ecology of geese, and the landscape that held geese at the very instant that he pulled the trigger, and that in fact much of his love and respect had come from learning just when and how to pull that trigger, was utterly foreign to my student. At its best, history is a chain of stories and encounters through which we both gain what we regard as facts and through which we can also get context and emotion. My student talked to me. I had talked to one of Leopold's sons and his daughter, people who had hunted and botanized with him, and knew first-hand as well as anyone could what he had felt about nature. I can tell my students stories of stories, and perhaps someday my students will tell others stories of stories of stories. The chain continues as long as we maintain the links.

Time *matters*, and it is important that we keep this in mind when we go to explain what people see and what they might think about history and the natural world. It is unfortunate that at the same time that members of our culture have rejected history as "boring," there has also been a collapse in our sense of time: everything is either "recent" or "ancient," whether we are talking about Nixon, Charlemagne, or Caesar Augustus. This is a mistake because it tends to undervalue or underappreciate the degree to which cultures and the land can change along any number of axes. Aristotle was born about as long after the social and ecological horrors of the Peloponnesian War as my students were after the horrors of the Vietnam War. In Aristotle's time, the destruction of the olive trees in Attica must have seemed just as horrific as the destruction of the mangroves and jungles of Southeast Asia seem to us, but it really has been a very long time since the Spartans rode out of Decelea, and many other things have impacted the Greek people and their landscape since then.

This book is intended to introduce the reader to some of the ideas, places, and people that have been important in the development of natural history over more than three millennia. I write almost exclusively from the European and Anglo American perspective, not because that is the only sort of natural history available to us, but because, first, I feel that there is a degree of internal logic and cohesion in such an approach, while a much more massive treatment would be required to write from a global viewpoint, and, second, because it is this form of natural history that gave rise to modern ecology.

Each chapter revolves around particular individuals or groups of individuals who made key contributions to the development of natural history as a discipline. This strategy is deliberate, in part because these were genuinely interesting people, and in part because science in general and natural history in particular are both very human pursuits, done by real people with a mixture of backgrounds, motives, and intents, but linked time and again by their joy of discovery.

Until probably as late as the eighteenth century, one can find elements of most, if not all, of the modern sciences being undertaken by people whom one might also consider natural historians. Many of these people were true polymaths—working equally well in what we might now call chemistry, physics, botany, and zoology—and also were deeply concerned with philosophy and theology. The nature of what constituted science was also somewhat in doubt from our perspective.

No modern science department would offer courses in astrology or necromancy with astronomy or anatomy, yet many of the founders of natural history had no trouble combining elements of each in their cosmology. This makes things somewhat confusing and lays me open to charges of playing favorites—why was *this* person included and *that* one left out? I can only plead guilty. I find some people inherently more interesting than others and some stories more informative. I do not pretend that this is a definitive history, but I hope that by the end I will have intrigued and annoyed you enough that you will go out and make your own list of heroes and heroines.

ONE . From Hunter-Gatherers to Kings of Kings

By definition, prehistoric peoples did not leave us a written record of who they were or what they did. We are forced to infer their stories from artifacts, from oral histories, or through comparative studies of more recent humans who seem to have made use of similar technologies and resources in similar environments. There are obvious dangers in all this, particularly when we must base our assumptions on what are often only fragments of a civilization or culture.[1] Some patterns, however, do seem to recur with enough frequency that it may be safe to suggest at least a working hypothesis on the role that aspects of natural history may have played in early human societies.

Many of the questions that God asks in the Book of Job inquire into just the sort of knowledge that would have been useful to nomadic peoples, and these questions may be regarded as an allegory for the loss of contact with the wider and wilder world that seems inevitably to accompany humans' settling down to live in one place. Today, with the luxury of precut, precooked, packaged foods, we feel this loss as primarily one of aesthetics; we can agree with Wordsworth that there is "little we see in Nature that is ours," but personal understanding and experience of nature are no longer a matter of survival, at least in the short run. Hunter-gatherers are very practical people; they have to be. Game and other resources are often highly seasonal in terms of both distribution and abundance, and individuals may be faced with superabundance at one moment and near starvation at the next.[2] Local human population numbers may have varied widely both within and between generations.[3] The traditional view of nonwestern societies as being in balance or harmony with a relatively stable nature has been challenged by more detailed analyses.[4] Survival required the development of detailed knowledge about the habits of game species. In this sense, natural history is very old, and it may well be the oldest of our sciences. People learned to read the environment long before they learned to read the printed page, and clouds and seas and the ways of animals and plants and seasons were not just interesting external phenomena, but essential elements of everyday life.

In a hunter-gatherer society, the success or failure of a particular hunt—and, ultimately, of any given social group—was in part a function of the abilities of local experts to find and in some cases to manage game within the constraints of social taboos and tribal needs. Patterns of growth, reproduction, and movement of prey species affected the development of cultural practices around methods of harvest. There are major advantages to specializing on particular food sources and developing a high degree of knowledge of prey species, but there is also a real risk of overspecialization in a varying environment. Beyond this, if one overharvests prey, the result may be socially or biologically disastrous.

Evidence suggests that the impact of overkill is by no means limited to any one cultural or geographic group. For example, the effect of technologically advanced humans on naïve prey species has been demonstrated repeatedly in Polynesia.[5] When the Maori reached New Zealand, they were confronted with a remarkably diverse avifauna, including some of the world's largest flightless birds, the moas *(Dinornis)*. The Maori had been sea peoples, capable of making long voyages and subsisting off fish and other marine organisms, although their ancestors had certainly also fed on island birds.[6] What they found in New Zealand was a veritable hunter's paradise: flightless birds unused to predation by organized terrestrial mammals. Flannery makes it clear in his discussion of the archaeological evidence that the resulting slaughter was enormously wasteful, with little or no attempt to consume large portions of the birds killed.[7] Within two hundred years, the majority of the moas had been wiped out, and by the time Europeans arrived, the New Zealand avifauna was a shadow of its former self.

Someone who understood the natural history of plants and animals considered suitable for food would be in a powerful position in any society. Although it is dangerous to project the culture of one group onto others not known to us, it seems possible that some variation on the habit of identifying individuals as experts in the ecology, capture, and processing of particular foodstuffs, as seen in recent Washoe, Paiute, and Shoshone cultures, may be a longstanding model.

The "rabbit boss" or "antelope boss" among Great Basin peoples was responsible for planning hunts and directing other members of a social group in the capture and preparation of game animals.[8] As such, the boss must have of necessity been highly familiar with life-history elements of his or her particular target species or other taxonomic group.

The boss was a natural historian in the sense that he or she closely studied a particular organism or taxonomic group and was recognized as the local or regional expert on that taxon. There is a distinctly different "feel" to this form of natural history, which we will discuss much later (see chapter 10) in Humboldt's encounter with the "poison master" in Venezuela. The activities of the local expert might differ little (at least in the field) from those of a Victorian natural historian, but the ultimate ends were different. In the case of the local expert, the intent was usually supremely practical in an immediate sense: you ate well or you didn't. The Victorian naturalist might eat well or badly regardless of the outcome of any particular study, but the intent was to satisfy curiosity and/or to gain social status elsewhere.

The exact nature of Paleolithic peoples' foraging behavior—and indeed overall lifestyle—is the subject of endless debate, ranging from the timing and method of human arrival in a particular area to the extent of their impact on particular species.[9] Although it is tempting to rely on theoretical ecological models of costs and benefits to support specialization or generalization, cultural norms and the passage of time inevitably affect what is considered valuable enough to harvest—and hence to study. Gender roles, for example, affected understanding of the landscape and environment,[10] although one should avoid being too glib in applying modern notions of men's work and women's work to societies very different from our own. It has been popular to focus on dramatic ideas of big-game hunting as being the centerpiece of prehistoric lifestyles, but few human cultures are likely to have lived exclusively off the products of large animals. Foraging, processing, and manufacture all required an increasingly intimate knowledge of the environment and set the groundwork for more abstract ideas of natural history that emerged millennia in the future.

As human culture changed from nomadic hunting and gathering to animal husbandry and finally to a sedentary, agrarian way of life, attention shifted from the immediate demands of the hunt to longer-term issues of controlled production and harvest. It seems likely that many hunter-gatherer societies appreciated complex systems of land management that enhanced access to game or the growth of desirable fruits and berries. There is plenty of evidence, from both oral histories and core stratigraphy, of regular cycles of burning in order to produce desired mixtures of trees, shrubs, and open grasslands. Many of the supposedly "natural" landscapes of the Americas and eastern Africa that were reported by early explorers appear, on further examination, to have been the products of sophisticated application of fire as a clearing agent and cultural practices, including patterns of migration, that maximized productivity in available food supplies.

Farming requires a new relationship between humans and the land. The more that one invests in a particular plot of earth, the more reluctant one is likely to be to give it up and move on. If one has taken a great deal of effort to clear a particular region, put up a substantial dwelling place, and select particular types of plants and animals that one wants to encourage (or discourage), a drop in local productivity is likely to be met with innovation, rather than simply migration to a new area. Tillage agriculture called for more immediate attention to particular locations than did a wandering existence, and it also had the potential to smooth out some of the variance that an otherwise uncontrolled environment might impose.

The transition from a nomadic lifestyle to a more sedentary existence seems essential for the development of a more abstract and less applied natural history. The ecological economics of this transition have been discussed by a variety of authors,[11] and it has occurred repeatedly in different times and places. For the purposes of this book, I concentrate for the moment on the history of the Near East: the region between India and Syria that contained the Fertile Crescent.[12] This region in general, and particularly that between the Tigris and Euphrates rivers, has long been regarded as the birthplace of western civilization.

Unlike in the Americas, there was a wealth of small to medium-sized mammals in Eurasia that could be transformed into domestic livestock. Domestication of goats and sheep occurred between nine and ten thousand years ago in the Near East.[13] Breeds of domestic cattle were developed from wild species at roughly the same time.[14] Oxen provided both meat and draft labor as agriculture became more intensive. Horses do not seem to have been incorporated into the domestic landscape until much later—perhaps as recently as 3500 BCE.[15] The first horse cultures developed in what is now Kazakhstan and other areas of Central Asia, rather than farther south, in the Fertile Crescent. Initially horses were used both as milk animals and for riding and drawing sledges. Eventually the advantages of mounted cavalry made the armies of Asia nearly invincible against their opponents to the east and west. It is no surprise that Europeans adopted horses as soon as they became available to them.

The practical natural history of the early hunter-gatherers must have morphed over time into a form of what we would call today agroecology. Successful farmers developed techniques for cultivating particular soil types and had deep knowledge of water requirements, the correct timing of sowing and harvest, and the types of crops that could and could not be grown together. They were also familiar with pests, plant diseases, and other potential sources of loss. Successful farmers, like successful hunter-gatherers before them, passed on useful techniques and abandoned efforts that took too much work or failed to yield a dividend. They might also have been regarded as having an "in" with the gods, or as being just plain lucky, but even today you can find racehorse breeders who shake their heads at too much science and say, "Breed the best to the best and hope for the best." One suspects that similar feelings have been common for as long as there has been organized agriculture and livestock rearing. Such early natural history was still not knowledge sought for knowledge's sake or for a wider understanding of the world, but it provided a basis from which later scholars could work.

The first evidence for an academic natural history comes from the Assyrians, an ancient people who ruled much of the Middle East under various kings until their final defeat by the Medes in the seventh century BCE. At the height of their power, the Assyrians were the masters of the lands from Egypt north into central Turkey and east to the western edge of modern Iran. With a heartland lying in the rich soils of the Fertile Crescent, the Assyrians were ideally placed to develop a complex civilization. They created a network of paved roads linking cities of their empire and facilitating trade throughout the Near East. They brought agriculture and animal husbandry into a recognizably modern condition, and they engaged in studies of astronomy, medicine, and philosophy that had a profound influence on later writers such as Pliny and Aristotle.

Assyrian reliefs illustrate torture, slave labor, and the destruction of opposing cities and armies, but they also show an increasing artistic sensibility and a growing emphasis on the depiction of nature in both a stylized and a more realistic form.[16] Assyrian rulers assembled hunting parks and "paradises" that contained selections of plants and animals from throughout the empire[17] and provided the opportunity for the study of animals in a more or less natural setting, while giving rise to stories of the Hanging Gardens of Babylon—one of the Seven Wonders of the ancient world.

Asurbanipal, who ruled in Nineveh and Babylon from 668 to 626 BCE,[18] might serve as a potential founding father of natural history as we think of it today. Other rulers in the Near East might have established a degree of scientific study of nature, but Asurbanipal provides evidence for a systematic study, drawing on the work of earlier writers in amassing texts for his library, the contents of which are the first surviving example of a broad interest in the structure of the world that goes beyond utilitarian usage.

Asurbanipal was the great-grandson of Sargon, an officer in the Assyrian army who had seized the throne in a coup d'état during the absence of the reigning king. Sargon's son and grandsons had plotted, schemed, and murdered their way through any opposition to both retain their hold on the throne and expand their empire. Asurbanipal proved to be a highly capable military commander, and he also used the rivalries and disorganization of his enemies to extend the frontiers of Assyria into regions never before annexed or explored.

Having smashed all opposition, Asurbanipal returned to Nineveh, where he ruled for another twenty years in what was to prove to be a golden age at the twilight of Assyrian civilization. The King of Kings seems to have been a great collector and also something of an aesthete. His royal palace was much more elaborate than those of his predecessors, decorated with sculptures and friezes. Excavations at Nineveh have revealed detailed relief panels depicting Asurbanipal hunting lions, contemplating his "paradises," and engaging in a variety of kingly and priestly tasks. Notable in many of these illustrations is a careful attention to detail in depictions of plants and animals that suggests that the king and his court might have been sticklers for a realistic interpretation of nature.

While the portraits of royal life alone would have made the finds at Nineveh of great importance, of even more interest was the discovery of a vast library of cuneiform tablets that must have at one point occupied a significant portion of the royal palaces. Piles of broken tablets covered the lowest floor of the palace to more than a foot deep, and their positioning suggests that they must have fallen through from an upper level, rather than simply having been consigned to basement storage. Many of these tablets have been translated, and often proved to be copies of still more ancient texts whose originals are lost to us. Among the treasures of Asurbanipal's library was the *Epic of Gilgamesh*—perhaps the oldest "book" now available—as well as descriptions of a flood that foreshadows the story of Noah in the Bible. Here also we have for the first time evidence of a systematic ordering of natural objects, in the context of trade, commerce, and medicine, including an extensive herbal describing over one hundred medicinal plants.

We have no evidence that the king himself ever engaged in active study of natural history, so my selection of *this* king and *this* moment in history as the starting point of natural history as a form of science rather than subsistence is admittedly arbitrary. Much of what is found in the translated portions of the library relating to plants in particular is utilitarian in that it relates to medical applications. In this sense, there is little difference between what the Assyrians were doing and what medieval monks and abbesses were still doing nearly two millennia later. The library at Nineveh and the images of the royal paradises hint at broader themes: with appropriate patronage, great things could be done; knowledge could be both advanced and stored for future generations; and the written word could provide a continuity and a precision that oral tradition lacked.

Unfortunately, Asurbanipal was not only the greatest king of Assyria; he was also the last great king. After his death, the empire came under increasing attack, and Nineveh itself fell to the combined armies of the Medes and Babylonian rebels around 607 BCE.[19] Enough remained of Asurbanipal's library more than two centuries later that, according to some authors, it inspired Alexander the Great to commission a library of his own—the Great Library of Alexandria—although it seems more likely that that library was the work of Alexander's general Ptolemy and his successors. Ironically, the contents of the older library were preserved because they were written on clay tablets, while the more modern Alexandrian library made use of flammable papyrus and thus was lost.

Even as Assyria went into decline, the city-states of Greece were showing signs of a degree of wealth and stability that would encourage the development of specialized knowledge of astronomy, medicine, botany, zoology, and mathematics. It was not until Greece herself was in decline, however, that we see the first truly encyclopedic description of the world under the direction of the first natural historian to receive that name without any likelihood of controversy: Aristotle.

TWO . A Wonderful Man

Aristotle and Greek Natural History

From his earliest days as a naturalist, Charles Darwin was a voracious reader who always rejoiced in the excitement he found in the works of earlier authors. In a letter written just two months before he died, Darwin said: "I had a high notion of Aristotle's merits, but I had not the most remote notion of what a wonderful man he was. Linnaeus and Cuvier have been my two gods, though in very different ways, but they were mere schoolboys to old Aristotle."[1]

Although much of Darwin's work was firmly lodged in the Aristotelian tradition of careful observation and recording of facts, and he would certainly have been exposed to Aristotle as an historical personage while in school and university, it is obvious from his correspondence that he never read him.[2] This is perhaps not surprising: Aristotle created the framework for modern biology, but by the nineteenth century his work had become so heavily overlaid with later studies that it was easier to skip to the moving present. A generation before Darwin, William Macgillivray, in his *Lives of Eminent Zoologists*, had dismissed Aristotle by saying, "The modern naturalist does not consult his volumes for information, but merely to gratify curiosity."[3]

This tendency has only grown greater over time, and it is a shame. If people think of Aristotle at all these days, they think of him either as a philosopher more or less contemporary with Plato, or as someone who assembled masses of information that served as source material for later scholars. This attitude undervalues Aristotle's central role in the development of a real natural history. Aristotle and his followers represented a major break in ways of thinking that allowed research to proceed. Some of the specific material in Aristotle is wrong, but he is right much of the time—and right on issues about which many later scholars made mistakes.[4]

Aristotle was born in 384 BCE in the city of Stageira, in northeastern Greece.[5] His father served as personal physician to Alexander the Great's grandfather, but Aristotle was orphaned at a young age and sent to live with a guardian. Like Darwin, the young Aristotle does not seem to have shown much early promise. Furthermore, lacking Darwin's advantage of a sensible uncle and stern father, he overindulged himself in wine, women, and song, and managed to spend his inheritance at a young age, and he was reduced to selling medicines in Athens.

In spite of encouraging youthful misbehavior, the move to Athens proved to be of key importance in Aristotle's life. Once he reached the city, he enrolled in the Academy, where he was introduced to ideas of philosophy and rose rapidly to be a star pupil of the then-aging Plato. Either shortly before or just after Plato's death, Aristotle left Athens, perhaps because of disagreements over who should take leadership of the Academy, or because of growing Athenian xenophobia toward anyone associated with the northern "barbarians," a qualification that Aristotle's father's ties to Macedon would fulfill.[6] In any case, in his late thirties he moved to Mysia, in Asia Minor, then under the control of the Persians.

Persia had risen on the ashes of the old Assyrian empire and became a great power after Cyrus the Great captured Babylon in 539 BCE.[7] The Persian Empire expanded steadily for the next fifty years, reunifying most of the former Assyrian possessions, including Egypt and Israel, and conquering what is modern-day Turkey. Athenian meddling in the Persian government of Asia Minor and the islands to the east of mainland Greece led to a full-scale revolt in 498 BCE. After suppressing the rebellion, the Persians set out to subdue Greece, which they regarded as a potential rival and source of troublemaking along their western border.

In spite of their numerical superiority, the Persians were never able to crush the Greeks, enduring humiliating defeats at the battles of Marathon in 490 BCE, Salamis in 480, and finally Platea in 479. Although failing at outright conquest, Persia continued to be actively involved in Greek affairs, playing one Greek city-state off against another. The Persians had a major role in the final stages of the Peloponnesian Wars between Athens and Sparta, providing the Spartan navy with money and arms that allowed the Spartans to win the decisive victory at Aegospotami.

A Greek living in Persian Asia Minor was likely to be tolerated but not trusted. After three years in Mysia, Aristotle found himself in the awkward position of being accused of conspiring against Persia with his sponsor, the governor Hermeias. Hermeias was executed on the orders of the king Artaxerxes, and Aristotle fled to the island of Lesbos, where he married Hermeias's adopted daughter. It was on Lesbos that he and his great friend and most important pupil, Theophrastus, may have begun their research into natural history.

Greek natural history certainly predated Aristotle,[8] with some authors suggesting Thales of Miletus (624–540 BCE) as the real founder of modern scientific ideas. Thales rejected mystical causes for events and things and sought a rational explanation for natural phenomena. It appears that at least some of Aristotle's ideas owed their foundation to Thales, but if Thales conducted anything like the level of research that is attributed to Aristotle, little of it has survived.

After Thales, Greek philosophy concentrated on increasingly abstract issues. Socrates and later Plato turned away from natural history, with Socrates's famous statement in the *Phaedrus* that "fields and trees will not teach me anything, but men in the city do."[9] This left Aristotle to develop his own studies in what had become a neglected arena since the departure of the pre-Socratic philosophers.

Aristotle approached many subjects in a manner remarkably similar to that of today's graduate student: first, look to see what else has been written on the topic. After you have consulted prior authors, consider what the present conception of the topic might be. Once you have satisfied yourself that there is something there worth studying, go out and make careful new observations and see whether what you have come up with fits into previous work or deviates sufficiently to be worth further study or publication.

Much of Aristotle's work was descriptive; he must have done or at least witnessed a great deal of dissection. Sections of *Parts of Animals* read like notes from a careful necropsy. Aristotle himself seems to have concentrated on zoology, while Theophrastus may have been responsible for at least part of the botany that appears under Aristotle's name. Precise authorship is hard to pin down, and many pieces ascribed directly to Aristotle are probably of the "school of Aristotle" or, in modern parlance, "from Aristotle's lab" or "Aristotle's lecture notes" rather than formally authored by the master himself.

Aristotle attempted to identify clear physical traits shared by some organisms but not by others in what was at least a first step toward systematic taxonomy. He succeeded to a degree at the level of genera and species, but did not really manage a more general hierarchy. Some of his choices seem arbitrary (for instance, his division of animals into those with or without red blood), but in spite of these quibbles, the sheer breadth of his investigations is remarkable. One can dip into the *History of Animals* at almost any point and find a gem worth consideration and follow-up.

Aristotle also addresses issues of what we would now call ecology or animal behavior. Throughout his writing, he mixes his own observations with what he has been told or had read. He also provides his readers with caution as to methodologies and observations. For instance, in Book IX of the *History of Animals,* he points out, "Of the animals that are comparatively obscure and short-lived the characters are not so obvious to our perception as are those of animals that are longer-lived."[10] This is just as true now as it was then. Later in the same book, he describes what we might now refer to as "trophic cascades," although to him they take the form of animals "making war" on each other. Again, some of this comes from direct observation and some is hearsay, as when he says of the oriole: "The story goes that he was originally born out of a funeral pyre."[11] Fanciful? Certainly. But at the same time, note the care Aristotle takes in stating "the story goes," and also the "originally born" that allows for a nonmythical contemporary hatching. Like Darwin, Aristotle consulted with practical people—beekeepers, sponge divers, fishermen, and the like—to get the benefit of their lifetime exposure to a subject.

Aristotle's developing philosophy was a refreshing break from the purely practical agroecology of earlier periods and the theistic explanations that had dominated much of western thought up until his time. If the answer to any "why" question about nature is simply "Because the gods so intended it," there is little room for scientific inquiry. Doubtless mindful of Socrates's fate, Aristotle avoids any obvious impiety, but his investigations are couched in such a way that the gods are unnecessary—one can believe in them all one wants, but Aristotelian science is conducted on lines of evidence rather than belief, and with this break, real research could begin. In quasiexile on Lesbos, Aristotle had the leisure to observe plants and animals; he would soon have the patronage he needed to expand his studies.

Macedon was regarded by the Greeks as little more than a barbarian kingdom during the Golden Age of Athenian ascendency, but the Macedonians were ambitious and effective warriors and resented being snubbed by Greece. Alexander the Great's father, Philip II, dreamed of uniting all the Greek states into a common empire that could compete directly with Persia, and he wanted to make sure that his son would have all the advantages of a good education. There could be no question of the heir to the throne being sent abroad to study, so suitable tutors had to be found and brought to the court.

From Lesbos, Aristotle was summoned to Macedon to teach the young

Alexander. This invitation carried with it both a tremendous opportunity and grave risks. The Macedonian royal family was clearly the rising star in Greek politics, and the opportunity to mentor the probable future ruler of the Greek world would have been enormously tempting. At the same time, Macedonian mastery was by no means certain. Going to Macedon was a clear statement to more conventional Greeks that Aristotle's loyalties were no longer with the old establishment, and if Macedon were to lose its struggle with either Greece on the one hand or Persia on the other, a philosopher who had been instrumental in instructing the heir of the losing side would be in an extremely difficult position.

Aristotle made the journey north in 343 BCE, perhaps accompanied by Theophrastus, and served as Alexander's tutor for the next four years.[12] Philip seems to have been sufficiently satisfied with Aristotle that he not only supplied the philosopher with money for further research, but also paid for the rebuilding of Aristotle's home city of Stageira, which the Macedonians had destroyed earlier in the war. Alexander eventually joined the army in the field and was at the battle of Chaeronea in 338 BCE, where his father defeated the combined forces of Thebes and Athens, leaving Macedon the unquestioned master of Greece. Two years later, Philip was murdered by a member of his own bodyguard just as he was about to begin an invasion of Persia.

In spite of some suggestion that he had had a hand in his father's murder, Alexander succeeded to the throne and continued the planned attack on Persia. Aristotle seems to have remained in Macedon throughout this period. Macgillivray believes it possible that Aristotle accompanied his erstwhile pupil as far as Egypt before returning to Athens in about 334 BCE.[13] While this is not clearly documented, it would have been tempting to any natural historian to have the opportunity to accompany one's wealthy patron on a journey through the Middle East. Military campaigns are hard work, however, and have their obvious dangers, and it would also not be surprising if Aristotle decided that discretion might be the better part of valor and retired early, first to the court in Macedon, and eventually to Athens, where his own schooling had matured.

We will never know the full extent of Aristotle's own journeys, but it is clear from some of the species of plants and animals that appear in his writings that he had the advantage of Alexander's eastern exploits in providing new specimens for study. Alexander's conquest of the East also granted access to ancient texts previously unavailable to the Greeks and also scholars who were familiar with entirely new realms of study. Aristotle and Alexander appear to have remained in contact as Alexander moved from triumph to triumph in his conquest of the Persian

Empire, but eventually they fell out, perhaps over Alexander's increasing adoption of Persian customs.

Aristotle's return to Athens was a success. The Athenians were grateful to the Macedonians for having spared them after the debacle of Chaeronea, and Aristotle's fame had preceded him. He established a school of his own in the Lyceum, and spent the next twelve years teaching and writing. His technique of teaching consisted of walking with his students through the city and surrounding countryside while he lectured them on philosophy or natural history. As a result of this teaching style, Aristotle's students were referred to as the Peripatetics, or Walkers, a name that has become synonymous with an entire school of philosophy. These Walkers would have provided a useful group of assistants as Aristotle continued to categorize both the physical and the intellectual world.

On a philosophical level, Aristotle proposed a "natural teleology" in which things happen for a reason that goes beyond mere accident of circumstance or will of the gods.[14] The goal of the philosopher (and hence of the natural historian) is to both describe conditions, objects, or organisms as carefully as possible and then to determine what causes them to be or do as they are observed being and doing. In determining why things happen, Aristotle proposed four forms of causation: material, formal, efficient, and final.[15] He suggested that the role of the scientist is in part to answer questions that come out of each of these causes. This structure is clearly at the heart of Niko Tinbergen's famous "Four Whys" for explaining the reason for behavior.[16] Neither Aristotle nor Tinbergen give absolute primacy to any one level; they leave that up to the original observer. Instead, they suggest that much useful work can be done at any of these levels, and they also believe that any solution approaching an "ultimate" answer would benefit from addressing as many levels as possible at any one time.[17]

Aristotle's natural teleology does not fully escape theistic interpretation. In insisting on an ultimate, final cause for things—the unmoved Mover that sets all things into motion and hence into being—he is performing something of a sleight of hand. One can imagine students at the Lyceum going away and wondering just how much the Mover differed from the gods. In spite of this, Aristotle's emphasis on direct study of what can be perceived with human senses made natural history useful in an intellectual sense to a degree that strictly theological explanations did not.

Aristotle doesn't expect the same types of causations or proofs for everything: one can determine a great deal about anatomy from dissection, and one can come up with a particular degree of certainty about the form of the liver after examining many livers, but one is unlikely to get very far with love by dissection. At the same time, both love and livers are worthy subjects for study and are capable of being described and classified.[18]

As well as providing a methodology for future workers, Aristotle assembled an enormous body of fact, written and organized in an accessible form and containing both careful descriptions and proposed function. A significant portion of the latter has proved to be wrong—for instance, although he is correct that birds have an auditory passage but no pinnae,[19] their skin is not "hard" and the lack of pinnae can't be blamed on skin structure—yet his observations are often worth examination.

In spite of his fame, Aristotle also had critics. Diogenes Laertius was not above a degree of gossip when he says that Aristotle had thin legs and a lisping voice and liked fancy clothes and jewelry. Moreover, he tells a story that Aristotle liked to bathe in warm oil "and then sell the oil."[20] Whether this is true is open to question, but Aristotle's relationship with the Athenians was always a mixed one. Many Athenians flocked to the Lyceum, but Laertius has Aristotle saying that the Athenians invented both wheat and laws, but that they made use only of the wheat and neglected the laws. Inevitably Aristotle fell foul of what laws there were, and was charged with impiety for writing a hymn to his friend Hermeias. Unlike Socrates, who stayed in Athens for sentencing, Aristotle retired to Chalcis, where he owned property, and died shortly thereafter.

Aristotle's friend and colleague Theophrastus was born in Eresos on Lesbos in 371 BCE and was originally named Tyrtanium, but Aristotle seems to have given him the nickname of Theophrastus ("godlike speech") for his abilities in argument. Like Aristotle, he attended Plato's Academy, and seems to have left Athens with Aristotle when the latter moved to Macedon.

Theophrastus is best known for his work on botany, to which he applied an Aristotelian methodology in classifying plants as being trees, shrubs, or grasses on the basis of overall height and stem composition.[21] He also engaged in extensive philosophical teaching and writing, much of which has been lost to us. He disagrees with Aristotle on the extent to which one can assign final causes to things and seems more willing to admit to chance, accident, or material necessity than some deeper and more final explanation.[22]

Theophrastus was clearly an important teacher. He took over the Lyceum following Aristotle's departure, building enrollment to over two thousand students. During the thirty-six years of his leadership, the Lyceum continued to develop and elaborate on the ideas and methodology that Aristotle had initiated, using both the extensive library left by the founder and additional work as it became available. Unlike Aristotle, Theophrastus seems to have been genuinely popular, and when he in his turn was accused of impiety, he seems to have gotten off largely because of this public favor.

There is a certain irony in the fact that most modern professors of biology have as their degree a doctorate in philosophy, yet it is a safe bet that few have studied philosophy, and fewer still worry about the specific questions of causation that took up so much of Aristotle's, Theophrastus's, and their students' time. Perhaps this is the trend in much of science: ultimate questions don't really get answered, the culture changes, the people involved die, and what constitutes an important question shifts. I think (and hope) that most of my colleagues would invoke evolution by natural selection as their final cause for many aspects of biology, and some of us would perhaps be freer with allowing for chance and accident than Aristotle or Theophrastus, but we can celebrate Aristotle's gift of methodology and honor him for an enormous amount of study that produced an initial view of the world that, however imperfect, has gone on developing down all the long years since his death.

THREE . The Spoils of an Empire

Alexander died in 323 BCE—a year before Aristotle's death—and his empire immediately came apart at the seams. In the absence of any adult biological heir (Alexander's sons were infants and easily disposed of), his generals carved things up into separate domains. Ptolemy (367–283 BCE), perhaps the most sensible of Alexander's successors, centered his dynastic kingdom at Alexandria, Egypt, protected on three sides by desert and on the fourth by the Mediterranean Sea.

Ptolemy was of the right age to have been in court when Aristotle was in Macedon. Whether he was actually part of the group of young men who were tutored with Alexander will never be known, but he clearly developed a taste for scholarship.[1] As soon as his kingdom was established, he began to develop in Alexandria a center of scientific and philosophical studies: the Mouseion or Museum, dedicated to the Muses. The first director of this establishment was Demetrios of Phaleron, who had been a student of Aristotle and Theophrastus in Athens.[2] Peripatetic philosophy thus got a new home across the Mediterranean at just the moment when Athens was sinking into decline, and the Middle East became a storehouse for the assembled knowledge of both Greece and Alexander's wider dominions. Demetrios almost certainly modeled the new institution after the Lyceum, including spaces for study and teaching and a library, which Ptolemy's heirs determined would be the greatest collection of knowledge in the world.

The Ptolemys seem to have raised book collecting to an art or passion that exceeded any previous efforts. In a time when all written work had to be copied painstakingly by hand, they preferred originals to copies. They often seized new books that entered their dominions, returning only a copy to the original owner. At one point the library contained half a million texts, possibly split among several sites within the city. There is clear evidence of structured bibliographic organization, close attention to originals, and curation, as well as facilities for copying, editing, and amending documents.

While the museum did not produce natural historians on the order of Aristotle or Theophrastus, it provided an academic environment for Euclid, within which he worked out the fundamental laws of geometry. Beyond any single accomplishment, however, the emphasis on teaching and scholarship within the museum and library ensured that Peripatetic philosophy would be carried forward to subsequent generations. It is almost certainly due to the work of the library and museum that many of the earliest works of natural history and philosophy, as well as literature and history, were preserved. It was fortunate that such a center of learning, supported by such consistent patrons, existed as the Greek world went into permanent eclipse and Rome asserted its dominion over regions that even Alexander had not imagined.

Rome had begun as little more than a hill town among many hill towns in central Italy, but under a succession of kings it had established itself as a significant force in the peninsula before converting to a republic in approximately 509 BCE. A combination of growing economic and military power allowed the Romans to expand north and south, taking over other Italian cities, incorporating other tribes into a common political and cultural unit, and eventually spilling over the Alps into Gaul (modern France). Julius Caesar made a somewhat half-hearted attempt to invade Britain in 54 BCE, but it was left to Claudius, nearly a hundred years later, to actually subdue the province and incorporate it into the imperial domain. Interestingly, Claudius's triumph was in no small part due to his use of elephants and camels against the British cavalry. Claudius was something of a scholar, and we can assume that he was familiar with the distribution and behaviors of large animals within the empire. Romans riding exotic creatures into battle must have been a huge shock to people largely confined to a small island. The British horses were terrified by the sight and smell of strange beasts, and they fled in disorder during the decisive engagement.

The Romans had been in increasing contact with Greek civilization for some time. Greece had established significant colonies in southern Italy and Sicily when Rome was barely getting started. These city-states had gradually been absorbed into the Roman sphere of influence with sometimes tragic results, such as when

Archimedes, arguably the greatest scientist of his era, was killed by a Roman legionnaire during the sack of Syracuse, supposedly when the great man asked the soldier to step out of his light as he worked on a geometric problem.

Much of what we call Roman civilization was actually a series of borrowings from and adaptions to the many cultures conquered by Rome, including that of Hellenistic Greece. Rome defeated Macedon and then the rest of Greece in a series of wars between 200 and 146 BCE that ended in the destruction of Corinth. Roman attitudes toward the Greeks and Greek philosophy were distinctly mixed, with Roman republicans such as Cato regarding the Greeks as degenerate and a negative influence on the development of a true Roman civilization, while others adopted Greek culture with enthusiasm.[3]

Ptolemaic Egypt maintained its independence a bit longer than Greece itself, although the library was partially destroyed by some of Julius Caesar's troops in 47 BCE.[4] This does not appear to have been a deliberate act of arson, or an attempt to suppress the contents or ideas of the Mouseion. Rather, the fire seems to have started in the nearby dockyards, either as the result of a riot or during the response to local resistance to the Roman presence in still nominally independent Egypt.

The expanse of the Roman Empire at its peak—spanning from the Scottish coast across France, southern Europe, and well into Asia Minor—meant that Roman philosophers had access to an enormous range of habitats, cultures, and subjects for study. The trade networks that fed the empire provided access to even greater spheres of interest that would have included South Asia and parts of the Baltic.

Rome's control of the Mediterranean basin ensured that scholars would have the potential to become familiar with over five hundred years of prior natural history research. While this was in one sense an advantage, it was also probably somewhat daunting—it would be easy to believe that the ancients had already worked out everything worthy of study. Although Rome produced some important pieces of literature, there is a feeling of borrowing and a reliance on previous authority, rather than the development of entirely new ways of looking at things. Rome still looked to Greece and the East for both medicine and philosophy, but she also produced some natural historians of her own, the greatest of whom was undoubtedly Pliny the Elder (Gaius Plinius Secundus).

Pliny was born in 23 CE, possibly in Verona or (more likely) Como in northern Italy.[5] He served in the Roman army as a young man, and rose quickly through the ranks before taking up the law and then engaging in further government service. Macgillivray cites Pliny's nephew (Pliny the Younger) for details about his life and work habits. Pliny was apparently something of an insomniac, using much of each evening for philosophy or writing and conducting his government business during the day. Macgillivray gives us a delightful portrait of the great man: "In summer, when he happened to have any leisure, he often lay in the sunshine, having a book read to him from which he carefully took notes. It was a saying of his, that no treatise was so meagre but that some part of it might afford instruction."[6]

Pliny was a compulsive reader, insisting on being carried in a sedan chair around Rome if he had to travel so that he would not lose any time that could be applied to studying. He traveled throughout the empire, both as a soldier and later on imperial business. He lived through the reign of the emperor Nero but was, perhaps fortunately, not a member of the court. Once Nero had been assassinated, Pliny came into prominence as a personal secretary or assistant to the emperor Vespasian, another insomniac, to whom Pliny the Younger says he reported to daily "before sunrise."[7]

Pliny's odd working hours gave him a great deal of time to indulge in his passion for collecting books and stories about the natural world. He was trained as a Stoic, and believed that one could obtain guidance on right behavior from the observation of natural order. Unlike Aristotle or Theophrastus, Pliny does not seem to have been much of a direct observer or experimenter. When one reads parts of Aristotle, one feels almost as if one is present during the dissection of a particular specimen. By contrast, Pliny's works show clear signs of a removed scholarship.

As a favorite of the new emperor, Pliny would have had access to whatever accounts existed of plants and animals within the reach of Rome. Although he had been in North Africa on army duty, there is no record of him traveling to Alexandria to consult the library, but undoubtedly copies of many texts would have been available in Rome, and the capital city was also a magnet for traveling philosophers wishing to share tales of distant regions and strange sightings. During the last years of his life, Pliny focused on assembling as much of this material as he could into a massive text, the *Naturalis Historia* (Natural History), which is the only major piece of his work still available to us.

The *Naturalis Historia* is an encyclopedic work covering all aspects of the sciences, and it is an odd mixture of truth, legend, hearsay, and gossip, organized in a somewhat arbitrary fashion, yet containing most of what was known—or thought to be known—by Pliny's contemporaries.[8] The thirty-seven books of the *Historia* were probably actually assembled between 77 and 79 CE, but they drew on years of reading and summarizing original works that are now largely lost to us. Pliny dedicated the work to Titus, the son of his patron Vespasian, and his book seems to have been well received and widely distributed.

Because Pliny did not do much personal observation, he had no way to check his sources except by comparing one text against another, and he often made mistakes or included statements that even the most preliminary examination would have revealed as false. His list of animals contains both real creatures and mythical beasts such as the phoenix. He did not attempt to develop his own philosophy or to set out much in the way of explanatory theorizing, and some authors complain that there is little science per se in his writing. But even his critics admit that he has a spare and simple style that can become animated when he addresses particular subjects.

Ironically, it seems that Pliny's one recorded attempt to see a major natural phenomenon in person led to his death. At the age of seventy, he was appointed commander of Roman naval forces stationed in Misenum, and was on station when Mount Vesuvius erupted, burying the cities of Pompeii and Herculaneum. Pliny ordered the fleet to stand in to shore and rescue survivors, and he set off in a small sailing ship to examine the situation first-hand. When his companions became afraid, he is reported to have said, "Fortune favors the brave, steer for the villa of Pomponianus."[9] After landing, he and his party were ashore for some time, eating and drinking and comforting refugees. Suddenly Pliny sat down, complained of a paralysis, and seems to have died on the spot. Although some histories suggest that he was overcome by poisonous gas from the volcano, it seems much more likely that he had a heart attack. All his friends and relatives on shore were rescued, and his body, partially covered in pumice, was recovered three days later.

Pliny saw himself as a compiler and organizer of what already existed, and his work was sufficiently comprehensive and his writing sufficiently satisfying that he became the central source whereby knowledge of Graeco-Roman natural history was passed forward through the Dark and Middle Ages. George Sarton sums up Pliny's work quite aptly in saying: "It is at once a sepulcher of ancient science, and a cradle of medieval lore."[10]

Besides Pliny, two other names from the Roman era are worthy of mention in any history of natural history, those of Galen (129–200 CE?)[11] and Dioscorides (40–90 CE).[12] Both Galen and Dioscorides were, strictly speaking, primarily interested in medicine, but the widespread use of different plants in the treatment of different ailments led them to build on the work of Theophrastus, as well as undoubtedly drawing on still older texts that may have extended back to Nineveh.

Dioscorides, like many doctors of the Roman era, was a Greek. He was born in southern Asia Minor and joined the Roman army as a field surgeon before going to Tarsus to study a wider medical curriculum.[13] His book *De Materia Medica* describes about five hundred plants and lists over a thousand treatments for different diseases. Although Dioscorides drew heavily on botanical knowledge, including descriptions of many herbs, his writings are in no way as thorough as those found in later herbals. He remains an important figure in natural history, however, because his writings served as the basis of much of the late medieval and Renaissance work that led in turn to a more systematic botany. His writings seem to have remained in print and in use much longer than those of other classical scholars, and were heavily commented on and amended.[14]

Egerton suggests that Dioscorides's main contribution was an emphasis on precise species identification and compares his work favorably with modern botanical texts. They acknowledge that there are limitations to his classifications, but stress the importance of his work in encouraging later authors to pay attention to geographic distributions of plants.[15] Like many of the other early naturalists, Dioscorides had no real system of classification above the species or type. He was still writing for very practical reasons—you needed to identify a particular plant because of its usefulness in medicine, not because it was related to another plant in any sort of evolutionary or greater hierarchical sense.

Galen was born at Pergamum in Asia Minor. He is reported to have studied medicine in part due to a prophetic dream of his father's. He was fortunate in his birthplace because at one point Pergamum had developed a library that was in competition with that at Alexandria for size and coverage, and his early studies of medicine at Pergamum and later at Smyrna would have benefited from this bounty. He eventually moved to Greece and then to Alexandria, where he became familiar with the museum and library.

After a brief return to Asia Minor, Galen went to Rome, where he remained on and off for the rest of his life, periodically fleeing the city either because of an outbreak of plague or because of jealous infighting among the physicians and philosophers in the capital. Thorndike stresses the degree of competition and dislike shown among professional physicians of the period. He quotes Galen as saying that many of his contemporaries were little more than "a band of robbers as truly as the brigands of the mountains."[16]

Much of the medicine practiced at the time seems to have been an odd mixture of folk treatments, charms, poultices of everything from herbs to various sorts of dung, and a reliance on different translations of ancient works gathered from the four corners of the empire. Galen was probably righteously contemptuous of the many charlatans who were drawn to the capital simply to make money, and he worried that little new thought was being brought to science.

Galen served as physician to emperors, including Marcus Aurelius, but his biographers make him out as something of a killjoy—he frequently complains about other people having fun to the detriment of their studies, and is constantly of the opinion that other physicians are stealing his work for their own profit. He traveled widely within the eastern half of the empire, collecting herbs and minerals for medical uses, and wrote extensive medical treatises, which, like Dioscorides's works, were considered essential medical texts at least until the Renaissance. Although Galen's reputation is based almost exclusively on his contributions to medicine, he also addresses fundamental questions about the nature of science itself. He is concerned with the balance among direct experience, logic, and reliance on primary sources. In discussing aspects of Hippocrates's treatments, he says: "I also think that you [Hippocrates] never travel far from home and have no experience of the differences between places."[17] Galen's somewhat whiney and accusatory tone comes through here quite well, but he goes on to make interesting suggestions about regional variations in responses to treatment. Later in the same text, he encourages physicians to themselves examine not only patients and the particular symptoms presented, but also to try to fit patient and illness into a broader context of environment, occupation, and relationships—good advice even two thousand years later.

Galen died somewhere around the year 200, but his extensive writings and the widespread regard that he had achieved among the Roman aristocracy ensured that his ideas would survive. Eventually copies of his various treatises formed a significant part of the required reading for medieval physicians, and were incorporated into a canon of ancient literature that had a stultifying effect on the development of both science and medicine. If the Ancients such as Galen had done things thus-and-so, who was a medieval physician to challenge the accepted practice?

By 642, the Arabs had taken Alexandria and pushed steadily westward along the North African coast, eventually occupying much of Spain. To the east, repeated thrusts reached the walls of Constantinople, eventually leading the emperors to ask the West for help, which came in the form of the Crusades. The Crusades were ultimately disastrous for the Byzantines. During the Fourth Crusade, the Venetians took time out from fighting the Arabs to sack Constantinople itself and strip the city of many of its most valuable possessions.[18] The empire never really recovered from this defeat, and in 1453 Constantinople was taken by Mehmet the Conqueror and the last eastern emperor died fighting on the city walls.

The exact fate of the library at Alexandria will never be known. Thiem says that all that is certain is that it was burned, whether by Caesar in the first century

CE, by order of Theodosius in the fourth century, by the Arabs in the seventh, or by a combination of some or all of the above.[19] The loss of the library is in part symbolic of a general decline in access to learning that, with the collapse of Rome itself, led to the extinction of anything resembling organized natural history in western Europe for an extended period. Fortunately, many of the Arab conquerors were very interested in scholarship,[20] and translations of many of the classical works of philosophy, medicine, and natural history were made from Greek and Latin into Arabic.[21]

In our age, when copying an entire manuscript is done with a mouse click and we can store libraries on a microchip, it is hard to imagine that books could be lost. It is important, however, to remember that prior to the development of the printing press, every copy of a text had to be written word by word by hand. This process could take weeks or months, and there was a strong probability of errors, omissions, and reinterpretations. Yet the Arab scholars, with access to many original texts in the Middle East, were in a wonderful position to preserve a wealth of classical knowledge. Texts that had originated in Greece or Alexandria were spread across the new Arab empire and into northern Spain. In time, this work would be available for retranslation in an awakening Europe, but that time would have to wait for the right person, with the right attitude and the right resources.

FOUR · An Emperor and His Descendants

It is often popular to view the thousand years between the fall of Rome and the beginning of the Renaissance as a miserable Dark Age, undistinguished by any real advances in the sciences or humanities. Huxley says: "From the end of the Classical period until the beginning of the 15th century, original thought and speculations about Natural History were effectively stifled."[1] Earlier authors were even more brutal. Nicholson gives a brief nod to Pliny and ignores other Roman authors entirely, saying: "With the death of Aristotle, the scientific prosecution of natural history practically came to a close, not for a short time merely, but for a period of many centuries."[2] After this, Nicholson jumps to the sixteenth century. Arber is much more sympathetic to the Middle Ages. She points out in her introduction the importance of the revival in learning characterized by the "rediscovery" of Aristotle in the ninth and thirteenth centuries.[3] Although there is certainly evidence to suggest that medieval scholars, like the Romans before them, mostly borrowed from earlier sources, there were at least *some* cases of originality.

With the decline of Rome, western Europe faced the real likelihood of becoming dominated by the Arabs. By 732 CE, the Arabs were sufficiently confident of their control of Iberia that they crossed the Pyrenees and invaded France. The invasion was initially successful, but as they moved north, loaded with spoils, the invaders encountered stiffening resistance. In what has been described as one of the most significant battles in western history, Charles Martel rallied the Franks and defeated the invaders at Tours, killing the Arab leader Abderrahman and driving his surviving troops back over the mountains.[4]

Charles Martel's grandson was Charlemagne—literally Charles the Great—who ruled first as king of the Franks and later as emperor of the Romans from 768 to 814 CE. Charlemagne was the first western monarch to acquire and hold a truly imperial realm since the fall of Rome, and under his patronage there was a revival in the arts and sciences.[5] Charlemagne encouraged scholarship at his court and was also a patron of monastic schools throughout his dominions. The most significant natural historian of the period was probably Rabanus Maurus (776–856 CE).[6] Rabanus entered a monastery when he was nine, but he showed such promise that he was subsequently sent by his abbot to Tours to study with Alcuin of York, whom Charlemagne had invited to France to personally instruct the emperor.

After finishing his studies with Alcuin, Rabanus was appointed to run the monastic school at Fulda. Soon thereafter, the monastery's abbot renounced teaching and insisted that Rabanus and his fellows employ themselves as manual laborers, building churches. Rabanus complained to the emperor, and the abbot was removed, allowing Rabanus to resume his teaching. Between 842 and 847 CE, he wrote his encyclopedic work *De Universo,* which drew heavily on translations of Pliny by way of Isidore of Seville.

Rabanus devotes a significant amount of his encyclopedia to botany, describing over two hundred species of plants. He wrongly believes that a tree is simply an herb that has grown large, but he discusses the importance of soil types in the growth of plants, identifies lichens as a distinct type of their own, and waxes eloquent on vines. Overall there seems to be little in his work that could not have been found in that of earlier authors, and his writing is filled with the "fables of the ancients" rather than the results of actual experiments, but one is inclined to agree with Hartwich that Rabanus "is one of the solid stones that are sunk one upon the other into the soft ground to be hardly ever seen again by the eyes of men—one of those who in quiet, busy toil have laid the foundation among the people which now bears a mighty structure."[7] He is representative of the European scholars who carried forward the idea of natural history, which might otherwise have fallen by the wayside.

Like Alexander before him, Charlemagne was unable to create an empire that would survive him for long. By 888 CE, the Carolingian Empire had been irreparably broken up, and the last Frankish emperor died in 924 CE, by which time the title of "empire" applied to only a limited part of Italy. In the meantime, the eastern portions of Charlemagne's realm, composed of a number of principalities in what is now Germany, had taken to electing their own leader. This was not done by a popular vote—rather, the princes themselves selected a sort of "first among equals," whose powers and responsibilities were unclear. In 962 CE, Otto was crowned emperor of the Romans and initiated what was eventually called the Holy Roman Empire.

It is enormously difficult to place medieval scientific pursuits into any one tidy category. Many of the people engaged in such studies bridged multiple disciplines and were driven by a broad range of enthusiasms. Nowhere is this more apparent than in the period's definition of natural history itself. Abstract study was often focused on theology or a somewhat more general philosophy, but many philosophers became interested in mathematics, and from there it was but a short step to astronomy and astrology. If there was a single overarching theory of natural history, it was probably the *scala naturae,* or great chain of being, which provided a degree of order and certitude in an otherwise chaotic period.[8] The *scala* was governed by three fundamental principles: plenitude, continuity, and gradation.

Under the principle of plenitude, God had created all *possible* species, including all those already known and all those that could be imagined. Thus there was no incongruity in a world containing both elephants and dragons—if the mind of man could conceive of dragons, how much greater diversity must the mind of God possess? If dragons had not yet been observed in the medieval European world, well, the outer world was wide, and there was plenty of room for them elsewhere. The principle of continuity suggested that there were no "gaps" or separations between species. One group seamlessly blended into the next, and this continuous chain provided a necessary linkage to the mind of God. Finally, the principle of gradation provided justification for the overall ranking of different groups. The inanimate world was at the bottom of the strictly linear hierarchy; it then gave way to simple organisms—mosses and lichens—which then gave way to more complex plants, animals, and the various "grades" of man. Above man one had angels, archangels, and finally God. Although the great chain of being had been largely rejected by the scientific community by the middle of the nineteenth century, it has had interesting intellectual echoes in twentieth-century ecology's ideas of ecological equivalence and niche theory, and in the modern environmental movement, with its beliefs in global interdependence and connectivity.

Hildegard von Bingen (1098–1179 CE) is perhaps best known to us for her musical compositions, but she was also engaged in studies of health and medicine.[9] She wrote an encyclopedic text, the *Physica,* which lists and partially describes nearly a thousand plants and animals, and a specifically medical text, *Causae et Curae,* which presents the application of various treatments to particular ailments. Although von Bingen's combination is not natural history as we have come to know it, she is clearly in the tradition of Aristotle or Pliny while retaining a distinctly Germanic component in the preparation and administration of particular cures.[10]

Hildegard is also worthy of mention in terms of the mixture of spirituality and practicality in her work. She practiced elements of science, yet she saw (and wrote about) visions from an early age. The nature of these visions has been argued over for some time, with modern authorities suggesting that she was a lifelong sufferer of migraine—some of her experiences sound remarkably like the aura that may precede an attack.[11] Hildegard describes migraine—and potential cures—without associating it with her own experiences. Assigning a modern causative explanation to what has been accepted as a religious experience is, arguably, excessively reductionist, but it does highlight the problems faced by the modern reader in interpreting the role of purely *experiential* explanations for events, as compared to those derived from experimentation.[12]

Natural history had been looking for a real hero since the death of Pliny; in 1194 CE, it finally got one. Frederick II of Hohenstaufen, Holy Roman Emperor, king of Sicily and of Jerusalem, was born in that year on the day after Christmas in Jesi, Italy. He was the son of Emperor Henry VI and Constance, queen of Sicily.[13] Although at least one modern source suggests that his mother gave birth to the future emperor in the town square in order to convince the public of his maternity, this is almost certainly a fable. It is true that Constance, at forty, was quite elderly for a delivery, and that her preceding eight years of childless marriage would have given rise to speculation as to the legitimacy of the heir apparent, particularly given the troubled nature of the times. A much more reasonable account of Frederick's birth is given in Busk, who says that "as many as fifteen ecclesiastics of high dignity are said to have in consequence attended."[14] One may wonder why any of this matters, but if Frederick were not actually Constance's son (and throughout his life various "witnesses" were put forth by his enemies to testify that they had sold his infertile "mother" a baby), he could not claim title to either Sicily or the Holy Roman Empire.

The exact nature of the Holy Roman Empire changed repeatedly over its eight-hundred-year existence. Voltaire comments rather snidely that it was "neither Holy, nor Roman, nor an Empire," but he was writing in the final years of the institution, and excessive use of the quote ignores the very real social and political importance that the emperors held periodically over the long course of the medieval and Renaissance periods.[15]

As the question of the legitimacy of his birth reveals, Frederick was born into troubled circumstances, with ambivalent relations to both the Church and most of the aristocracy. His father, Henry, died in 1197, when Frederick was not quite three years old. Constance died a year later, but not before her son had been crowned king of Sicily. The boy seems to have been shuffled around various royal and semi-royal palaces for the next several years and was remarkably lucky not to have been murdered by the many rivals to his titles. Constance was cleverer than any of the claimants to the throne—before her death, she named the pope the official guardian of her son. Pope Innocent III was a shrewd and calculating man who was determined to establish the papacy as the supreme arbiter of things temporal as well as spiritual. Probably believing that he would be able to manipulate his young ward, Pope Innocent fended off rival claims to Sicily and kept alive at least the possibility of Frederick becoming emperor.

The pope seems to have done a remarkably good job in overseeing the upbringing of the young Frederick. The kingdom of Sicily was torn with almost continuous civil war throughout Frederick's childhood, but Pope Innocent found it strategically important to pay for armed forces to act on behalf of the young king. He also arranged for Frederick's schooling, and Kington mentions that some of his tutors were Musselmen—presumably Arab philosophers—who would have had direct access to copies of Aristotle and other classical authors.[16] Frederick had a knack for languages (he was eventually fluent in six) and was trained in history, philosophy, and mathematics.

Frederick's inheritance from his mother was an interesting mixture of peoples and cultures. The island of Sicily, lying as it does in the central Mediterranean, was equally close to Christian Europe, Muslim North Africa, Orthodox Greece, and Catholic Rome.[17] The kingdom of Sicily consisted of both the actual island and also much of what is now southern Italy. After an extended period of rule by the Romans, Germanic invaders, and the Byzantines, insular Sicily had been captured by the Muslim Saracens in the ninth century, but the invaders had never managed to maintain a hold on mainland Italy. By the end of the eleventh century, Norman mercenaries had been brought in to drive out the Muslims and retake the island for the Christian kingdom. A substantial Arabic-speaking population remained, however, and Frederick would have had the opportunity to be exposed to both the culture and the ideas of the East in the form of the empire's remaining Greeks and Arabs.

In 1212, the seventeen-year-old Frederick was encouraged to come to Germany to assert himself as emperor in place of Otho, who had claimed the throne upon the murder of Frederick's uncle Phillip. Pope Innocent somewhat reluctantly decided to support Frederick's claim, although its outcome was very much in doubt. Frederick barely escaped capture by Otho by making a daring crossing of the Alps, after which an increasing number of German princes declared for him. He was proclaimed emperor-elect at the end of the year.

The First Crusade, at the end of the eleventh century, had established the kingdom of Jerusalem, and for the next two hundred years successive crusades attempted either to enlarge Christian control of the Middle East or to win back territory that had been lost in the interim. It was widely regarded as one of the duties of the Holy Roman Emperor to play a major part in this effort. Yet given the enormous cost of going on crusade and the necessity of being away from one's major power base for months or years—not to mention the very real danger of death in fighting or from disease—the possibility of glory on the field of battle or spiritual benefit from the rescue of sacred sites or relics might have seemed unattractive.

In spite of the clear expectation of Pope Honorius—who had succeeded Innocent upon the latter's death—Frederick was, perhaps unsurprisingly, reluctant to leave Germany for a crusade as soon as he had managed to establish a degree of peace, but the failure to obey the pope meant the likelihood of excommunication and further civil war. Frederick put off his ascension to the throne, but finally, in 1220, he traveled to Rome for his formal coronation as emperor of the Romans. As part of this ceremony, he was required to reaffirm his obedience to the pope, who continued to remind him of his sworn oath that at the first opportunity he would lead the armies of Europe to rescue the kingdom of Jerusalem from the Arabs.

Frederick spent the next several years restoring order in the kingdom of Sicily, and outraged many Italians by moving a large number of Muslims to the mainland, where they served as a sort of army reserve for the empire. This was a particularly shrewd strategy, as the Muslims would have had no scruples about making war on the pope should the need arise. On a less belligerent note, Frederick also established the University of Naples in 1224. This was one of the first universities in Europe, and it remains the oldest state university in the world. It was also the first clear sign of the emperor's growing interest in scholarship.

Finally, in the summer of 1227, Frederick set off for the Middle East, bringing with him as many as forty thousand fighting men.[18] After being at sea for three days, the emperor declared himself too sick to continue and put back to Italy. The pope was furious and publicly excommunicated Frederick.

The crusade was relaunched in late June 1228. Unlike his predecessors, Frederick seems to have had both a good understanding of political and cultural nuances in the Arab world and a desire to gain as much as possible by negotiation rather than by ruinous warfare. If he had had the cooperation of the Church, he might well have secured the whole of Palestine with minimal trouble—the Muslim caliphate was in disarray, with its most impressive leaders dead and their heirs either children or at odds with one another.

In some senses, Frederick did very well, negotiating with Sultan Al-Kamil Muhammad for the return of Jerusalem itself and the protection of pilgrims traveling to other holy sites. The sultan and the emperor seem to have become friends without ever meeting, exchanging a variety of presents, such as a large number of interesting wild animals for Frederick, which he included in the traveling menagerie for which he was already famous. There are also accounts of the two monarchs sending each other philosophical and scientific questions and in general behaving as intellectual equals rather than hereditary enemies. While one would think that this bloodless success would have pleased everyone, it was exactly the sort of intercourse with heathens that enraged the Church.

Frederick's return home in June 1229 was greeted enthusiastically by his subjects. The emperor had been on the move almost continuously since he had set off for Germany eighteen years earlier to claim his patrimony. His life had consisted of a series of intrigues, plots, counterplots, civil wars, and uprisings, and he had been lucky to spend as much as a year in any one place. A temporary reconciliation with the pope at last allowed him the breathing space to settle down and devote himself to his passion for scholarship. At some point in this period (different authors vary widely in their accounts), Frederick encountered a remarkable person who was to have a profound impact on both the emperor and the revival of natural history in Europe. This was Michael Scot, the famous mathematician, scholar, astrologer, and perhaps sorcerer.[19]

Scot was born in Britain but seems to have traveled to Paris early in his education. In Paris he specialized in mathematics, and may have taken holy orders. A hundred years later, Dante would depict Scot, "practiced in every slight of magic wile," in the eighth circle of Hell with the other astrologers and fortunetellers,[20] but at the time that Frederick took him into his court, Scot was most famous for his ability with languages and his knowledge of Greek philosophy and science.

Scot's encounter with Greek philosophy probably occurred in Toledo, where the archbishop had encouraged the translation of ancient Greek texts from Arabic into Latin. Scot prepared a series of these translations, adding in some cases his own commentaries on the original, or appending or abbreviating particular texts to suit his purposes. It is noteworthy that he dedicates a number of his books to Frederick, and it seems certain that Frederick himself was keenly interested in reading as much as he could about both the philosophy and the natural history of Aristotle.

We have here a remarkably circuitous journey. The works of an ancient Greek were translated into Syriac and traveled to Alexandria, where they were eventually retranslated into Arabic. They were then transported the length of North Africa and passed across the sea to Spain, where they were translated into Latin by a Scotsman to be read by an Italo-German emperor who wished their contents to be spread throughout his empire. One cannot but believe that Aristotle himself would have been very amused.

Scot probably brought plenty of material to Frederick's court from Toledo, and it is clear that Frederick was delighted to have someone available who could do translations for him and respond to questions about science and philosophy. Besides working on Aristotle, Scot admitted to having some books on demons and magic, and he was extremely interested in astronomy and its "practical" form for the age: astrology. He does not seem to have believed that the stars *cause* events to happen; rather, he felt that the constellations serve as signs whereby the future can be told.[21]

Scot's relationship with the emperor seems to have been a mixture of serious mutual respect and simple fun. Haskins reports one occasion when Scot demonstrated principles of trigonometry to the emperor, using a church tower to calculate "the distance to the starry heavens." After Scot had made his calculations, Frederick secretly had the tower reduced in height and then asked Scot to redo his calculation. Scot did so and reported that the tower had either sunk into the ground or the distance to the heavens had decreased, neither of which was possible. Frederick congratulated him on his accuracy and presumably explained the trick.[22]

Scot predicted his own death, saying that he would be killed by a falling stone. In order to ward off this fate, he made himself a small steel helmet, which he wore everywhere. Unfortunately, in 1232, while in church, he removed his headpiece for Mass, and a stone falling from the roof struck him on the head and killed him exactly as he had predicted. After his death, later scholars such as Roger Bacon accused him of having made poor translations of Aristotle and lacking much originality, but there is a strong feeling of professional jealousy in these charges.

Without a doubt, Frederick's greatest claim as a natural historian is his masterful treatise on ornithology, *De Arti Venandi cum Avibus* (The Art of Hunting with Birds), which he worked on between 1244 and his death in 1250. Frederick had always enjoyed animals, a behavioral trait so well known that Sultan Al-Kamil Muhammad had wisely won his heart by sending him an elephant and other exotic beasts during the crusade. Unlike most other monarchs, Frederick was unwilling to be simply a patron of science; he wanted to make his own contributions as well.

Even Frederick's harshest critics admit to his scholarship, and there can be no doubt that he was the actual author of *De Arti Venandi*. Falconry had been a passion since childhood, and Frederick constructed several beautiful fortified hunting lodges in Apulia that can still be seen towering over a countryside that every autumn and spring serves as a stopover for thousands of songbirds migrating between Africa and northern Europe. This landscape is perfect for falcons, and Frederick took great pride both in the raising and care of a variety of birds of prey and in his studies of predator and prey.

De Arti Venandi begins with a general overview of the ecology, behavior, and anatomy of birds. Some of this draws on Aristotle and other ancient sources, but much is new and has the feel of a serious observer working through his own exhaustive notes. Frederick distinguishes between waterbirds, land birds, and "neutral birds" such as plovers and curlews, which alternate between land and water.[23] Frederick is clearly Aristotelian in his method of classifying species by a mixture of specific traits and behaviors. He correctly identifies pelicans as being totipalmate (having all four toes linked by webbing) and splits off raptorial birds from other groups, based again on both morphology and behavior. Whereas Frederick follows Aristotle in terms of method, he has no hesitation about stating his disagreement with the classics when his own observations differ.

Again and again, as one moves through the text, one finds clear evidence of direct observation and personal experimentation. Frederick is fascinated with incubation. He experiments with placing eggs from a variety of birds under chickens or simply exposing them to sunlight. He considers the problems of migration; he explores feather structure, internal anatomy, and gross morphology. Once he has fully developed the biology of birds, he moves to the more specialized questions of falconry. Here one finds guidance in identifying and capturing suitable birds for hunting, the preparation of jesses and hoods, the gentling of a hunting bird, training techniques in the field, correcting errors in a mistrained falcon, and so forth.

In all, *De Arti Venandi* represents a gigantic leap forward in scientific research. Gone is any trace of Pliny's and his successors' reliance on the work of others. Frederick makes use of earlier references, but only as a springboard to his own research. He is clearly fascinated with birds in general and the behavior of hawks in particular. The writing is clear, organized, and comprehensive. He is careful to lead the reader through his arguments step by step, indicating his intentions at each point and illustrating arguments with examples. While the bulk of the text deals with raptors, Frederick goes to great pains to include a broad variety of other birds, and whereas some of his speculations have proved false, there is more than enough truth here that *De Arti Venandi* could make a fine text for a modern course in ornithology.

Unfortunately, Frederick did not live to complete his masterwork. Succeeding popes went out of their way to undermine Frederick's authority and to encourage his enemies. Civil war broke out in northern Italy and in Germany. Frederick put down many of these revolts and survived another round of excommunication, and each time that he seemed on the verge of defeat, he managed to stage a comeback. He was in his fifties, not by any means a great age even for those times, but he was clearly growing tired. By 1250, he no longer led his armies in person, and after he fell into his final illness, death came quickly. He was buried in a massive tomb in Palermo, in his beloved Sicily, although legends still have him sleeping in some Alpine cave, waiting like King Arthur to return someday to save his people from invaders.

Frederick is the first person worthy of the term *ornithologist*, and the first since Aristotle to insist on personal observation and experimentation. I can think of no nobler epitaph for this remarkable man than his own statement that "entire conviction of the truth cannot come from mere hearsay."[24] Unfortunately, after his death there was nobody even approaching Frederick's stature to carry on his work. His sons soon lost political control of the empire, and natural history, which for a glorious moment had become central to learning, was forced to retreat into the isolated domains of specialists. One cannot but wonder what might have been accomplished if so much of Frederick's time and energy had not been squandered by endless quarrels with the Church.

Of the natural historians who succeeded Frederick and Michael Scot, Roger Bacon (1214–94 CE), like Scot, is touched with a tinge of wizardry. Both Bacon and Scot were credited at different times as having split Eildon Hill (on the border of England and Scotland) into three parts. Bacon supposedly did this with the help of the Devil. Legend has it that Bacon had raised the Devil through practice of the dark arts; the difficulty was that he had to keep the Devil busy, or he would turn on his master and rend him in pieces. Bacon first told the Devil to ring all the bells in Notre Dame, and the Devil did it in a night. Then Bacon told the devil to split Eildon Hill in three, and the Devil did it in a day. Finally, in despair, Bacon told the Devil to weave Solway Sands into rope, a task that the Devil is still trying to accomplish. This, I was told when I was a little boy, is why when you go down to the shore at low tide, you see rippling lines in the sand. It is the Devil trying to do his weaving, though Bacon is eight hundred years dead. Unfortunately for the storyteller, Eildon was known as Trimontium ("three mountains") to the Romans hundreds of years before Bacon or Scot was born, so we will have to fall back on less romantic geological explanations for the distinctive three peaks.[25]

Bacon is also credited with having made a brazen head that could answer any question put to it.[26] The manufacture of oracular brazen heads and other machines that could talk was quite a popular pursuit of medieval alchemists, and Bacon's was but one of many. Unfortunately for its creator, Bacon had supposedly hired an incompetent assistant. As the head was set to cool, the exhausted Bacon retired to sleep, having first instructed his assistant to wake him if the head spoke. After some time the head said, "Time is." The assistant was so terrified that he failed to wake Bacon. Later, the head spoke again: "Time was." Again, the assistant cowered in the corner, not waking his master. Finally the head spoke one last time—"Time has been"—and then shattered into pieces. One gets the sense that Bacon would actually have been offended by these stories. Accounts from the period suggest that he was something of a conservative, and although he dabbled in alchemy, he was much more interested in mathematics and theology.[27] He did eventually run afoul of the pope, but this likely had more to do with questions of scripture than with deliberate attempts to raise the Devil.

It is probably no accident that many of these people come down to us with the trappings of wizards—for the common people of the time, an "unhealthy" interest in dead bodies and the mixing of potions and chemicals would make even the straightest philosopher suspect of witchcraft. Bacon is sometimes credited with discovering gunpowder, an ideal substance for confirming him as a wizard.[28] He does seem to have made use of it in some of his experiments, but he may have been building off common knowledge rather than developing it by original experimentation.[29]

Another important alchemist and botanist of the period was Albertus Magnus (approx. 1193–1280?).[30] Albertus was born into a wealthy family and was apparently regarded as remarkably stupid, to the point that he was about to give up any hope of education. Legend has it that at this moment he had a vision of the Virgin Mary, who offered him the possibility of becoming great in science or in religion.[31] Albertus chose science, and Mary granted his wish, with the caveat that at the end of his life he would sink back into his former stupidity. Albertus went on to become a widely respected teacher and philosopher and, in keeping with the prophecy, developed what sounds like Alzheimer's disease late in life and sank into dementia.

The extent of Albertus's contributions to natural history is somewhat debatable. He does not seem to have been part of Frederick's collection of scholars, perhaps because of his affinity for the Church. His greatest student was St. Thomas Aquinas, and both seem to have engaged in the study of philosophy, medicine, and alchemy. Like Bacon, they constructed a brazen head, but—so the story goes—their head kept speaking, to the point that it so interrupted Aquinas's thoughts that he seized a hammer and smashed it. Albertus is another example of the return of Aristotelian thought to European scholarship. He certainly worked with (and extracted from) portions of Aristotle as well as a number of other authors.[32] His most significant contributions seem to have been in botany, and he may have constructed specialized botanical gardens during his services in different monasteries.[33]

Magic and science were never far from each other in the public's perception of a scientist. Besides the construction of brazen heads, the public attributed to Albertus the power to change seasons at will. There is a delightful account of Albertus inviting a visiting count to dinner in his garden in the depths of winter. The count, annoyed by some slight, is about to ride off when Albertus magically transforms the snow-clad landscape into a summery scene filled with flowers. Lockyer suggests that this story is perhaps better explained by a winter garden, deliberately planted with cold-hardy perennials, but again we see the likely interface between medieval natural history and beliefs in magic.[34]

In the 1920s, Lynn Thorndike produced a massive overview of the odd mixture of people and the various branches of science and astrology, alchemy, prophecy, theology, and mathematics that made up much of serious thought during the Middle Ages.[35] Thorndike's thesis is that both what we call magic and what we call science share a common root, often have common practitioners, and may be indistinguishable in terms of methodologies and even outcomes to any but the careful student. This idea has not gone unchallenged, but is certainly worth considering.[36]

Two events important for natural history occurred in the early fifteenth century. First, in 1417, Poggio Bracciolini discovered the only surviving copy of Lucretius's (99?–56? BCE) poetic treatise *De Rerum Natura* (On the Nature of Things).[37] This text both argues against reliance on religious explanations for causation and presents the concept of an atomistic universe whose mechanisms can be worked out by careful study. In 1426, Guarino da Verona republished *De Medicina*, an extract from a much larger work by Aulus Cornelius Celsus (25 BCE–50 CE). Celsus's text proved highly readable, and it provided new incentives to examine old sources and evaluate general medical knowledge.

Like magic and science, medicine and natural history were deeply entwined during much of the early histories of both disciplines. Medical practitioners needed to be able to identify particular plants—or even parts of plants—that could be used in cures, and knowledge of animal anatomy was also useful, both in the preparation of medicines and the treatment of particular injuries. The result of this very practical set of needs was the production of a large number of herbals throughout the Middle Ages, some of which concentrate on plants available locally and others of which might contain selected excerpts or fragments from Galen, Dioscorides, Aristotle, or Theophrastus. In spite of their name, herbals often contain a mixture of botanical and zoological information, including in some cases ecological information on range and even behavior. As such, some of these texts may be regarded as lying in the realm of general natural history, rather than being strictly medical science.

The development of the printing press had a very positive effect on the production, standardization, and distribution of herbals as well as books in general. By the late fifteenth century, illustrated works such as Konrad von Megenberg's *Das Buch der Natur* began to appear, though the text itself may be at least a hundred years older.[38] The *Gart der Gesuntheit*, published in 1485, is noted for the quality of its illustrations.[39] Perhaps the most famous of all the herbals is the *Hortis Sanitaris*, published six years after the *Gart* and containing over a thousand illustrations, though it is of lesser quality than its immediate predecessors.

The *Hortis Sanitaris* focuses primarily on plants, but it also includes some discussion and illustration of animals, including quite recognizable peacocks. The *Hortis* contains many species commonly employed in medieval medicine, but it also has its share of mythological plants and animals, including unicorns and the Tree of Life. It was enormously popular and went through several editions before its final release in 1539 as *Le Jardin de santé*. By this stage, however, Europe was grappling with an entirely new botany and zoology—Columbus's and his successors' voyages to the Americas had revealed completely new forms that would have to be dealt with. At the same time, the quickening development of science and engineering was beginning to outpace reliance on ancient knowledge. Europe was no longer in awe of a lost past, and was reaching out, both physically and mentally, to embrace an exciting future.

FIVE . New Worlds

By the end of the fifteenth century, Europeans had known for some time that the world was much larger than their studies of Greek and Roman texts might suggest. Early mapmaking had relied heavily on the depictions of the world produced by Claudius Ptolemaeus or Ptolemy (90–168 CE). Ptolemy had created both a system of mapmaking and a series of maps of his own, but no originals have survived.[1] Ptolemy's maps had depicted rough outlines of the coast of India, and had extended as far as Indochina, with even hints of Japan, but they seriously underestimated the distances involved. For much of the medieval period, mapmakers seem to have been content to depict the outer limits of their experience in a pre-Ptolemaic style that bordered the known world with a vague "River Oceanus" that effectively limited travel.[2]

Muslim dominance of the Middle East and Asia Minor following the fall of Constantinople disrupted trade routes to the east, providing greater impetus for maritime explorations to the south and west. In 1469, Ferdinand of Aragon married Isabella of Castille, uniting the two largest Spanish kingdoms and creating a grand alliance that would drive the Arabs out of southern Europe. Granada, the last major Moorish citadel, fell to the Spaniards in 1492, the same year that Columbus set off on his first attempt to find a short sea route to Asia.

The next hundred years have been called the era of the "discovery of the sea."[3] It seems probable that at least some account of the Viking voyages to Vinland (Newfoundland) and Markland (Labrador) nearly five hundred years earlier had reached Spain and Italy, but Columbus and his sailors had no real concept of the ocean vastnesses that lay ahead of them, or of the continents that separated them from their goal, China. Yet within fifty years the world had been circumnavigated, and we can find remarkably "modern" maps showing recognizable continental outlines that became only more detailed in the ensuing centuries.[4]

Reliance on ancient authors such as Pliny and Aristotle had served as a brake on new discovery for centuries. Pliny in particular may have been a cause of the retardation of original work. He is in some ways like the attic of an enormous old house, full of interesting objects, some partially broken, others whose use or origin has long since been forgotten. Nothing in Pliny or Aristotle could prepare Europe for the wealth of new information that was about to sweep across the Atlantic as the Americas were opened for conquest and colonization.[5] Crossing the Atlantic was not in and of itself sufficient to bring about a revolution. Leif the Lucky's explorations had produced no land rush to the west; the Vikings came, saw, and went home. What Columbus achieved—besides a remarkable feat of navigation—was to present the far side of the ocean as a place that was worth visiting and even settling.

The ecological impacts of the European discovery of the Americas and the subsequent development of circumglobal trade and movement were enormous. Crosby describes this eloquently: "The seams of Pangaea were closing, drawn together by the sailmaker's needle. Chickens met kiwis, cattle met kangaroos, Irish met potatoes, Comanches met horses, Incas met smallpox—all for the first time."[6]

Perhaps most impressive about the Age of Exploration is how rapidly it changed not just the European view of the world, but the ability of Europeans to move around in it. In 1491, venturing across the Atlantic seemed a voyage for madmen. People genuinely believed that one might be lost forever in the Ocean River. By 1600, any merchant with sufficient cash, four years to spare, and the right connections could book a voyage around the world. The European powers, which had spent the previous millennium squabbling over a relatively small pool of resources, had to deal with the concept of global empires that would create and destroy whole markets and nations as new products and new sources of old commodities became available. Whether Europeans themselves could survive extended contact with the new lands and new species that were being discovered was an open question—one which natural historians might have been in a position to answer.

The sixteenth century saw an explosion in the production of herbals and other books addressing various aspects of natural history. The volume and scope of these productions have been explored in some depth by Rohde, who, while concentrating on English examples dating back to late Anglo-Saxon documents, gives us a fairly comprehensive bibliography of source manuscripts.[7] Of particular note is the herbal of the Dutch botanist and physician Rembertus Dodonaeus (1517–85), who served as the court physician to the emperor of Austria. His herbal was originally published in Dutch in 1554,[8] then translated into French, and from French retranslated into English by Henry Lyte in 1578. In 1583, a second English translation was begun by a "Dr. Priest" of the College of Physicians in London.[9] Priest died before he could complete the translation, and the task passed to John Gerard, who published an amended and illustrated version under the somewhat ponderous title *The Herball or Generall Historie of Plantes Gathered by John Gerarde of London* in 1597.

The *Herball* is important in a number of ways. First, it was widely published, edited, republished, excerpted from, and used as a model. Second, it provides clear evidence of both the decline of superstition and the rise of a truly global perspective in botany. Examples of both abound throughout the book, which is organized so that each species gets a basic description (illustrated in later editions), a rough range estimate, a synonymy, and its "Temperature and Vertues," which consist of possible medical applications and preparations, often with reference to earlier authors.

Gerard includes the mandrake *(Mandragora)* in his catalogue, but he is downright dismissive of what he refers to as the "old wives' tales" surrounding this plant.[10] Contrary to earlier opinion, he rejects the notion that the plant can be harvested only by attaching it to a dog, which will be killed by the mandrake's screams as the plant is uprooted. He also rejects "many fables of loving matters, too full of scurrility to set forth in print, which I forbear to speak of" (205). The gossip in some of us might have enjoyed such "loving matters," but "all which dreams and old wives' tales you shall from henceforth cast out of your books and memory knowing this: that they are all and every part of them false and most untrue" (205). Gerard is also very firm that he has himself safely "digged up, planted, and replanted very many" (205) mandrakes and assures us that the plant does not look like a human.

Gerard's medical applications run the full gamut, from an enormous variety of "purges" to the treatment of what we might now regard as psychological ailments. He cautions that drinking a concoction of the "Prickly Indian Fig" may result in red urine to the degree that a patient may fear for his life, but he assures us that the color is simply from the plant itself. Quite charmingly, he speaks of the seed of basil, which "cures the infirmities of the heart, takes away sorrowfulness that comes of melancholy, and makes a man merry and glad" (28). Would that it were so.

While there is still a strong hint of medievalism in some of the "cures" that he espouses, there is also a new energy and a new willingness to directly examine both forms and results. This insistence on personal study harkens back to Aristotle rather than Pliny, and one gets the feeling that Gerard would have made an interesting and useful member of Frederick's court.

Gerard gets himself in trouble when he goes beyond what he himself has actually seen. In the third volume of the *Herball,* he allows plants and animals to mix by admitting the strange story of the barnacle goose *(Branta leucopsis),* which has been discussed by a number of authors.[11] As early as the twelfth century, stories had come out of India of a marvelous tree that produced fruit that hatched into birds or at least birdlike creatures. Gerard believes that the barnacles that are found on driftwood off the west coast of Scotland and Ireland must come from a similar tree, and that they hatch into the great flocks of wintering geese (barnacle geese nest in the high Arctic, moving south only in late autumn) seen along the coasts. It is interesting to note that this story had been rejected by both Roger Bacon and Albertus Magnus, but was sufficiently widely discussed to be the subject of debate in the Royal Society of London as late as the seventeenth century.[12]

Gerard was by no means the only person publishing on botany or natural history in the period. Another natural historian who fell for the story of the barnacle goose was William Turner.[13] Turner was born in England in approximately 1508 and trained for the ministry. Highly unorthodox in his religious views, he had to spend a substantial amount of time in exile on the continent. This was not a bad thing for his other passion, ornithology, as he befriended Conrad Gesner (1516–65), who was in the process of compiling a series of books on botany and also a massive illustrated encyclopedia entitled *The Natural Histories of Animals.* The two naturalists seem to have been on the warmest terms, and Turner probably spent time with Gesner in Switzerland while he was on one of his periodic outs with the Church in England. Turner probably began his *Short and Succinct History of the Principal Birds Noticed by Pliny and Aristotle* while he was in Europe, and his notes on additional species, including the puffin (one of which he hand-reared for eight months), are directly addressed to Gesner.

Although, as his title implies, Turner draws on Pliny and Aristotle, he is not above criticizing them, and he attempts to relate ancient and Mediterranean observations to "what I have seen with mine own eyes." He concludes the book by pointing out the advantages of patronage, in a rather plaintive cry to his reader to consider the difficulties of trying to construct a comprehensive treatise with limited means: "The well known Alexander, the greatest and most renowned of all kings . . . presented Aristotle with 480,000 crowns, when he was about to write on animals, since he knew that the philosopher could not carry out that task with his private means. . . . If such an Alexander existed anywhere today, I should not doubt that a new Aristotle would be born for us from somewhere."[14]

Turner's complaint is not without foundation. Due in part to his conflicts with various religious authorities, perhaps made worse by his acknowledged cutting wit, Turner was frequently at a loss for funds. He mentions at one point that he is without house or land and cannot go to his book "for the crying of the childer [children]."[15]

Turner's friend and correspondent Conrad Gesner is worth mentioning on his own merits. He was born in Zurich in humble circumstances and lost both of his parents at a young age.[16] In spite of this, he was determined to have a professional career and traveled to Paris, where, Macgillivray complains, he "indulged to excess his literary appetite" (107) while being supported by a young Bernese nobleman. After this, he returned to Switzerland, got married, and briefly taught in a grammar school. Before long he was recognized for his talent and sent at government expense to Basel to study medicine. His ability in classics got him a job as a professor of Greek before he finally finished his medical studies in 1541. Four years later, he published the *Bibliotheca Universalis,* which was intended to be a catalogue of every book ever written. He seems to have been actively engaged in the study of natural history throughout the latter half of his life, and was appointed a professor of natural history in Zurich in 1555. For the last nine years of his life, he worked on the *Historia Naturalis Animalium,* which was incomplete at his death but was finished by a student and widely published, including in a shorter English translation. Macgillivray dismisses this work as being "chiefly composed of extracts from Aristotle, Aeolian, and Pliny, without order or discrimination, but intermixed with numerous original observations, and illustrated by rude engravings" (107). This is a brutal critique, and, happily, modern readers have the opportunity to render a different judgment. While Gesner does indeed owe a debt to the ancients, he, like Turner, includes interesting observations of his own, and the woodcuts are anything but "rude," consisting of many charming images, and often including key characteristics that leave the viewer in no doubt as to what species is being illustrated. Gesner does include many fantastical creatures out of myth, including unicorns, satyrs, and so forth, but his book is a key breakpoint: an author is moving beyond Pliny into a new comprehensive examination of species. Gesner's death bordered on the heroic. He refused to leave Zurich when the plague broke out, and continued attending his patients until he himself contracted the disease. He then instructed his assistants to carry him to his study, where he set about ordering his papers until he died.

The sheer abundance of texts produced in the sixteenth century is quite remarkable.[17] Rohde gives us ten pages of various editions of herbals published in the period.[18] Many contain similar information, and in some cases were copied directly one from another. Among those worthy of special mention is *A Greene Foreste or a Naturall Historie* by John Maplet.[19] Maplet was born in approximately 1540, taking a BA at Cambridge in 1564. He subsequently became a vicar in a country parish in Middlesex—one of a distinguished tribe of country parsons turned naturalists. His book was published in 1567 and is noteworthy in part because Maplet actually uses the term "Naturall Historie" in his title. Beyond this, however, his writing does not really live up to the example of more original thinkers such as Turner, and he looks more to the past than to the future. It is clear that Maplet wished to address everything from geology to zoology, but most of what he records is derived from translations of Aristotle, Pliny, and Albertus Magnus.

Maplet recognizes classical forms of classification—for instance, he breaks plants down into "herbs," "shrubs," and "trees" and follows Aristotle in talking about animals "with blood" and "without blood," though he also mentions behaviors and body forms as ways to separate species. In the actual structure of the text, his chief innovation is organizing everything alphabetically within more general groups. He seems quite proud of this and is certain that this will aid the reader in finding what he wants.

The third "booke," or division, of the *Foreste* is about animals and is the most charming (the other two deal with gems and plants, respectively). Maplet does not seem to bother with examining organisms himself, even species that must have been readily available to him. The book is full of wondrous mythical animals that settle in comfortably beside common ones. Next to common birds of Britain, we find the griffin, "a foulle of plentifull and thicke fethe, and four footed withal" that lives in "Hyperborea, right under the North Pole" and is also said to "keepe the Precious stones such as the Smarage, jasper and so forth."[20] If we return to the first book, we find that the "Smarage" is the emerald, and that it can be used in divination of things to come.

Elephants, so Maplet believes, have some knowledge of astronomy, and use the stars to time their ritualized washing and purging. They are also good natural historians, and both males and females make use of the mandrake, which in elephants increases the male's "earnest desire" and in the female aids her in conception. Elephants are great friends of humans but are afraid of mice. Their bitterest enemy is the dragon, from which they will protect human riders. Elephants attack dragons by rushing at them and crushing them, unless the dragon leaps first on the

FIGURE 1. Illuminated elephant and dragon, from the *Aberdeen Bestiary*, 1542, illustrations circa thirteenth century. (Courtesy of the University of Aberdeen.)

elephant's back and bleeds it to death. Even if the elephant manages to fall on the dragon, both animals may be killed in the encounter.

The story of battling elephants and dragons—one of the longest descriptions of behavior in the entire text—is both entertaining and initially baffling. Maplet is unlikely to have been exposed to real elephants, much less dragons, but he is clearly fascinated by them. The presence of text about and illustration of elephants and dragons in contemporary texts such as the *Aberdeen Bestiary* of 1542 suggests that the story may have been widely believed.[21]

One source of the elephant and dragon story can be found in Pliny.[22] Earlier Roman authors had told stories of giant African snakes devouring elephants, so perhaps it was not too much of a jump for Pliny to turn snakes into dragons.[23] Maplet may have had a more direct link to the story, however. John Mirk (1318?–1414?) had published a *Festial*, or series of sermons appropriate for different feast days. Someone as well read as Maplet was likely familiar with this text, in which, in a description of customs and practices of the Feast of St. John, we find the war between elephants and dragons. Maplet may have gone back to the original, or simply contented himself with the account listed by his fellow clergyman. In any case, the story captures the risks of the authoritarianism that still dogged the development of natural history—a mixture of Roman myth, fifteenth-century Christian ritual, and sixteenth-century attempts at comprehensive study and cataloging. Maplet himself is not yet modern, but he senses the need for an order to his thoughts and a system with which to work.

In the meantime, the Spanish exploration of the New World generated material for an expanded natural history. Francisco Hernández (1514–87) arrived in Mexico, in the New World, in 1570, after several years spent in Toledo translating Pliny.[24] His mission in America was essentially what we would now call ethnobotany—he was to seek out plants that could be used for medicinal purposes. Hernández was also instructed to collect and prepare specimens of plants and animals that were to be sent back to the court in Spain for further study, as well as to develop paintings and written descriptions of new rarities.

Hernández did his task almost too well: upon his return to Spain, in 1577, he brought with him descriptions of over a thousand plants and thirty-eight folio volumes of information. This wealth of information seems to have been more than Philip II really wanted—the manuscripts were reedited before being published long after Hernández's death as *Treasure of the Medical Things of New Spain*. The zoological component of Hernández's work was eventually translated into English as *The History of the Animals of New Spain*. The originals of much of Hernández's works were unfortunately destroyed in a fire in 1671, but copies survived to be edited and republished.

Settlement in the New World generated increasing interest in both the land itself and its human and nonhuman inhabitants. In 1637, Thomas Morton (1579–1647) published an odd little book entitled *New English Canaan or New Canaan, Containing an Abstract of New England*, which includes descriptions of the American Indians in New England and a discussion of the landscape in general, the "wild beasts" that were to be found there, and the trees and herbs of the region.[25] A much more detailed description, bordering on a real natural history, is John Josselyn's (1610?–75?) *New England's Rarities Discovered*, originally published in 1672.[26] Josselyn had an excellent eye for nature, and besides describing a broad variety of plants and animals native to New England, he also includes a list of introduced species that had arrived in the brief period since the coming of the first colonists.

Josselyn is not above mistakes and fancies: he describes the "caribou" as having a third straight horn in its forehead "wreathed like an unicorn's horn" (56), although he admits that such creatures are very rarely found. Josselyn also describes a "jaccal" as "a Creature that hunts the Lions prey"(57)—could this actually be a coyote?—which he regards as proof of stories of there being lions in the Americas. He is clearly delighted with turkeys, and he assures the reader that he himself has dined on birds weighing at least thirty pounds, although he says that some speak of monsters of over fifty pounds. He also describes an enormous bird of prey, larger than any eagle, which "dines on fawns and jaccals" (41), although again, as with the three-horned caribou, he admits that it is seldom seen.

William Wood visited New England from 1629 to 1633, and describes the general natural history of the countryside in *New England's Prospect*.[27] Wood hopes to be "laying downe that which may both enrich the knowledge of the mind-travelling Reader, or benefit the future Voyager" (2). This he does in his interesting text, which was reprinted several times (Thoreau makes repeated reference to him in the *Journals*). Wood gives us excellent descriptions of a variety of animals, including the beaver, which, he says, builds its house "three stories high" (48); he is also impressed by the hummingbird, "as glorious as the Raine-bow" (50), and he gives an account of the vast migration of passenger pigeons: "I have seen them fly as if the Aerie regiment had beene Pigeons; seeing neither beginning nor ending, length or breadth of these Millions of Millions" (50). The "experimental" nature of his writing (mentioned in the full title of his book) refers to his insistence on relying as much as possible on what he himself has seen. When he is relying on other people's accounts, he makes this clear, and overall he is more reluctant to do so than John Josselyn.

The growing internationalization of science meant that it became more important to make clear to a wide audience just what a researcher was speaking of when describing a plant or animal. Formerly "common" names might lead to rampant confusion as natural historians confronted the same species at opposite ends of its range, or tried to lump American, African, or Asian species in with familiar European forms. As collectors amassed larger catalogues of species, it became obvious that higher degrees of relatedness than mere species or genera should be suggested. There was a growing need for some sort of systematic approach that would make a permanent break from the constraining boundaries provided by Aristotle. It would take a century and several false starts and partial successes to arrive, but a new order was clearly on its way.

SIX . Ray, Linnaeus, and the Ordering of the World

The seventeenth and early eighteenth centuries marked a remarkable period for science in general and natural history in particular. The first decade of the new century saw the staging of Shakespeare's *The Tempest*, featuring Prospero, almost the archetype of the medieval sorcerer-scientist. By the end of the century, Isaac Newton had published his *Principia*, John Ray and his colleagues had moved botany out of the realm of the herbalists, William Harvey had demonstrated the circulation of the blood in vertebrates, and science and magic had parted ways once and for all. Of particular importance to the creation of a modern science was the increasing freedom of travel and communication for a broad range of people. In spite of wars, revolutions, and plague, natural historians found it increasingly easy to both move about and experience a broad range of climates and species, and also to send and receive letters from a growing circle of fellow researchers.

The founding of the Royal Society in 1660, and its subsequent support and publication of research across a broad range of subdisciplines, brought science into the mainstream in a way that had not been common before. The society's motto, *Nullius in verba*, or "Take nobody's word for it," made an explicit break with the past and encouraged direct experimentation over reliance on authority. Science had moved beyond the university and cloistered religious contexts and now was also the province of the gifted "amateur," who could count on a widening circle of learned friends to discuss, debate, and communicate new ideas.

Other boundaries were beginning to break down. The increasing precision of optics permitted new advances in both cosmic and microcosmic research. Galileo and his telescope are justifiably famous examples of the effect of this new technology in the late sixteenth century, but the development of the microscope was equally important, and it had a far greater impact on the study of natural history. The first really popular account of the microscopic world was *Micrographia*, by Robert Hooke (1635–1703), which was published in 1665. A possible reason for the success of *Micrographia*—which was republished, reedited, and rereleased multiple times—was its inclusion of large copper-plate etchings.[1] Of perhaps equal beauty was the work of Nehemiah Grew, who published detailed studies of the structure of plants in 1682, including *Anatomy of Plants*.[2] Like Hooke, Grew illustrated his work with lavishly detailed etchings that showed a degree of detail previously unavailable to readers (see figures 2 and 3).

The sheer number of new organisms that were being discovered, and the need for a more universal system of naming and organizing this wealth of material, required a real science of taxonomy. Traditionally, the concept of taxonomy, or systematics, is credited to Linnaeus, but many people had their hand in its creation, and foremost among them was the quiet English theologian and natural historian John Ray.

John Ray was born the son of a blacksmith in 1628, in rural England.[3] His life spanned one of the most difficult periods in English history. By the time Ray finished his MA at Cambridge in 1649, the English Civil War had been fought, Charles I had been tried and executed, and Oliver Cromwell was ready to invade Ireland. Ray remained at Trinity College, Cambridge, throughout the Commonwealth and the Protectorate, teaching Latin and Greek and rising through the college's hierarchy.

Ray seems to have been interested in natural history from an early age, though his first overtly biological publication, an alphabetized catalogue of the plants of Cambridgeshire, did not come out until 1660.[4] Prior to this, Ray had taken a series of extensive walking tours in England in order to examine botanical and other specimens for himself. Ray was also remarkably lucky in his pupils. He had befriended Francis Willughby (1635–72), a young man of significant fortune, who shared his interest in natural history and had a particular fascination with ornithology. Together they resolved to explore the British Isles, Ray to botanize and Willughby to pursue birds.

Willughby came from a family of landed gentry and was in a position to devote his life to scientific study without having to worry much about making a living. He was one of the first fellows elected to the Royal Society.[5] Toward the end of his life,

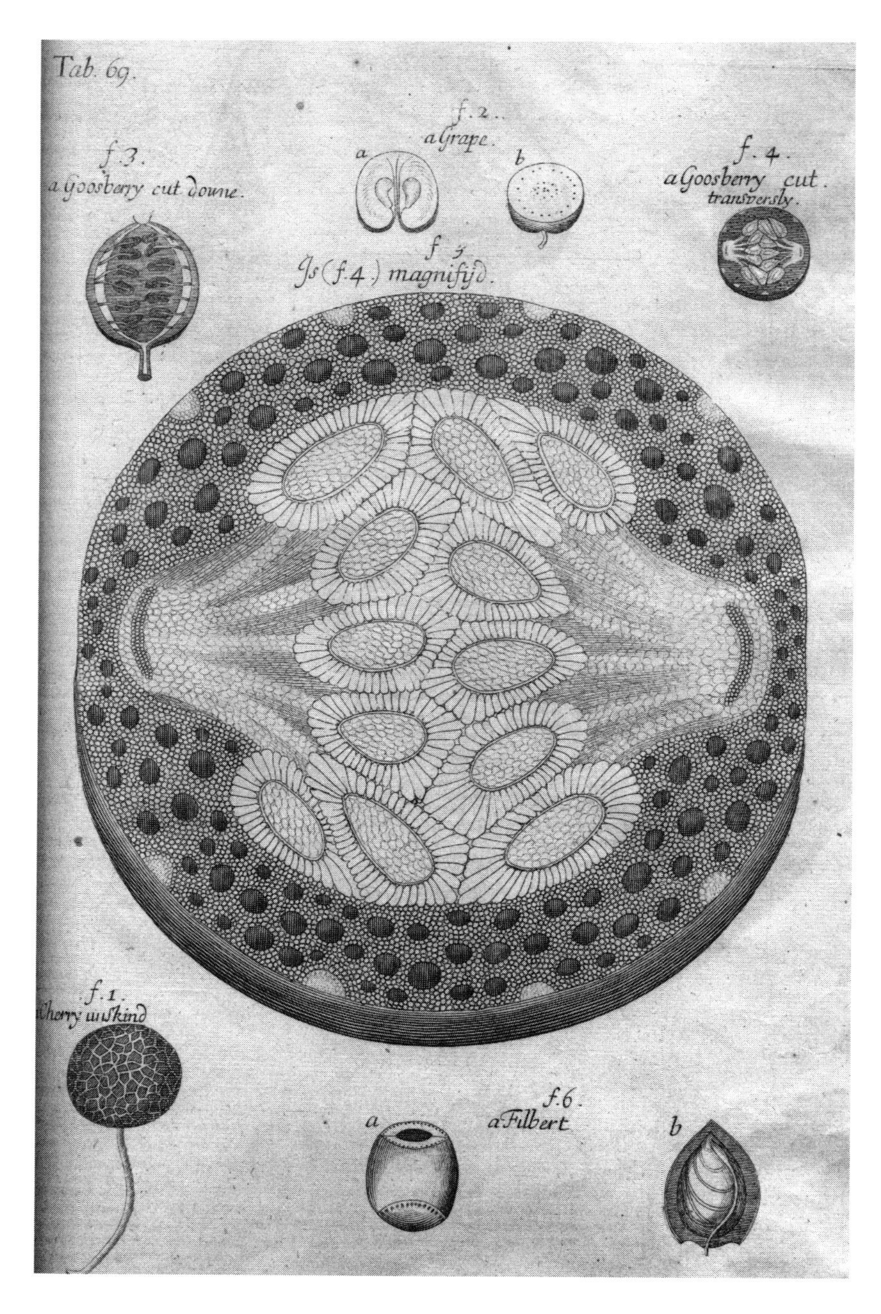

FIGURE 2. Cross-section of a gooseberry, from Nehemiah Grew's *Anatomy of Plants*, 1682. Note the quality of the depiction of the magnified image. (Author's collection.)

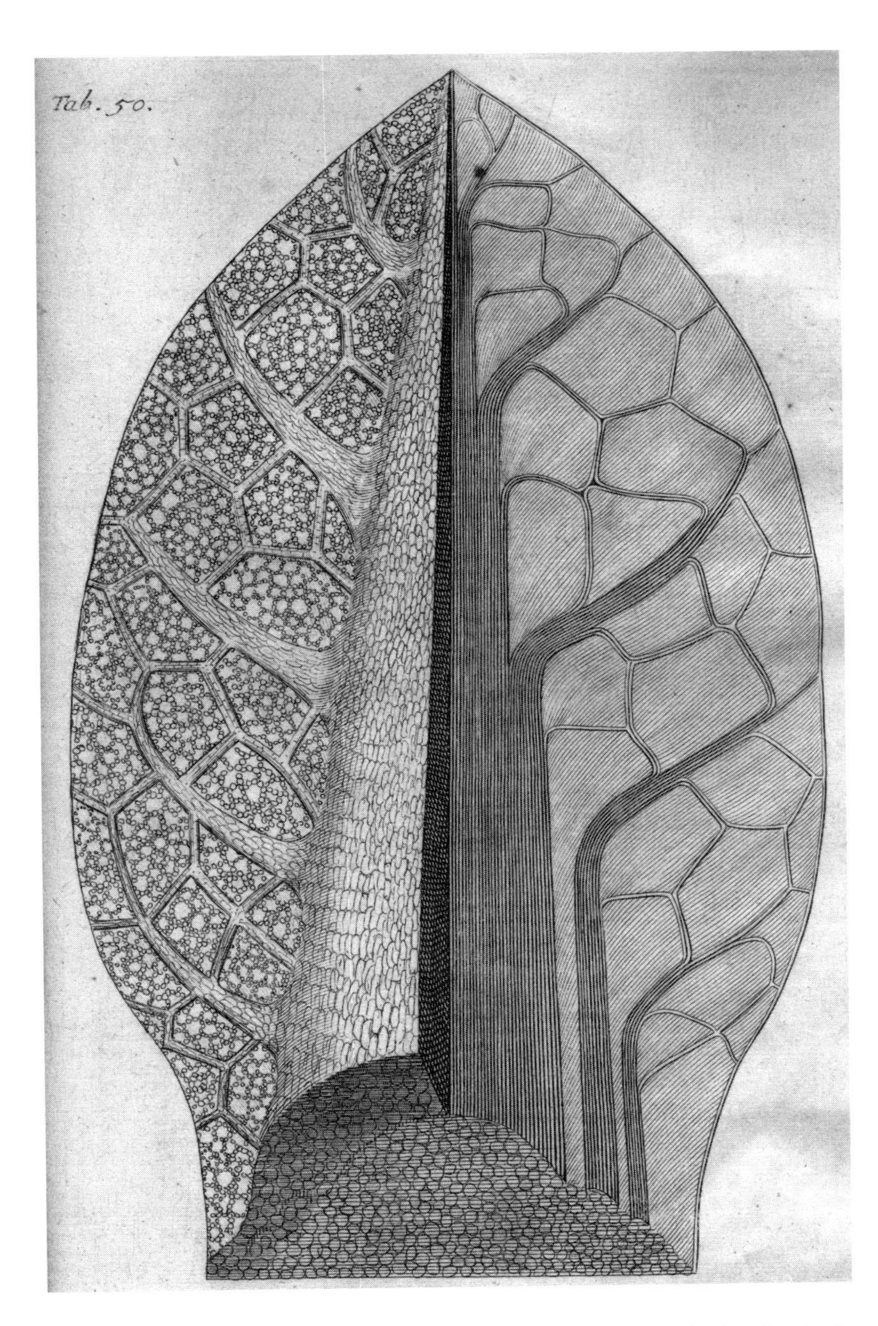

FIGURE 3. Dissection of a leaf, from Grew's *Anatomy of Plants*. (Author's collection.)

he came into a sizeable inheritance that required some management, but overall he was free to pursue his education as he thought fit, and what better education could he hope for than what amounted to an extended tutorial with his favorite teacher?

The two naturalists traveled north in 1661, venturing over the border into Scotland. Ray recorded several of his travels, including this one, with detailed notes on the botanical and zoological observations that he made and also more general (and often very acerbic and witty) comments on the people whom he met and places that he passed through. These notes were probably not intended for publication, at least not without editing, but they appeared posthumously as *Ray's Itineraries* in parts of other collections. Even three centuries later, they make excellent reading as a travelogue and in many respects are more interesting than some of Ray's more polished writing.

Ray, like so many Englishmen, does not seem to have liked the Scots much, making any number of disparaging remarks about their habits, their houses, their persons, and their food: "They have neither good bread, cheese, or drink. They cannot make them, nor will they learn. Their butter is very indifferent, and one would wonder how they could contrive to make it so bad."[6] Ray's reaction to the Scots (and, doubtless, their reaction to him and Willughby) was at least in part due to the politics of the time. Scotland had suffered extensively in the Civil War, and would face further invasion, occupation, revolt, and suppression for the next five generations. Two English academics searching out birds and plants were not likely to endear themselves to a people already tired of repression from the south.

Once they reached Dunbar, they visited the enormous seabird colony on Bass Rock, near Edinburgh, and after giving a nice description of the nesting gannets (he calls them Soland geese), Ray says that "the young ones are esteemed a choice dish in Scotland, and sold very dear (1s. 8d. [about twenty dollars in contemporary money] plucked). We eat of them at Dunbar."[7] Ray comments that the owner of the island was making the princely sum of £130 in selling eggs and birds, and that would-be egg collectors were killed in falls every year. Having dealt with the birds and economics, Ray goes on to list the plants that he found on the island.

The next spring and summer, Ray and Willughby set off again, traveling this time through Wales, including a climb on Snowdon, where Ray made notes on alpine flowers, and then on through Cornwall and the south coast of England. Throughout the account of their travels, one gets the sense of their twin passions for birds and plants. Ray also records the legends and stories of the local people, but he makes clear when he believes something and when he leaves it up to the reader to make up his or her own mind. An interesting example: He is told that on

Christmas Day the salmon will allow anyone who wishes to catch them by hand. His private response is to quote St. Augustine: "Credit qui cupit," or, in other words, "Those who want to make a mistake believe what they wish, not what is."[8] This is a notable shift from the level of credulity that had been popular in natural history even a century earlier.

Upon their return from these travels, in the summer of 1662, it seemed as if Ray could look forward to a life of peaceful scholarship. He had taken holy orders in 1660, but avoided being caught up in the religious controversies that had swept the country during the civil war. In late 1662, however, he was confronted with the demand that he swear to uphold the Act of Uniformity (which set specific boundaries on religious practice), and, upon his refusal, he was forced to resign from Trinity College.[9]

Upon Ray's resignation, he and Willughby decided to make the best of the situation by setting off on a journey through Europe to visit other scholars and universities and to collect specimens.[10] Together they roamed over much of Western Europe for the next several years, in many cases buying fresh birds in the open markets and carefully dissecting them and recording anatomical details.[11]

Willughby briefly enrolled in medical school while in Europe to enhance his anatomical skills, while Ray continued working on botany. Both were inveterate note-takers, and it is unfortunate that many of their notes were lost in transit to England. Eventually Willughby went on to Spain and thence back to Britain in 1664. Ray continued to wander in southern Europe and visited Sicily, Malta, and Switzerland before going home in 1666. The narrative of this journey was published in 1673, and, as are the *Itineraries*, it is a fascinating mixture of scientific observation, travelogue, and essentially gossip about places and peoples.[12]

It is clear from the tone of surviving letters and Ray's dedication in the edited publication of Willughby's *Ornithologia* (1676) that the two were on excellent terms as friends as well as colleagues. Some of the language in the letters may surprise a modern reader: for instance, Willughby, writing to Ray from Spain, says, "And now I would advise you by all means to make a little tour in Spain . . . but to go no further than Cardona, unless you resolve upon a Canary voyage, or have a mind to an Andalusian whore."[13] Not exactly what one would expect in an exchange between teacher and pupil, but Willughby would have been barely thirty, and for all his having taken holy orders, Ray was certainly not one to be overly shocked by earthy language or reference to distinctly nonclerical ways of the world. Just a few years later, he was to write in the preface to his delightful *Compleat Collection of English Proverbs:* "But though I do condemn the mention of any thing obscene, yet I cannot think all use of slovenly and dirty words to be such a violation of modesty as to exact the discarding all Proverbs of which they are ingredients."[14]

Willughby wanted to travel as far as possible and see as much as could be seen. In the same letter that mentions the "Andalusian whore," Willughby suggests that the Royal Society might fund an expedition by one or both of them to the Peak of Tenerife, a site that we will encounter in future chapters. Willughby also planned to visit America, although he did not live long enough to do so, and one can only wonder how much he might have contributed to natural history had he lived to fulfill these plans.

The two made one more joint trip through the south of England before Willughby got married in 1667. Although the beginnings of domesticity and fatherhood (Willughby and his wife had three children in the next four years) must have been somewhat distracting, they did not pull him entirely away from research, as he and Ray wrote a paper on tree sap in 1669. In the meantime, Ray had traveled alone to Yorkshire before returning to write up his *Catalog of English Plants*. This book was a significant extension of his earlier Cambridge catalogue and drew on the trips through the United Kingdom that he had taken with Willughby and by himself, as well as on extensive correspondence with other naturalists. The *Catalog* was published in 1668, and it seems that Ray and Willughby had decided to work on a common system of nomenclature within a general encyclopedic natural history, with Ray covering botany and Willughby zoology.

Unfortunately, Willughby's health, never good, deteriorated steadily. By 1672, it became obvious that he might not survive, and he drew up a will appointing Ray as the tutor of his children, settling on him an annuity of £60—enough to allow Ray to live independently, if frugally, for the rest of his life. Willughby died in the summer of 1672, leaving his zoological work unfinished. Ray got married in 1673, and, after several moves, he returned to his native village of Black Notley, where he spent the rest of his life writing and conducting research.

Ray's greatest contribution to natural history was his development of a hierarchical taxonomy that went well beyond that of Aristotle. He seems to have begun to work on this in his original botanical studies in Cambridge, initially simply alphabetizing species, with only minimal attempts to eliminate redundancies. As his work expanded (the *Catalog of English Plants* was followed in 1673 by a catalogue of plants "not native to England"), he saw the need for a better system of identification and ordination.

Before he could fully concentrate on botany, Ray felt that he had an obligation to finish the work that his friend Willughby had begun on ornithology. Ray edited and published Willughby's *Ornithologia* in 1676. Some authors have suggested that Ray was responsible for much of the work, but this suggestion has been rejected by others who believe that Willughby had played a major part from the first both in developing the taxonomy of birds and in analyzing avian anatomy and behavior.[15]

The book divides all species of birds into terrestrial or aquatic forms, in a manner similar to that of Frederick von Hohenstaufen (Frederick's "neutral" class is absent). This reliance on location for an initial division is rejected in Ray's later solo botanical classification, which lends support to the idea that the *Ornithologia* was Willughby's at heart. The terrestrial group is further subdivided by bill shape and claw structure, then by feeding habits, then further divided by whether a species is nocturnal or diurnal, and so forth. Aquatic birds are divided first into swimmers and waders, and then further divided by foot structure and bill structure.

Nomenclature in the *Ornithologia* is still quite clumsy, with Ray and Willughby usually using a single Latin word for the equivalent of a generic, a single word for the specific if it was alone in its genus, and two or more Latin words for the specific label if there were several species within the genus.[16] They also tend to include English names in identifying particular birds, and one senses the hand of Ray in the inclusion of multiple common names for a species, particularly if the name has an odd story attached or is odd in and of itself. Thus the woodpecker is listed as also being called the woodspite, the pickatrees, the rainfowl, the highhoe, and so forth. Ray's interest in country proverbs and odd words, which shines out in his *Compleat Collection of English Proverbs* and in a later collection of words "not generally used," is allowed here to provide both extra—and sometimes extraneous—information and a synonymy, which to a modern reader is either a quaint attraction or a minor annoyance, but was doubtless useful to ensure identification in Ray's time.

Willughby's widow was responsible for supervising the engraved illustrations to the text, and biographers hint at strains between her and Ray.[17] There is nothing of the quality of John Gould or even Audubon in the images, but given the overall state of engraving, many of the prints probably served their purposes well. The tongue of the woodpecker (figure 4), for instance, is nicely depicted in an illustration of a dissection, and several other birds are attractively done.

With Willughby's major book out of the way (a second Willughby-Ray treatise, *De Historia Piscium*, on fish, was published in 1686,[18] and a third, *De Historia Insectorum*, covering insects, also attributed at least in part to Willughby, was published after Ray's death), Ray could concentrate on botany. His *Methodus*

FIGURE 4. Woodpecker, from Francis Willughby's *Ornithologia*, 1676. Note the detail on the articulation of the woodpecker's tongue. (Author's collection.)

Plantarum Nova was published in 1682 and marks a major step forward in the classification and understanding of plants. After rejecting classification by either distribution or human use, Ray suggests that the only true method of organization uses the actual structure and form of a plant as the basis for splitting up or lumping together groups.[19]

Ray acknowledges the earlier work of the Italian botanist Andrea Cesalpino (1524–1603), who also used the structure of fruits to classify plants, but Ray goes much farther, incorporating a wide variety of traits into his classification scheme. He is careful to caution the reader against making mistakes based on the plasticity of form exhibited by many plants, and he rejects many previously considered "species" as being nothing more than varieties induced by local climate, soil type, or cultivation. In keeping with what we would now call the biological species concept, Ray says that only variations that breed true and are passed on to subsequent generations make an adequate basis for taxonomy. He keeps to Aristotle's division between "herbaceous" and "woody" plants, but he creates what amounts to a dichotomous key for species using a combination of traits from fruits, flowers, leaves, and so on, which is presented as a series of tables in the text.

Between 1686 and 1704, Ray worked on his comprehensive *Historiae Plantarum*, which was eventually published in three volumes and included English-to-Latin botanical nomenclature.[20] This work was clearly part of the original Ray-Willughby master plan for a comprehensive encyclopedia of natural history. Ray was greatly aided in the preparation and eventual publication of the books by his friendship with Sir Hans Sloane (1660–1753). Sloane had the means to both support interesting natural historians in their studies and to take the passion for collecting interesting artifacts that was already the rage among the British and European elite to its logical extreme. His private collection ultimately became the basis for the British Museum, and there is no question but that he provided incentives to Ray to keep working.

Besides his more scientific work on natural history, Ray was best known for his ability to mix theology and science. While he was still at Cambridge, he was responsible for delivering periodic Sunday lectures, or "commonplaces," to the students and faculty. His most important sermon, *The Wisdom of God Manifested in the Works of the Creation*, probably started out as one of these commonplaces, although it is not clear just when he first delivered it.[21] The text went through a number of revisions both before and after initial publication, and forms a basis for the natural theology subsequently espoused by William Paley.[22] Ray's sermon is remarkable in a number of ways. He draws upon the ancients, citing Pliny, among others, but the sense throughout is that of Ray the scientist, insisting on direct observation of fact or communication among contemporaries. As the sermon's title states, Ray is caught up in a vast teleology, in which absolutely everything must have a purpose, which, for living things, rests within a sort of hierarchy: things done for the good of the individual, to things done for the good of the species, to things done for the good of Man, and ultimately to things done to show the glory of God. If we step away from this purposefulness, however, there is plenty of evidence for ideas that would not seem unusual in a modern biology seminar. As one small example, Ray precedes David Lack by nearly three centuries in suggesting that birds lay only the number of eggs that will maximize their reproductive success, rather than being limited by their ability to produce eggs.[23] He cites experiments involving egg removal from both chickens and swallows as support for the hypothesis. Ray is, of course, using all this in an attempt to prove the beneficence of God rather than the workings of natural selection, but it is still interesting to see how ideas can in some cases have long foreshadows.

The success of *The Wisdom of God* led Ray to produce several other treatises on science and religion, including, in 1692, three essays on the creation, maintenance, and eventual "dissolution" of the world.[24] Again, Ray is in some respects remarkably ahead of his time. He invokes what will become known as uniformitarianism—the application of presently observable phenomena such as erosion or volcanic action—to both explain the creation of the world and to examine its possible endings. He correctly describes fossils as being the remains of once-living creatures, and he suggests that the world may end only when the sun dies.

In 1690, Ray published *Synopsis Methodica Stirpium Britannicarum*, which Macgillivray believes to be the "most important work on British plants that had hitherto been written."[25] In 1695, he responded to attacks on his botanical classifications with the *Dissertatio Brevis*, which summarizes his arguments. Preparation of the final volume of his *Historiae Plantarum* probably took up much of the period between 1688 and 1704, and he was also working on and editing his text on insects, which Willughby had begun more than thirty years earlier. His death in 1705 was not unexpected, and he was widely eulogized, both for his contributions to science and for the kindness of his character.

Ray's and Willughby's publications significantly altered the landscape of taxonomy, and evolutionary biologist Tim Birkhead says that Ray was "arguably the most perceptive naturalist of all time," but there was still a great deal of work to be done.[26] The two naturalists attempted to provide a standardized system for both nomenclature and identification, and to identify literally key characteristics by which plants and animals could be divided or combined into species and genera.

The biggest weakness of their classification scheme is that it all too often relies on single characteristics that are perhaps more plastic or less distinctive than they had hoped, and as a result they split up otherwise related groups.

The man who was to supplant Ray in terms of both reputation and methodology differed from his predecessor in origin and temperament. Carolus Linnaeus was born in Sweden just two years after Ray's death. By all accounts, he was interested in botany from a very young age.[27] His father, the village pastor, indulged him in this passion while he was a boy, but his parents hoped that he would follow his father into the ministry, and sent him to a grammar school in a nearby village, where he was supposed to learn Greek, Latin, and the classics. He was not a very good pupil—instead of studying the prescribed texts, he preferred to be out in the woods, collecting plants and observing animals. By the time he reached high school, Linnaeus was seriously behind in his studies, to the extent that his teachers complained to his parents, and his father decided to take him out of school entirely and to apprentice him to a cobbler.

A local doctor had taken notice of Linnaeus, and convinced his father that Linnaeus's abilities and interests might lend themselves to the study of medicine. Linnaeus moved into the doctor's household for the next two years. Linnaeus then attended the University of Lund, where he was befriended by a professor who not only provided him with food and housing, but also encouraged him in his studies of natural history.

In spite of the kindness of his sponsor, Linnaeus grew tired of studying at Lund and decided that he would be better off at the more prestigious University of Uppsala. In an act that can be regarded only as self-centered and rude, he walked out on his host without bothering to thank him or to explain his reasons for leaving, and transferred to Uppsala. Once he arrived in Uppsala, he found himself nearly destitute and lived by relying on the kindness and generosity of a new set of friends.

Even in the depths of poverty, Linnaeus had one of the lucky encounters that so marked his career. He was walking in the botanical gardens when he met the theologian Olaus Celsius (1670–1756).[28] Celsius inquired of him about some of the plants in the garden, and was so impressed by Linnaeus's answers that he investigated who this ragged student might be. Celsius invited him into his home and gave him access to his books and papers. Linnaeus assisted Celsius in his botanical researches, and it seems likely that it was while reading the texts available to him in Celsius's library that he came up with the idea of using the structure of flowers as a basis for a botanical taxonomy.

Celsius also introduced Linnaeus to Olof Rudbeck the Younger (1660–1740), who had visited Lapland in 1695. Lapland, the northernmost province of Sweden, was at that point a largely uncharted region of mystery that held great promise for a natural historian. Rudbeck, who was professor of botany at Uppsala and had already done preliminary studies in Lapland, was sufficiently impressed with Linnaeus's knowledge that he obtained special dispensation for him to lecture for fees at the botanical gardens, an unusual privilege for a young man still lacking a degree. Rudbeck also arranged for Linnaeus to be hired to repeat and expand on his own earlier exploration of Lapland.

Linnaeus tells of his remarkable five-month journey through Lapland in *Lachesis Lapponica*.[29] The journal still carries with it a remarkable degree of spontaneity and some charming descriptions, ranging from detailed botanical sketches to descriptions of how the people of Lapland rock their children to sleep. Linnaeus starts off with a list of what he wore and what he carried with him on his "Tour." This included a bag containing "one shirt; two pair of false sleeves; two half shirts; an inkstand, pencase, microscope, and spying-glass; a gauze cap to protect me occasionally from the gnats; a comb; my journal, and a parcel of paper stitched together for drying plants, both in folio: my manuscript *Ornithology*, *Flora Uplandica*, and *Characteres generici*. I wore a hanger at my side, and carried a small fowling-piece, as well as an octangular stick, graduated for the purpose of measuring."[30] Only this for what was to turn out to be over four months of trekking and paddling through hundreds of miles of largely unexplored territory.

Linnaeus's travels took the form of a series of east-west transects from the coast of the Gulf of Bothnia inland and then later along the coast of modern Finland. The exact extent of his movements is subject to some debate. Macgillivray cites a fairly popular figure of "about 3800 English miles," which he probably got from the appendix of the *Lachesis Lapponica*.[31] This translates into over twenty-five miles (forty kilometers) a day, *every* day, for the 150 days that Linnaeus was on the road. We know from Linnaeus's own journal that he periodically stopped for a time, either to botanize or because of weather conditions. Gourlie calls at least one section of Linnaeus's claimed travels "a little fib"; other authors are less kind and essentially accuse Linnaeus of fraud in exaggerating both the distances covered and the dangers encountered.[32]

Rather than dwelling on Linnaeus's shortcomings, it is perhaps better to return to the details of the *Lachesis Lapponica*, which is a truly remarkable document, in some ways comparable to Darwin's *Voyage of the Beagle*, only more candid in that it was not originally written for publication. Where else can one find several pages on the marriage customs of the Lapps followed without a pause by a discussion of local names for *Angelica* and other species of plants? Any field ecologist who has been driven half-crazy by biting insects cannot but be both amused and impressed by the following:

> I have long ago related my sufferings from gnats in the course of my Lapland expedition. In this place I was still more incommoded by some very small flies, about a line in length and very narrow. Their breast was of a blueish gray. Front of the head whitish, with black eyes. Wings pellucid. Body grayish, oblong and narrow. A white scale was placed on each side at the insertion of the wings. . . . What rendered them peculiarly troublesome was their manner of running over the face, and flying into the nose, mouth and eyes.[33]

The degree of detail in this description is remarkable. Even allowing for subsequent editing and translation, Linnaeus is clearly thinking and writing with an eye to future taxonomic keys, but he is also human enough to conclude with a complaint. A paragraph earlier, Linnaeus describes having to run between flaming tree trunks in escaping a forest fire, saying, "We were not a little rejoiced when this perilous adventure terminated."[34]

Not a little rejoiced indeed, but one cannot but wonder whether the constant torment of biting flies and mosquitoes wasn't worse than the occasional run-in with real danger, whether from fire or swollen rivers. Overall the reader feels that these are the notes of a very *young* man, and also a very remarkable one who knows that given a chance he will excel and must have as much material as possible to work with in the future.

Upon his return from Lapland, in October 1732, Linnaeus was elected to the Royal Society of Sciences at Uppsala, the group that had funded his expedition, but this honor did not carry any material reward, and he began to give lectures on natural history for a fee in order to pay his bills. Linnaeus had still not completed any degree, and his behavior soon attracted unfavorable attention from university officials. Nicholas Rosen, the professor of anatomy, complained to the academic senate, which prohibited Linnaeus from engaging in any more teaching. At this juncture Linnaeus exhibited either a complete loss of control or an indulgence in showmanship. He ambushed Rosen and attempted to stab him to death with a sword. Fortunately for everyone, Linnaeus either was a bad swordsman or was only playacting, and passersby were able to wrestle the sword from him before any damage was done. Assault on a faculty member could not be taken lightly, however, and it took the best efforts of Celsius to prevent Linnaeus's immediate expulsion. Linnaeus got off with a reprimand, but one has the sense that it was generally agreed that it would be a good idea if he left town for a while.

Around this time, Linnaeus decided that he could perhaps get out of poverty by marrying the right girl. Such a bride soon presented herself in the form of Sara Elisabeth Moraea, the daughter of a doctor who was one of the richest inhabitants of Falun, Sweden. Sara seems to have been quite taken by Linnaeus, but her father was more cautious, insisting that the couple wait to get married until Linnaeus had finished his degree and proved himself for three subsequent years. The difficulty, of course, was that Linnaeus was short on funds for travel and was also persona non grata in Uppsala. In what we can regard only as either a leap of faith or a surprising degree of passionate commitment, Sarah supplied her fiancé with enough money to go abroad in search of an institution willing to grant him a degree.

Linnaeus traveled to Holland, and there, in June 1735, he finally completed his medical degree. This essentially involved the preparation and successful defense of a dissertation. Completed within a week of his arrival, Linnaeus's dissertation was on the causes of fever.[35] Although it was subsequently roundly criticized, it was regarded as good enough to get him his degree.

Rather than hasten back to Sweden, Linnaeus seems to have enjoyed his time in Holland. He moved to Leyden and, to be blunt, found a new group of friends and sponsors to sponge off. He had already spent most of his and Sara Elisabeth's money, so in Leyden he was forced initially to live in a garret. This in no way deterred him from his pursuit of natural history, and his time in Holland was incredibly productive in terms of writing. It is obvious from the Lapland journal that Linnaeus had been thinking about how to create a structured taxonomy for some time, but he had put off writing down his thoughts, perhaps due to the disorganization of his personal life. His friends in Leyden, however, persuaded him that it was time to get on with it, and Linnaeus's first publication, the *Systema Naturae*, came out in 1735.

The first edition of the *Systema Naturae*, or to be more precise, the *Systema Naturae sive regna tria naturae systemice proposita per classes, ordines, genera, et species* (The System of Nature by the Three Natural Kingdoms According to Classes, Orders, Genera, and Species), consisted of a mere fourteen folio pages. The book went through thirteen editions, the final version appearing after Linnaeus's death, and each edition would prove substantially longer as more details—and more species—were classified and ordered.

Linnaeus's system is in part "artificial" in that higher levels of classification (kingdoms, classes, orders) are based on traits selected for the convenience of the observer. He regards only the relationships of genera and species as being "natural" and reflecting some biological or even theological meaning. Linnaeus sees three kingdoms in nature, the perception of which reflects the understanding and definitions not only of his time, but of a lineage extending back through Ray to Aristotle: minerals lack life and sensibility, vegetables are alive but lack sensation, and animals have both life and sensation and are able to move at least at some point in their lives.

Beneath the level of kingdoms, Linnaeus divides organisms into classes. Among the animals, he recognizes six classes: mammals, birds, amphibia (which include the reptiles), insects, fish, and worms. This latter class seems to be a catch-all for anything that didn't fit the other groupings, and it is no surprise that it was the first to be eliminated by subsequent authors. Within each class Linnaeus places orders that share more specialized traits, and within each order the ultimately "natural" genera and species have a clear biological affinity to each other. The most lasting of Linnaeus's taxonomic reforms was his insistence on a Latinized binomial for every species. This is the form that all modern scientists use for the technical name of an organism; thus *Homo sapiens* signifies "human being" the world over, and scientists from different backgrounds and speaking wildly different languages can be confident that they at least share a common species in any discussion.

From the first, Linnaeus recognized the great diversity of the botanical world. He developed his system of classification based on the structure of the sexual components of the flower—stamens, pistils, and so forth. As with animals, genera and species were determined by a combination of other shared characteristics. The advantage of this classification scheme was that it was relatively simple, could be applied to most (but not all) of the organisms that a botanist was likely to encounter, and was based on easily observed traits as long as one had a specimen in flower.

Holland in the 1730s must have been an exciting place to be a natural historian. The Dutch had been a seafaring people for centuries, and had established colonies in Southeast Asia, particularly among the islands of modern Indonesia. They were also engaging in active trade with the Americas, Africa, and China, and a flood of species of plants and animals came in with the ships of the Dutch East India Company. With his usual luck or skill at picking up a good sponsor, Linnaeus found a patron in John Burmann, a professor of botany in Amsterdam. Burmann was impressed with Linnaeus's skills in identifying species of plants—Stoever says that they initially argued over the correct classification of a species of bay tree[36]—

and convinced him to remain longer in Holland in order to assist in the publication of a flora of Ceylon (Sri Lanka).

In 1736, Burmann and Linnaeus were invited to the estate of George Clifford, a director of the East India Company and an enthusiastic collector of natural history. Clifford kept a number of large greenhouses to cultivate exotic tropical plants, and also had a private zoo full of animal curiosities from around the world. He too was enormously impressed with Linnaeus's knowledge, and "bought" him from Burmann in exchange for a copy of Sir Hans Sloane's *Natural History of Jamaica*, of which Clifford had two copies. Linnaeus does not seem to have minded being treated as a useful commodity to be passed between wealthy enthusiasts; he was clearly moving up in the world, and Clifford would be able to supply him with a comfortable living as well as access to rare specimens.

Linnaeus took advantage of his position with Clifford to further expand his classification scheme and to publish a number of works that had been in progress for some time, including, in 1737, the *Genera Plantarum*, which describes nearly a thousand genera of plants; the *Fundamenta Botanica*, which outlines basic principles of botanical study; and a catalogue of Clifford's collections entitled *Hortus Cliffortianus*. Linnaeus also took advantage of his proximity to a number of excellent libraries to assemble the *Bibliotheca Botanica*, which contains extracts from nearly a thousand books. Clifford was an obliging patron, and paid to send Linnaeus to London, where he visited Ray's friend Sir Hans Sloane. Sloane was initially unimpressed by Linnaeus, but he consented to allow him to see his library—estimated to contain more than fifty thousand volumes—and collection of artifacts before sending him on to Chelsea Botanical Gardens, of which Sloane was the major patron. Here also Linnaeus was initially met with some hostility, until he was able to convince the staff that he knew what he was talking about.

From Chelsea, Linnaeus went on to Oxford in hopes of obtaining specimens from the University Botanical Gardens for his patron Clifford. Unbeknownst to him, Johann Dillenius (1687–1747), who had published an updated version of Ray's botanical works, had obtained an advance copy of Linnaeus's *Genera Plantarum*. Dillenius had been infuriated by many of Linnaeus's reclassifications, and set out to test the young man on his knowledge. Linnaeus spoke no English, so the scholars addressed each other in Latin. At one point Dillenius turned to an assistant and said, "And *this* is the man who confounds all Botany."[37] Linnaeus understood enough to know that he was being dismissed and began to take his leave, but before he departed, he asked Dillenius what had offended him so much. Dillenius showed him the copy of Linnaeus's book, heavily marked up with disagreements and corrections. They fell into debate, and Dillenius's opinion of Linnaeus was sufficiently changed that he allowed him to obtain a variety of specimens from the botanical gardens and also introduced him to a number of other Oxford professors, some of whom would prove useful correspondents in Linnaeus's later career.

Upon his return from England, Linnaeus threw himself into writing, and besides the previously mentioned books, he also completed a supplement to his *Genera Plantarum* and wrote up a flora of Lapland based on his earlier expedition. One gets the sense that Linnaeus might have remained happily and indefinitely in Holland, but things at home were not as they should have been. He had been away from his fiancée for a long time, and in the meanwhile the friend through whom he had been writing her (one may assume that her father had forbidden direct correspondence) had decided that he would make a better suitor than Linnaeus.[38] In spite of this, Linnaeus still showed no hurry to return, stopping off in Paris for an extended stay, attending lectures and salons, and generally seeming to have a good time of it.

After several months in France, he did eventually make his way back to Stockholm, and while he was restored to Sara Elisabeth's good graces, her father still insisted that he have a reasonable job if he was to support a family. He began to practice medicine, and after a slow start received a government appointment to the navy. This was followed by a request from the king that Linnaeus serve as the royal botanist. These advances allowed him to get married at last, and he wed his long-suffering fiancée in June 1739.

In 1741, Linnaeus was appointed professor of medicine in Uppsala, and eventually he became director of the University Botanical Gardens, which he expanded and reorganized along his own taxonomic lines. For the next nine years, he made a number of exploring trips within Sweden accompanied by students, revised and edited his previous books, and published a number of floras. His taxonomic system had many enemies, and Linnaeus's personality seems to have both charmed some and offended others, but the straightforward logic that marked so much of his system was such a relief from the preceding chaos that he steadily gained adherents.

In 1750, Linnaeus was appointed rector of Uppsala University. He continued to teach, mixing regular lectures with "labs" in the botanical gardens and weekend field trips into the surrounding countryside to collect species of plants. By all accounts he was an extremely popular professor, and he gathered around himself a group of particular favorites whom he called his "apostles," who not only spread the gospel of Linnaeus's taxonomic system but also traveled abroad and sent their old professor interesting specimens from new colonies around the globe. One of the most famous of these apostles was Peter Kalm (1715–79), who traveled through the eastern parts of North America between 1748 and 1751 before returning to Sweden with extensive descriptions of the landscape and hundreds of species of plants and animals, many of them previously undescribed.[39] Kalm also noted the impact of European settlement on the native flora and fauna, expressing concern for the ultimate loss of species as colonization continued.[40]

Other apostles traveled with James Cook on his voyages to the South Seas, ventured into Africa, and visited Japan. In an oddly prescient hint of future controversy, Haller comments that "Linnaeus considered himself as a second Adam, and gave names to all the animals after their distinctive marks, without ever caring for his predecessors. He can hardly forbear to make man a monkey or the monkey a man."[41]

In 1751, Linnaeus published his *Philosophia Botanica,* which summarizes his earlier books on taxonomy and also was intended to serve as a guide to field study and the care and cultivation of plant specimens. This was followed in 1753 by the *Species Plantarum,* which contains over seven thousand species of plants, organized according to his system. These activities led to further royal notice, and Linnaeus was given a knighthood of the Order of the Polar Star, an honor usually reserved for the military and nobility. The royal family continued to be grateful for the fame that Linnaeus was gaining for Sweden, and he was made a noble in 1761, changing his name to Carl von Linné.

By 1772, Linnaeus's health was failing, and he resigned as rector, retiring to his farm outside the city. Two years later, he suffered the first of several strokes, each of which had a progressively more serious impact on his physical and mental health. A final stroke in late 1777 reduced him to helplessness, and he died in January 1778.

The fate of Linnaeus's personal books and collections is a fascinating one. Originally the British naturalist Sir Joseph Banks (1743–1820) expressed an interest in them, but he decided against pursuing the matter. Banks had befriended James Edward Smith (1759–1828), a wealthy young man with a strong interest in natural history. Smith came from an interesting background: his great-grandfather had distinguished himself by marrying six wives and squandering a sizeable fortune in canal and drainage schemes in the fenlands of East Anglia.[42]

Smith was keenly aware of the importance of Linnaeus's work, and he happened to be having breakfast with Sir Joseph Banks when Banks received a letter from Sweden saying that Linnaeus's collections were for sale for a thousand guineas (approximately two hundred thousand dollars in modern currency). Banks suggested that Smith buy the materials. There followed a delightful exchange of letters between Smith and his father in which the younger Smith is obviously thrilled at the prospect of getting his hands on the complete works of his botanical hero and his father is understandably cautious. Eventually the deal was struck, and Linnaeus's collections, manuscripts, and private papers were loaded onto an English brig, the *Appearance*. A popular story has it that once the ship set sail, the Swedes, realizing their mistake, sent a warship after the *Appearance* but failed to catch her. The story *should* be true—many scientists in Sweden deeply regretted the loss of what amounted to a national treasure—but, alas, Blunt says that the story is "without foundation."[43] Ten years later, Smith founded the Linnean Society of London, which is dedicated to "the cultivation of the science of Natural History in all its branches." The society still houses many of Linnaeus's artifacts and was, as we shall see, the venue chosen for the first reading of Darwin's and Wallace's ideas on natural selection, eighty years after Linnaeus's death.

The modern focus on evolutionary phylogeny ironically has confounded some of the goals that Ray, Willughby, and Linnaeus were striving to achieve. Willughby would have been enormously appreciative of *Peterson's Field Guides* or their equivalent. He wanted a book that could be used to quickly and clearly identify what the observer was seeing in front of himself, and he wanted it organized in a way that "made sense," in that it would use characteristics that were easily perceived and agreed upon by everyone. When taxonomists focused on evolutionary relationships and began to use molecular genetics as a standard for differentiation, they were embarking upon what Yoon has called "their own strange new journey."[44]

Yoon has rightly indicated that there is a "clash between instinct and science" in taxonomy, and she makes much of the "non-scientific" approach of taxonomists such as Linnaeus and Ernst Mayr, who said that two species differed on the basis of "arbitrary" characters. She suggests that traditional taxonomists relied on an *umwelt*—a sort of instinctive sense of order and of which features should be used to constitute that order—in making their taxonomic decisions. Ultimately this system gave rise to a degree of authoritarianism: a species was a species because, well, Mayr or Linnaeus or whoever was in fashion said it was. I think this rather misses the point. Although there have been some startling revolutions in taxonomy as we have come to understand increasingly finer structures, down to the level of the individual DNA sequence, at the same time an enormous number of species, initially defined by the *umwelt* of the "authority," have remained useful taxonomic groups. Linnaeus or Ray may not have known (and, based on their worldview, probably did not care) how many of their groups were "related" to one another, but they could tell a pelican from a cormorant, and that was what mattered.

Another example of the ability of a good naturalist to detect pattern in nature with little more than the naked eye can be found in Vladimir Nabokov's pioneering work on butterfly distributions and taxonomy.[45] Besides his literary career, Nabokov worked as an amateur lepidopterist for much of his life (readers of *Ada* may remember the heroine's fascination with butterflies) and proposed that certain species of blue butterflies had spread to the Americas from Asia. At the time that he proposed this novel idea—based largely on classical morphological analyses—Nabokov was disbelieved by scientific colleagues. Yet in 2011, his suggestion was confirmed in virtually every particular through exhaustive study of DNA samples.[46] One imagines that he would have been both pleased and amused at this "more scientific" confirmation of his hypothesis.

SEVEN . Journeys Near and Far

Linnaeus's travels in Lapland in the second quarter of the eighteenth century were part of a much more general trend of naturalist-explorers who took it upon themselves to go and see and bring back for study examples of the expanding natural world. Sometimes these intrepid adventurers went with the support of wealthy patrons or the learned societies that were springing up throughout Europe; sometimes they relied on their own resources to get them where they wanted to go. Some came back to fame and position, some were soon forgotten, and some never returned at all. But between 1700 and 1900, they did a remarkable job in mapping, cataloguing, and in a sense explaining their world.

One of the earliest women to go into the field was Maria Sibylla Merian (1647–1717).[1] Merian was born in Frankfurt at a time when it was highly unusual for a woman to travel on her own, much less work as an active, practicing scientist. Merian was an artist who was also fascinated by natural history, particularly that of insects. Her family raised silk moths for commercial trade, and Merian studied the process of metamorphosis—the transformation from egg through caterpillar and chrysalis to moth or butterfly. Contemporary belief, which could be traced back to Aristotle, suggested that most insects arose through spontaneous generation from earth or rotting meat. Merian mapped out the true pathways of insect life cycles and illustrated her work with painting and drawing. She published the results of her studies as *The Miraculous Transformation of Caterpillars* in 1679. This book made something of a name for her, at least in popular society, as it was written in German rather than the more "scientific" Latin, but this choice may also have limited her audience.

After raising a family, Merian became acquainted with the governor of Suriname. Suriname, in South America, was at the time a Dutch colony, and very much a frontier—not the sort of place frequented by a European woman alone. One of her daughters married a trader in the colony, and in 1699 Merian traveled to visit her and to investigate in situ the tropical insects that were being brought back to Europe. Merian spent two years sketching and painting the insects for what became her *Metamorphosis Insectorum Surinamensum*, published in 1705.

Another notable artistic traveler to the New World was Mark Catesby (1682?–1749).[2] Catesby, likely born in Essex,[3] early on developed an interest in natural history, and moved to London to study with fellow naturalists in the city. Catesby's sister Elizabeth had married Dr. William Cocke, the secretary of state for the colony of Virginia, "against her father's wishes."[4] In spite of this, relations in the family were pleasant enough that Catesby traveled to Virginia in 1712, ostensibly to visit his sister. He spent the next seven years in America, taking a side trip to Jamaica in 1715, but he seems to have done little in the way of natural history beyond sending back some specimens to colleagues in Britain.

Upon returning to England in 1719, Catesby was befriended by Sir Hans Sloane, whom we have already encountered in relation to Ray and Linnaeus. Sloane had visited Jamaica in 1707, and this gave the fabulously wealthy and famous president of the Royal Society and the relatively unknown Catesby something in common. Sloane was in the process of building up his collections of plants and animals and was always on the lookout for a new source of interesting specimens.

With Sloane's patronage, Catesby returned to America in 1722 and remained there for nearly four years. He centered his operations in Charlestown and ventured throughout much of what is now the southeastern portion of the United States. He also made a voyage to parts of the West Indies for further collection and cataloguing. Catesby's attitude about the state of the country and its inhabitants is both curious and revealing. In the preface to *The Natural History of Carolina, Florida, and the Bahama Islands*, he says: "The inhabited parts of Carolina extend west from the sea about sixty miles, and almost the whole length of the coast, being a level, low country."[5] "Inhabited" clearly means "inhabited by English settlers." There is no mention of prior occupants, and in fact he makes it clear that other areas that he visited were "uninhabited." Catesby spent his first year collecting and exploring in the inhabited zone before heading into the wilds. Interestingly, he includes Indian names for the plants that he collects as well as English and Latin descriptors, so he is aware of the Indians, but at the same time they do not constitute inhabitants in a meaningful sense.

Besides his observations and collections in Carolina, Catesby went as far south as Florida, and contemplated visiting Mexico, but it seems that a lack of funds and the reluctance of the Spanish government to grant him a passport prevented this extension of his adventures. By this time Catesby had become an accomplished artist, and he is justly famous for having produced some of the first color engravings of plants and animals, to illustrate his *Natural History of Carolina, Florida, and the Bahama Islands*, which was published under the sponsorship of the Royal Society in 1731 and republished in 1754.

After his return from America, Catesby seems to have spent the rest of his life in and around London, studying natural history, working on his books, and raising a family. Besides the *Natural History*, he also wrote the *Hortus Britanno Americus, or A Collection of 85 Curious Trees and Shrubs, the Production of North America, Adapted to the Climate and Soil of Great Britain*. It seems likely that this book was in part the result of experiments with naturalizing species of plants that he had had shipped back from America in earthen tubs, to be grown in various botanical gardens by his friends. As with the collections of curious artifacts that were becoming the rage among the scientific aristocracy, there was also a good deal of interest and no small amount of competition in raising live specimens, either in greenhouses or on country estates. Catesby, with his network of wealthy sponsors, was perfectly positioned to study the success or failure of these introduced New World species in Britain.

Besides his two books, Catesby also wrote a paper, published in the *Philosophical Transactions of the Royal Society of London*, on migration, or "birds of passage." The popular theory, which persisted until at least the beginning of the nineteenth century, was that many birds did not actually migrate; rather, they flocked together in deep caves and hibernated through the winter. Catesby rejects this notion, saying that "the reports of their lying torpid in Caverns and hollow Trees, and of them resting in the same State at the bottom of deep Waters, are so ill attested, and absurd in themselves, that the bare Mention of them is more than they deserve."[6] He suggests instead that birds respond to changes in food supply by moving north or south as the seasons allow. He also suggests that the vast nocturnal migrations of songbirds are timed to avoid predators, a perfectly reasonable hypothesis. He notes the effects of the introduction of grain farming in America on the distribution of species of migratory birds and changes in behavior as a result of the growth of farming. A version of this paper was also published in the more popular *Gentlemen's Magazine*, and away from the stern eye of the Royal Society, Catesby feels freer to speculate, at some cost to the truth. In this second article he suggests that migratory birds start their flight by flying straight up until they reach an altitude from which they can see their destination and then simply glide down an inclined plane to reach it.[7]

Catesby died around 1749. By this time, medicine had become increasingly specialized and secular, but the study of nature itself had taken on religious connotations—clerics justified their studies as a form of both understanding and glorifying God through the study of his creation. John Ray's famous sermons were one example of this development, but the most successful example of the "reverent naturalists" is Gilbert White (1720–93), who was born in the small village of Selborne, approximately ninety miles southwest of London.[8]

In the storms of development that have burst over the south of England in the past three centuries, Selborne seems somehow to have escaped the worst of the transformation. The village is still isolated from the world by deep, narrow, twisting country lanes. The Hanger, the great hill behind White's house, still dominates the landscape, although it now has more trees on it than it did when White walked on it, composing his sermons and letters. Many of the surrounding farms are gone, but their fields have grown over with trees rather than housing developments, and it is easy to see, sitting in the quiet of the churchyard, how this environment would have lent itself to a leisurely contemplation of the natural world.

White's family home, the Wakes, sits on the main road through the village. St. Mary's Church and the pub are both a stone's throw from his front door. Basingstoke, the nearest town of any size, is far enough away that there is no hint of the noise and bustle of the twenty-first century. The church has been restored since White's day, but it still has its great Norman arches, dating from the twelfth century, that would be instantly recognizable to White and his fellow villagers. The coffin lid of the Knight Templar is still embedded in its floor, only a little more worn now than when White examined it in the 1780s. Only the great yew tree that once stood by the church, and was reputed even in White's day to be over a thousand years old, is gone, blown down in a great gale in 1990.

Gilbert White and his village have an ability to sneak up on you in a way that some of the more flamboyant or heroic figures in natural history do not. White was born in Selborne, spent almost his entire life in Selborne, and died in the house that he had lived in for over thirty years. He is buried beneath a simple stone marked only with his initials in the yard of the church where he preached hundreds of Sunday sermons. He left us a single book, *The Natural History and Antiquities of*

Selborne in the County of Southampton, made up of a series of letters to two friends, and it would be easy to see how White and his book might have vanished completely.[9] With what can be described only as remarkable prescience, the warden of Merton College at Oxford said of at the time of its publication: "[White] has sent into the world a publication with nothing to call attention to it but an advertisement or two in the newspapers; but, depend on it, the time will come when very few who buy books will be without it."[10] Since then, more than 275 editions of the book have been printed; it has never been out of print, and it remains today an acknowledged classic of early ecology.

In contrast to Linnaeus, Catesby, and Merian, White never traveled overseas. Most of his journeys were within a hundred miles of his home, and he was content to get to know one small corner of the world very well, rather than to get a somewhat fuzzier picture of a wider landscape. Sir Robert May, possibly one of the greatest theoretical ecologists of the twentieth century, describes White's book as "arguably the first ecological text."[11]

White's paternal grandfather was the vicar of Selborne, and this explains White's birth in the village parsonage on July 18, 1720.[12] Gilbert was sent to grammar school in Basingstoke and thence, in 1740, to Oriel College, Oxford, where he studied divinity. White graduated with his AB in 1743 and began attending lectures in mathematics. In 1744, he was elected a fellow of his college, a position that he held for the rest of his life. This allowed him a small income and required only minimal attendance at college, so it was ideal for someone whose heart was clearly set on country life. Besides attending lectures, Gilbert spent time with his many relations, the most immediately important of whom was his aunt Rebecca Snooke, who had a pet tortoise called Timothy. White was obviously quite taken by Timothy, and years later, after his aunt's death, White dug Timothy out of hibernation and brought him back to Selborne, where, as we shall see, he would feature prominently in White's seasonal notebooks and also was the subject of a variety of nonintrusive experiments.[13]

In 1746, White received his MA, and, in 1747, his holy orders as a deacon from the bishop of Oxford. This latter distinction allowed him to become the curate of Swarraton, near Selborne. At that period, particular "livings," or parishes within the Anglican community, were parceled out to individual colleges at Oxford, which had the exclusive right to assign the job of parish priest to one of their graduates. Unfortunately for Gilbert, Oriel did not have the "living" of Selborne in its roster, so although he was to play the part of parish priest in his home village for most of his life, he was never allowed to officially assume the title (or salary).

For the next several years, White seems to have enjoyed himself by visiting a variety of college friends and members of his family throughout southeast England and going up to Cambridgeshire on family business. His letters and those of his friends suggest that he had a good eye for detail and was already taking notes on his surroundings.[14] His attendance at college functions was sporadic, but in spite of this he rose through the university hierarchy, becoming proctor of Oxford in 1752 and also dean of Oriel.

In 1758, White's father died, and White moved permanently into the family house in Selborne. The property included a fairly large piece of arable land and is bordered on one side by the Hanger. The steep, wooded hill's summit was accessible only by a fair scramble until Gilbert and his brother John (1727–80; John seems to have done much of the actual digging) created a path known as the Zig-Zag because of its switchbacks, which gave a hiker an easier climb. White was enormously interested in gardening, both in raising flowers for their aesthetic beauty and in growing vegetables for purely practical uses. Upon moving back into the Wakes, he almost immediately began to experiment with plans and treatments for growing vegetables, and he often rode about the parish inquiring of farmers how they succeeded with particular crops.

Although he seems to have been somewhat casual about his duties as curate in the various parishes that he was responsible for, he was well known for his generosity, both financially and in sharing the product of his labors in the gardens.[15] Cultivation of the soil thus gave him several important benefits: he was able to stretch his relatively small salary, help his parishioners, and also make careful note of seasons and patterns of growth.

White's fame rests on the painstaking and deliberate observations that he began to make once he determined that his destiny lay in Selborne. From 1751 through 1767, he kept what he called the *Garden Kalendar,* which describes his activities in tending his garden, the growth of plants, and noteworthy weather events. Of necessity, the *Kalendar* has many gaps in it that mark when White was off in Oxford or on other travels, but it still has a wonderfully "fresh" feel to it, as White builds his garden, plants his vegetables, and records the results. On April 6, 1756, for instance, he records: "Made a Cucumber bed for three hand-glasses with two dung-carts of Parson's Dung. The trench is sixteen feet long, two & an a half broad, & one & half deep: the dung did not reach to the level of the Ground by some Inches."[16]

There is nothing heroic here, no romantic exploration of farthest Lapland or long venture across the Carolinas, and it would be easy to dismiss the whole work

FIGURE 5. Early-nineteenth-century print of Selborne. The "Zig-Zag" is visible on the hillside slightly to the right of the church tower. (Author's collection.)

FIGURE 6. The Wakes, Selborne, from the back lawn. (Author's collection.)

as the typical gardening notes of someone who perhaps took his work more seriously than others, but was in no real way different from thousands of other smallholders who were trying to get a jump on spring in their vegetable beds. White was, however, also an experimenter from the first. On April 10, 1756, he made a memo to himself: "Those melon-plants that were once seized with a mouldiness constantly dy'd-away by degrees, 'till they were quite devour'd by it; except those plants on which I tried the experiment of clipping-off the infected part with a pair of scissors: when they recover'd, & afterwards grew pretty well."[17] Again, nothing heroic, but the key is that White is *paying attention*, taking careful notes, and building up a store of experience for the long run. He never pretends that he is developing a general text for a wide area; in fact, his whole philosophy seems to rest on the importance of many local specialists, each responsible for detailed description and analysis of places that they know very well.

In 1766, there is a change in White's style and a refinement of focus. He abandons the title *Kalendar* and instead presents the *Flora Selborniensis with Some Co-Incidences of the Coming & Departures of Birds of Passage & Insects & the Appearing of Reptiles for the Year 1766*. In this work, he explicitly draws on Ray for plants, insects, and reptiles and on Willughby for birds.[18] One thus gets the chance to see Ray and Willughby "in action," as it were—their work is no longer simply catalogues; they have passed into a usable form in which they are references for practitioners. White gives us day-to-day occurrences, noting the presence and activity of particular species, each of which usually also receives its Latin name to ensure clarity. The style is very telegraphic: things "bloom," "blow," "emerge," "sprout," and "budd." Weather information is also reduced to a single line: "Snow and thick frost"; "Snow melts very fast in sunshine."[19]

Animal behaviors are also included in the *Flora:* "The more-hen, or water-hen, *Gallinula chloropus major;* chatters; and sports in the water."[20] Note the care with which White gives us alternate names for the same bird, as well as Willughby's trinomial. None of these notes is anywhere near as detailed as Linnaeus's Lapland notes, but they are designed for a different purpose. Linnaeus was looking to classify hitherto unknown species or habitats. White is immersed in the familiar—the naming has already been done by others. White is attempting to identify an order and flow within his immediate surroundings.

White's brother John shared Gilbert's interests in natural history. After an initial false start at university (he was initially sent down for misbehavior, but eventually was reaccepted), John also took holy orders, joined the army as a chaplain, and was sent to Gibraltar. This put him in an ideal position to observe the fall and spring migrations between Europe and Africa across the narrow Strait of Gibraltar, and Gilbert and he shared an active correspondence over the movement of particular species of birds. John was also a correspondent of Linnaeus, who wrote him several letters discussing taxonomy and zoology.[21] Partially at his brother's urging, John assembled a manuscript on the natural history of Gibraltar, but the book was never published, and most of it has been lost.

One of the really important aspects of the histories of the eighteenth and nineteenth centuries is that many people in both the middle and upper classes were dedicated letter writers—and they kept their letters. Letter writing (and handwriting, for that matter) was an art, with writers doing their best to convey often vivid descriptions of places and events. From the vantage point of two centuries, one cannot but be moved by these accounts from people whose living present was to become our history, and, in the case of Gilbert White, a significant moment in natural history.[22]

White had two correspondents of particular note to natural history: Thomas Pennant (1726–98)[23] and Daines Barrington (1727–1800).[24] Pennant, who probably met White at Oxford, came from a wealthy family and never had to worry about sources of income. He attended Oriel College (White's college) but never graduated, and spent his life writing more or less "popular" books.[25] Lysaght describes Pennant as "the most able British zoologist between Ray and Darwin," but he also acknowledges that little of what Pennant did was original and that he had the unfortunate habit of taking the work of others without giving full credit where it was due.[26] He seems to have made a point of knowing everyone worth knowing, and it was through him that White was introduced to Barrington.

Barrington was born into the aristocracy, became a judge, and for much of his life contributed notes and observations to the Royal Society.[27] Both Barrington and Pennant were well known in their day, both published a number of scientific and popular articles, and both were elected fellows of the Royal Society.[28]

Barrington was essential in organizing White's notetaking into a more formal and easily accessible format. It seems likely that Barrington's training in the law influenced his desire to have a clear record of fact from which to work, and he developed a particular format for notetaking that White adopted and used for the rest of his life. In 1767, Barrington sent White a *Naturalist's Journal*, which consisted of a bound notebook laid out with twelve columns per page waiting to be filled in.[29] These columns were headed "Date," "Place" (almost always "Selborne"), "Barometric Pressure," "Temperature," "Wind Direction," "Rainfall," "General Weather Notes," "Trees in Leaf and Fungi Appear," "Plants First in Flower," "Birds and Insects First Appear and Disappear," "Observations with Regard to Fish and Other Animals," and "Miscellaneous Observations."

White immediately saw the advantage of this structure, and starting in January 1768 he began entering data on a daily basis, employing a caretaker to record the measurements if he happened to be absent. He also set out to chronicle both the human and the nonhuman artifacts of his parish and to create a detailed phenology in which he carefully records the arrival and departure of species of birds, the first snowdrop to flower in the garden, the first frost, and so forth. Once he had obtained Timothy the tortoise from his aunt, he used Timothy's activities as an additional "standardized" tool for phenological measurement, recording when the tortoise first emerged from hibernation, what its activities were in the garden, and when it retired for the winter.

If all that White had done was to maintain this careful, systematic description of his immediate surroundings, he would have created an invaluable record for anyone interested in everything from climate change to the first hints of industrial pollution in rural England (he mentions periodically the arrival of a "London Haze" when the wind blew from the right quarter).[30] It is apparent, however, that his correspondents, Pennant and Barrington, had ideas toward a wider circulation. The three men engaged in a spirited correspondence in which White provided details of his observations in and around Selborne. These letters formed the basis of *The Natural History and Antiquities of Selborne.*

Barrington encouraged White in quantification, suggested additional avenues to pursue (he applauded White weighing Timothy the tortoise, and suggested that this should be an annual event, which it came to be), and presented some of White's work to the Royal Society.[31] Barrington also made some suggestions that White ignored, such as marking individual swifts by clipping their toes to see if indeed particular birds returned to the same nest each year.

Throughout his life, White was intrigued with the question of bird migration, or the "birds of passage" that had also fascinated Catesby. Gilbert's brother John's tenure in Gibraltar—a major migratory chokepoint—resulted in a good deal of discussion of both the timing and direction of migrations, and Gilbert seems to have been largely on the right track regarding both causes and consequences of migration. That he falls back into the earlier belief that swallows hibernate rather than migrate seems to be the result of overreliance on testimonials from numerous informants who claimed to have seen the birds in hibernacula or frozen under the ice of ponds, only to be revived upon gentle warming.[32] White was also bothered by the irregular appearance and disappearance of swallows in contrast to the regularity of other species.

One possible reason that White succeeded in catching and holding an audience for over two centuries is that he was writing to be read. Many other examples of natural history texts from the period were encyclopedic in form, designed to be used as a quick reference or to adorn library shelves as indicators of learning, rather than to be actually enjoyed as narratives. White's format—a series of edited letters that he wrote first to Pennant and then to Barrington—gives one the sense of dropping in on a fascinating conversation between friends. One can either read the book cover to cover or open it at random and be more or less guaranteed interesting insights into plants, animals, and the landscape in which they live.

More than seventy years after White's death, Lowell described White's writings as "Adam's journals in paradise."[33] One can applaud the sentiment, but at the same time it is important not to let sentiment get in the way of White's very real contribution to science.

On June 3, 1769, we know that the barometer stood at 29.5, the temperature was 58 degrees, and there were "Great Showers" at Selborne, yielding 0.3 inches of rain, after which it was "Fine." This was just as well, because in the "Miscellaneous Observations" column of the *Naturalist's Journal*, Gilbert White records, "Saw the planet Venus enter the disc of the sun. Just as the sun was setting the spot was visible to the naked eye. Nightingale sings, wood-owl hoots, fern-owl chatters."[34] Other eyes were watching the Transit of Venus, too.

Joseph Banks (1743–1820) was born to a wealthy family in London, and was sent to Harrow and then Eton for his early education before going up to Oxford in 1760.[35] He describes his interest in natural history as having started during his time at Eton, and being further advanced by the discovery of John Gerard's *Herbal* among his mother's books when he returned home for a holiday. Life as a young natural historian, even in the peaceful English countryside, was not always easy. There is a wonderful story of Banks as a teenager: searching for new species of plants in a ditch beside the highway in Chelsea, he was arrested on suspicion of being a highwayman. Banks was taken up to the Bow Street Court before the mistake was discovered and apologies offered all round.

Even more wonderful is the tale told many years later by one of Banks's school friends of traveling with the young man through Yorkshire: "The most amusing to me was the jump of a frog down the throat of the said Sir Joseph; he held it in the palm of his hand . . . to convince his three followers that there is nothing poisonous in this animal."[36]

When Banks arrived in Oxford, he discovered that there was nobody there capable of or willing to teach him the botany and natural history that he so wanted to study. Being by this point a young man of means (his father had died, leaving him a large estate), he went to Cambridge and hired his own tutor in botany and mathematics. Banks left Cambridge in 1763 before taking his degree, but he continued to study natural history with enthusiasm. He soon made friends with Thomas Pennant, who introduced him to many of the chief natural historians of the day. As a result of these connections, Banks was made a fellow of the Royal Society in 1766, when he was only twenty-three. At the end of April 1766, Banks joined the company of HMS *Niger*, which had been detailed to build a defensive blockhouse at Chateau Bay in Labrador.

Banks was able to use his position aboard ship to obtain a variety of specimens of plants from Newfoundland and to gain invaluable field experience. At the end of the season, the *Niger* ran in to St. John's, where she briefly shared the harbor with HMS *Grenville*. Onboard *Grenville* was Lieutenant James Cook, who had been sent to Newfoundland and Labrador in 1763 and had surveyed Chateau Bay as well as constructing other detailed maps of the region. Although no record exists of the two men meeting at St. John's, it is hard to imagine that they did not; in any case, they would soon play a major role in each other's lives.

From St. John's, the *Niger* sailed back to Europe, stopping in Portugal before returning to England. Banks's return with his interesting and detailed collections from America put him in a very good light with the government and the British natural history community in general. He was friends with Lord Sandwich, who served periodically during the eighteenth century as first lord of the admiralty and as such was in a position to provide favorable opportunities, or at least strong recommendations, to deserving candidates.[37]

The dates of the Transit of Venus had been determined by the astronomer (and fellow of the Royal Society) Edmund Halley earlier in the century, and the fellows had agreed that it was vital to send an expedition to the South Pacific for additional observations. They persuaded George III to fund the venture, which would also allow the navy to conduct an extended circumnavigation of the world that would include stops in New Zealand and the still largely hypothetical Australia. Cook, home from his successful survey of the Labrador coast, was the logical man to command the expedition. Banks's connections, his ability to subsidize any scientific studies, and the success and quality of his recent experiences gained him the berth of naturalist for the voyage.

The expedition, generally referred to as Cook's First Voyage, followed a track that would be repeated by multiple cartographic and natural history ventures over the next two centuries. Departing from Plymouth in August 1768, HMS *Endeavor* sailed to the coast of Brazil. From there she made her way southward, rounding Cape Horn at the extreme southern end of the continent, before making off to Tahiti for her rendezvous with the Transit of Venus. Unlike Darwin in the *Beagle*, more than sixty years later, the *Endeavor*, with Cook and Banks aboard, did not spend much time on the coast of South America and never went near the Galapagos. Instead, the expedition made directly for Tahiti, where they observed the transit from the appropriately named Point Venus on Saturday, June 3, 1769, just as Gilbert White was observing the same phenomenon in the late afternoon in his garden at Selborne. We know from Cook's journal that, unlike White, the expedition had no "Great Showers" to contend with, but they also had to do without the song of the nightingale.

Prior to leaving England, Cook had been given sealed orders for the second part of the voyage. These orders were necessarily vague, but encouraged Cook to proceed as far as 40 degrees south latitude in search of a then hypothetical southern continent and, if he found no new lands, to stand west for New Zealand.[38] *Endeavor* had a rough passage south, and finally at 40 degrees, 20 minutes south latitude, Cook turned northwest. The ship arrived in New Zealand in October and conducted a detailed survey of the two main islands. From New Zealand, the voyagers steered west, hoping to reach Van Diemen's Land (modern-day Tasmania), but they were driven somewhat northward and reached the east coast of Australia.

Endeavor worked her way north along the coast, with Cook mapping as much as possible and Banks doubtless wild to go ashore. They reached Botany Bay (modern Sydney) in late April 1770 and finally had the opportunity to investigate the land at first hand. Banks and his companions were particularly taken by the kangaroos, but they were also fascinated by the native vegetation and collected large numbers of specimens, while the painter Sydney Parkinson (1746–71) painted and sketched landscapes, flora, and fauna.[39] As *Endeavor* moved north, she grounded on the edge of the Great Barrier Reef and was seriously damaged. This required an extensive stay ashore while the ship was repaired and gave Banks still more opportunities to collect and observe the strange new plants and animals that were appearing on every hand.

Once the ship was repaired, they proceeded around the northern point of Australia, stopping in the Dutch East Indies for supplies and further repairs before sailing west once more, around the Cape of Good Hope, visiting St. Helena (later famous as Napoleon's final place of imprisonment) before returning home to England in July 1771. Cook and Banks were greeted as heroes on their return, although it seems that Banks made the most of his newfound fame, and some biographers chide him for excessive boastfulness that left Cook rather in the shade. Banks had done a great deal for natural history in his collections and notetaking throughout the voyage, and he had assisted Cook in supplying the crew with sources of vitamin C to prevent scurvy during the long voyage, but there is no question that it was Cook's skill as a navigator and seaman that had saved the ship on the Great Barrier Reef and had brought them safely home after a remarkable voyage through largely uncharted waters. It was Banks, however, who received an audience with the king—an audience that led to a long-lasting friendship that was to benefit science in general and natural history in particular.

Banks and Cook seem to have remained friends in spite of Banks's initial tendency to overshadow his captain. A more serious issue came up almost immediately, however, over the possibility of a second voyage. Banks was enthusiastic, and at his own expense began recruiting a team of scientists to accompany him and to purchase instruments and materials for their studies. The true cause of the resulting dispute between the natural historian and various naval authorities will probably never be absolutely clear, but it would seem that in spite of his experiences on *Endeavor,* Banks may have underestimated the sheer nuisance of accommodating eighteen supernumeraries on a small ship. He insisted on substantial modifications to *Resolution*, the flagship of the flotilla that was to conduct the new adventure. These included adding sufficient deck housing to render the ship seriously top-heavy, to the point where the pilot was reluctant to take her into the Channel, never mind around the world. The officers objected strongly to the new construction, the admiralty sided with the officers, and Banks, in a fury, quit the planning of the expedition and stormed off to Iceland instead.[40]

Once Banks had gotten over what we can refer to only as his hissy fit, he returned to London and got on with promoting the study of natural history. His friendship with King George literally blossomed when he convinced the king to pay some royal attention to the botanical gardens at Kew. It was largely through Banks's efforts and the king's patronage that Kew Gardens began their rise to their present stature as one of the most important botanical collections in the world.

Banks's personal life is perhaps worth a passing note. Here again he was very different from the retiring Gilbert White. We know that Banks kept at least two mistresses, despite being married in 1779. Adultery was both widely practiced and at least partially ignored among the upper classes, although George III was notoriously disapproving of any out-of-wedlock carnality. Banks's friend and patron Lord Sandwich was reputed to have been a member of the infamous Hellfire Club, which was the subject of much public gossip throughout the late eighteenth century.[41] Banks's actual marriage appears to have been relatively peaceful, but he had no acknowledged children. His death marked a major transition in both science and society. Darwin was too young to have known Banks personally, but one cannot but believe that Banks's example of the world-traveling scientist who returns home to develop his ideas and results must have been on Darwin's mind when he set off on the *Beagle*.

While England and the continent were producing a crop of globe-trotting natural historians, North America was developing its own homegrown varieties. John (1699–1777) and William Bartram (1739–1823) were a remarkable father-and-son duo who between them laid a solid foundation for a real North American botany. According to legend, John was initially "but a ploughman,"[42] but, as he says in a letter to Catesby, "I believe have taken more pains after the study of Botany, and the operations of nature, than any other that was born in English America, notwithstanding my low fortune in the world, which laid me under a necessity of very hard labour for the support of my family."[43]

John Bartram was an avid correspondent ideally placed in eastern North America at just the moment when an intelligent and careful botanist could be of the most use to a European scientific community increasingly eager to sample the flora of the New World.[44] John wrote to Catesby, to Johann Dillenius at Oxford, to Sir Hans Sloane in London, and to Linnaeus in Sweden (Bartram assisted Linnaeus's "apostle" Peter Kalm during his visit to America). He obtained specimens for colleagues seeking additions to their herbaria and botanical gardens, he identified new species on his own, and he brought the Linnaean ideal of an organized taxonomy into the growing American science.[45] John Bartram's hunger for new knowledge is palpable in his writings, and one cannot but love someone who says, "Before Doctor Dillenius gave me a hint of it, I took no particular notice of Mosses, but looked upon them as a cow looks at a pair of new barn doors; yet now he is pleased to say, I have made a good progress in that branch of Botany, which really is a very curious part of vegetation."[46]

This hunger for knowledge traveled both ways across the Atlantic, with English natural historians sending whole shopping lists of questions and desired specimens and rewarding Bartram with a mixture of monetary payments and, perhaps even more welcome, copies of books not yet available in overseas colonies. There were hints of things to come in a letter from a Dr. Fothergill: "I am pleased that thy son William is engaged in describing the Tortoises of your country. America seems to abound with this species of animal, more than any other country. As the inhabitants increase, these, as well as native plants, will be thinned; and it is therefore of some consequence to begin their history as soon as possible."[47] It is particularly interesting to see that at the same time that orthodox theology more or less excluded the possibility of extinction, natural historians were already fully cognizant of the likelihood of anthropogenic "thinning."

Naturalists in Britain funded some of John Bartram's longer expeditions, including a journey from Pennsylvania to Lake Ontario, and he and William traveled through Florida at the conclusion of the Seven Years' War. In one letter, he comments, "I have performed my journey through Maryland and Virginia, as far as Williamsburgh, so up the James River to the mountains, in many very crooked turnings and windings . . . betwixt my setting out and returning home, I travelled 1100 miles in five weeks' time; having rested but one day in all that time."[48] One assumes that he was on horseback for much of this journey, but it is still an impressive distance to have covered. In addition to payments for his collecting and trips, his English friends lobbied George III to give him the title of king's botanist for North America, with an attached pension that must have been welcome to the former plowman.

In part to facilitate his ability to supply his European colleagues, and in part to provide a place for study and reflection, Bartram established what seems to have been the first truly systematic general botanical garden in North America, just outside Philadelphia. This garden contained a broad range of flowering plants, including both recognized medicinal species and plants collected simply for their rarity or beauty. The garden remained within the Bartram family until the mid-nineteenth century.

Bartram's writings do not seem to have met with much favor in his own time period. His friend Benjamin Franklin, with whom he helped found the American Philosophical Society, commented when writing to a fellow scientist about the elder Bartram that "I make no Apologies for Introducing him to you, for tho' a plain illiterate Man, you will find that he has merit."[49] This is more than a little patronizing. Bartram's letters show him to be a careful, thoughtful observer of nature—hardly illiterate—and a number of them were read into the *Philosophical Transactions of the Royal Society*, on topics ranging from mussels, wasps, and snakes to the aurora borealis. More recent biographers refer to him as "the Father of American Botany," which seems a fair enough designation, but how many modern botanists (or scientists of any era, for that matter) could say, "I have split rocks seventeen feet long, and built four houses of hewn stone, split out of the rocks with my own hands"?[50] These were the same hands that could gently pack up a moss or a bullfrog to send to a friend on the other side of the Atlantic. Bartram's garden was spared by British troops advancing from the Battle of Brandywine Creek, but he died before the results of the Revolutionary War could be known.[51] He is buried in an unmarked grave in the Friends Burying Ground in Philadelphia.

William Bartram, as noted, traveled extensively with his father, and he carried on the family business of botanizing. William was the third of the nine children whom John had by his second wife, Ann (his first wife, Mary, had died in 1727, after giving him two children). Besides working closely with his father on developing the family botanical garden and trade in specimens, William was a talented artist, painting and sketching many of the specimens of plants that he and his father collected, as well as expanding into illustrating his other passion: the avifauna of North America.

William had accompanied his father to Florida and later attempted to set up a plantation there, underwritten by his father. The attempt failed disastrously.[52] In spite of this, he determined to explore as much of the southern region as possible, and under the sponsorship of his father's correspondent John Fothergill, the younger Bartram set off on an extended collecting trip in the spring of 1773.[53] This journey lasted over four and a half years and took him through Florida, the Carolinas, modern Alabama, Georgia, Mississippi, and the then French province of Louisiana.

William's expedition resulted in the publication of the *Travels of William Bartram*.[54] The *Travels* are one of the most complete depictions of late colonial eastern North America available. William often traveled alone, sometimes on foot, sometimes by boat. He was often in real physical danger, yet throughout he took careful notes of his surroundings and sketched what he saw.[55] Overall, his writing displays a remarkable degree of objectivity, mixed with a sense for a good yarn. Even when confronting large groups of alligators (and beating away one with his club), he still assesses the surrounding environment, concluding that the abundance of predators is almost certainly due to the enormous number of fish in the river down which he is paddling.

After the Revolutionary War, Bartram spent much of his remaining years close to home. He continued his correspondence with the great and the powerful. Letters between him and Thomas Jefferson discuss seeds that Bartram supplied Jefferson for plantings at Monticello;[56] when Jefferson organized the Lewis and Clark Expedition, he encouraged Bartram to consider accompanying the team for at least part of its journey. Bartram refused, citing his advancing years. Bartram was encouraged to offer courses in botany, but he declined this also. However, he was a great supporter of the young Alexander Wilson as Wilson began to develop his plans for an illustrated text on the birds of North America.

Bartram's own artistic renditions of what he saw in his travels or grew in his garden are mixed in terms of overall accuracy. In his writing, he makes it clear that he is often overwhelmed by the beauty of what he sees, and some of his botanical illustrations are very fine indeed. But by contrast, in spite of (or perhaps because of) several close encounters, his alligators resemble medieval dragons rather than anything likely to be seen in the swamps of Florida.

Bartram was born in an America not much different from that depicted by Mark Catesby: a thin band of colonies bordering a vast, unknown wilderness occupied by savage beasts and savage humans. Yet by the time he died, the United States was already making much of its Manifest Destiny to occupy the continent from coast to coast. Between them, the Bartrams had ushered in a new age of scientific botany suitable for the new nation that had come into being while they quietly collected and sketched the plants and animals that would be under that nation's guard.

EIGHT . Before the Origin

Darwinian biology, or Darwinism, as Alfred Russel Wallace christened it, was deeply rooted in natural history.[1] Both Charles Darwin and Wallace were supremely confident natural historians and keen observers of a broad range of phenomena; both traveled widely during some part of their careers; and both were fully aware of the attempts of their predecessors to study and make sense of the natural world.

The primary elements of Darwinism were born from studies of natural history and the taxonomy that was built out of it.[2] Natural selection itself is one of those ideas that, after the fact, simply makes sense (Thomas Huxley, Darwin's chief champion, commented, "How extremely stupid not to have thought of that!" after reading *On the Origin of Species*).[3] In essence, Darwin says that if you observe variation in form (observable from studies of morphology), and if some of these variations are heritable (observable in the domestic pedigrees of plants and animals), and if some of these heritable variants are associated regularly with the production of more or fewer young (potentially observable in detailed behavioral studies), then, given enough time, a population will change.

That Darwin and Wallace did not develop their ideas in a vacuum should be obvious, and enormous amounts of scholarship and ink have already been spent on examining where these ideas originated, who Darwin and Wallace actually were, and what they were actually saying.[4] It would be impossible to completely encapsulate the life of either man in a single chapter, but it is important to consider the role of natural history in their work and their impact on natural history as a form of biology.[5]

Regardless of the degree of religious belief or skepticism that one senses in various natural historians' writing (and there is evidence of both), it is worth considering how the "deep program" of biblical accounts may have impacted others' thought processes.[6] Hildegard von Bingen, John Ray, Gilbert White, William Bartram, and Darwin himself would all have been exposed to the first book of Genesis long before they started examining the world as naturalists.

If one defines *evolution* as "change over time," the book of Genesis can be regarded as evolutionary in some senses. A creation story in which a creator simply wills the world into existence all at once was entirely possible. Such stories do exist in other religions, but in Genesis the world comes into being through a series of steps, and is in essence built up logically. The deep program here is profoundly developmental. One moves from nothingness to being, from an implied disorder to ultimate order.

Three critically important differences between the evolution in Genesis and the evolution in Darwin and Wallace are that, first, Genesis assumes an author of the process, analogous to, but even more personified than the "un-moved Mover" in Aristotle. Second, there is a specific endpoint to Genesis's evolution: everything is completed in six "days," and on the seventh God rests. After this there can be no further creation, no further change. Finally, there is a normative judgment at the end of each day of creation: God examines what is now there, and finds it "good."

Another potential deep program emerging from both a biblical form of creation and classical Greek philosophy is typology. Plato suggests that the world of our perception is filled with mere "shadows" of ideal forms, which can only be approximated in the physical world. This suggests that there could be better or worse "shadows" or copies of any particular organism, and places the entire question of variation in an interesting light. Taxonomists were encouraged to select the "best possible" or "most typical" sample of a species as the type specimen against which all other individuals could be measured. That the actual selection of a type specimen was often quite arbitrary could be forgotten, and possession of type specimens within a collection was an indicator of the overall status of the collection. The Platonic notion of shadows of some perfect form also fit well with a biblical creation in which organisms would have initially been created in ideal forms, and any subsequent variation would be a lapse from grace rather than an essential element of an evolution that is supposed to have ended with the initial act of creation.

The increasingly detailed and comprehensive studies and catalogues of natural historians, and the decreasing proportion of the world left blank on the map, exerted ever greater pressure on a tidy biblical creation. One can sense Ray's deep frustration in the differences between the evidence of his senses, which tell him that a single Deluge never could have produced the landforms that he sees, and his belief in the truth of scripture. Other naturalists avoided the question of origins entirely, contenting themselves with describing what they saw as they saw it, but the evidence they collected could only raise more questions.

One of the most popular encyclopedias produced for a general audience was the *Histoire naturelle générale et particuliére* of Georges-Louis Leclerc, the comte de Buffon, known typically as Buffon.[7] Buffon (1707–88) was born in the same year as Linnaeus, but unlike Linnaeus, who had to struggle to afford an education, Buffon was born into the aristocracy and could afford to study and travel as he pleased.[8] Buffon immersed himself in the natural history of his day, communicated with a broad range of other scientists, and conducted research of his own. He was a polymath, intrigued by all branches of science, and believed that it was important to provide information in a form that would be accessible to a wide audience.

In 1739, Buffon was appointed director of the Jardin du Roi, the French equivalent of the Royal Gardens at Kew in England. Buffon seems to have been much more comfortable with animals than with plants, but he took his job seriously, and set about writing what was intended to be a comprehensive description of everything in the natural world. Buffon adopted a three-kingdom structure in his *Histoire naturelle*, but completed only the minerals and animals in the thirty-five large volumes that were published between 1749 and 1788, the year of his death. Sufficient notes remained for nine additional posthumous volumes, but it is ironic, given his professional position, that plants get such short shrift. Buffon does not stick to a strict Linnaean taxonomic structure below the most general level of kingdoms. Instead he organizes his books by degrees of presumed familiarity to his readers, beginning with domesticated species and working gradually outward to more exotic examples. He also emphasizes temperate species before dealing with tropical varieties, and makes it clear that within any hierarchy humans must be regarded as the most perfect of forms.

As Mayr has pointed out, a taxonomy based on familiarity is "as unsuited as [it] can be to serve as a basis for evolutionary considerations."[9] Buffon's insights are remarkable, but so is his unwillingness to follow through and accept his conclusions: "If, for example, it were true that the ass is but a degeneration from the horse—then there would no longer be any limit to the power of nature, and we should not be wrong in supposing that, with sufficient time, she has been able from a single being to derive all the other organized beings."[10] He is almost there, so incredibly close! Common descent, multiplication of species, gradualism—one can feel how close he comes to Darwinism. But then it all falls apart: "But this is by no means a proper representation of nature. We are assured by the authority of revelation that all animals have participated equally in the grace of Creation and that the first pair of every species issued fully formed from the hands of the Creator."[11] In an era in which reliance on authority was being challenged on almost every front, this final Authority would persist for at least two more generations.

Buffon believes that species' outward forms are dictated in part by a need to match their physical environment. As a result, besides cataloguing species on the basis of familiarity or importance to humans, he groups organisms by where they are found. Although this sort of classification may seem almost facile at first glance, by doing this Buffon moves into the realms of biogeography and ecology. A strictly morphological or cladistic scheme of classification may lose or obscure relationships that a geographic ordination will preserve. In this sense, Buffon precedes more commonly recognized biogeographers, such as Humboldt and Wallace, by a century. Buffon made natural history fun, and it seems likely that many of the successors who supplanted his ideas with new information got their start by wandering through his text and marveling at the variety of organisms and landscapes waiting to be explored.

Another important French contributor in the run-up to Darwinian evolutionary theory was Jean-Baptiste Pierre Antoine de Monet, the chevalier de la Marck, known to most of his readers as Lamarck. Lamarck was born in 1744 in a small village in Picardy.[12] His father hoped that he would become a priest and sent him to a Jesuit school in Amiens. The senior de la Marck died when his son was sixteen, and the following year Lamarck joined the army and served for seven years before being pensioned and going to Paris.[13] There Lamarck worked in a bank and studied botany and medicine while publishing a three-volume treatise on French flora, which brought him to the attention of Buffon. This flora is remarkable in its use of specific dichotomous keys to identify each plant. It also had the advantage of being published in French, which opened it to a wider domestic audience. In 1779, Lamarck was elected to the French Academy of Sciences, and he continued to support himself with writing and part-time jobs until 1788, when he was appointed a keeper of the herbarium in the Jardin du Roi. Lamarck's most significant writing up to this point was the botanical volume in the *Encyclopédie méthodique,* which is, at 186 volumes published over 40 years, perhaps the most massive of the great encyclopedias of the Enlightenment.

FIGURE 7. Birds, from Buffon's *Histoire naturelle générale et particuliére*, eighteenth century. (Author's collection.)

Lamarck's experiences during the Revolution (1789–93) are somewhat unclear. He continued working at the Jardin du Roi, but the outbreak of Republican fervor and the subsequent Terror made any sort of elitism suspect.[14] Lamarck's position was in jeopardy, but he published a series of pamphlets on the importance of the collections in which he strategically changed the garden's name to the Jardin des Plantes, and as such both it and he survived the regicide. The First French Empire provided opportunities for both the physical expansion of the Jardin's holdings (captured and confiscated herbaria were added to the collection) and for Lamarck's professional advancement. In 1793, he was appointed "professor of zoology, insects, worms, and microscopic animals."[15]

Until this point, Lamarck seems to have shared the common eighteenth-century view of the fixity of organisms and structures since some original moment of creation. His geology, by contrast, suggests a process of transformation and degeneration, with mineral structures beginning as highly organized forms and gradually dissolving into simple crystals. The idea seems silly from a modern perspective, but it is important in that it provides a clear break from an unchanging, ordered world. Lamarck's excursions into geology were important in another sense: they required him to confront the question of fossils head on. The Paris Basin is notoriously rich in fossils, and careful study of various layers convinced Lamarck of the antiquity of the earth. In discussing the nature of change on a global scale, Lamarck likens human experience to that of insects with a lifespan of a year trying to describe the history of the building in which they live: "For twenty-five generations there has been no change: hence the building is considered eternal."[16] This is enormously important. The official position on the possible age of the earth tended to rely exclusively on scripture. In 1650, Archbishop James Ussher, basing his calculations on the often almost parenthetical ages of biblical figures, had estimated that the earth had come into existence in the late afternoon of October 22, 4004 BCE.[17] While other scholars had hedged a bit on Ussher's precision, the overall accuracy of his estimate was widely accepted, with unfortunate results for science. An earth that was less than six thousand years old could not possibly produce organisms through any sort of gradual change. Lamarck's explicit rejection of this estimate and the changelessness that often accompanied it was an important foreshadowing of things to come.

By 1801, Lamarck was back to biology, producing a text on invertebrates in which he begins his discussion of the possible transformation of species for which he is most famous.[18] This work was completed between 1815 and 1822 as he prepared a comprehensive natural history of the invertebrates in seven volumes.

Lamarck's ideas on an evolutionary origin of species involved a combination of the cumulative effects of the environment and the great swaths of time that his geology allowed. Lamarck's most important contribution here is that he sees a clear relationship between taxonomy and phylogeny—organisms not only *are* more complex as one moves through a taxonomic sequence, they have *become* more complex—that is to say, there has been real evolutionary transformation from simpler forms to more complex ones in such a way that what might have started out as one species has, with enough time, become another.

Much has been made of Lamarck's proposed mechanism for evolution—the so-called inheritance of acquired characters, or the importance of the use and disuse of a feature in its preservation, extension, or loss. Lamarck is quite clear when he says, "Each species has been submitted to the influence of the circumstances which it has encountered and, from this it has acquired the habits which we now know and the modifications in their parts which we now observe."[19] Essentially, the environment creates a "need" for a feature or the expansion of an existing feature; the organism responds; and the result is passed on to subsequent generations until some sort of temporary equilibrium is reached. The resulting organism may differ so much from its parental stock that the taxonomist places the new organism in a new taxonomic classification. Alternately, the organism makes use of an existing feature (or, inversely, ceases to use it) and as a result the feature is enhanced or discarded, again eventually leading to a reclassification. Lamarck points to the obviously highly modified giraffe's neck as an example supporting his theory. Although the example is zoological, one cannot but wonder how much Lamarck was influenced by his early exposure to and concentration on botany. Plants are notoriously plastic in form, and clearly respond to environmental conditions by adjusting patterns of growth. That the *plasticity* may be what is heritable, rather than any particular change, does not seem to have entered into Lamarck's calculations, and it would take more than a century for this issue to be addressed in a perhaps definitive form.[20]

Sadly, Lamarck's final years were dominated by poverty and growing blindness. His ideas fell out of fashion as French science became increasingly dominated by Georges Cuvier (1769–1832). Cuvier's studies of the fossil record established once and for all the reality of extinction, but he was firmly opposed to evolutionary thought and was a strong proponent of catastrophism: the idea that the earth's history has been dominated by periodic floods and upheavals interspersed with periods of stability. Lamarck's eyesight began to fail in the late 1810s, and he was completely blind by 1822. Some of his final works were dictated to his daughter, as he could no longer write. In 1824, he was forced to sell his herbarium, and he died relatively ignored or forgotten in 1829. Many of Lamarck's ideas have proved to be wrong, and he was often prone to speculating without providing adequate evidence, but he was a real pioneer in opening up the possibilities of organic evolution, and it would no doubt give him some satisfaction to see how many bright young graduate students stumble over his work nearly two centuries later and say, "Hmm . . . just suppose . . . " The Baron Cuvier has been sidelined as perhaps the last great guardian of traditional eighteenth-century natural history. By contrast, Lamarck, although he died before Cuvier, heralded the nineteenth century and the future.

Meanwhile, in a Britain rapidly growing as an industrial and imperial power, the Darwin family was beginning to take the first steps that would make their name a household word. From their writing—particularly their private letters—the Darwins seem to have been droll, ironic, remarkably fun people, engaged in serious pursuits but also fully appreciative of one another and the world around them.

Examples of Darwin humor abound. In the "Preliminary Notice" to a life of his grandfather Erasmus (1731–1802), Charles cannot resist including letters to and from his grandfather and his great-aunt Susannah Darwin in which they discuss their fasting for Lent.[21] Susannah wants to be reassured that pork is in fact "fish" and therefore acceptable during Lent, citing the fate of the Gadarene Swine.[22] Erasmus assures her that she is justified in her assumption and continues: "For my own part have lived on Puding, milk, and vegetables all this Lent; but don't mistake me, I don't mean I have not touch'd roast beef, mutton, veal, goose, fowl, &c. for what are all these? All flesh is grass! . . . P.S. Excuse Hast, supper being called, very Hungry."[23]

I suppose that one either finds this very funny (particularly the postscript) or one doesn't. What is apparent here and elsewhere is that the Darwins liked one another, teased one another, and were well-read intellectuals who "got" one another's literary allusions without prompting. Erasmus Darwin died before Charles's birth, and he has often been overshadowed by his famous grandson and also by a hint of scandal, but he was a formidable figure in his time, and it is clear that Charles was familiar with his writings and legacy when he set off to make a name for himself.

Erasmus was born in 1731 at the family seat of Elston Hall in Nottinghamshire, England. After getting his BA and medical degrees from Cambridge, Erasmus moved to Lichfield to practice medicine, and in 1757 he married Mary Howard, who was eight or nine years younger than himself. Charles includes another wonderful letter, from his grandfather to Mary, written three days before their marriage, in which Erasmus tells his fiancée of finding an old family notebook that contained recipes "to make Pye-Crust" and "to make Tarts," but that his eye had fallen on a recipe "To make Love":

> "This Receipt" says I, "must be curious, I'll send it to Miss Howard next Post, let the way of making of it be what it will"—Thus it is "To make Love. Take of Sweet-William and of Rose-Mary, of each as much as is sufficient. To the former of these add of Honesty and herb-of-grace; and to the latter of Eye-bright and Motherwort of each a large handful: mix them separately, and then, chopping them together, add one Plumb. Two sprigs of Heart's Ease and a little Tyme. And it makes a most excellent dish.

He goes on to find a recipe "to make an honest Man": "'This is no new dish to me' says I, 'besides it is now quite old Fashioned; I won't read it.' Then follow'd 'To make a good Wife.' 'Pshaw,' continued I, 'an acquaintance of mine, a young Lady of Lichfield, knows how to make this Dish better than any other Person in the World, and she has promised to treat me with it sometime.'"[24]

So was gentle courtship in the eighteenth century![25] Erasmus and Mary seem to have been very happy together; they had five children, three of whom, including Charles's father, Robert, survived infancy. Sadly, Mary died in 1770 after a long illness. Erasmus hired a governess to look after Robert and eventually had an affair with her that resulted in two daughters. These children were supported by Erasmus, but their mother eventually married a local businessman. Erasmus then fell passionately in love with Elizabeth Pole, who was already married to a war hero nearly thirty years older than herself, by whom she had three children. Descriptions of Erasmus at this time are hardly flattering. His love of food—hinted at in his letter to his sister—had already begun to affect his weight. He was heavily pockmarked by smallpox, and, while his medical practice supported him and his family, he was by no means rich. He also had a lifelong stutter, which affected his ability to articulate his thoughts but may have also made him a sympathetic listener. By contrast, Elizabeth had been born into the aristocracy, was beautiful, articulate, and wealthy, and had, as the saying goes, "married well."

Elizabeth's husband died in 1780, and, much to the surprise of everyone, she married Darwin soon afterward. Again, it seems to have been a love match on both sides, and, though Elizabeth outlived her second husband by thirty years, she never married again. They had seven children together, six of whom survived infancy. Elizabeth insisted that Darwin leave his house in Lichfield and live with her just outside Derby. She also made it clear that she had no intention of being stranded forever in the countryside, and periodically made Erasmus accompany her to London.

Erasmus was primarily interested in medicine, but he wrote widely on a variety of topics, and mixed them together with a degree of grace. Between 1783 and 1785, he worked on a translation of Linnaeus into English.[26] In *The Loves of Plants*, Erasmus sets Linnaeus to highly allegorical poetry, accompanied by detailed notes on the meaning of each stanza.[27] It was this poem in particular, when encountered by less accepting Victorians long after Erasmus's death, that probably led to charges that he was a pornographer. A culture reluctant to expose table legs must have had a difficult time with a poem based entirely on sex, even if it was largely of the vegetable kind. I suspect that my grandmother would have found the following sort of thing "unnecessary":

> The freckled Iris owns a fiercer flame,
> And three unjealous husbands wed the dame.
> Cupressus dark disdains his dusky bride,
> One dome contains them, but two beds divide.[28]

The notes attached to each verse make it clear what Erasmus was up to, but one has to wonder whether Linnaeus really needed this sort of transmutation.

In terms of original work, Erasmus's *Zoonomia* is intended to be a system of medicine, but it is also to a great degree an analysis of both the causes and functions of behaviors.[29] Its first part centers on an analysis of the motions of humans, animals, and plants. Erasmus then goes on to an interesting discussion of instinct, and moves from there into his medical system. He includes some surprisingly modern experiments in vision in which the reader is encouraged to stare at a colored dot or set of circles and then look away in order to experience an optical effect. Similar illustrations can be found in textbooks in the twenty-first century. Charles says, in his account of his grandfather, that Erasmus was reluctant to publish the *Zoonomia*.[30] Erasmus himself says in its introduction that that the bulk of the text had "lain by him for twenty years" for fear of ridicule—an interesting similarity to Charles's own reluctance to publish *The Origin of Species*.[31]

Erasmus's *Temple of Nature* is a poem whose repetitive rhyming scheme makes it difficult to read at length and easy to parody.[32] Charles comments rather sadly that he doubts that anyone of his generation has read even a line of his grandfather's poetry, although it was popular in its day.[33] In spite of this, much of Erasmus's poetry is worthy of attention if one is seeking potential sources for later ideas. Contained within it one finds clear evidence of thoughts that Erasmus's grandson would address in more sober terms decades later:

> So human progenies, if unrestrain'd,
> By climate friended, and by food sustain'd,
> O'er seas and soils, prolific hordes! would spread
> Ere long, and deluge their terraqueous bed;
> But war and pestilence, disease and dearth.
> Sweep the superfluous myriads from the earth.[34]

Much has been made of the impact of Malthus on Charles Darwin's ideas, but here we have a Malthusian world in which animals are capable of reproducing much more than they actually do because of the impact of disease and conflict, all set to snappy verse. Portions of the poem and the attached "philosophical notes" hint at transformation in a variety of senses, and in the notes one reads that "God created all things which exist, and that these have been from the beginning in a perpetual state of improvement."[35] This is a remarkable change from the fixity and completion of the medieval great chain of being. The *scala naturae* was not yet abandoned, but it had begun to show its age.

Erasmus was friends with some of the most interesting and active thinkers, inventors, and industrialists of his day. Politically speaking, he was liberal to the point of being a radical. He supported both the American and French revolutions, although he would have been horrified by the Terror. He was friends with Benjamin Franklin, with whom he discussed electricity and the alphabet.[36] He was also a founding member of the informal Lunar Society, which included some of the most innovative manufacturers and thinkers of the era.[37] Erasmus had been elected to the Royal Society in 1761, but he rarely attended, and his widespread interests in the applications of science and his love of invention drew him to a less aristocratic and more practical crowd.[38] Another member of the Lunatics was Josiah Wedgewood, who was in the process of becoming a millionaire through his development of cheap, high-quality pottery and his investment in a canal system to transport it.

Josiah became Erasmus's best friend, and the Wedgewoods played a major role in the Darwin family from then onward. Josiah's daughter Susannah married Erasmus's son Robert. They in turn had four daughters and two sons, the youngest of whom was Charles. Josiah's son Josiah II had four sons and three daughters.[39] Josiah III married Charles's sister Caroline, and Charles himself married Josiah II's youngest daughter, Emma.

Erasmus Darwin died very suddenly in April 1802. He had been busy writing all morning, felt cold, and moved closer to the fire. He took faint, was moved to the couch in his study, and died peacefully shortly thereafter. He was buried in the local church, and his monument reads in part, "Physician, a Poet and a Philosopher." Erasmus Darwin was all of that and more. He died too soon to even see his most distinguished descendant, but one cannot but feel that he would have been thrilled to know that evolutionary thought, fueled by a strong dose of natural history, was only a generation away.

NINE . Forms Most Beautiful

Darwin

Charles Robert Darwin (1809–82) was the fifth of six children born to Dr. Robert Darwin and Susannah Darwin *née* Wedgewood. By the time Charles was born, the Darwin and Wedgewood family fortunes were well established. Charles's father had followed Erasmus Darwin into medicine and had also taken advantage of the family's Lunar Society connections to become very well off. His marriage to Susannah also brought with it a piece of Wedgewood capital and cemented what had already become a multigenerational friendship between the families.

Robert constructed the Mount, a substantial Georgian house for himself and his growing family, in Shrewsbury, Shropshire, and settled down to practice in the surrounding region. Like his father before him, Robert was an extremely large man (he weighed in at well over three hundred pounds), and according to many contemporary observers could be quite daunting on first meeting. In spite of this, he seems to have been an excellent listener and was regarded as being particularly sensitive to what at the time were called "women's complaints"—the sort of thing that Freud would label "hysteria" a century later. From what we know of Robert's practice, he may have anticipated Freud in using talking cures, in which the patient essentially works through anxieties with the help of the physician.

Darwin's accounts of his childhood (admittedly masked and edited by time) are of a relatively happy period.[1] He was certainly bossed around by big sisters (he mentions thinking, before coming into a room for lessons from his sister Caroline, "What will she blame me for now?"; 22), but he also had many friends, and remembers being well liked. He enjoyed long walks and making up stories (he says at several points that he feels that he was "a naughty boy"; 22), but schoolwork was not a strong point. Overall he had the sense that he was at best of middling intelligence—not the stupidest boy in the class, but also not particularly bright. He says of his father that on the one hand "many people feared him," but also that "he was the kindest man I ever knew" (28). Of perhaps greatest interest to those wishing to delve into psychohistory is Charles's extensive testimony on his father's ability to judge people's characters and his assessment of Charles's own ability: "You care for nothing but shooting, dogs and rat-catching, and you will be a disgrace to yourself and all your family!" (28). Falser words, of course, were seldom spoken.

The grammar school that Charles attended after he became too old for home-schooling focused almost exclusively on the classics, at which he failed to excel, but he says that by the time he went to school: "My taste for natural history, and more especially for collecting, was well developed. I tried to make out the names of plants, and collected all sorts of things, shells, seals, franks, coins and minerals. The passion for collecting, which leads a man to be a systematic naturalist, a virtuoso, or a miser, was very strong in me, and was clearly innate, as none of my sisters or brother ever had this taste." He also mentions reading a book which he calls the *Wonders of the World*, to which he suggests he owes some of the wanderlust that encouraged him to travel.[2]

Realizing, perhaps, that Charles was wasting his time in school, Robert Darwin resolved to send him to university early. Charles's brother Erasmus (1804–81) had already gone to Cambridge for an undergraduate degree, but Robert must have thought enough of Charles that he was willing to send him straight to medical school. Darwin had already been out with his father on his rounds, and the elder Darwin had assigned Charles some patients of his own, and Charles's son Francis remembers his father being very proud of having cured some of their ailments.

To say that Charles was not happy in medical school would be an understatement. He found the lectures enormously dull, dissection made him queasy, and he recounts attending actual surgery only twice: "I also attended on two occasions the operating theatre . . . and saw two very bad operations, one on a child, but I rushed away before they were completed. Nor did I ever attend again, for hardly any inducement would have been strong enough to make me do so; this being long before the blessed days of chloroform. The two cases fairly haunted me for many a long year" (48).

Probably the best part of Edinburgh for Charles was membership in the Plinian Society, a short-lived natural history club that met regularly in an underground chamber at the university. The society had been founded by Robert Jameson, the Regius Professor of natural history, shortly before Charles arrived in Edinburgh, and it gave him an opportunity to both hear and present short "papers" on studies of plants and animals. Darwin gave his first presentations on marine invertebrates and algae, but the society kept no list of presentations, so there is no permanent record of what Darwin might have done there. Charles also attended lectures at the Wernerian Society, where he heard John James Audubon lecture about the birds of North America.[3] Darwin was not very taken with Audubon, feeling that he had treated other ornithologists badly, particularly on the question of food detection in vultures. The debate must have deeply impressed Darwin in some way, for on April 27, 1834, he recorded from South America, "This day I shot a condor" and then described a series of experiments that he conducted on captive condors' power of smell.[4]

There has been a good deal of debate over the years as to Darwin's attitude about race, ranging from accusations that he was a racist to assertions that he was an enlightened liberal well ahead of his time.[5] There is no question but that abolitionism was a longstanding issue in both the Darwin and the Wedgewood families. Erasmus senior had spoken and written against slavery in the eighteenth century, and the Wedgewoods had produced a memorable china plaque depicting a slave with the motto "Am I not a man and a brother?" Darwin was clearly opposed to slavery as an institution, a stand that was to cause him trouble on the *Beagle*.[6]

There is certainly evidence that Darwin did not regard all humans as equal in either a physical or a mental sense—he was enormously taken aback by the Fuegians, whom he regarded as "savages," but it would seem that here, as in most everything else, Darwin was applying the evidence at hand to evaluate the situation. The Fuegians behaved like "savages," so savages they were to him. When Darwin encountered intelligence, courtesy, and humanity, he immediately reciprocated. The first immediate test of this came in Edinburgh when Darwin met "a negro [who] lived in Edinburgh, who had travelled with [Charles] Waterton and gained his livelihood by stuffing birds, which he did excellently; he gave me lessons for payment, and I used often to sit with him, for he was a very pleasant and intelligent man."[7] These lessons in taxidermy, which doubtless also included tales of travels in South America, may well have been the most useful things that Darwin got from his time at Edinburgh. He later bitterly regretted not putting more time into studying dissection, which would have been enormously useful for his future work.

Erasmus left Edinburgh after one year, but Charles stayed on to take classes with Jameson, although he describes the great man's lectures as "incredibly dull." Instead of being inspired, he developed "the determination never as long as I lived to read a book on Geology or in any way to study the science" (52).

Darwin spent his summer holidays at the Wedgewood estate of Maer, which was located approximately thirty miles from Shrewsbury. He adored his "Uncle Jos."—Josiah Wedgewood II—and the feeling seems to have been returned. Wedgewood would play key roles throughout Charles's early life.

After the summer of 1828, Robert seems to have given up hope that Charles would ever become a doctor. Making a living would never be an issue—Robert had plenty of money from investments in canals, roads, and later railroads—but there remained the question of doing something worthwhile, rather than simply joining the idle rich. With medicine a nonstarter and Charles showing no interest in law, there remained only the Church. Somewhat reluctantly, Robert withdrew Charles from Edinburgh and sent him to Cambridge to take holy orders.

Darwin loved Cambridge, but not for the reasons his father had hoped. It is fairly obvious from Charles's letters that his experiences and behavior were those of a fairly typical undergraduate.[8] He says himself that he "got in with a sporting set, including some dissipated young men" (60). This is not to suggest that he constantly indulged in drunken orgies—the family dislike of alcohol was a permanent feature of his character (he told Francis that he had gotten really drunk only four times in his life)—but he and his friends certainly drank a fair bit, they liked to eat well (letters speak of the Glutton's Club), and they liked to hunt and ride and generally do pretty much anything except study. In those days, "gentlemen of the College" were expected to be in their rooms by curfew (although it was almost a point of honor to find ways to slip in and out after hours, escaping the watchful eyes of the porter). Darwin regularly broke curfew and was in danger of being sent down or "rusticated"—in modern terms, expelled.

Charles was rising twenty, and, as if the distractions of college life weren't enough, he also had his eye on a serious girlfriend. The young lady in question was Fanny Owen, the daughter of William Owen, a retired military officer with an estate near Shrewsbury. Fanny was a good friend of Darwin's sisters; he had known her since childhood, and she seems to have been born to flirt. Just how far the romance went is unclear. At least some of Fanny's letters are preserved in the Darwin archives at Cambridge (although Darwin's letters to her are—perhaps unsurprisingly—missing). She comes across in these as energetic and athletic (she loved to ride) but essentially empty. She writes of horses, parties, and local gossip, and she teases Darwin about his scholarly pursuits without much sign of real understanding or interest. Browne suggests that the relationship may have been more one-sided than Darwin might have imagined.[9] Fanny was a year older than Darwin, had already been engaged once, and obviously enjoyed any male attention she could get. Darwin, with his interest in insects and his official sights set on the ministry, might have seemed very dull to her.

We know from the *Autobiography* that Darwin had read Gilbert White before he went to Edinburgh,[10] and it seems likely that in some respects a married version of White and Selborne may have been his ideal when wrote from the *Beagle:* "Although I like this knocking about—I find I steadily have a distant prospect of a very quiet parsonage, & I can see it even through a grove of Palms."[11] Whether he was ever really serious about this idyll is debatable. Charles must have known early on that, unlike White, he would never have to worry about finances, and it is hard to imagine him interrupting his studies to dash off a sermon or go minister to the sick. Intellectually, Darwin never seems to have been particularly interested in religion, although he says in the *Autobiography* that he was very much impressed by Paley's natural theology.[12] He took the required classes, but his tutor warned him after his first year that he was certainly not ready for his qualifying exams.

What saved Darwin was almost certainly his choice of teachers. In his second year at Christ College, he began to sit in on lectures in botany given by John Henslow (1796–1861). Like Darwin, Henslow had been drawn to natural history from an early age. Becoming a professional natural historian, however, was a fairly formidable task. At the time Henslow arrived at Cambridge, in 1814, natural history and botany—indeed any of the natural sciences—were not regarded as suitable subjects for a degree, and were not to become so until 1861.[13] In the university system of the day, the exact role of a professor was unclear; students worked closely with their tutors, but attendance at lectures was distinctly optional, and many professors chose to give few or none. Henslow's enthusiasm for science took him past these obstacles, and he instituted a full series of lectures on botany, including the anatomy and physiology of plants.

Besides "labs" in which he encouraged students to dissect vegetation, Henslow was a nineteenth-century Peripatetic: he took his students outdoors on field trips around Cambridgeshire, on barges down the River Cam, and on coach trips to distant field sites. He also held evening tea parties at his home, at which other professors and favored undergraduates had the opportunity to mingle socially and to discuss topics of interest.[14] Darwin was very much a favorite student; besides the more formal tea soirées, he remembers being frequently invited to dine at the Henslow family home. Indeed, he spent so much time in Henslow's company that some of the other professors started referring to him as "the man who walks with Henslow."[15] In her commentary on the Henslow-Darwin correspondence, Darwin's granddaughter Nora Barlow suggests that Henslow might now be known as "the man to whom Darwin wrote."[16] This is perhaps a little unfair: Henslow was a remarkable natural historian in his own right, and encouraged many other significant figures, including Audubon, who named Henslow's sparrow after him.[17]

Henslow encouraged Darwin to return to the geology that he had abandoned after his bad experiences at Edinburgh. This included spending time with Adam Sedgwick (1785–1873), who was recognized as one of the most important geologists at Cambridge. Sedgwick was in the habit of taking a large portion of the summer break to engage in field studies, and in 1831, Henslow convinced him to take Darwin with him on a geological collecting trip in Wales.

Although Darwin's time with Sedgwick was relatively short, it proved important in a variety of ways. This was Darwin's first real field season with a highly trained supervisor watching over him, instructing him, and giving him responsibilities for data collection and interpretation. Darwin was enormously impressed by Sedgwick's ability to pull together an entire picture of ancient landscapes on the basis of assembled data, and Sedgwick made a point of teaching him techniques that Darwin would soon use on a much wider stage. Sedgwick made sure that Darwin was familiar with the use of map and compass, assigning him transects where he was to follow a bearing across the hilly landscape with minimal deviations to the right or the left so as to get an accurate picture of particular formations. Darwin returned from his travels excited about geology and actively seeking opportunities to put his new enthusiasm to work.

Both Henslow and Darwin had the itch to travel. Henslow had long contemplated an exploring trip overseas, perhaps into southern Africa. As Darwin read accounts of explorations by Humboldt and other naturalists, he started to dream in earnest of going abroad as soon as he was finished with his degree. Darwin set his heart on traveling to the Canary Islands to climb the peak of Tenerife, the very journey that John Ray and Francis Willughby had contemplated long before. He encouraged Henslow to consider accompanying him—what could be more fun than that teacher and student should travel together to see exotic lands and vegetation firsthand? Unfortunately, Henslow was by this stage too much a family man to simply take off on a journey of even a few months' duration.

In August 1831, when Darwin was returning home from his travels with Sedgwick, thinking only of the fun he would have shooting with his Uncle Jos at Maer, Henslow received a letter. It informed him that a certain Captain Robert Fitzroy (1805–65), who had been engaged in a survey of the South American coast some years previously, was to continue the survey around Tierra del Fuego and home via "many of the South Sea Islands." The vessel, the *Beagle*, would be "fitted out expressly for scientific purposes, combined with the surveys: it will furnish a rare opportunity for a naturalist & it would be a great misfortune that it should be lost."[18] Fitzroy hoped to find a suitable young man to accompany him on the voyage, both to serve as an intellectual companion and to assist the expedition by collecting and cataloging interesting artifacts of natural history.

Henslow wrote to Darwin to see if he was interested. He assured Darwin that Fitzroy was not looking for a "finished Naturalist" and that Darwin was "the best qualified man I know who is likely to undertake such a situation."[19] One suspects that by this time Henslow had realized—even if Darwin had not—that it would be unlikely that Charles would wind up as the curate of some quiet country parish. In contrast, the *Beagle* voyage was just the thing he would have loved to have done at Darwin's age, and it is a mark of his intelligence and charity that he immediately passed on the suggestion.

Robert Darwin was most definitely not enthusiastic. He presented his son with a list of reasons why he was unwilling to consent to the scheme, but he gave Charles one possible cause for hope: "If you can find any man of common sense, who advises you to go, I will give my consent" (71). Darwin fled to Maer to seek comfort from his Uncle Jos and his Wedgewood cousins. Josiah Wedgewood was known to be a man of few words (Sydney Smith commented to Emma Darwin's mother, "Wedgewood's an excellent man—it is a pity that he hates his friends"),[20] but Charles had long been a favorite nephew. Wedgewood was very supportive, and offered to first write to Robert Darwin and then to drive Charles back to Shrewsbury himself so that he could discuss the matter with The Doctor directly. Charles wrote also, and one can sense a degree of almost defiant joy in his words as he says that "all the Wedgewoods" view the voyage in a different way from how "you and my sisters do."[21] Wedgewood's letter is still available, and for all the formality in his point-by-point refutation of Robert's objections, you can sense a deep affection and concern for young Charles's well-being.[22] Given that Robert "had always maintained that he [Josiah] was one of the most sensible men in the world" (72), Robert's objections were set aside, and Darwin was given leave to at least interview with Fitzroy.

Robert Fitzroy is in some ways the most enigmatic and tragic figure of the whole Darwin story. By all accounts he was a brilliant seaman, surveyor, and navigator. He was a pioneer in weather forecasting, and a humane and sensitive commander, generous to a fault, and passionately dedicated to doing his best. He was only four years older than Darwin, but his life had been very different from the start. Fitzroy's mother was the daughter of a marquis, his grandfather was the Duke of Grafton, and his uncle, Lord Castlereagh, had been secretary for war. Fitzroy was sent into the navy at the age of twelve, and at fifteen he made his first voyage to South America. Fitzroy returned to England in 1822 and was promoted to lieutenant before being sent out to South America again, to serve as flag-lieutenant to Admiral Robert Otway in 1828. While Darwin was enjoying himself as a student at Edinburgh and Cambridge, Fitzroy was on station, sailing in some of the most challenging waters in the world.

Shortly after his second arrival in South America, Fitzroy found himself in a position of more responsibility than he might have expected. A surveying team, consisting of HMS *Adventure* and HMS *Beagle*, accompanied by the schooner *Adelaide*, had been surveying the extreme southern tip of South America near Cape Horn, justifiably known for its hideous weather and unforgiving coastline. Accounts of this expedition, in spite of their understatement, make it clear the conditions under which men and equipment had to operate.[23] Even at the height of the southern summer the land was often buried in rain and drizzle. Gale-force winds could spring up at a moment's notice, sometimes lasting for days, other times blasting through as wild "williwaws" that were over before captain or crew had time to react. Systematic observation and mapping were constantly at the mercy of the weather, and the project seemed to have no clear ending date in sight.

After a series of setbacks, the *Beagle*'s commander, Captain Pringle Stokes, shot himself to death. In spite of this, the survey had to continue, though it turned back to Brazil until a new commander could be appointed. Admiral Otway had been enormously impressed by his flag lieutenant and decided to pass over *Beagle*'s temporary captain and give the command of the ship and responsibility for the survey to Fitzroy. The *Beagle* was just about 90 feet long, with a beam of 24 feet.[24] She displaced 235 tons and drew slightly over 12 feet of water. She was small and she was plump, but she had good capacity for stores, could sail well in most airs, and, with a good captain, could be counted on to deal with most of what the ocean threw at her.

The small squadron again proceeded south to Tierra del Fuego. In the Straits of Magellan, the adventurers encountered their first indigenous peoples. The Fuegians were the ultimate extension of the great movement of humans across the Americas that had begun more than fourteen thousand years earlier. For all practical purposes these people had reached the end of the world: to the south lay a sea of monstrous waves, over which the winds blew all the way around the globe, and south of that lay only the ice of Antarctica, though it is unlikely that they had any knowledge of the southern continent, so hostile was the intervening water.

The Fuegians had adapted to a completely unforgiving environment. They ate what was available—marine mammals, seabirds, shellfish, seaweed, whatever wild berries were available in the short summer season. They lived in "wigwams" made of branches and driftwood and thatched with native grasses, and insulated and waterproofed their bodies by smearing them with grease from seal carcasses. To Fitzroy and his men, these people must have seemed the antithesis of everything that British civilization stood for; that the Fuegians might actually be doing remarkably well under difficult circumstances was not something easy to contemplate.

In late autumn, the ships sailed through the Straits and spent the worst part of winter in the Pacific, anchored under the lee of Chiloé Island, repairing damaged equipment, working up data, and preparing for the next field season. Again, one cannot help but compare Darwin's and Fitzroy's lives at this moment—Darwin was walking with Henslow, attending polite Cambridge tea parties, going to Maer on the holidays to shoot for fun; Fitzroy, by contrast was living in incredibly cramped quarters off a rainy Chilean island, shooting for fresh meat if such was to be had and otherwise living off ship's rations, which, if not quite as bad as in Captain Cook's day, were still very foul by Shropshire or Cambridge standards.

As spring developed in the south and Fitzroy took the *Beagle* back along the treacherous southern edge of Tierra del Fuego, Darwin was headed back to university. At Cambridge, the greatest worries would have been examinations; doubtless it was growing chilly in ancient college rooms, but there was always a warm fireplace and good conversation to be had at the Henslows'. In Tierra del Fuego, Fitzroy was facing the coast that had broken his predecessor in the loneliness of command. By custom the captain of a king's ship maintained a distance between himself and his officers. The lives of every man aboard were literally in his hands, and he often dined alone, and he kept his thoughts, plans, and, above all, his fears to himself.

The *Beagle* had no engine to get her out of trouble; there was no fleet of brightly colored Zodiacs sporting ninety-horsepower engines in which to zip ashore, no GPS to get a firm fix, no radar to tell where an unmarked island might lie. For much of this period, ship and crew had only themselves to rely on. If they got into trouble, they would have to get themselves out of it. If something broke, they had to fix it or go without. Extracts from the narrative of the voyage capture conditions quite well: "Such constant rain fell during this evening, that it was not until after much trouble that we at last made fires. Carrying dry fuel in the boats we found indispensable. . . . Raining so steadily all day, that it was useless to proceed; I could neither see my way, nor notice any thing but wind and rain."[25] In all, it was both a hellish experience and an amazing training ground for any captain who could survive it—and Fitzroy was just such a captain.

With a mixture of courage and dogged determination, Fitzroy and his crew worked their way along the coast, pulling ashore in the *Beagle*'s whaleboats, standing off in bad weather (and the weather was mostly bad), and doing their best to complete as much of their task as possible during the short summer months. The ship's boats were essential for much of the survey, as the *Beagle* herself could not come in to an undeveloped shore to transfer men or supplies, and the nearest dock or wharf was hundreds of miles away. In order to triangulate on key locations, it was important to land small parties of men on points and headlands with optical transits, sighting compasses, theodolites, and so forth and take as many fore- and back-sightings as the often limited visibility permitted. On many occasions, a detachment would take one of the ship's boats on an independent mission to map out a particularly tricky spot or to capture the location of a point or cove while the rest of the ship's company was employed elsewhere.

On one of these detached journeys, the ship's whaleboat was stolen by a party of Fuegians, who slipped away in it under the cover of darkness. Fitzroy was furious. The rough weather that they had been exposed to throughout the expedition had already taken a toll on boats and supplies, and there was nothing to spare. Besides the impact that the loss of the boat would have on further surveying, Fitzroy had become interested in the Fuegians as representatives of a form of "savagery" that he felt it his duty to relieve. One senses that he had long contemplated some sort of intervention in Fuegian society, and the theft of the whaleboat gave him a perfect excuse.

Once it became obvious that the missing boat could not be found by a simple search, Fitzroy decided to take some Fuegians hostage for its release. A large party of crewmen landed near a Fuegian village and stealthily encircled the area from the landward side. The crew hoped to surprise the Fuegians, but the village dogs alerted their masters of their danger. In the resulting scuffle, one Fuegian was killed and several of the *Beagle*'s crew were injured, but Fitzroy had his hostages.

To Fitzroy's surprise, the Fuegians seemed to take little interest in the concept of "hostage," and as the days passed the possibility of recovering the boat vanished. The *Beagle*'s crew resumed their survey as best they could with the remaining boats, and a number of the hostages escaped. Just when Fitzroy decided to take the remaining Fuegians back to England is unclear, but from his notes it appears that by the time the *Beagle* rounded Cape Horn, preparing to head north for Rio and home, he had some idea for a form of "mission."[26] Two more Fuegians were added to the two who had remained on the ship, and in early June 1830, ship, crew, and captive Fuegians (three men and one girl) left Tierra del Fuego and moved up the Atlantic toward what for the Fuegians must have seemed an entirely different planet.

Once they arrived in England, the Fuegians were feted, showered with gifts, and given an audience with the king. Fitzroy, however, was deeply unsatisfied. The *Beagle*, her captain, and her crew had done the best they could with the time and resources available, but there still remained many gaps and blank spaces on the charts that Fitzroy was laboring to produce for the admiralty.

Fitzroy was determined to both finish the survey and keep his implied promise to the Fuegians to return them to South America. At one point he contemplated fitting out a ship for himself and went so far as to charter the *John*, a small London-based merchant ship, to act as transport back to Tierra del Fuego.[27] At the eleventh hour, the navy decided, somewhat reluctantly, to continue the survey and selected HMS *Chanticleer*, a similar ship to *Beagle*, to carry out the mission. *Chanticleer* had also seen hard service in the southern ocean, and upon careful examination it was found that she was in no condition to go to sea anytime soon.[28] Fortunately the *Beagle* was waiting to be recommissioned, and the lords of the admiralty placed Fitzroy in command.

Doubtless a significant factor in Fitzroy's appointment was the young captain's personal fortune and his willingness to spend it in the furtherance of his task. Many of the modifications that the *Beagle* received, including the addition of two extra whaleboats and no fewer than twenty-four chronometers, were bought at Fitzroy's expense.[29] The chronometers were of particular importance if accurate surveys and navigation were to be done. The admiralty had declared that an arbitrary line from pole to pole, running through the Royal Observatory in Greenwich, just outside London, would be the prime meridian against which all measurements east or west would be measured. The difference between "local noon," which could be obtained with a sextant, and "Greenwich noon" allowed a navigator to calculate his or her precise longitude. Fitzroy's insistence on extreme redundancy was unusual, but by no means without cause. Only eleven of the twenty-four chronometers were still running when the *Beagle* returned from her voyage.[30]

Darwin's interview with Fitzroy did not go particularly well at first. Fitzroy was a believer in phrenology and felt that Darwin's nose suggested that he would be weak-willed and unsuited to the difficulties of the voyage.[31] Fitzroy stressed that they were likely to be gone at least two years, the exact itinerary of the trip was highly uncertain, and there were very real dangers in challenging what from a sailor's point of view were some of the most dangerous regions in the world. Darwin was determined to go. Fitzroy stressed that there could be no hope of monetary remuneration; the ship's naturalist was a supernumerary in terms of crew and would have to pay for anything that he consumed. Darwin assured him that this was not an issue. (In the *Autobiography*, Darwin says that he told his father "that I should be deuced clever to spend more than my allowance on the *Beagle*," but Robert answered him with a smile and said, "But they all tell me that you are very clever" (9). In point of fact, Darwin was to spend much more than his allowance on the journey, as shown by several apologetic letters home, but there is no evidence that Robert regretted this extravagance. Once he had accepted Charles's plan, his support was unstinting.)

Reassured by Darwin's obvious enthusiasm and energy, Fitzroy accepted him as part of the team. On September 5, Darwin wrote to Henslow of his enthusiasm for Fitzroy and said that the voyage would last three years, but that he did not mind as long as his father had no objections.[32]

Darwin immediately threw himself into a frenzy of preparation, obtaining supplies for collecting and preparing specimens and new guns and pistols for birds and whatever else might require shooting. Perhaps most important, in light of subsequent events, Fitzroy gave him a copy of Charles Lyell's book on geology.[33]

Charles Lyell (1797–1875) was born in Scotland but studied the classics at Oxford before following his father into the law. After a brief practice, he went up to Edinburgh, where he attended Jameson's lectures on geology, and unlike Darwin, he found the subject immediately fascinating, and began studies of geology in earnest. He was appointed professor of geology at King's College in London, and he proceeded to write a series of extremely influential books on the topic, which were widely read and republished throughout the century. Lyell was a confirmed "uniformitarianist" in the tradition of James Hutton. The uniformitarians were at particular odds with the religious orthodoxy because their theory depended on vast expanses of time, not allowed by biblical literalists. Lyell and Darwin later became close friends, but Lyell resisted biological evolution for most of his life.

The *Beagle* voyage was the only major field excursion that Darwin was to undertake throughout his long career as a scientist. He had made forays into

Wales and Scotland while at university, but none of these came close to what he undertook during his time on the *Beagle*. It is important to realize the scale of the expedition that Fitzroy proposed: a circumnavigation of the world, with multiple stops along the way, some in areas hitherto unexamined by serious natural historians. Besides the actual circumnavigation, there were a number of extensive trips onshore, some lasting for weeks or even months, any of which would have been noteworthy on their own. Finally, in comparison to Joseph Banks's voyage with Cook, which lasted just under three years, much of it at sea on long passages, Darwin was out for nearly five, with plenty of time ashore for botanical and zoological studies.

For some people, it has been easy to dismiss Fitzroy as a Bible-waving extremist, clinging to an outworn ideology in spite of the evidence before his eyes and opposing Darwin's ideas at every turn. This would be a gross misreading of much of Fitzroy's life and particularly the *Beagle* years. Fitzroy was a scientist in his own right. He had experience in geology, was a brilliant surveyor and mathematician, and was keenly interested in the lands and species that he encountered while traveling. Darwin and Fitzroy read Lyell together, and both were intrigued to apply his theories to the reality of the coasts of South America. Fitzroy collected specimens carefully and systematically—years later, Darwin had to go to Fitzroy to round out his collection of "Darwin's finches" because he had failed to note from which island he had obtained which specimen. The more methodical Fitzroy had done a better job at notetaking. That Darwin and Fitzroy would eventually part company over the issue of evolution is one of the tragedies of the whole story. On the *Beagle*, they could be young men together, off to encounter the newness of the world.

The *Beagle* was not able to sail until after Christmas, and in his diary Darwin laments not sailing on Boxing Day because most of the crew are too inebriated from Christmas celebrations.[34] He is also upset by the severe punishment (flogging and "clapping in irons" for public drunkenness), but at last, on December 27, 1831, the *Beagle* slipped out of Devonport, heading southwest across the Bay of Biscay toward Tenerife, and beyond that the Cape Verde islands, and beyond them the coast of South America.

Darwin was enormously seasick. There is no other way of describing it, and he seems to have never really gotten over it. He describes his state quite carefully in his entry for December 29: "In first place, the misery is excessive, and far exceeds what a person would suppose who had never been at sea more than a few days. . . . I found the only thing my stomach would bear was biscuit and raisins; but of this, as I became more exhausted, I soon grew tired."[35] Not exactly the

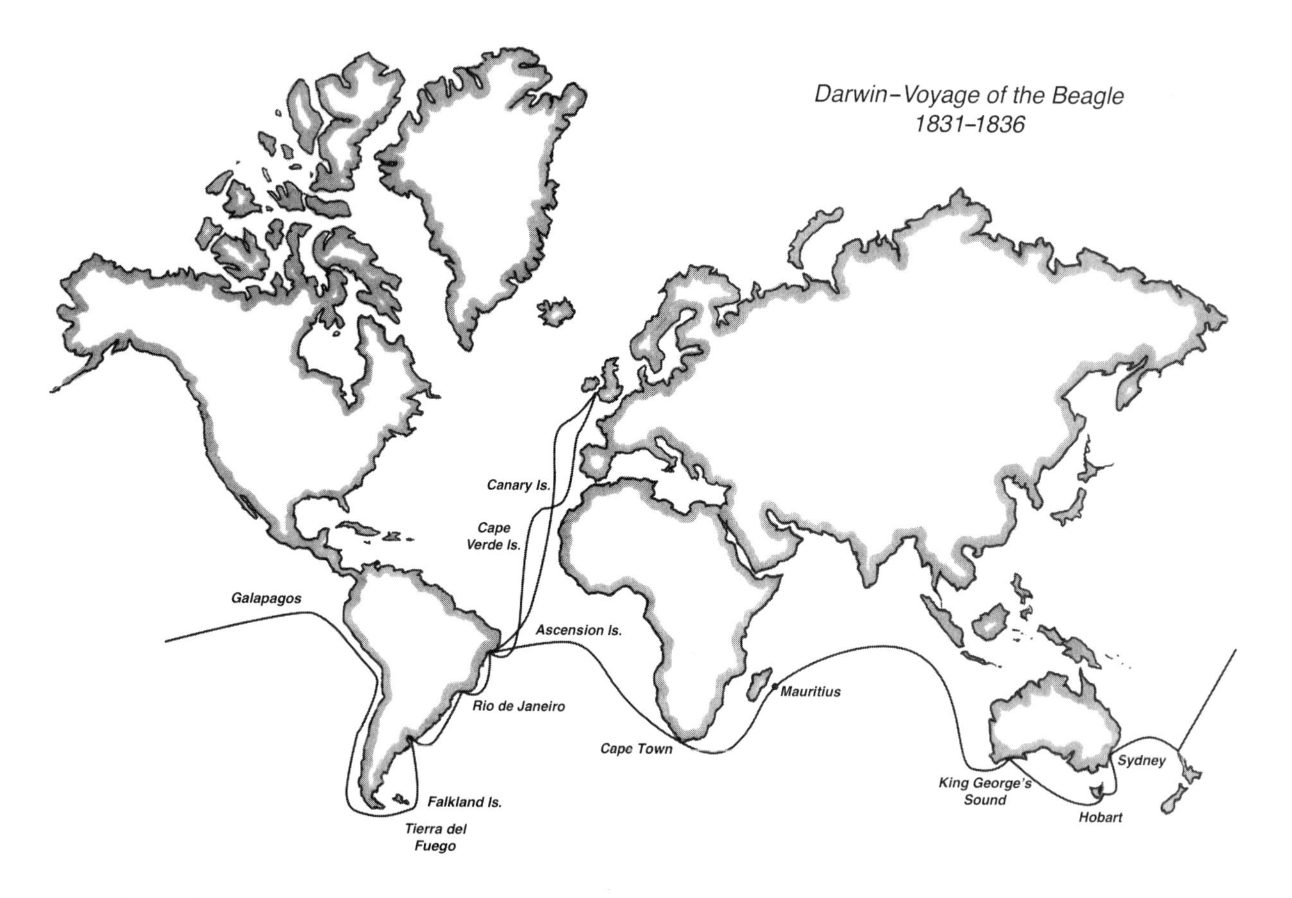

MAP 1. Route of Darwin's voyage in the *Beagle*, 1831–36. (Cartography by Robin Owings.)

image of the heroic young adventurer off to make new discoveries that one feels that Darwin had been imagining himself! The seasickness may have been both a blessing and a curse. Because of it, Darwin took any opportunity to go ashore and to stay ashore, rather than beating up and down the coastline with the surveying team. As a result, he was able to make many of the observations that would have such a profound effect on him over the ensuing years. In the meantime, there was what must have seemed an eternity of the Bay of Biscay to cross: "30 December At noon lat 43 South . . . across the famous Bay of Biscay: wretchedly out of spirits and very sick. I often said before starting that I had no doubt I should frequently repent of the whole undertaking. Little did I think with what fervor I should do so. I can scarcely conceive any more miserable state than when such dark and gloomy thoughts are haunting my mind as have today pursued me."[36]

A week later they were in sight of Tenerife, but Darwin's hopes of time onshore were shattered by the port captain, who declared a strict quarantine of all ships coming into the harbor. Fitzroy decided that they could not spare twelve days sitting at anchor, and ordered all sails to be set for the Cape Verdes. All Darwin can say is "Oh misery, misery . . . "[37]

Darwin's official account of the journey, which was first released as the *Journal of Researches* but is more commonly known as *The Voyage of the Beagle*, is probably his most-read book.[38] It was his first (in the *Autobiography* he says it is the one of which he is most proud), and it is also exactly the sort of book that a much younger brother might write, knowing that three bossy elder sisters were going to read every word. There is very little in any of the *Journal* of sickness, real hardship, or girls. Darwin describes his observations, both on ship (though these are noticeably abbreviated) and onshore, but there is little more than the occasional hint here and there that Darwin might have any regrets or concerns. In stark contrast to the unhappiness of his private diary, Darwin mentions being seasick only once in the *Journal*, and that in reference to Jemmy Button, one of the three Fuegians: "When the water was rough I was often a little sea-sick, and he used to come to me and say in a plaintive voice, 'Poor poor fellow!'"[39]

This is quite a different picture from what he kept to himself and was obviously known to everyone onboard. As for ladies, the word appears three times in the *Journal* ("girl" appears twice; "young woman" also appears twice), perhaps most famously in Buenos Aires, where Darwin is asked whether "ladies in any other part of the world wear such large combs?" Darwin "solemnly assured" his questioner "that they did not."[40] Left to itself, *The Voyage of the Beagle* is an almost too "nice" a travelogue, and we can only be grateful that so many letters were preserved to give us a truer account of both events and author.

Fanny Owen dumped him almost as soon as the *Beagle* left Britain, rushing off to get engaged to a somewhat disreputable older man. It was up to Darwin's sisters to break the news to him by letter once he had reached South America. Eventually a somewhat shamefaced Fanny also wrote, as did her father, which suggests there might have been more to the romance than mere nods and becks. Interestingly, although there is no hint of any Wedgewood romance before this point, Darwin writes in a miserable letter to his sister Caroline on April 2, 1832: "Whilst really melting with tenderness I cry my dearest Fanny why I demand, should I distinctly see the sunny flower garden at Maer."[41]

Any letters from Emma to Darwin have not been preserved, and there is very little mention of Emma in the surviving letters from Darwin's sisters, other relatives, and friends, so we have no way of knowing if the mention of the "sunny flower garden" at the Wedgewoods' house was other than a passing spell of homesickness. Whatever his feelings, England was now thousands of miles behind him and years in his future, and he had much to see and do to take his mind off romance.

The ship made a brief stop at St. Paul's Rocks in the middle of the Atlantic. Darwin went ashore for a much-needed—if brief—break from the rolling of the sea, taking the opportunity to collect geological specimens and observe nesting seabirds. From there they proceeded to Brazil, where Darwin had his first real encounter with the diversity of the tropics. It is here, as Darwin comes into his own as a field biologist, that one really gets the sense of the power of natural history that will illuminate and inform all of his work. Darwin is interested in *everything*. His notebook entries are telegraphic jottings, but in their very structure one gets the sense of the immediacy of the encounter.[42] Darwin had never seen anything like what he was now exposed to on a daily basis. On a journey near Rio on April 17, 1832, Darwin was caught in the romance of the tropics: "Twiners entwining twiners, tresses like hair beautiful lepidoptera. silence hosannah. Frog habits like toad. slow jumps. Iris copper coloured colours become fainter Snake. Cobris de Corrall Fresh water fish. edible Blaps musky shell. stain fingers red. . . . "[43]

Surely there has seldom been a better brief description of the neotropics than these lines. Darwin was also keeping a more formal journal, which he tended to write in each day. The journal was written both with an eye to being read by others and to serve as the immediate source for a future publication. The April 17 notebook entry gets translated thusly: "The woody creepers, themselves covered by creepers, are of great thickness, varying from 1 to nearly 2 feet in circumference.—Many of the older trees present a most curious spectacle, being covered with tresses of a liana, which much resembles bundles of hay . . . wonder, astonishment & sublime devotion fill & elevate the mind."[44] This is certainly more grammatical and contains additional detail, but one loses some of the immediacy and the poetry of the encounter. Darwin had read Humboldt's *Personal Narrative*, which we will discuss in the next chapter, and he probably had something similar in mind from the first.[45]

In Brazil, Darwin and Fitzroy had their first serious disagreement, which revolved around the constant thorn of slavery. As mentioned earlier, Darwin was an abolitionist coming from abolitionists on both sides of his family. Britain had abolished slavery in the United Kingdom in the eighteenth century, and by the beginning of the nineteenth century, the Royal Navy was tasked with suppressing the slave trade from Africa. Full abolition of slavery throughout the British Empire occurred in 1833, while the *Beagle* was still at sea. As a loyal officer in the navy, Fitzroy was sworn to uphold royal decrees, and doubtless would have acted efficiently and effectively if confronted with a slaver during the passages across the Atlantic. At the same time, as a conservative member of the aristocracy, Fitzroy seems to have had more in common with the slave-owning landholders of Brazil than with the liberal Darwin.

One day Fitzroy commented that a slave that he had interviewed seemed perfectly happy with his status.[46] Darwin replied that perhaps the slave's response was affected by the presence of the overseer. Fitzroy was furious, and for a time it seemed that Darwin would have to find his own way home. Fortunately, after a few hours, Fitzroy apologized for his temper, and the relationship was mended.

On April 22, Darwin gives us perhaps a little more insight into feelings unsuitable for the *Journal:* "At the vendas seldom see a woman. not worth seeing distances most inaccurately known.—not above a score of murders or crosses.—In Heavens name in what are blacks better off than our English labourers?"[47] Remove the oddly placed period in the first line and place it after "seeing," and the sense of the beginning of the note becomes apparent. For the rest, Darwin's fundamental humanity and dislike of the infliction of pain or misery is a repeated theme.

From the coast of Brazil, the *Beagle* worked her way south, periodically repeating a segment of the coast if Fitzroy was dissatisfied by the results of a particular survey. These back-and-forth transects were particularly satisfactory to Darwin, as they allowed him to step off the ship for an extended period onshore and either rejoin her on the return or establish some sort of rendezvous farther along the route.

Along the banks of the Río de la Plata, Darwin unearthed a variety of fossils, which he shipped home to Henslow. Henslow, in turn—ever the teacher—wrote long, encouraging letters back, instructing Darwin on how to collect samples and how to package them, and sometimes including books for his further edification. Henslow clearly saw the importance of Darwin's observations and stressed the importance of both good notetaking and of including sketches of everything that he saw: "Avoid sending scraps. Make the specimens as perfect as you can, root, flowers & leaves & you can't do wrong. In large ferns & leaves fold them back upon themselves on one side of the specimen."[48]

Henslow also sent a caution familiar to every modern writer about the need for backups: "Wd it not be a good precautionary measure to transmit to England a copy of your memoranda, with your next packet? I know it is a dull job to copy out such matters—but it is highly expedient to avoid the chance of losing your notes."[49]

For all of Henslow's gentle instruction, a transformation began to come over Darwin's correspondence as he headed south to Cape Horn. He was no longer the inexperienced young naturalist writing to his mentor. He was becoming seasoned in an arena immeasurably bigger than Cambridgeshire, his notes and specimens were valued by people whose opinions he valued, and although he dreaded the southern ocean, there was also a part of him that had come to appreciate adventures.

The journey south to Cape Horn was grueling. A side trip to the Falklands was but one example of many that Fitzroy insisted on in the interest of comprehensive mapping. At the time it must have seemed an annoying tangent to Darwin, but as later results would reveal, it may have been quite important in setting him up to view the special biology of island archipelagos that would make the Galápagos so famous.[50]

After an initial easy rounding of Cape Horn, the *Beagle* ran into heavy gales and shipped a great sea that smashed one of her whaleboats. Writing home to his sister Caroline, Darwin comments: "I am quite astonished, to find I can endure this life; if it were not for the strong & increasing pleasure from Nat. History I never could."[51]

Fitzroy was determined to set down the Fuegian hostages and a volunteer English missionary who was to accompany them in as favorable circumstances as possible. When he dropped off the Fuegians and their companion, however, he did so in a spot where it would be easy to return and check up on them after a short surveying venture.[52] It was fortunate that he did so. Almost as soon as the *Beagle* moved over the horizon, York Minster, the elder Fuegian, took up with Fuegia

Basket, the young female hostage, and made off with as many of the mission supplies as possible. Other Fuegians beat and robbed the missionary, and by the time the *Beagle* returned, he was more than happy to be rescued and taken away. Sadly, within two generations, the Fuegians had been essentially exterminated by disease and persecution brought by subsequent voyagers. The wild coastlines that Darwin saw are now a jumping-off spot for wealthy tourists heading for an Antarctic experience, and Ushuaia, the capital of the province, has a population of over sixty thousand, all of them immigrants from the north.

Throughout this section of the voyage, one is struck by Darwin's fitness and athleticism. In Argentina, he impressed the gauchos—some of the toughest cowboys in the world—by getting off his horse when it grew tired and running alongside across the broad pampas. In the deep south, when the ship's boats were almost smashed by a great wave sweeping in from a calving glacier across the bay, it was Darwin who raced down the beach to pull them to safety.

Once the ship rounded the Horn and began to move up the west coast of South America, Darwin made several important excursions ashore, including a two-month trek into the Andes between July and September 1833. Darwin was particularly intrigued by the great beds of marine shells that had been raised up by geological activity. As he climbed higher and higher, he noted: "Who can avoid wondering at the force which has upheaved these mountains, and even more so at the countless ages which it must have required."[53]

He also witnessed the results of a massive earthquake in Valdivia and Concepción, Chile. Both he and Fitzroy had by this point read the second volume of Lyell's *Principles of Geology*, which had caught up with them en route, and both were fascinated to see first-hand evidence of significant geological events that could produce enormous landscape changes, especially given enough time. A real sense of the depth of time was one of the greatest gifts that Darwin received from his expedition into the Andes. A less welcome gift may have been the parasite that was to haunt him for the rest of his life. In a primitive hut high in the mountains, Darwin reported being bitten by a large bloodsucking insect. Unfortunately we do not know the precise identity of this bloodsucker, and we cannot know for sure whether it was infected with some persistent microorganism it passed to Darwin, but we do know that from that point onward, Darwin suffered periodic episodes of unexplained sickness that would at times completely debilitate him.[54]

By the time the ship and crew reached the Galápagos, Darwin was more than tired of the whole affair. There was the possibility of catching a merchant ship that could take him up to the Isthmus of Panama from any of a dozen ports on the west coast, and from there it would be but a short landward trip to the eastern shore and then a matter of weeks, rather than years, before he would be home. Instead he chose to stick it out on the *Beagle*, knowing full well the horrors that a long blue-water sail might inflict on his protesting stomach. The Galápagos chapter is one of the shortest in the *Voyage of the Beagle* and has none of the energy or enthusiasm that one sees in Darwin's accounts of Brazil or Argentina. There are no "twiners entwining twiners." Instead he says in his journal: "The black rocks heated by the rays of the Vertical sun like a stove, give to the air a close & sultry feeling. The plants also smell unpleasantly. The country was compared to what we might imagine the cultivated parts of the Infernal regions to be."[55]

Darwin had looked forward to the Galápagos primarily for their geology—it would be a chance to see recent volcanoes up close. Once he arrived, however, he seemed to have been taken with aspects of the archipelago's fauna. He found the great land tortoises particularly appealing, and was also impressed with the general tameness of the islands' birds. Although he mentions finches in his notes, it is the mockingbirds that first attracted his attention: "The Thenca very tame and curious in these islds. I certainly recognize S. America in ornithology, would a botanist?"[56]

This is actually quite important, as it shows that Darwin was actively comparing the species that he was finding in the archipelago to those on the mainland. His curiosity was further piqued when he examined his specimens and found different species of "Thenca" (mockingbirds) on different islands, and was told that locals could identify which island tortoises came from by the shape of their shells. Of perhaps the greatest importance is the frequently cited statement in his ornithological notes in which he pulls together his observations of the (now extinct) wild foxes on the Falkland Islands and the tortoises and mockingbirds of the Galápagos and says: "If there is the slightest foundation for these remarks, the zoology of archipelagoes will be well worth examining; for such facts would undermine the stability of species."[57]

It is just this careful assembly of fact upon fact—the "one long argument" that became *The Origin of Species*—that Darwin so excelled at. For all practical purposes, the voyage might as well have been over after the Galápagos, with one possible exception. After a desperately (for Darwin) long passage, the travelers reached Tahiti, stopping at Point Venus, where Cook and Banks had seen the Transit of Venus so long before. Cruising through the coral atolls of the south Pacific, Darwin mused on the origin of these islands, musings that would become a book of their own in later years.[58] The rest of the time at sea was one long anticlimax. Darwin had little to say about or learn from New Zealand, Australia, or the Cape of Good Hope. Just before the end, there was one final dash across the

Atlantic to check a survey point in South America (Fitzroy really was a perfectionist to beat all perfectionists!), and then home at last on October 2, 1836. As soon as they had anchored, Darwin more or less jumped ship, much to the annoyance of Fitzroy, who was left to bring the *Beagle* up to London and offload specimens, notes, and stores from the expedition.

Darwin had left England a little-known and inexperienced young naturalist fresh out of college. He returned very much the talk of the British scientific establishment. Henslow had strategically released a number of Darwin's specimens as well as reading some of his letters at various society meetings, and people were anxious to hear more. Darwin had had the fun field component of what was to be his life's work; what came next was the intellectually more challenging task of fitting the pieces together and filling in the blank spaces as best he could. He also had to get on with the other aspects of his life.

Darwin resolved to live in or near London so as to be at the center of scientific conversations. It was obvious to everyone by this point that a "little country parsonage" was not in the picture, and Robert Darwin settled enough money (and investment advice) on Charles that he knew he would never have to work for a living. Charles's somewhat surprising and whirlwind courtship of his cousin Emma Wedgewood was a highly satisfactory event for both families, and seems to have been a genuine love affair on both sides.[59]

The young couple settled initially in London while Darwin wrote up his draft of the official report of the zoology of the *Beagle*'s voyage and began organizing his notes for further publication. For reasons that can be neither explained nor forgiven, in the first draft of the preface to the *Journal of Researches*, Darwin failed to adequately acknowledge Fitzroy's role in giving Darwin the opportunity to accompany him. Fitzroy was furious, in part because of what seemed a personal slight and also because Darwin failed to acknowledge the kindness of the officers and crew, who, among other things, had shared their own finds with Darwin.[60] The lapse is particularly inexplicable given Darwin's usually generous personality. This was the beginning of a real estrangement between two people who had survived five years of storm, privation, exploration, and debate in extremely close quarters. Things were patched up for the moment, but Fitzroy may also have felt that Darwin's family wealth (by this point much greater than his own) allowed Darwin to concentrate on benefitting from the results of the expedition, while he, Fitzroy, had to continue in government service.

As mentioned earlier, Darwin's health was never really good after South America, and he eventually decided to move out of the city. The family settled in

FIGURE 8. Down House. (Photo by the author.)

the village of Down, within range of London so that Darwin could attend scientific meetings if he chose to do so, but far enough away that there was space for experiments and quiet for writing. Perhaps the best portrait of life at Down is provided in snippets by his granddaughter Gwen Raverat, who was born a few years after Charles's death but knew her grandmother Emma and her uncles very well.[61] Down House figures large in her memories of her childhood, and every indication is that it was a happy place to grow up, in spite of the deaths of three of Darwin's children in infancy or childhood.[62]

The similarity of Down to Gilbert White's Selborne is striking. Both are tiny country villages that somehow have escaped the ravages of the twentieth century. Like the Wakes, Down House sits on a sizable parcel of land that Darwin cultivated in part for flowers and vegetables for home use (although, unlike White, he never had to stretch his funds to cover food) and partially for experiments. The village is—as he himself said—"only sixteen miles from London Bridge," yet it was far enough out that people had to really want to come to visit, and even in a modern automobile, navigating the narrow lanes of Kent can be quite an adventure.[63] Down lacked a steep Hanger up which to walk while meditating on natural history, but Darwin constructed a Sandwalk, around which he could pace several times in a morning as he worked out details of his next book. The house itself was large enough for a growing family (seven children survived to adulthood) and a steady flow of visitors, which, over time, included all the greats of British natural history.

FIGURE 9. Charles Darwin's study. (Photo by the author.)

Darwin's methodology, once he had settled at Down, resembled a refinement of his research during the *Beagle* voyage. His chief criticism of his grandfather was that Erasmus had hypothesized too freely with too few facts at his disposal. Charles went at things from the exact opposite perspective: he assembled vast numbers of facts from a broad range of sources and only then linked them in a complete hypothesis. His genius was in his ability to take seemingly disparate organisms (foxes, tortoises, and mockingbirds) and distill out of them explanatory ideas that could then be projected onto the larger world. He was also the sort of scientist who sees the obvious and asks the one key question that will give vast insights. Countless farmers, horticulturists, and scientists had seen earthworms over millennia. Gilbert White had been intrigued by them, but it took Darwin to deliberately set up a "Worm Stone" and then patiently wait year after year, measuring the rate at which the stone was buried due to the passage of soil through the worms' bodies.[64]

Darwin always liked going directly to the source. His correspondence is a delightful mixture of letters to and from the great and famous, as well as doctors, lawyers, farmers, and pigeon fanciers. Anything and anyone could catch his eye and be quietly absorbed into the brewing crucible that would become *The Origin of Species*. Just when Darwin put the pieces that constitute Darwinism into one form is impossible to tell. He clearly arrived at some conclusions in the early 1840s, but he was content to seemingly get sidetracked into studies of barnacles for years. His plan seems always to have been to pull his studies together in one big book that would explain everything from corals to plants to worms to humans, but he was forestalled by the arrival of a brief manuscript from a young admirer, Alfred Russel Wallace, who had also chosen to travel to distant lands, to seek out new and strange plants and animals, and to ask profound questions of origin and form.

Wallace's manuscript arrived at Down during the terminal illness of Darwin's young son Charles. Darwin was obviously in no condition to do much about anything, but his friends Joseph Hooker and Charles Lyell convinced him that both Wallace's paper and Darwin's earlier "sketch" of his ideas on natural selection, coupled with copies of letters that Darwin had written to the American botanist Asa Gray, should be read into the records of the Linnean Society of London. This was done on July 1, 1858, but there was little, if any, comment on the idea then or for much of the rest of the year. In his concluding remarks summarizing the society's business for the year, Thomas Bell, the president of the Linnean Society wrote: "The year which has passed has not, indeed, been marked by any of those striking discoveries which at once revolutionize, so to speak, the department of science on which they bear."[65]

There the matter might have rested without further support. Wallace was far away and largely unknown, and the scientific establishment was split on how far it wished to go with ideas of speciation. It would take a serious marshalling of evidence to change many minds, and Darwin was the ideal naturalist to do just that. Although flustered by pressure to publish sooner than he felt ready, Darwin had been wrestling with the idea for at least sixteen years.

Rather than delaying further to fully complete his big book, Darwin edited what he called an "abstract" of his major ideas and supporting evidence and published it in 1859 as *On the Origin of Species by Means of Natural Selection, or the Preservation of Favored Races in the Struggle for Life*.[66] The full title of the book essentially summarizes the thesis; the book itself presents the evidence. As such, parts of the *Origin* may seem dull or repetitive to the modern reader, but Darwin rightly saw that unless he addressed as many objections as possible with specific examples, the theory ran the risk of being dismissed as either wrong or trivial. Although Darwin had a wealth of exotic experiences to illustrate his ideas, he often wisely chose the mundane and familiar—there are pages and pages on the selective breeding of the domestic pigeon, a subject of great interest to nineteenth-century animal husbandry and one more likely to be immediately comprehended than mockingbirds or tortoises on distant islands.

Unlike the yawn that had greeted Darwin's and Wallace's initial presentation at the Linnean Society, the *Origin* immediately sold out and had to be reprinted. Revisions to the book became Darwin's continual task for the rest of his life as he added new facts and observations to bolster his initial ideas.

Darwin continued to regard himself as a natural historian throughout his life, working quietly on orchids, earthworms, insectivorous plants, and so forth. He never wrote his one big book, but taken together, the more than twenty volumes that he did produce added up to a much more manageable whole than a single encyclopedic text could have done. He also had the support of an ever-wider group of brilliant associates, as well as that of an extremely tolerant family (one of his most charming books is *The Expression of Emotion in Man and Animals*, which features his children as study specimens). Ill health was a constant plague and source of frustration, but he had remarkable champions in men such as Thomas Huxley and Asa Gray, who were willing to go before the public and defend as well as advance his ideas. At his death, at home in Down, his last words were supposedly "I am not the least afraid of death."[67] He had done more in a lifetime to advance our understanding of the power of natural history than most of the generations behind him. After millennia of descriptive effort, natural history had finally produced a truly synthetic theory to work with.

Perhaps the most troubling aspect of the *Origin* to some of its readers was recognition that if you followed Darwin's logic to its conclusion, any notion of a fixed period of creation would have to be abandoned. The final sentence of the book is perhaps its most powerful: "There is grandeur in this view of life, with its several powers, having been originally breathed by the Creator into a few forms or into one; and that, whilst this planet has gone cycling on according to the fixed law of gravity, from so simple a beginning endless forms most beautiful and most wonderful have been, and are being evolved."[68]

Here you have it. Darwin is twenty-eight years and thousands of miles away from "twiners entwining twiners," yet the aesthetic of the true natural historian is still very much with him: "forms most beautiful and most wonderful." Is there not a faint echo of that "hosannah" in the stillness of the Brazilian rainforest? Then we have the final revolution: "have been, *and are being* evolved." Nothing would ever be the same, in the natural world or in science itself.

TEN . The Geography of Nature

Humboldt

When Darwin departed on his circumnavigation of the globe, he was following in the footsteps of a growing army of natural historians who were taking advantage of the ever easier modes of travel that were opening up the world to settlement and study. Joseph Banks had been an early model, and we know from Darwin's letters that he had read accounts of Cook's voyages, and indeed was thrilled to see some of the very sights that had so impressed the earlier explorers. Darwin's interest in traveling through South America was also fired by another traveler, who wrote, some time before 1807: "Devoted from my earliest youth to the study of nature, feeling with enthusiasm the wild beauties of a country guarded by mountains and shaded by ancient forests, I experienced in my travels, enjoyments which have amply compensated for the privations inseparable from a laborious and often agitated life."[1]

Alexander von Humboldt (1769–1859) was one of the most dashing explorers ever to set off on travels of discovery. Apart from his personal mastery of an enormous range of subjects, he was to serve as the inspiration for at least two generations of travelers, including Darwin and Wallace. In his exploration of South America, he set a world's record for altitude and, more than any other individual, laid a foundation for modern ideas of biogeography. During his lifetime, Humboldt was widely regarded as one of the most knowledgeable and influential men in Europe, and one can sense an almost palpable joy in Darwin's response after Humboldt contacted him in 1839: "That the author of those passages in the

FIGURE 10. Alexander von Humboldt in middle age, from K. Schlesier, *Lives of the Brothers Humboldt, Alexander and William*, 1853. (Author's collection.)

Personal Narrative, which I have read over and over again, & have copied out, that they might ever be present in my mind, should have so honoured me, is a gratification of a kind, which can but seldom happen to anyone."[2] Darwin was still very young, natural selection was still years in the future, and neither of the two could have foreseen a time in which Darwin would be world-famous and Humboldt largely lost to view.

Humboldt was born into the German nobility, the son of a Prussian officer and a widowed baroness.[3] He grew up in the family castle, and met Goethe when he was nine or ten. While attending university at Frankfurt, Humboldt became acquainted with George Forster, who had accompanied Cook on his second voyage of exploration, and it seems that this friendship sparked a desire for travel. In Humboldt's own words: "I felt an ardent desire to travel into distant regions, seldom visited by Europeans. This desire is characteristic of a period of our existence when life appears an unlimited horizon, and when we find an irresistible attraction in the impetuous agitations of the mind, and the image of positive danger."[4]

Humboldt's writing is immediately engaging: it is easy to imagine the young Darwin nodding his head over this sort of passage and reaching for a map of the world. Like Darwin, Humboldt was fascinated by geology. After brief travels in Europe, Humboldt was determined to go abroad. He originally hoped to visit

Egypt and travel up the Nile, studying the geology of the river valley as he went. Politics in the form of continuing hostilities between France and Britain intervened, and the journey to Egypt had to be put aside. Humboldt then hoped to take part in a French circumnavigation whose itinerary was eerily similar to that eventually of the *Beagle*, but again, political troubles, this time in the form of Napoleon's coup d'état, ended any immediate hope of a French voyage of exploration, and Humboldt found himself stranded in the south of France, contemplating a trip to the Atlas Mountains of Morocco.

According to his *Personal Narrative of Travels to the Equinoctial Regions of America, during the Years 1799–1804*, Humboldt was only a day from sailing, delayed by the insistence of the ship's master to keep livestock in the main cabin (Humboldt stresses that he was more concerned about the possible effect of the animals on his scientific instruments than about personal inconvenience), when word came that any passengers arriving in Morocco from France would be immediately thrown in prison. This effectively ended any hope of getting to Africa, and Humboldt moved on to Spain in the hopes of new prospects. Once he reached Madrid, he found himself welcomed as a scholar and given access to the natural history collections of the national museum. After a successful audience with the king, he was granted leave to visit Spanish possessions in the Americas. This was actually more important than it seems in the modern age of world-traveling global citizens, when many of us assume that the only thing that could prevent us from going anywhere is the cost of airfare. Passports or "papers" and letters of introduction from government officials were essential for crossing borders, and travelers could expect to be asked to present them at any moment.[5]

Humboldt's reputation as a geologist had preceded him, and he was given almost unheard-of license to travel and explore where he liked. He departed for La Coruña to take ship on a blockade runner (Spain was at that point at war with Britain) bound for Cuba.[6] Once clear of the coast, the captain made for Tenerife, in the Canary Islands. This was an ideal landfall for Humboldt, as Mount Teide, the peak of Tenerife, is one of the highest volcanoes in the world, with a summit of over twelve thousand feet. Humboldt was delighted with the tropical vegetation of the island at sea level, and pleased with the warm welcome that he received from everyone he came in contact with. It was particularly pleasant to be in an area that had not yet been studied by a learned mineralogist, and Humboldt felt confident that he could gain useful information that would be of interest to colleagues at home.

Although Humboldt was interested primarily in the physical structure of the

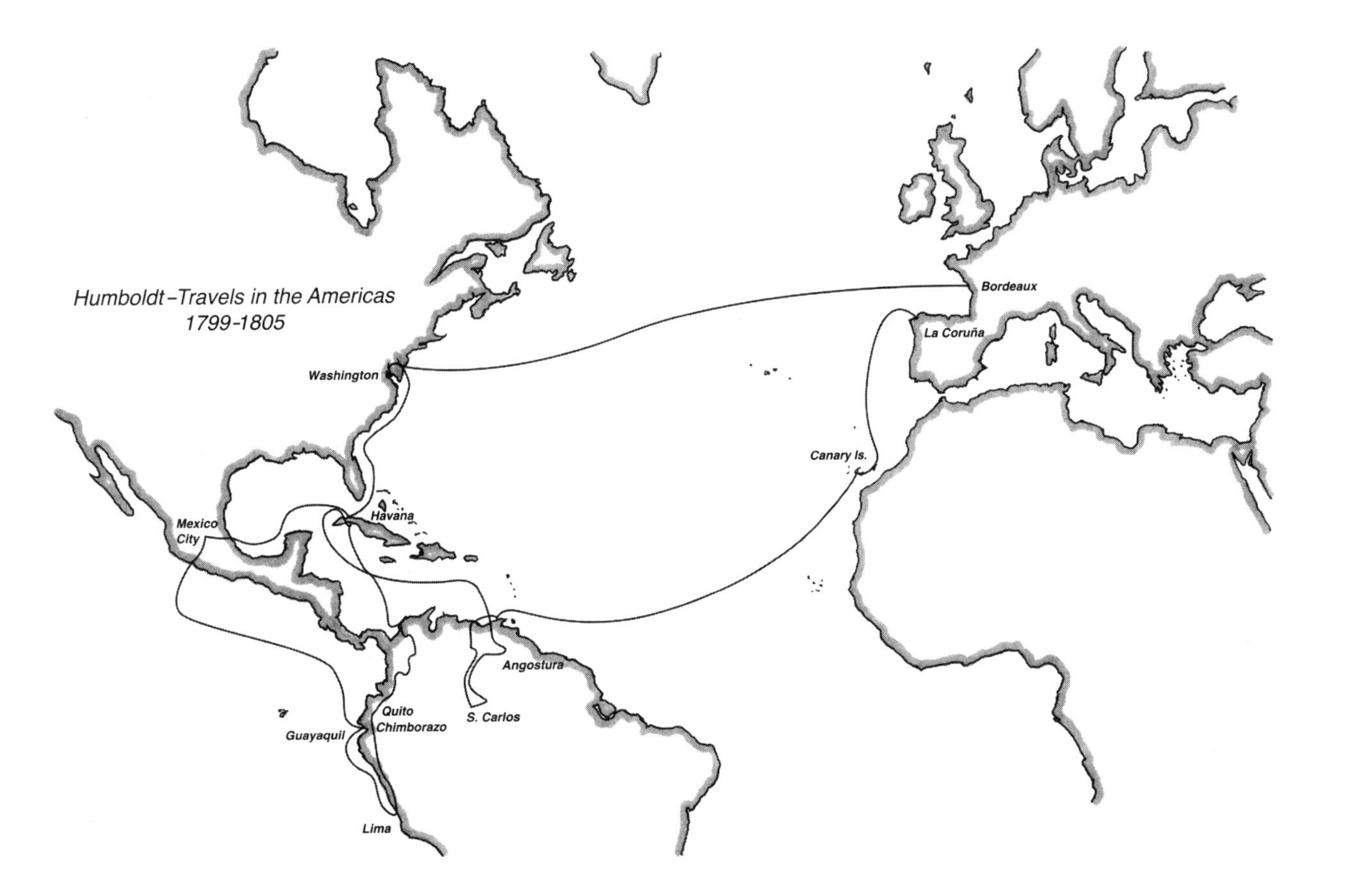

MAP 2. Humboldt's travels in the Americas, 1799–1805. (Cartography by Robin Owings.)

peak (the *Personal Narrative* goes into some detail outlining the forms of rock encountered), he clearly is writing for a broad, if educated, audience whom he recognizes will want information about more than just geology. Like Darwin, he had an abhorrence of slavery, and he comments periodically on both the state of the local peoples and their villages, houses, and customs.

Unlike Darwin, whose greatest contributions to biology were still ahead of him when he wrote his travelogue, the Humboldt of the *Personal Narrative* has clearly edited his text in light of his later understanding. Reflecting on the summit of Tenerife, he records: "We behold the plants divided by zones, as the temperature of the atmosphere diminished with the elevation of the site. Below the Piton, Lichens began to cover the scorious and lustrous lava: a violet . . . takes the lead not only of the other herbaceous plants, but even of the gramina . . . . below the retama lies the region of ferns."[7] It is this eye for detail and patterns that will go with Humboldt across the Atlantic and be immortalized in his studies of the Andes.

In general, Humboldt is instructing his reader on aspects of geology and natural history, but he knows that he will be read by future travelers, and he is anxious to ensure that they have the information they need to get the most out of their journeys. A clear example of this is Humboldt's note to his readers after returning from the peak: "As a great number of travelers who land at Santa Cruz, do not undertake the excursion of the Peak, because they are ignorant of the time it occupies, it may be useful to lay down the following data: In making use of mules as far as the Estancia de los Ingleses, it takes twenty one hours from Orotava to arrive at the summit of the Peak, and return to the port."[8] He then goes on to give a detailed itinerary, with times from place to place. This is altogether a very different style than what one finds in Darwin. Humboldt is, in essence, inviting his reader along, suggesting that you too could climb the summit or cross the ocean if only you made time for it among your doubtlessly busy affairs. It is no wonder that Humboldt's readers in the first quarter of the nineteenth century found themselves poring over maps and looking longingly at portmanteaux and trunks suitable for voyaging.

From Tenerife, Humboldt and his companion, the French botanist Aimé Bonpland (1773–1858), sailed west through the Sargasso Sea, encountering flying fish, which gave Humboldt the chance to digress on his philosophy of narrative: "Nature is an inexhaustible source of investigation, and in proportion as the domain of science is extended, she presents herself to those who know how to interrogate her, under forms which they have never yet examined."[9] Humboldt is such a master of his topics that rather than finding this sort of education by tangent disconcerting, one wanders along with him, enjoying what one is hearing and at the same time looking forward to new surprises in the next paragraph or page. One is reminded of Aristotle and the Peripatetics. It would have been wonderful to travel with Humboldt, but reading him is the next best thing. The travelers passed Trinidad and Tobago, but a fever broke out onboard ship, causing the death of a passenger, so Humboldt and Bonpland resolved to land in Venezuela rather than continuing directly to Cuba.

The decision to stop in what was then known as New Andalusia proved a fortunate one. Humboldt and Bonpland were immediately taken by the vegetation and wildlife of the region and resolved to do some serious exploring. Humboldt's interest in geology was further piqued by accounts of major earthquakes in the area, one of which had destroyed much of the capital, Cumaná, two years previously. Again, Humboldt cannot resist a subtle hint to future naturalists: "Each part of the globe is an object of particular study; and when we cannot hope to penetrate the causes of natural phenomena, we ought at least to endeavor to discover their laws, and distinguish, by the comparison of numerous facts, that which is permanent and uniform from that which is variable and accidental."[10] A better description of the methodology that Darwin took as his own cannot be imagined.

Humboldt and Bonpland took their time in beginning exploration of the interior countryside. Humboldt was anxious to establish his location as accurately as possible, and had brought an impressive array of surveying and astronomical equipment with him for just that purpose. His estimate of latitude was extremely accurate—within a few hundred yards of his actual location—but his estimate of longitude, at least for Cumaná, was out by nearly 150 miles. The naturalists found themselves a comfortable house in town (although it proved to be distressingly close to the slave market) and set about preparing instruments and exploring the surrounding coast and lagoons before turning toward the mountains.

In general, Humboldt seems to have been much less interested in animals than in plants, and less interested in either of them than he was in geology and landforms. One of the most interesting zoological finds during the early months of their expedition was the *guácharo,* or oilbird *(Steatornis caripensis),* which nests in large colonies in caves around the Caribbean basin.[11] Humboldt and Bonpland visited one of the largest nesting caves primarily out of interest in its geology, but they were extremely impressed by the vast numbers of birds and their relationship to local Indian and missionary customs of harvest. Humboldt was fascinated by the birds' nocturnal behaviors, their blue eyes, and their survival in spite of regular persecution.[12] Typically, he gives a detailed description of the species, which had previously not been described by a scientist, and then he immediately shifts over to a discussion of the geology of the nesting cavern.

Humboldt's observations on human affairs were often well ahead of his time. He makes it clear that he is not in sympathy with what he calls the "reduction" of the local Indians, and he has the insight to remark: "It is a common error in Europe, to look on all natives not reduced to a state of subjection, as wanderers and hunters. Agriculture was practiced on the American continent long before the arrival of Europeans. It is still practiced between the Orinoco and the river Amazon, in lands cleared amidst the forests, places to which the missionaries have never penetrated."[13]

This is one of those facts that are painfully obvious once one thinks things through, but all too often is lost in a mist of preconceptions. Much of the landscape of the Americas had been radically altered by generations of cultivation long before the colonial era, but the massive die-offs of native peoples that occurred in the immediate aftermath of the conquest lead to rapid shifts in both the pattern of vegetation and the cultures of the survivors. By the time Europeans documented what they saw, they were witnessing not some longstanding natural condition, but rather a series of landscapes in motion, denuded of the human populations who had affected them for centuries.

After four months of exploring the region around Cumaná, Humboldt and Bonpland decided to move westward to Caracas. Bonpland suffered severely from seasickness, so he accomplished part of the journey on foot, botanizing as he went, while Humboldt stayed with the ship the entire distance to Caracas.[14] The two naturalists liked what they saw of the town (Humboldt describes the nights in June and July as "clear and delicious"), and made it their base for the next two months, climbing some of the nearby mountains, comparing the floras at different elevations, and planning the next stage of their adventure.

Humboldt proceeded to the Orinoco by a somewhat zig-zag route, paying attention to hot springs, lakes, and other items of "peculiar interest" as he went. Their route took them across the *llanos*—the broad savannahs to the north of the Orinoco—and Humboldt speculated on the effects of the introduction of cattle and repeated burning on trees and shrubs in the region. Much to Humboldt's delight, once they reached Calabozo, in north-central Venezuela, they encountered a local scientist, Carlos del Pozo, who had been experimenting with electrical phenomena, including a homemade battery and various models of lightning rod. The three scientists exchanged notes, and Humboldt demonstrated some of the equipment that they had brought with them, before they set off to examine the electric eels for which the region was infamous.

Humboldt's description of their capture of large electric eels is frightening—horses were driven into ponds occupied by the eels and the eels attacked the animals, shocking them repeatedly until two horses drowned. Eventually the eels' ability to generate further shocks was exhausted, and the Indians were able to capture them using harpoons attached to dry strings. Humboldt gleefully reports some eels over five feet in length. He was nothing if not a participant observer—he talks of the extreme pain he got from the shock of standing with both feet on a large eel that had just been removed from the water, and he continues: "I can assert that, after having made experiments during four hours successively with *gymnoti*, M. Bonpland and myself felt, till the next day, a debility in the muscles, a pain in the joints, and a general uneasiness, the effect of a strong irritation of the nervous system."[15] One can certainly see why four hours of periodic shocks, some potentially strong enough to kill a horse, might fatigue even the most intrepid researchers.

Having satisfied themselves with a complete description of the effects and basic anatomy of the electric eel, Humboldt and Bonpland continued across the *llanos* toward the Orinoco. It is clear from their descriptions of the hot, dusty march that this was not the favorite portion of their travels, but Humboldt must have been a delightful traveling companion. He was like a sponge, soaking up every story or piece of information that came his way, whether it was hibernation in crocodiles or the use of the dorsal muscles of boas for guitar strings ("preferable to those furnished by the intestines of the alouate monkeys").[16] It must have been fascinating and frustrating to work with Humboldt—in his writings he has no difficulty in sliding instantaneously from observation of river dolphins to the effects of a passing thunderstorm on his electroscope. Thunderstorms remind him of weather patterns, which in turn lead to discussions of seasonality in the tropics. One imagines oneself uncomfortably on muleback, listening with half an ear to his happy chatter, while wondering what will be for dinner and where on earth one is going to spend the night.

Once the party reached San Fernando de Apure, they purchased a large canoe and proceeded down the Río Apure to the Orinoco. Humboldt is his usual cheerful self about conditions for recording information: "I noted down day by day, either in the boat or where we disembarked at night, all that appeared to me worthy of observation. Violent rains, and the prodigious quantity of mosquitos with which the air is filled on the banks of the Orinoco and the Cassiquiare, necessarily occasioned some interruptions; but I supplied the omission by notes taken a few days after."[17]

Apart from the mosquitos and the violent rains, the descriptions are enough to either chill the blood or, in the case of readers like Darwin, increase the wanderlust:

> Having passed the Diamante we entered a land inhabited only by tigers, crocodiles, and chiguires; the latter are a large species of the genus Cavia of Linnaeus. . . . You find yourself in a new world, in the midst of untamed and savage nature. Now the jaguar,—the most beautiful panther of America,—appears upon the shore. . . . In those desert countries, where man is ever wrestling with nature, discourse daily turns on the best means that may be employed to escape from a tiger, a boa, or a crocodile.[18]

Humboldt himself had a narrow escape from a "tiger"—actually a large jaguar—when he ventured onshore and disturbed its sleep under a tree. Fortunately Humboldt had already determined that the best means to be employed in escaping from a jaguar was to walk away from it without looking back, and he reached the boat in safety.

Movement on the Río Apure was by paddle. Once the boat reached the broader Orinoco, the native guides hoisted sail, and they proceeded upriver in the direction of the first cataract. At Uruana, a mission on the river, a local man came to examine Humboldt's surveying instruments. He appeared deeply puzzled as to why the travelers insisted on going upstream: "'How is it possible to believe,' said he, 'that you have left your country, to come and be devoured by mosquitos on this river, and to measure lands that are not your own?'"[19] The question captures much of natural history: this is exactly what natural historians have always done. Humboldt and Bonpland continued upriver, encountering Indians harvesting turtle eggs, which caused Humboldt to meditate on how jaguars might break through turtle shells when preying on adults and how they might find eggs when hunting along riverbanks. At one point the boat almost capsized when the captain chose to show off by sailing too close to the wind. Humboldt comments in relief that "only one book was lost,"[20] but he acknowledges that he and Bonpland both had some restless nights thinking about the possibilities of shipwreck deep in the jungle. The mosquitos might be fierce, but they lead Humboldt into a discussion of body painting and ornamentation. Jaguars were increasingly common, but Humboldt had monkeys to fascinate him, too. In all, even allowing that the *Personal Narrative* was written once Humboldt had reached the comforts of home, one cannot but admire the bravery and persistence of the little expedition.

The trip on the Orinoco lasted nearly three months. Once they had passed the first set of rapids, they had to switch into a much smaller boat—essentially a hollowed-out tree trunk three feet wide and forty feet long.[21] Into this unstable and unwieldy contraption were piled crew and passengers—a total of twelve adult men—plus a large dog, books, instruments, journals, specimens (alive and dead), and food to get them through periods when hunting failed them. It is perhaps no surprise that Humboldt commented: "It is difficult to form an idea of the inconveniences that are suffered in such wretched vessels."[22]

The only shelter on the boat was a small covered area at the stern, and passengers and captured specimens of birds and monkeys—which were kept in small cages attached to the superstructure—suffered badly from the sun. By the end of the journey they had acquired seven parrots, eight monkeys, two manakins, a motmot, two guans, a toucan, a macaw, and a kinkajou. It is understandable that their local guide "whispered some complaints" about this ever-growing collection.[23]

A major point of the expedition was to try to map out the relationships among the rivers feeding into the headwaters of the Orinoco and the Amazon and to see if it was possible to make a link with the Río Negro. Through a series of paddles and portages along a variety of tributaries, the explorers were able to reach and pass down the Río Negro. Humboldt had hoped to enter Brazil, but he found that his passports from the Spanish king were, if anything, a hindrance in Portuguese Brazil, and in fact a warrant had been let out for him, ordering border officials to seize his instruments and notes and take him down the Amazon and across to Lisbon for questioning. He was able to avoid arrest, but wisely turned back up the Río Casiquiare, rejoining the Orinoco for the return journey.

In the village of Esmeralda, Humboldt was introduced to a "poison master" who showed him the preparation of curare, which was used by the Indians in hunting and warfare. This "chemist of the place" had his own laboratory where he boiled down and tested concoctions of extracts from different plants. Plantain leaves were used to filter the preparations, which were boiled in large earthenware vats. Humboldt gives us a complete account both of the preparation of curare and of its weaponization, in which the poison is mixed with a glutinous extract from an unknown tree (he complains about how often the most interesting plants are not in flower or fruit just when you want to key them out). The combination of the poison with this binding agent allows it to be smeared effectively on arrowtips.

Here we see some of the themes discussed in the first chapter. Humboldt is the "natural historian" throughout. The local expert is regarded as an interesting character who has useful information that will be recorded by the natural historian for later publication. Humboldt appreciates the man's knowledge, but he is not likely to regard him as any sort of intellectual equal, even though the poison master has a much deeper understanding of the plants and animals of the surrounding jungle than any European. It would be easy to dismiss this relationship as one of racial or class prejudice in a simplistic sense, but I suggest that what is really demonstrated here is the distinction of natural history by intent. The question that Humboldt and Bonpland faced from the local mentioned earlier, who could not believe that they were subjecting themselves to great inconvenience "to measure lands *that are not your own*" (emphasis added), captures much of the issue. The poison master learned about plants and animals for very practical reasons. By so doing, he put meat in the pot, defended himself from enemies, and gained status among his peers as a master. Humboldt the natural historian, by contrast, was gaining nothing of a practical nature by his studies. True, he would enhance his reputation by publishing accounts of his travels and he would gain status through recognition of his knowledge, but there were many far less uncomfortable and dangerous ways for a member of the German aristocracy to gain status, recognition, and material reward than spending months in a crude canoe in mosquito- and jaguar-infested jungles.

The poison master made use of what was available for obvious benefits to himself and his society. Humboldt had the luxury of impracticality. It didn't really matter in a broad sense whether he understood electric eels or curare, but he was willing to go to great trouble to find out things that he really didn't need to know, and thus his activities would be instantly recognizable to any other natural historian, regardless of language or era.

Humboldt was interested in reports of potential medical uses for curare (in his writings he is never without at least *some* eye to practical applications), and he comments at length on the effects of the poison when swallowed compared to those observed from contamination of the blood. This in turn leads him to a discussion of why animals killed with poisoned arrows are perfectly edible and do not carry the toxin to the consumer.

After leaving Esmeralda, Humboldt and Bonpland proceeded downstream to Angostura. There the stresses of their journey finally seem to have caught up with them, and both developed fevers. Humboldt recovered quickly, but Bonpland was much more seriously ill and required several weeks of rest before he was able to continue onward. Once he had recovered, the travelers proceeded back across the *llanos* toward the coast. Now it was Humboldt's turn to be seriously ill, and they were forced to remain in New Barcelona for a month. Humboldt and Bonpland both had fond associations with their original base of operations in Cumaná, and they resolved to return there to sort their specimens and plan their next steps.

The easiest mode of transport was by sea, but this risked capture by a British warship. Sure enough, almost as soon as they put to sea in a smuggler's sloop, they were overhauled and fired on by a privateer. Fortunately a genuine English man-of-war showed up and Humboldt was invited onboard to discuss his adventures with the captain. It is worth noting that Humboldt's exploits on the mainland were familiar to the captain and officers of the warship, the HMS *Hawk*, "from the English newspapers,"[24] so we must assume that Humboldt had already attracted a good bit of fame. After a pleasant evening aboard, Humboldt was allowed to return to his own ship, taking with him additional astronomical information that he could use for his mapmaking.

Humboldt's original plan was to continue more or less immediately to Cuba, taking advantage of what he had been led to believe were frequent passages by traders among the Spanish Caribbean possessions. Unfortunately, the British blockade of the coast had seriously disrupted traffic, and though Humboldt, as a neutral, would have been free of concern about arrest, such immunity would not have extended to Bonpland. In any case, few ships were available. As a result, the pair spent over two months in Cumaná, writing up their notes, doing some local exploring, and arranging to send their live specimens back to France.[25]

The travelers departed from Venezuela in November 1800. The voyage to Cuba was a hard one, taking nearly twenty-five days, most of them in various forms of bad weather. They spent three months in Cuba, visiting the tomb of Christopher Columbus in Havana and exploring the countryside around the city. In the spring of 1801, Humboldt received news that Captain Nicolas Baudin, with whom he had originally intended to do a circumnavigation of the globe, had sailed at last and would be working up the west coast of South America in the coming months. Humboldt was wild to catch the ship, as it offered the opportunity to visit Australia and the East Indies. Humboldt and Bonpland immediately divided up their collections from Venezuela and sent duplicates of everything to Cadiz and to England, where they were entrusted to Sir Joseph Banks, who would forward the material to Humboldt's home in Germany. There is something remarkably comforting about the degree of cooperation among scientists. Prussia and Britain were allies against France and Spain, but Humboldt and Bonpland, citizens of countries that were regularly at war, were able to get along for years at a time, and could count on an international network of colleagues who would pass their specimens and notes across warring frontiers.

In March 1801, Humboldt chartered a small ship to take them to Central America, with the intention of then traveling overland to the Pacific coast and heading south to join the French exploring team. After a voyage of sixteen days from the south coast of Cuba, Humboldt and Bonpland arrived in Cartagena, in what is now Colombia, and proceeded up the Río Magdalena as far as Honda and so by mule to Bogotá, where they remained for four months, exploring the mountainous terrain surrounding the city. After this stopover, they continued to Quito, in modern Ecuador, which they used as a base of operations for six months while they ventured higher into the Andes.

In Quito, they learned to their dismay that Baudin had sailed east by the Cape of Good Hope and thus around Africa, rather than west around Cape Horn. There was now no prospect of a scientific circumnavigation, and Humboldt would have to content himself with further travels in the Americas. Unfortunately, the *Personal Narrative*, or at least the published form of that book, does not take us much beyond Cartagena,[26] and we have to rely on his *Views of Nature*, the *Vue des caudilleras*, and more explicitly scholarly treatises to get a sense of the latter half of his travels.

The stay in Quito may not have been what Humboldt had hoped for, but it allowed him to fully immerse himself in the botany and geology of some of the highest and most dramatic mountains on earth. In June 1802, Humboldt and Bonpland, accompanied by local guides, attempted to climb Chimborazo, which was then regarded as the world's highest mountain.[27] It is a testimony to the travelers' physical fitness and sheer determination that they got within 450 meters of the summit. They reported bleeding from their lips and eyesockets, and were forced to more or less crawl the last part of their journey, only to be stopped by a deep crevasse. Probably most annoying for Humboldt, their hands were so numb with cold that they could barely operate their scientific instruments.

Overall, Humboldt felt that although they had set an altitudinal record that would not be topped for nearly fifty years, the scientific results of their attempt had been minimal. This may have been true in some senses, but the attempt on the summit and Humboldt's later interpretation of the importance of altitude (which, as we have already seen, was clearly on his mind in Tenerife) led to one of the most dramatic and truly multiple dimensional works of scientific illustration ever produced. This was the *Tableau physique des Andes et Pays voisins* that accompanied the 1807 *Essay on the Geography of Plants*, arguably the real foundation of modern biogeography.[28] In the *Tableau physique*, Humboldt and Bonpland lay out the dif-

FIGURE 11. Chimborazo. This rather fanciful early-nineteenth-century print includes carefully posed "exotic" plants, animals, and people and barely hints at the detail of Humboldt's analyses. (Author's collection.)

ferent zones of vegetation that they have recorded, from the depths of the sea to the highest summit of Chimborazo, and also depict the climatic elements that they feel are responsible for this pattern of zonation.

The *Essay* itself is essentially a commentary on this remarkable graphical depiction, going over many of the ideas that are alluded to in the *Personal Narrative* but presenting them in a more concentrated and telegraphic scientific framework. The list of topics covered in the *Tableau* is remarkable: vegetation, animals, geology, cultivation, air temperature, perpetual snowline, chemical composition of the atmosphere, "electrical tension," barometric pressure, decrease in gravity, color of the sky, refraction, and the boiling point of water. Humboldt had engaged in measurements of all these things in Tenerife and along the Orinoco, but the *Tableau* and *Essay* allowed him to pull them all together into what amounts to one figure and an extra-long explanatory caption.

After Chimborazo, Humboldt and Bonpland continued down the Andes, crossing over to explore the extreme upper reaches of the Amazon. They moved on to Lima, distracted on their way by an eruption of the volcano Cotopaxi. From Lima, they took a ship to Guayaquil, arriving early in 1803 before sailing on to Acapulco in Mexico. The pair then traveled overland to Mexico City, where they remained for several months, with Humboldt taking advantage of local natural historians and libraries to compile extensive notes for what was to become his *Political Essay on the Kingdom of New Spain*.[29] Humboldt was already hoping to link together the biological and physical sciences with what we would now call sociology, economics, and geography. What Humboldt was actually practicing can best be called human ecology, although the term was still a century in the future.

Rather than heading straight home, Humboldt resolved to pay a visit to the United States on the way. This had been part of his original alternate plan before he had been distracted in Cuba by the possibility of joining Baudin's circumnavigation. At that time he had hoped to explore the Mississippi basin, but now he seemed more interested in scientific conversation. Sailing first to Cuba and thence up the eastern seaboard to Philadelphia, Humboldt and Bonpland were welcomed by the scientific establishment in the fledgling United States.

The travelers were invited to Washington to meet Jefferson, who had long held a deep interest in the sciences and, as we shall see, had just been responsible for sending the Lewis and Clark Expedition across North America. Humboldt and Bonpland would doubtless have thoroughly approved of the Corps of Discovery (one can easily imagine them signing on had they been in the States at the appropriate time), and Humboldt and Jefferson seem to have developed a warm professional friendship in spite of the latter's slaveholding. The travelers then returned to Philadelphia to receive a *laisser passer* from the British consul before boarding a ship back to France.[30]

Bonpland and Humboldt found France significantly changed from how they had left it more than five years earlier. While they had been exploring the jungle, climbing mountains, and observing strange and exotic plants and animals, Napoleon Bonaparte had risen from general, to first consul, and then to emperor of France. He had turned the energies of the Revolution outward and made war on much of the rest of the world. What Humboldt, with his republican sympathies, must have thought of this can only be imagined.[31]

Although some of the specimens and notes that they had sent back to France had been lost in transit, Humboldt and Bonpland still had over six thousand botanical specimens to sort through, as well as thousands of pages of notes and a vast array of additional specimens in need of cataloguing. Besides the highly popular *Personal Narrative* and the *Essay on the Geography of Plants* discussed above, Humboldt published more than seventeen important works between 1805 and 1826. These books' topics range from straight botany and geology to discussions of the political situation in the New World.

Bonpland's later career was less dramatic than Humboldt's. He was friendly with the imperial family (he had served in the French army prior to going overseas with Humboldt) and was appointed gardener to the Empress Josephine at the Botanic Gardens at Malmaison outside of Paris. The fall of the emperor and the political unrest that followed made this position less desirable, and in 1816 he accepted a professorship in Buenos Aires and departed for Argentina. He continued explorations in South America, but was arrested in Paraguay in 1821 and held captive for a decade, during which time he resumed his earlier practice as a medical doctor. After his release, he returned to Argentina and continued to work there until his death in 1858 in what is now Uruguay.

Humboldt's exploits in the Americas and his subsequent books and papers established him as one of the most important men of science of his era. The king of Prussia supported his research when Humboldt's personal fortune began to run out and sent him to London as a diplomatic representative. Humboldt also attended the peace conference at Aix-la-Chapelle that worked out the division of Europe following Napoleon's final defeat, and he used the opportunity to make contacts that he would find useful in a planned visit to Asia. In the meantime, he launched a lecture series at the university in Paris on a topic that perhaps only he could fully engage: the universe.

In 1829, Humboldt left Paris for Berlin, where he learned that Czar Nicholas would support an expedition to Russian Asia. This was an important piece of news, as Humboldt had by this stage almost entirely exhausted his inheritance on publishing his South American work and in supporting research by young scientists. He proceeded to St. Petersburg, drawing on the contacts that he had made at the peace conference eleven years earlier. Humboldt was pleasantly surprised by the warmth of his reception in Russia. The royal family was excited about his planned expedition and made a point of dining with him informally on a regular basis. This mark of favor made both the support and the conduct of the journey immeasurably easier, although the distances and terrain that were to be crossed still imposed significant natural barriers.

From St. Petersburg, Humboldt traveled to Moscow and thence eastward across the Urals to the Mongolian border before retuning to Berlin with a stopover on the Caspian Sea. Much of his time was spent in examining the broad range of mines that were being developed in eastern Russia, but this journey, while considerably shorter than his travels in the Americas (he was gone just under nine months), also allowed him to do some serious comparisons between the geology of South America and that of Central Asia. The visit to the Caspian, in typical Humboldt style, had the dual objectives of conducting an analysis of the water and also of obtaining rare species of fish for anatomical studies by Cuvier in Paris. For much of the journey, Humboldt either rode in carriages or traveled on horseback, and although some of the regions through which he passed were notorious for stinging insects, it was probably much more comfortable than the Orinoco. The expedition covered approximately nine thousand miles in twenty-five weeks, or a remarkable fifty miles a day. This would have been possible only with the imprimatur of imperial approval—one biography says that over twelve thousand post horses were used in relay for travel.[32]

Humboldt's next project was intended to be his masterpiece: nothing less than a complete encyclopedic discussion of essentially everything. We have seen that this tendency to attempt the compilation of a complete picture of the physical and biological world goes back at least as far as Aristotle (one could suppose that with his great library, Asurbanipal was perhaps engaged on a similar project). The scope of such a work had expanded enormously since Aristotle's time. Bonpland returned from South America with an estimated six thousand species of plants; Linnaeus, only fifty years earlier, had listed a *global total* of seven thousand. Besides the increasing biological diversity revealed by two millennia of natural history, the physical sciences had become much more sophisticated and detailed than anything imagined by Aristotle or Pliny. Still, if anyone was capable of pulling it all together, it would be Humboldt.

His five-volume work known as *Cosmos* probably began as lecture notes for the courses on the universe that he had given in Paris in the 1820s. The first volume came out in 1845, and succeeding volumes were published periodically until Humboldt's death in 1859. Humboldt also continued to encourage and support other scientists with fewer advantages than his own. When Louis Agassiz was about to give up his studies in Paris for want of funds, Humboldt sent him fifty pounds and told him to consider it a loan, repayable whenever he was able. This generosity allowed Agassiz to continue his studies with Cuvier, with results that we will see in a future chapter.

Besides being a brilliant scientist and polymath, Humboldt was an enormously *humane* human, generous to a fault and constantly delighted by the world around him. He died in May 1859. His last words, speaking of the sun through his window, were "How grand those rays, they seem to beckon Earth to Heaven."[33] A little under a year earlier, the mail at Down House in Kent had included a small package from one enthusiastic reader of Humboldt to another. Charles Darwin had received the manuscript on natural selection from Alfred Russel Wallace.

ELEVEN . Hearts of Light

Wallace and Bates

There is a literary tradition, exemplified by Joseph Conrad, in which a supposedly civilized European or American penetrates into some savage backwater and proceeds to regress into a form of bestial savagery that makes a lie of everything that he or she is supposed to represent. There is something very appealing about this idea: the thin veneer of civility is ripped away by the harsh reality of untamed nature. The trouble is that, as with all such fables, it isn't necessarily true. In chapter 10, we have already seen Humboldt and Bonpland, two of the most civilized naturalists on record, pass into, through, and out of the jungle with their humanity fully intact. Alfred Russel Wallace (1823–1913) and Henry Walter Bates (1825–1892) form another example of this sort of "anti-Conrad" story: civilized men who go into the jungle, up long rivers, through constant dangers, and emerge, if anything, more civilized than when they went in. Beyond this, each is able to carry with them not Kurtz's "horror" from the *Heart of Darkness*, but rather a deep appreciation and even empathy for the peoples and places they see. In the case of Wallace, he also brought back an intellectual gem that was one of the crowning achievements of the nineteenth century: the theory of evolution by natural selection.

There is something enormously appealing about Wallace. He was born sufficiently after Darwin and lived sufficiently longer than Darwin that we have a whole series of photographs of him. These range from Wallace the young man to Wallace the Edwardian sage. In contrast to the often sad and aged photographs of

Darwin, those of Wallace start with a distinctly gawky youth, move on to a self-confident, hat-wearing young explorer, continue with the serious scientist, and end with what I can describe only as everyone's favorite great-uncle. Darwin never smiles. In his later pictures, Wallace positively twinkles—you could see him playing Santa Claus in any number of children's films. One feels that Wallace is perpetually bemused that he has achieved so much more than he ever had imagined in his wildest dreams.

Wallace demonstrates that wealth, position, formal education, and standing in the scientific community are all very well and certainly help, but with a lot of hard work, a little luck, and a bit of natural genius, it is possible to make major contributions in a variety of fields. When we are looking for an excuse to not do things, we can shake our heads and say, "Well, Humboldt *was* a baron, after all," or "Well, Darwin *did* come from a wealthy family and went to an outstanding university," but this doesn't work with Wallace; he is just himself, fascinated with beetles in Brazil, life on Mars, and most everything in between.

In the last twenty years, there has been a growing industry in "rediscovering" Wallace, and at one point there was almost a mania for using Wallace as a way to undercut and belittle Darwin. I feel that Wallace would have been saddened by this sort of behavior. There is no evidence in any of his writing that he feels other than respect, admiration, and gratitude toward Darwin, whom he rightly credits with establishing the validity of their mutual theory of evolution. Wallace was far too busy to be troubled by issues of priority. The idea, and the ability to continue searching out new ideas, was what mattered. Wallace loved new things, whether they were new places, new species, or new explanations for old observations. Above all else, Wallace, like Humboldt, seems to have been an enormously humane person. One has but to look at his later portraits to see that he was also a very *nice* man.

After his one great spasm of traveling, Darwin turned inward, spending most of the rest of his life in a narrow geographic orbit while throwing his mind across the whole expanse of deep time to some absolute origin. The quiet of Down provided a safe haven from the difficulties of an industrializing Britain, and Emma made sure that Charles's life was as untroubled as possible so that he could get on with his work. Humboldt and Wallace, by contrast, never really stopped traveling; they were out *in* the world, and to a great extent their thoughts and actions were *of* the world. Like Humboldt, Wallace was widely heralded in his own day, and, like Humboldt, his reputation went into eclipse after his death. In the end, Wallace chose to go in thought to places where neither Darwin nor Humboldt would tread.

His insistence on the existence of Mind as something that transcended even natural selection was the only real source of fierce disagreement between him and Darwin.

Wallace was born on January 8, 1823, in Usk, Monmouthshire, in the right country at exactly the right time. Britain was the rising power of the age. The era that is the topic of one of his later books, *The Wonderful Century*, saw the industrial and scientific revolutions that made much of his travel and science possible.[1] With enough time, a few resources, and sufficient good health, a British traveler could go just about anywhere, do just about anything, and know that he had the backing of a truly global network of power and influence. It was ironic that the same advances that eased transportation and communication and provided an economic base for world travel and natural history on a global scale also created a foundation for the horrors of child labor, mechanized warfare, and repression that so outraged first Humboldt and then Wallace. In spite of this, Wallace never lost hope, and at the end of *The Wonderful Century*, he writes: "True humanity, the determination that the crying social evils of our time shall not continue; the certainty that they can be abolished; an unwavering faith in human nature, have never been so strong, so vigorous, so rapidly growing as they are today. . . . The flowing tide is with us. We have great poets, great writers, great thinkers to cheer and guide us; and an ever-increasing band of earnest workers to spread the light."[2] Wallace himself was, of course, one of the great thinkers and also one of the earnest workers, although he probably would have been embarrassed at such praise. He was born at the height of the Age of Sail; by the time he died, airplanes, telephones, and global communication had become realities. He would have hated most of the twentieth century.

Wallace's father held a variety of odd jobs throughout Wallace's childhood, including that of a librarian and a schoolteacher.[3] What little additional income the family had was lost in a bankruptcy, and, as a result, the family was constantly on the move in search of employment or cheap rent or both.[4] Wallace's formal schooling was limited to a few years of grammar school, complemented by a short stay at boarding school. In his autobiography, he says rather sadly that most of the lessons were little more than mindless memorization of names, dates, or places, and he doesn't seem to have objected when the process of schooling was cut short by a further decline in family fortunes.

Probably the most important influence on Wallace's developing thoughts were the books his father brought home or had sent to him via a book club. His reading list was extensive, including a huge array of novels, but in his autobiography he also mentions being fascinated by Mungo Park's tales of travel in Africa, and it

FIGURE 12. "M. Park's First View of the Niger," from Mungo Park, *Travels in the Interior Districts of Africa Performed in the Years 1795, 1796 and 1797*, 1816. Scenes such as this one inspired the young Darwin and later Alfred Russel Wallace and John Muir, all of whom cite Mungo Park's writings as a source of their desire to travel. (Author's collection.)

seems likely that this early exposure to exotic locales may have influenced his own desire for adventure.[5] Wallace left school at fourteen and traveled to London to live with his elder brother John, who was an apprentice joiner. Wallace helped around the shop and went out on the town with his brother, both for amusement and also to attend lectures on socialism and workers' rights, topics that would be central to Alfred's later years. The work in the joiner's shop would also prove useful once Wallace was in the East Indies and needed to make himself collecting boxes and basic instruments for his studies.

After a few months in London, he was sent to his brother William to learn surveying. Surveying showed Wallace the application of mathematics to real-world problems, and William's interest in geology also proved infectious. Wallace began his own collections of fossils found in the course of his travels. He also became interested in botany and worked out the best ways to dry and preserve specimens while developing a personal herbarium. Surveying work took the brothers over much of England, exposing them to a variety of landscapes and giving Wallace time to develop his skills as a naturalist. This idyll did not last long: Wallace's father died in 1843, and surveying work dwindled to a point where Wallace decided to try his hand at teaching and applied for a job at a small private school in Leicester.

In Leicester, three important events occurred that had a profound effect on the entire course of Wallace's life. The first two came in the form of books. He found a copy of Thomas Malthus's *Essay on the Principle of Population*, which described the inevitable consequences of an exploding population and a limited food supply.[6] He also came across Humboldt's *Personal Narrative*, which fired his interest in the tropics. The third big influence was his meeting H. W. Bates, a young man who was, like Wallace, almost entirely self-taught in natural history, but who had a particular interest in insects. Bates's family was better off than Wallace's, but they also lacked much formal education.

Wallace was immediately captivated by entomology, and joined Bates in collecting expeditions in the countryside around Leicester. Besides collecting, we know that the pair engaged in exciting discussions of the mysterious book *Vestiges of the Natural History of Creation*, which had appeared anonymously in 1844 and had provoked a storm of controversy over its proposal that species might be mutable.[7]

In 1846, Wallace's brother William died suddenly, leaving his surveying tools to Alfred, who was able to make use of them in the great railway bubble that dominated the country that year.[8] Before the bubble burst and surveying became unprofitable once more, Wallace had saved enough money that he could propose to Bates that they try their hand as professional natural history collectors in South America. This was a distinctly risky proposition. Governments and private collectors were willing to pay significant sums for the rare and the beautiful, but travel still had its real dangers and, as Humboldt and Bonpland had found, getting specimens—especially fragile specimens of butterflies and moths—safely back to Europe was no mean feat.

Wallace and Bates must have looked around them and realized that they faced the choice of a rather dull lower-middle-class existence in Britain or potential fame and economic reward if they went abroad. Perhaps most important, both had caught the travel bug from their reading, and they were both interested in questions about the origin and diversification of species. If they were to go, the time was now. Neither were married; both were young, fit, and ambitious. A suitable destination was obvious: South America was opening up. Soon it would be overrun with collectors of all sorts, and, as Wallace himself puts it in a letter to Bates, he had two examples before him who had demonstrated the value of travel in tropical America: "I first read Darwin's Journal three or four years ago, and have lately re-read it. As a Journal of a scientific traveler, it is second only to Humboldt's 'Personal Narrative'—as a work of general interest, perhaps superior to it."[9] Both Bates and Wallace had also read the American entomologist William Edwards's account of his journey on the Amazon, which included a description of the countryside around Pará, and this further increased their resolve to go to Brazil.[10]

Fieldwork in and around Leicestershire had given Bates and Wallace plenty of experience in collecting and preserving insects, but they were now going to take what had been a hobby to a new level. They traveled to London to consult with experts at the British Museum on appropriate ways to pack and ship specimens, and Wallace also took a crash course in shooting and stuffing birds. Equally important, they sought out an agent who would act as the recipient of any specimens that they sent home ahead of them and who would find buyers for as many specimens as possible. Unlike Darwin or Humboldt, neither of them had the prospect of checks from home to tide them over difficult periods, and the continuation of their travels, as well as their entire financial well-being, depended on the ability of the agent to find a market for what they collected. They visited Kew to meet with William Hooker, who was in the process of expanding the Botanic Gardens. Hooker assured them that he would be delighted to receive any interesting plants that might come their way. Back in London, Edward Doubleday, the curator of Lepidoptera at the British Museum, told them that the northern portions of Brazil were still largely unknown to collectors, and this further convinced them of the wisdom of their choice of destination.[11]

Once these preparations had been made, Wallace and Bates embarked on the 190-ton schooner *Mischief,* bound for Brazil. Like their predecessors, they found the Bay of Biscay extremely rough, and Wallace was very seasick for the first week of the voyage. Fortunately, he got his sea legs once they were past Madeira, and the weather from that point onward was fine. They reached the mouth of the Amazon at the end of May 1848 without incident. Both naturalists were disappointed by their first views of the New World. Edwards's dramatic accounts of the flora and fauna had led them to expect that they would immediately be overwhelmed by biological diversity, but Wallace was uninspired by what he saw.[12] Bates got into the spirit of things more quickly, writing about the noisy fiesta that was going on as they arrived and reveling in the foreignness of everything, but Wallace wanted monkeys and exotic butterflies. The town of Pará (modern-day Belém) was small and dusty, and the edge of the true tropical forest was some miles away. Birdlife was relatively scarce, and the commonest animals were lizards that eluded the grasp of novices.

After a short stay in the house of the local consul, the travelers moved to a villa on the edge of town that served as a base of operations for some months. From there they could explore the local forests and begin the serious work of collection. Life in Pará sounds rather blissful in some ways. Mornings were spent in the jungle, collecting and observing. Once the heat of the afternoon arrived, most insects disappeared, and this was a ready excuse to retire for a siesta before resuming activity in the late afternoon. Bates specialized in insects, but Wallace was interested in everything. Mindful of Hooker's requests for plants, he made collections and notes of as many botanical specimens as possible—notes that would lead to his first book.[13] He quickly got over his initial disappointment, as one sees from his early writing: "Huge trees with buttressed stems, tangled climbers of fantastic forms, and strange parasitical plants everywhere meet the admiring gaze of the naturalist fresh from the meadows and heaths of Europe."[14] Palm trees fascinated him the way that tortoises in the Galápagos had fascinated Darwin—to his naive eyes, each species was slightly different from the next, yet each was recognizably a palm: "To the lover of nature Palms offer a constant source of interest, reminding him that he is amidst the luxuriant vegetation of the tropics, and offering him the realization of whatever wild and beautiful ideas he has from childhood associated with their name."[15] Wallace was a long way indeed from the valleys of Wales, but he had much farther to go.

Venturing into the jungle, Wallace encountered his first wild monkeys, several of which were shot for collections. Wallace exhibits an interesting mixture of humanity and pragmatism in this encounter: "The poor little animal was not quite dead, and its cries, its innocent-looking countenance, and delicate looking hands were quite childlike. Having often heard how good monkey was, I took it home and had it cut up and fried for breakfast."[16]

Natural history in its heyday was not for the squeamish. Collecting went well once Wallace and Bates became more familiar with the jungle landscape. Soon they had over three thousand specimens ready to be sent back to England for sale. Wallace also boxed up several hundred plant specimens for Hooker, but the great botanist seems to have been unimpressed with Wallace's efforts, at least to the extent that he was later to publish a negative review of Wallace's *Palm Trees of the Amazon and Their Uses*.[17]

After ensuring that their specimens were safely on their way, Wallace and Bates joined a local mill foreman for an extended trip up the Tocantins, a subsidiary of the Amazon. They sailed in a much more seaworthy and comfortable vessel than Humboldt and Bonpland had used on the Orinoco nearly fifty years earlier. This craft was twenty-eight feet long—shorter than Humboldt's—but at eight feet in diameter, it provided more room to move around while underway, and it had two covered spaces to keep passengers and cargo out of the elements. At the start of the trip, the travelers were accompanied by a crew of four, but at their first stop the pilot jumped ship, soon to be followed by two of the crew. As a result of these desertions, they were forced to accept the loan of two slaves from a nearby plantation.

After this journey, Wallace and Bates decided to operate independently, collecting in different locations. None of the biographies of the two men and none of their own writings sheds much light on the reasons for this separation. There is no evidence of a major quarrel, and most authors seem to agree that the desire for independence was more a matter of general differences in personality, perhaps enhanced by the confines of the river trip, than of any particular disagreement. Regardless of the immediate cause of the split, it does not seem to have hurt their overall friendship. Both wrote to each other while Wallace was in Malaysia and Bates still in Brazil, and upon their respective returns to Britain, they continued their correspondence until Bates's death in 1892.

Wallace soon gave up on insects, concentrating instead on collecting birds, which he shot and stuffed for transshipment back to Britain.[18] He was entranced with the hummingbirds that could be found around, it seemed, every flowering bush. Vampire bats, on the other hand, were less appealing. Wallace heard tales of the bats killing hundreds of cows a year, and of the slaves on the estate he was staying at killing thousands of bats in return. After a solo expedition, Wallace returned to Pará, where he was joined by his brother Herbert, who had given up hopes of teaching in Britain and thought he would try his hand at natural history in the New World.

The two brothers obtained a sailing canoe and proceeded up the Amazon, collecting as they went. Wallace's account is significantly different from Humboldt's. It is written very much as a travelogue, with some nice descriptions of particular animals and locations, but there are none of the wonderful tangents on meteorology, geology, and culture that are so entertaining and so distracting in the *Personal Narrative*. It was all very new and in part wonderful, but one also gets a strong sense that Wallace was not at ease in the backcountry, particularly with his fellow humans. The Wallace who writes the *Travels on the Amazon and Rio Negro* is still a bit of a prude: "And then it is the fashionable visiting time, when every one goes to see everybody, to talk over the accumulated scandal of the week. Morals in Barra are perhaps at the lowest ebb possible in any civilized community: you will everyday hear things commonly talked of, about the most respectable families in the place, which could hardly be credited of the inhabitants of the worst part of St. Giles's."[19]

A month's sailing and paddling brought the brothers to Santarem, over four hundred miles in a straight line from their starting point—and considerably more by river, even without counting side journeys in pursuit of specimens. After pausing at Santarem to ship specimens home, Wallace continued up the river, passing and being passed by Bates as each collector tarried in one choice spot or leapt ahead in hopes of better finds. Another 360 miles upriver, they reached Barra (modern Manaus). Wallace found little about the town that appealed to him, so he set off up the Rio Negro. This side venture netted him twenty-five specimens of the umbrella bird, a species of cotinga, including a live individual, which was captured after being wounded by a shot from Wallace's gun. Wallace kept the bird alive for some weeks by force-feeding it fruit. It eventually died, but not before Wallace had begun to observe its behavior—the first real sign that he was going beyond collecting for the sake of collecting.

Back in Barra, the rainy season set in with a vengeance. Bates had also arrived, and the half dozen or so European expatriates in town made the best of things by entertaining one another, talking, arguing, and comparing notes of travels accomplished and travels planned. Wallace was anxious to be off. As he resumed traveling, Wallace's prose grew more descriptive and more enthusiastic: "But what lovely yellow flower is that suspended in the air between two trunks, yet far from either? It shines in the gloom as if its petals were of gold. Now we pass close by it, and see its stalk, like a slender wire a yard and a half long, springing from a cluster of thick leaves on the bark of a tree."[20]

The rainy season had brought orchids to flower, as well as turning much of the Amazon basin into a confusing and delightful maze of channels, lakes, and blind alleys, all available to an intrepid collector whose growing confidence was drawing him ever farther afield. His brother Herbert had decided that he had had enough of the tropics, and was anxious to return to England as soon as he could save up enough money for passage, so Wallace would be continuing on his own, accompanied by whatever guides and rowers he could muster.

A major object of the early part of this journey was to obtain specimens of the gallo, or cock of the rock (genus *Rupicola*, a particularly brightly colored cotinga). Wallace initially based himself in an Indian village on the banks of the Rio Negro, but soon found that the birds were more common in the nearby mountains. He set off with a party of Indians to assist him in obtaining specimens. Once again, his account slides between enthusiasm and distaste: "Gigantic buttress trees, tall fluted stems, strange palms, and elegant tree-ferns were abundant on every side, and many persons may suppose that our walk must necessarily have been a delightful one; but there were many disagreeables. Hard roots rose up in ridges along our path, swamp and mud alternated with quartz pebbles and rotten leaves."[21] There is no real trace here of Humboldt's calm, phlegmatic view of the difficulties of travel; Wallace had a hard time moving through the jungle, and he wants his readers to be fully aware of it.

The next day the group finally encountered gallos: "At length, however, an old Indian caught hold of my arm, and whispering gently, 'Gallo' pointed into a dense thicket. After looking intently for a little while, I caught a glimpse of the magnificent bird sitting amidst the gloom, shining out like a mass of brilliant flame . . . . [I] fired with a steady aim, and brought it down. . . . In a few minutes . . . it was brought to me, and I was lost in admiration of the dazzling brilliancy of its soft downy feathers."[22] In all, they were successful in shooting a dozen gallos as well as a number of other birds including manakins, barbets and ant-thrushes.

Wallace then proceeded upriver and across the border into Venezuela. Unlike Humboldt, he had no trouble crossing between Brazil and the now independent former Spanish colony. As he reached San Carlos, he finally intersected Humboldt's path from fifty years earlier, and one gets a sense of real accomplishment as he finally encounters landscapes seen by his hero.

Wallace spent three months in the village of Javita, the only European among some two hundred Indians, and it is a mark of his maturation as a naturalist that he seems to have been reasonably comfortable in this position. He had also learned that the Indians were enormously effective at catching specimens for him if they could be persuaded to do so. By September 1851, Wallace's supplies were running low, and he needed to ship off his collections, so he determined to return downstream to Barra before planning any further extended trips. There he was greeted with the news that far from being safely back in Britain, his brother Herbert had caught yellow fever in Pará just before he was to embark for home and was dangerously ill. The letter was several months old, and Wallace had no way of knowing that his brother had died in an epidemic that had caused widespread mortality along the coast. Bates, who had also returned to Pará, had nursed Herbert as well as he could before developing the disease himself. Bates recovered; Herbert did not.

Wallace set out once more, determined to explore additional tributaries of the Amazon. He contracted a bout of fever and a case of dysentery, both of which responded fairly quickly to a combination of fasting and quinine. A few weeks later, however, he came down with a much more serious fever and hovered for some weeks at death's door until he was finally able to eat again. This episode helped him decide to finish collecting in the Rio Negro region and then return to Pará for the journey home. This he did, and accompanied by a menagerie of live specimens, including monkeys, macaws, and parrots, reached the port in July 1852. He was still suffering from bouts of fever, but was determined to get home as quickly as possible—a determination only reinforced by signs of the yellow fever epidemic in Pará and a sad visit to his brother's grave.

On July 12, he boarded the brig *Helen*, laden with specimens alive and dead, looking forward to a swift passage home. It was not to be. Wallace's intermittent fever kept him in his cabin for much of the three weeks of the voyage, reading, resting, and doubtless dreaming of the reception he and his collections would receive in Britain. One morning, however, the captain came to him and said, with remarkable understatement, "I am afraid the ship is on fire, come and see what you think of it."[23] Sure enough, fire had broken out in the hold, which had been packed with inflammable India rubber and balsam. Dense smoke soon started pouring out of the hatchways, preventing the crew from getting at the fire. As the flames increased, the captain decided that there was no hope of saving the ship and ordered the crew to lower the small boats. Wallace grabbed a "small tin box" containing a few clothes, a couple of notebooks, and some sketches of palms, but the bulk of his journals and drawings, and all the specimens that he had brought with him, were lost.

As the flames swept upward, passengers and crew floated nearby in the lifeboats, watching in horror as the monkeys and parrots that Wallace had hoped to bring to England flew or climbed into the rigging, only to be consumed by the fire. The ship burned all night, and in the morning the lifeboats set sail for Bermuda, seven hundred miles away. At first it seemed that they would reach Bermuda within a week, but then the wind veered, dropped, and died away, only to come on from an unfavorable direction. Supplies began to run low, and water was an increasing problem. At last, after ten days in the open boats, they were picked up by a passing ship, still two hundred miles from Bermuda.

Fortunately for Wallace's financial security, his agent had insured the lost collections for two hundred pounds. This, coupled with money remaining from the sale of materials shipped back earlier, ensured that he was not destitute. The loss to his scientific ambitions was much greater. Many of his notes and the all-important journals of his travels had been destroyed in the fire, and he had to decide whether he would be able to reconstruct anything worth publishing, and whether he should take his recent brush with death as fair warning that future travels were inadvisable. To his undoubted pleasure, he found that a number of his letters home had been read at the Entomological Society and the Royal Geographical Society, and he was by no means unknown among the scientific establishment in London.

In spite of the loss of notes and specimens, Wallace wrote up his book on palms, which, as we have seen earlier, was dismissed by William Hooker, who referred to it as more of a coffee-table book than a real work of botany. He also wrote his *Travels on the Amazon and Rio Negro*, drawing largely from surviving letters home and his prodigious memory. The result, while interesting and containing some attractive passages, was certainly not up to the standard of either Darwin's or Humboldt's travel narratives, nor was it as careful or thorough as his later writing, when he had the benefit of a full set of notes at hand.

In the meantime, Bates had seriously considered giving up on natural history when he returned to Pará. Work on the river had been exhausting and marginal in terms of profits, and letters from home informed him that industry was booming. He could expect a warm welcome from his family and employment in the family business. After much thought, he resolved to stay on in Brazil, continuing to travel and collect, concentrating primarily on insects, of which he eventually amassed a total of over *fourteen thousand* species (remember that only two centuries earlier John Ray had imagined a *global* total of a few thousand species).[24]

Bates remained in Brazil for a total of eleven years, returning just in time for the excitement over the publication of the *Origin of Species*. He had discussed evolutionary ideas with Wallace at the beginning of their time in South America, and it is obvious from correspondence that he thought a great deal of Darwin, and that Darwin returned the sentiment. Bates wrote his own narrative of his travels, which Darwin was to describe as "the best book of Natural History Travels ever published in England. . . . It is a grand book."[25] It is indeed a grand book and deserves to be much more widely read and acknowledged. If we hearken back to Darwin's blissful rhapsody during his first encounter with the Brazilian rain forest, it is perhaps worth seeing what longer exposure to the landscape and its biology could mean in the hands of a writer who had had the opportunity to experience the outcomes of the struggle for existence. In describing the *sipo matador*, or murderer liana, Bates writes:

> It is not essentially different from other climbing trees and plants, but the way the matador sets about it is peculiar, and produces certainly a disagreeable impression. It springs up close to the tree on which it intends to fix itself, and the wood of its stem grows by spreading itself like a plastic mould over one side of the trunk of its supporter. It then puts forth an arm-like branch . . . and the victim, when its strangler is full-grown, becomes tightly clasped by a number of inflexible rings. . . . The strange spectacle then remains of the selfish parasite clasping in its arms the lifeless and decaying body of its victim, which had been a help to its own growth.[26]

This is a long way from happy "twiners entwining twiners," yet Darwin was immediately drawn to it. In a review of the manuscript, he says: "It is, in my opinion excellent—style perfect—description first rate (I quite enjoyed rambling in forests). . . . Matador very good—Better than very good."[27]

Darwin was enormously enthusiastic about Bates in general, recommending his book to many important friends, writing to his own publisher to encourage publication of *The Naturalist on the River Amazons*, supporting Bates in quarrels with other entomologists, and helping him to find jobs. Part of his motivation may have been that Bates provided excellent support to Darwin's evolutionary ideas without any hint of rivalry or competition, but part of it was also the recognition of the enormous amount of work that Bates had done and the overall quality of his writing. Bates married in 1861, and died in 1892. The bulk of his private collection wound up in the Museum of Natural History in London.

Upon returning to London, Wallace was faced with something of a dilemma. If he was to succeed as a naturalist, he would have to resume his travels. Three obvious areas presented themselves to someone who was experienced in the tropics: a return to South America, Central Africa, or the Far East. Illness, shipwreck, and the death of his brother may have put Wallace off further explorations in South America, and besides, he had relinquished his position in Brazil to Bates, and other collectors were streaming into the region. Africa may have been a real temptation, and indeed he proposed at one point to venture into the mountainous regions of that continent, but in the end he settled on an extended collecting expedition to the little-known archipelago of islands then known as the Dutch East Indies.

He still had money left from his South American collections (in some senses he had done better financially than Bates, who said later that eleven years of hard work in South America had netted him only about eight hundred pounds), but not enough to outfit an expedition of any length. He spent a number of months making contacts and establishing connections that might be helpful both in getting to the East Indies and in logistical support once he was there. Among these contacts was Sir Roderick Impey Murchison (1792–1871), president of the Royal Geographical Society and "one of the most accessible and kindly men of science," who was willing to propose that the Geographical Society support Wallace's endeavors.[28] After a couple of false starts, Murchison was able to procure free passage for Wallace and an assistant on a P&O steamship to Singapore.

Singapore was a suitable base from which to become acclimated to the Far East. Wallace arrived there in April 1854. He spent the next three months reading up on the region, assembling supplies, and preparing for serious travel. One of the most important books that Wallace reports having taken with him everywhere was the *Conspectus Generum Avium*, the first real "birds of the world," by Napoleon's nephew Charles Lucien Bonaparte (1803–57), who had also updated Alexander Wilson's *Birds of America* and had been friends with Audubon. In his autobiography, Wallace notes approvingly that the book had particularly wide margins, which allowed him to write additional material, including key characteristics not in the original, so that "during my whole eight years' collecting in the East, I could almost always identify every bird already described."[29]

Much of what we know of Wallace's time in Malaysia comes from what he presents in his next travelogue, *The Malay Archipelago*.[30] This book is clearly intended for a popular audience, as is shown by the dramatic frontispieces, the rather gory "Orang Utang Attacked by Dyaks," the "The Red Bird of Paradise *(Paradisea rubra)*," and the more sublime "Natives of Aru Shooting the Great Bird of Paradise" (figures 13–15).[31] The book is dedicated to Charles Darwin, "not only as a token of personal esteem and friendship, but also to express my deep admiration for his genius and his works."[32] In terms of writing, it represents a significant step up from the earlier *Travels*, in part because Wallace was able to use more complete notes and in part because he was becoming more seasoned as both a traveler and a travel writer.

Among the many colorful characters that Wallace spent time with was Sir James Brooke (1803–68), the first of the White Rajahs of Sarawak, who was then in the process of establishing his family's rule over an immense portion of Borneo.[33]

FIGURE 13. "Orang Utan Attacked by Dyaks," from Alfred Russel Wallace's *Malay Archipelago*, 1869. At least here the orang appears to be winning. (Author's collection.)

that the weather was unprecedentedly bad, considering that it ought to have been the dry monsoon. For near a month we had wet weather; the sun either not appearing at all, or only for an hour or two about noon. Morning and evening, as well as nearly all night, it rained or drizzled, and boisterous winds, with dark clouds, formed the daily programme. With the exception that it was never cold, it was just such weather as a very bad English November or February.

THE RED BIRD OF PARADISE. (*Paradisea rubra.*)

FIGURE 14. "The Red Bird of Paradise *(Paradisea rubra)*," from Wallace's *Malay Archipelago*. (Author's collection.)

FIGURE 15. "Natives of Aru Shooting the Great Bird of Paradise," from Wallace's *Malay Archipelago*. Wallace employed locals wherever he could to assist in collections. (Author's collection.)

Brooke was periodically accused of brutality in some aspects of his government, but Wallace says that the rajah "possessed in a pre-eminent degree the art of making every one around him comfortable and happy."[34]

Wallace spent two Christmases with the rajah in Sarawak, and perhaps he had need of someone who could make him comfortable and happy given that much of his travel was by small boats along poorly charted coasts or treks into jungles that continued to be the home of headhunting tribes long after Wallace's departure.

Brooke invited Wallace to come to Sarawak immediately, and Wallace seemed glad of the invitation. He based himself out of the rajah's house and, in a style reminiscent of his Amazon days, he used rivers to move through the jungle, stopping to collect as he went. After four months in Sarawak, he decided to move at least temporarily east, to a large coal mine that was being developed deep in the jungle. He mentions that "during my whole twelve years' collecting in the western and eastern tropics, I never enjoyed such advantages in this respect as at the Simûnjon coal works. . . . The number of openings and sunny places and of pathways were also an attraction to wasps and butterflies; and by paying a cent each for all insects that were brought me, I obtained from the Dyaks and the Chinamen many fine locusts and Phasmidae, as well as numbers of handsome beetles."[35] In all, he collected (or had collected for him) two thousand species in Borneo alone.

The most exciting vertebrate that Wallace discovered in Borneo was the flying frog *(Racophorus nigropalmatus)*, whose unique expanse of webbing allows it to glide from tree to tree.[36] Wallace could not help noting: "And it is very interesting to Darwinians, as showing that the variability of the toes, which have been already modified for purposes of swimming and adhesive climbing, have been taken advantage of to enable an allied species to pass through the air like a flying lizard."[37] Of course, Wallace was writing this in hindsight, as he was still not at his breakthrough to natural selection when he encountered the flying frog, but the plethora of new adaptations and forms must have been weighing on him. Besides finding new or rare species, a major goal of Wallace's travels at this point was to find, study, and collect "Orang-utangs" or "mias" (genus *Pongo*). In this he was extremely successful, shooting four adult orangutans in a few weeks near the mines, and adopting the baby of one female that he had shot.

Wallace's description of his attempts to rear the baby orangutan is heartbreaking.[38] Baby orangutans hang on to their mothers' fur for much of the early part of their lives, and the orphan tried desperately to cling on to anything within grasp. Wallace attempted to construct an "artificial mother" out of a bundle of buffalo skin, but the baby almost choked to death on a ball of hair, so he was forced to remove the imitation. He lacked any source of milk, so he fed the animal on rice milk until it was old enough to take some solid food, and washed and combed it as best he could. The baby orangutan survived for three months before contracting some sort of fever, which killed it after a miserable week.

The experience of trying to raise the young animal did not affect Wallace's desire to procure more adult specimens. Over the next few weeks, he shot thirteen additional orangutans, some of which he was unable to collect, as they remained stuck in the trees. As with the bird collecting described in Wallace's book on the Rio Negro, there is something remarkably cold-blooded to a modern reader in the descriptions of shooting each individual orangutan, a feeling that can only be heightened by our knowledge of the extreme likelihood that these intelligent and fascinating apes may become extinct in the twenty-first century, victims of habitat loss and poaching. What makes this scene even harder to understand is the following pages, where Wallace goes into great detail about the habits of the orangutan—he had obviously spent a significant amount of time observing some before he shot them—but again, we can only place this in the context of nineteenth-century natural history, where a physical specimen took primacy over just about anything else.

Christmas 1854 was spent as the guest of Brooke in Sarawak, after which Wallace spent time at the mouth of the Sarawak River, organizing his specimens and working on a paper that he entitled "On the Law Which Has Regulated the Introduction of New Species."[39] This is his first technical statement of evolutionary ideas. Far off in England, Darwin read the paper with some alarm. It was obvious that Wallace was hot on the track of a mechanism for speciation. None is given in the paper, although Wallace draws on Darwin's account of the Galápagos in discussing islands and their flora and fauna as possible crucibles for new species. Immersed in a vast archipelago, Wallace had seen immediately what had taken Darwin years to tease out: geographic isolation can have profound effects on seemingly continuous populations.

From November 1855 to January 1856, Wallace traveled through the interior of Borneo in a series of canoes, navigating the network of rivers and making observations on the tribal villages that he encountered. Some of his canoes rivaled Humboldt's in terms of discomfort—he describes one that was "about thirty feet long, and only twenty-eight inches wide" that the Dyaks propelled by poles.[40] Many of the villagers had seen few or no Europeans before, and Wallace often found himself the center of attention. The Dyaks were generally very friendly, although the children were more reserved or frightened by the strange man among them. At one point Wallace performed shadow puppets, using his hands to make animal impressions in order to please his audience. He also had his first encounter with a ripe "durion" (durian—genus *Duno*) fruit, which he says caused him to "at once [become] a confirmed durion eater."[41] After some comments on the general natural history of the durian, Wallace cannot but break out into lyricism: "Then there is a rich glutinous smootheness in the pulp which nothing else possesses, but which adds to its delicacy. It is neither acid, nor sweet, nor juicy, yet one feels the want of none of these qualities, for it is perfect as it is. It produces no nausea or other bad effect, and the more you eat of it the less you feel inclined to stop. In fact, to eat durions, is a new sensation worth a voyage to the East to experience."[42] He does go on to warn the traveler that when ripe durian fruit falls from a tree, it can injure or even kill unwary passersby.

Wallace returned to Singapore for several months, shipping off specimens, working on notes, and practicing his languages, before setting off once again, this time to the island of Bali. This journey was of profound importance for the subsequent history of biogeography. Wallace spent time on both Bali and the nearby island of Lombok. Here he had two islands of similar size and topography, separated by a narrow but deep strait. To his excitement, the more he looked, the more he realized that the floras and faunas of the two islands were radically different. Species such as cockatoos that were common in islands east to Australia were present on Lombok, but not on Bali. From these observations he began to develop his idea of biological provinces. To this day we call the gap between Bali and Lombok a key part of Wallace's Line, which separates the Australian and Oriental biological regions.

The remainder of Wallace's time in the Malay Archipelago proceeded in a somewhat similar fashion—if explorations of such a diverse and complex area can ever be referred to as similar. Returning to Singapore only for mail and supplies, he traveled by schooner, dugout, canoe, or whichever craft would carry him within and between the islands of this bewildering Eden. Darwin wrote to him, asking about different species that he was observing on the islands. He collected butterflies and beetles, birds of paradise, ducks, vegetation—anything and everything that might be of interest back in England. All the time he pondered on what he was seeing: the patterns of similarity and variance across the islands of the archipelago.

At the beginning of 1858, Wallace arrived on Ternate, a large volcanic island well supplied with durians and mangoes, which had been visited by Sir Francis Drake during his circumnavigation in 1579. Wallace rented a house in the largest town and used it as a base for the next three years while he explored the sur-

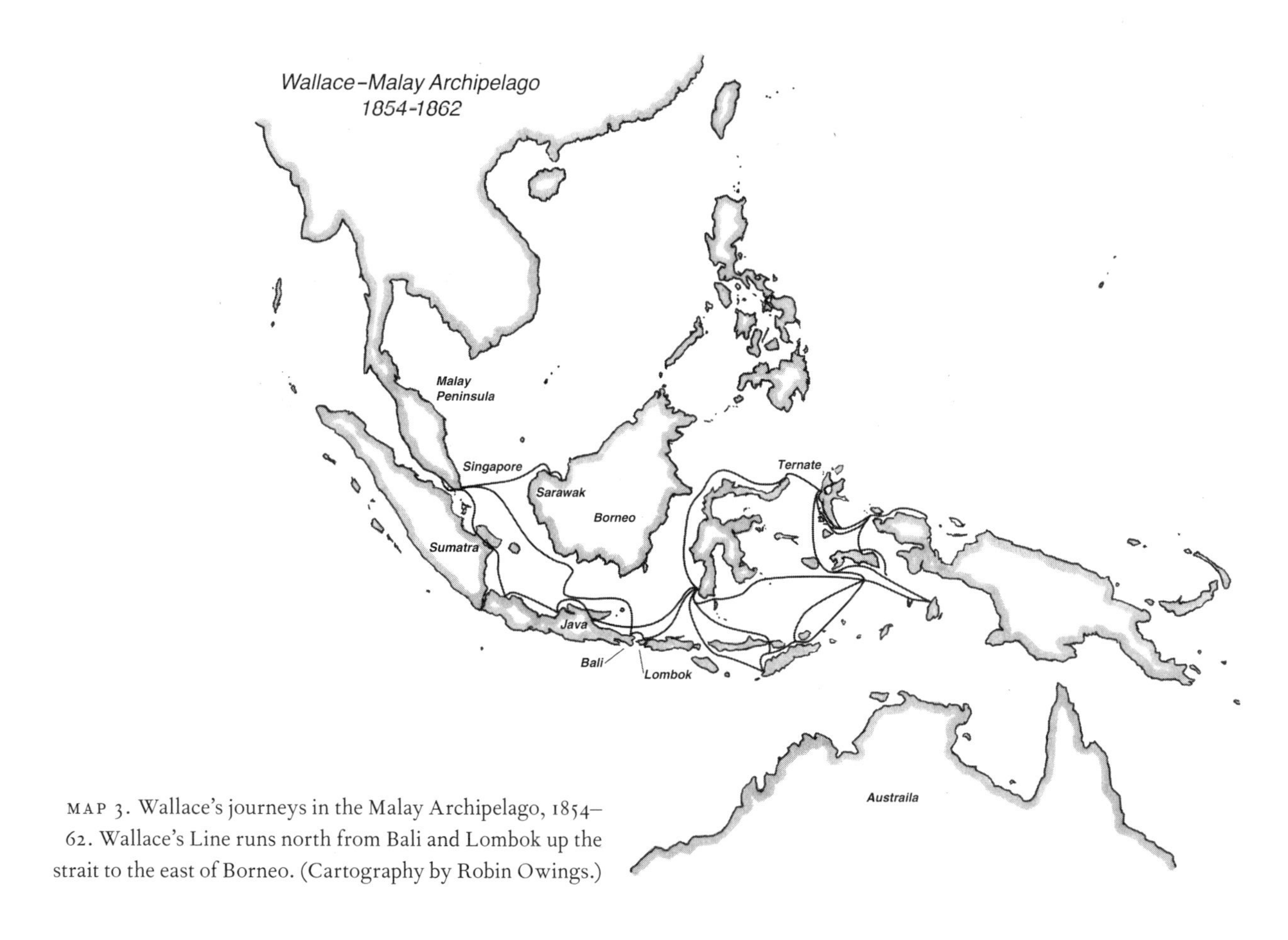

MAP 3. Wallace's journeys in the Malay Archipelago, 1854–62. Wallace's Line runs north from Bali and Lombok up the strait to the east of Borneo. (Cartography by Robin Owings.)

rounding islands. It was here on Ternate, recovering from a bout of fever, that his mind was drawn to Malthus's essay on the struggle for existence that the difference between food supply and reproductive capacity must engender. Darwin had seen the importance of this concept years earlier, but had drawn back, wanting to amass an overwhelming weight of evidence before speculating further. Wallace was a very different person. As soon as he recovered from his illness, he sat down to write a short, clean paper that he entitled "On the Tendency of Varieties to Depart Indefinitely from the Original Type."[43] The only person who could possibly really understand what he was getting at was Charles Darwin, so it was to Darwin that he sent it.

Darwin was clearly shocked and dismayed by the possibility of losing "priority" for a theory on which he had worked for years, but he was also unwilling to behave badly just for the sake of that priority. Hooker and Lyell wanted to look after their friend (remember, Darwin's son was dying at the time), but they were also far too serious scientists to have put up with any bad behavior. The result, the joint publication of Wallace's paper and the outline of Darwin's "sketch" accompanied by his letters to Asa Gray, accomplished two important ends. First, it forced Darwin to finally stop dithering and get his book out. Second, it put Wallace once and for all at the high table of natural history and evolution. He could return home at any time and be assured of an enthusiastic welcome.

Wallace traveled to New Guinea in search of birds of paradise; he examined small atolls and larger reefs. He moved on to Timor, once again noting the similarities and differences that its flora and fauna held compared to other islands along his line. Besides the importance of specimens for future theorizing, Wallace knew that his future financial independence depended in no small part on what he could get for his collections. His agent in London had done a wonderful job in placing specimens with wealthy bidders, but every sale helped when one had the rest of a lifetime to provide for. Finally, in March 1862, it was time to go home.

Wallace arrived in England in April 1862; he had been gone for eight years. In some senses, everything had changed; in others, things were depressingly the same. Money was still tight in spite of the successful sale of specimens: both his sister and his mother expected support, and he poured money into his brother-in-law's unsuccessful photography business. Recognition of his role in the development of natural selection brought him attention and membership in scientific societies, but recognition paid no bills, and in job hunting his social standing and lack of formal education worked against him. Darwin was very supportive, writing references and contacting other members of the scientific establishment with positive assessments of Wallace's work, but one also gets a sense of reticence on Darwin's part. Darwin had not been very impressed by Wallace's South American books (remember that Darwin's best friend, Joseph Hooker, who would inherit the direction of Kew Gardens, was the son of William Hooker, who had panned Wallace's palms book), and he very much wanted Wallace to write up his eastern travels in a more formal way.

Wallace was thirty-nine. The last year of travel had been much harder than it would have been a decade earlier, and he wanted to settle down while there was still time. Darwin invited him to Down, but initially he felt too ill to go.[44] When he finally did, Darwin's house must have seemed an ideal naturalist's retreat, but, lacking Darwin's fortune, it was a retreat beyond Wallace's grasp. The two evolutionary pioneers walked the Sandwalk, doubtlessly admired the plants in Darwin's garden, and discussed the latest revisions to the *Origin* and the state of the debate in both the scientific and the public arenas. Another appealing aspect of life at Down must have been the whole noisy, cheerful Darwin family. Wallace wanted to get married and start his own family; publication of a new book could come later.

At first things seemed to go well on the domestic front. His attention was drawn to a certain "Miss L———," who was the daughter of someone with whom he had started playing chess.[45] Initially the young lady rebuffed him, although in such a gentle fashion that he continued his courtship for another year, at which point she consented to get engaged. Everything seemed to be organized, the date had been set, the details worked out, when suddenly Miss L——— broke off the engagement and refused to see Wallace again. Wallace was deeply hurt and went into a distinct depression for some months before pulling himself together and getting back to writing. Two years later he married Annie Mitten, the daughter of a botanist friend. The couple had three children, but, as happened to Darwin, a favorite child died young, and this doubtlessly affected some of Wallace's later fascination with spiritualism.

Wallace's account of his eastern travels, *The Malay Archipelago*, finally came out in 1869, much to Darwin's relief. The book is much better than *Travels on the Rio Negro* and makes clear references to examples of natural selection at a number of points. There were plenty of signs of storms to come however. Wallace was extremely concerned about the condition of the poor and working classes—a group to which he had very nearly belonged. He lacked both Humboldt's tact and Humboldt's position, but both men had been struck by some of the contrasts in outlook and prospect of the tribes they had encountered overseas and the people whom they saw in the streets on their return home. At the end of *Malay*

Archipelago, Wallace makes clear where his mind is going: "If we continue to devote our chief energies to the utilizing of our knowledge of the laws of nature with the view of still further extending our commerce and our wealth, the evils which necessarily accompany these when too eagerly pursued, may increase to such gigantic dimensions as to be beyond our power to alleviate."[46]

Wallace was deviating from Darwin on two fronts. First, he was moving explicitly into the political realm, and second, his whole concept of which forces could have produced humans had moved in a new direction. In some respects, Wallace was a more extreme Darwinian than Darwin. He wanted everything to have a functional cause, and if there was no clear link between selection for or against a perceived trait, something else must be responsible. Darwin's encounter with the Fuegians had been interesting to him, but in the long run it did not shake his faith in selection. Humans came in varieties, and they could share many features, but there would also be inherent differences. Wallace, on the other hand, had seen the tribes of the Americas and Malaysia very differently. They possessed brains at least as large as his, they survived and reproduced, yet their notion of civilization was on such a reduced scale that surely they had no need for such brains. Beyond this, Wallace wondered at the selective value of artistic sensibility, mathematical ability, and music. He had held a baby orangutan in his arms; how, he must have wondered, could we have gone beyond the level of the orangutan by blind selection alone? Darwin was horrified, writing: "I hope you have not murdered too completely your own and my child. I have lately, i.e. in the new edition of the 'Origin' been moderating my zeal, and attributing much more to useless variability."[47]

Darwin is absolutely right here Many traits are what we have come to call "exaptations": they persist not because they have been selected for, but rather because they have not been selected against. Under changing conditions, what was selectively neutral can become an advantage or a disadvantage, but everything does not require a continuous "Just So" story to be explained.

Wallace might not have been a murderer, but he was out of the box and gone when it came to humans. He had been interested in psychic phenomena from his earliest years, and he became increasingly caught up in the notion of some higher power that must have governed the development of mind. In an even more radical turn to the unorthodox, Wallace became involved in the Victorian passion for communicating with spirits, with all its paraphernalia of table knocking, automatic writing, strange lights, and ectoplasms. He invited Darwin and Huxley to séances (both declined); he took charlatans at face value and, in the opinion of many members of the scientific community, ran the risk of bringing discredit on everyone.

Beyond this, Wallace wrote extensively in the next few years on land reform, on socialism, and against vaccination (he was the first person to do a serious statistical analysis of the outcome of government vaccination programs. He was right to be critical of the government numbers, but wrong in his basic assumptions). Wallace's arguments are interesting and his motives are admirable, but one can also see why his scientific colleagues (not to mention his critics) might start looking askance at his positions.

Fortunately for natural history, he still had two major publications up his sleeve. The first of these was *The Geographical Distribution of Animals*, which is in some ways his real masterpiece.[48] At a scale worthy of Humboldt, Wallace says in the preface: "My Object has been to show the important bearing of researches into the natural history of every part of the world, upon the study of its past history. An accurate knowledge of any groups of birds or of insects and their geographical distribution, may enable us to map out the islands and continents of a former epoch."[49]

He then goes on to do just that. He focuses exclusively on what he calls the "Land Animals," as he lacks data on marine organisms. He gets a lot wrong: he had no knowledge of continental drift, although he incorporates a remarkably dynamic earth into his model, with land masses rising and falling and being connected and broken apart over the course of evolutionary time. In spite of his errors, there is an awful lot here for any reader, and ideas for a hundred doctoral dissertations. He incorporates Ice Ages and the likely influence of changes in vegetation patterns on animal distribution and abundance. He discusses the effects of introduced species on isolated native flora and fauna. In all, much of what he says is remarkably modern. This is no longer straight descriptive natural history; this is its application in a grand synthesis of ideas, with the potential for great explanatory power.

Humboldt does not get much mention, probably because Wallace felt that Humboldt had focused mostly on vegetation, and this was intended to be an animal book. It is odd, however, that Wallace either does not see or does not choose to incorporate more of Humboldt's examples of the role of climate and elevation on species distribution to back up his own discussion of animal communities. Wallace mentions Humboldt several times in his autobiography, but mainly in relation to the *Personal Narrative*. He quotes an early letter to Bates in which he says that he hopes to read *Cosmos* at some time, but it is unclear if he ever did.[50] Humboldt had died before Wallace returned from the Far East, and it would seem that his star was eclipsed in the debates over Darwinism. What use Wallace makes of him is primarily in relation to geology, the effects of volcanoes on their surroundings, and Humboldt's estimates of the range of global elevations.

The most significant and lasting element of *The Geographical Distribution* is probably Wallace's "Zoological Regions"—a concept that had crystallized for him in the distinctions in the flora and fauna of Bali and Lombok. It was his particular genius to take this relatively "local" idea and expand it to a truly global scale. The seven regions—Australian, Oriental, Asian, Nearctic, Neotropical, Ethiopian, and Palearctic—are broadly defined by the species that are common within each but are absent from others. Each region is then divided into subregions based on further degrees of endemism. Wallace admits that the generality of the model makes it somewhat crude, but he also feels that there is enough here to be worth further thought.

One odd feature of the book, given Wallace's time in Malaysia, is that in spite of the massive nature of *The Geographical Distribution*, very little space is devoted to islands. Wallace rectified this omission in 1880 with *Island Life*, which is in some ways the "third part" of the two-volume *Geographical Distribution*.[51] As in the earlier book, Wallace envisions a dynamic world in which continents "undulate" over time, rising up above sea level in some parts, and sinking below in others. The combination of elevation and flooding was thought to explain both the geology of particular regions and some of the discontinuities in flora and fauna. By 1880, Wallace was able to draw on some of the information from the voyage of HMS *Challenger*, which had circled the world from 1872 to 1876, conducting the first comprehensive oceanographic survey. Wallace cites many of the results from *Challenger* to refute former ideas of continental stasis. Many of the climatic ideas that Wallace alludes to would have further impact in a modified form in the early twentieth century as ecology began to replace natural history.

Wallace published many more books, including several on evolutionary theory. He depended for a significant portion of his income on his writing, in spite of the government pension that Darwin helped to secure for him. He visited the United States on an extended lecture tour that took him across the continent to California, where he met John Muir and saw giant sequoia. One of his last books relating to natural history was a scathing attack on the astronomer Percival Lowell's assertion that he had seen structures on Mars and that these were evidence of the presence of intelligent beings.[52] Lowell had frightened and intrigued the world with his claims that there was a vast network of canals on Mars that had supplied water to an ancient Martian civilization. Humboldt doubtless would have been pleased to find his estimates of temperature in relation to altitude used to demolish a foolish hypothesis. Wallace died in 1913, widely hailed as the last of the Great Victorians. He had outlived them all—Humboldt, Darwin, Bates, even Joseph Hooker, to whom he had dedicated *Island Life*.

The rescue of Darwin by the Modern Synthesis of R. A. Fisher, Sewall Wright, and J. B. S. Haldane that united Darwinian evolution with Mendelian genetics seems to have left Wallace behind.[53] Let us hope that this error is now being rectified. In conclusion, I think it is only fair to let Wallace end the chapter in his own words:

> Can we believe that we are fulfilling the purpose of our existence while so many of the wonders and beauties of the creation remain unnoticed around us? While so much of the mystery which man has been able to penetrate, however imperfectly, is still all dark to us. . . . It is true that man is still, as he always has been, subject to error; his judgments are often incorrect, his beliefs false, his opinions changeable from age to age. But experience of error is the best guide to truth, often dearly bought, and, therefore, the more to be relied on . . . what is it but the accumulated experience of past ages that serves us as a beacon light to warn us from error, to guide us in the way of truth? But . . . truths once acquired are treasured up . . . for posterity, and each succeeding generation adds something to the stock of acquired knowledge, so that our acquaintance with the works of nature is ever increasing.[54]

TWELVE . Spoils of Other Empires

From the fifteenth through the first third of the twentieth centuries, the nations of Europe moved outward, conquering much of the rest of the world, destroying or subduing local human populations, and in some cases transforming large areas of other continents to resemble the European homeland. At its peak at the beginning of the twentieth century, the British Empire ruled over a quarter of the land surface of the earth and also over more than 425 million people, out of a global population of fewer than two billion.[1] Other European countries never quite achieved this scale, but not for want of trying.

In a world in which envoys could take months to travel out from a capital, see what there was to see, and return home for consultation, a great deal of discretion inevitably had to be left to the people on the spot. In addition, particularly in the case of the British Empire, private enterprise often led the way, with government coming along later. Much of what was to become first the Indian Empire, and later modern India, Bangladesh, and Pakistan, was originally put together by the East India Company and taken over by the Crown only after the Mutiny. Likewise, the borders and much of the development of modern Canada were in large part the results of the private Hudson's Bay Company, rather than an act of deliberate planning on the part of London. Where this all becomes important in terms of a history of natural history is that the blending of commercial and political interests, coupled with the high degree of autonomy granted to people willing to live on the frontiers, created both the space and the need for detailed information about the plants, animals, climate, and geology of areas acquired in an often haphazard way by rival imperial powers. One may abhor the politics, cultural impact, and loss of lives, but the gain to science was enormous.

As a note before we continue, it is worth considering what we mean by "discovering" a place or naming a plant, animal, or place. With the exception of Antarctica, humans had been discovering, naming, and living in most of the world for tens of thousands of years before the age of empires. When we say "discovered," we mean discovered to our own meanings and culture and time. It has become popular in recent years to emphasize the negative side of empire and exploration—thus Columbus has been transformed in my lifetime from hero to villain. Truth is seldom that simple; we are all heroes in our own stories but often knaves in someone else's. Again, I think it is possible to regret the negatives while at the same time acknowledging that these explorers were very brave people in very particular situations that often brought out both the best and the worst in human nature.

At the beginning of the Imperial Age, many voyages of exploration and discovery were fairly explicitly about loot when everything went well, and survival when it didn't. The first European crossing of North America was accomplished by Álvar Núñez, also known as Cabeza de Vaca.[2] De Vaca (approx. 1490–1557) was shipwrecked on the west coast of Florida in 1528. The survivors of the wreck had little if any idea of their location or the distances involved in reaching Mexico, their goal. They proceeded on foot and eventually by raft to modern-day Galveston, where they subsisted with the local Indians for some time. Eventually de Vaca and the three other remaining members of the expedition set off to the northwest, looking for signs of Spanish settlement and the possibility of a ship to take them back to Spain. They wandered through much of western Texas and northern Mexico until they reached the Sea of Cortez and eventually found their way to Mexico City, returning home in 1537.

The account of de Vaca's journey, which was published in 1542 as *La Relación*, gives a variety of details about the lands and peoples that de Vaca had encountered or imagined. Some of this material qualifies as natural history, but besides lacking any specific training, not to mention any supplies for making notes in the field, de Vaca was too busy trying to survive to really do more than provide intriguing hints and anecdotes that drew future explorers north along his trail in search of gold and trade opportunities.

A specific eighteenth-century example of the mixture of natural history and commercial interests was the activities of the naturalists employed by the

Hudson's Bay Company. The Governor and Company of Adventurers Trading into Hudson's Bay, as the organization was first named, was founded in 1670 with a royal charter from Charles II. Europe was then in the grip of the Little Ice Age and the demand for fur had never been higher.[3] The charter gave the governor and his fellow adventurers an exclusive monopoly over the fur trade throughout the entire watershed of Hudson's Bay. For all practical purposes, this made the company potential rulers of a vast area of nearly five million square kilometers, or more than a tenth of the total surface area of North America.

The selection of Hudson's Bay as the center of trade was no accident. French Canadians had moved west from the Maritimes and into the drainages of the Mississippi and Missouri rivers in search of beaver, lynx, and mink. The entire economy of French North America depended on the fur trade, and France was willing to fight to maintain a stranglehold on any fur exports. The Hudson's Bay Company constituted an end run around French control of the Gulf of St. Lawrence, which had been the traditional route into and out of the northern heartland.[4] Initial exploratory ventures by the Hudson's Bay Company, or HBC, as it is often referred to, showed that the lands around the bay were capable of producing furs of a better quality and at higher volumes than were produced in traditional French areas. Tension over who would control the fur trade led to a series of attacks and counterattacks by English and French forces.

Fortunately for the HBC, and perhaps also for natural history, John Churchill, the duke of Marlborough, was both one of the heroes of the wars with France and a former governor of the HBC. When the next round of hostilities was ended by a peace treaty in 1713, he played a significant role in ensuring that the whole of Rupert's Land—as the Hudson Bay watershed was known—was granted to Britain, and the HBC was allowed to take over any French trading posts in the region. The HBC steadily expanded its web of factories and trapping posts across the Arctic, in a vast network ruled from its headquarters in London. The final defeat of France in the Seven Years' War gave the company effective control extending into the Mississippi drainage and west as far as the Canadian Rockies.

Trappers and traders were encouraged to maintain careful records of what they caught and also additional information about the plants and animals around their trapping runs. These HBC "factors" were responsible for major trading posts, and were also instructed to collect weather information, including daily temperatures and phenological data, and to obtain specimens of rare or new species of animals that they encountered.

The result of this emphasis on data collection was the development of a remarkably comprehensive sampling system for much of the high Arctic. Specimens from the HBC factors went to Linnaeus and to the Royal Society. A disproportionately large number of birds endemic to polar latitudes was first collected and identified by HBC naturalists, who were recognized throughout the eighteenth and nineteenth centuries as important sources of information on the region. Thomas Pennant, Gilbert White's correspondent, based portions of his book on the Arctic on results sent home by the HBC.[5] The weather data collected at the trading posts provides one of the best really longterm runs of temperature information and is invaluable to studies of climate change. Finally, it was HBC trapping data that allowed Charles Elton, one of the most significant population ecologists of the twentieth century, to quantify and map the cyclic oscillations of snowshoe hare and lynx populations.[6]

While the men of the Hudson's Bay Company patiently collected their counts of skins, recorded temperatures, and sent rare birds back to London, the British colonies in North America turned from the mother country and declared independence. The young United States found itself surrounded by powerful neighbors caught up in a struggle for global dominance and eager to draw the new nation into the fray.

The original thirteen colonies hugged the eastern coast of North America, and it took several generations before serious efforts were made to examine what the interior of the continent might hold. Part of the reason for this was the harshness of the environment, particularly in the Northeast, and the presence of less than friendly Indians across the frontier.[7] Even after the loss of Québec, French North America laid claim to enormous areas of the continent, including the Mississippi watershed, but it lacked the European population to hold on to its claims.[8] By 1803, Napoleon had realized that the only real question was whether Louisiana would become British or American. The British government, its traders focusing on the richer fur areas of the north, was slow to investigate the center of the continent.

The United States had been negotiating to acquire the port of New Orleans for some time, and in 1803 Napoleon decided to sell the whole of Louisiana to the United States for what he could get rather than see it simply taken by the British later. To Jefferson's surprise, Napoleon offered him the entire territory, much of it unmapped, most of it unsettled by the French, for fifteen million dollars. Jefferson accepted, instantly doubling the size of the country.

Having bought Louisiana, Jefferson was eager to initiate an official government-sponsored transcontinental expedition to examine what he had bought. In many respects, Lewis and Clark's expedition was organized around a mistaken notion of the structure of the North American continent.[9] Early cartographers seem to have been obsessed with ideas of symmetry—somewhere in the center of the continent lay a ridge of mountains from which all rivers would flow either east or west. Some took this idea even further and suggested a pyramidal scheme in which there would be a centralized Continental Divide from which rivers would flow into the four oceans surrounding North America. Discovery of this central node would allow a traveler to pass across the continent either east-west or north-south almost entirely by water, with only limited portaging in the vicinity of the central node itself.

Eighteenth-century maps depicted the then hypothetical sources of the Missouri rising in a thin chain of mountains and flowing southeast until the river eventually joined the Mississippi. To the west of the mountains, a large river, beginning immediately on the other side of the Divide, flowed westward into the Pacific. To those sitting comfortably in Washington, it must have seemed that sending a party up the Missouri, across the thin band of mountains, and then down the western river to the sea would be a relatively simple matter. Once this was accomplished, an effective crosscontinental water network, with all the advantages to trade and commerce, would be established.

Jefferson's interest in natural history was a significant element in the formation and makeup of the Corps of Discovery, as the Lewis and Clark Expedition was formally known.[10] Jefferson was perhaps the most literate president whom we have yet seen.[11] Earlier in his career, he had published *Notes on the State of Virginia,* which included details of the plants and animals of the mid-Atlantic coastline, mostly extracted from other authors, and a savage response to Buffon, who had had the temerity to state that North American animals were inferior to their European counterparts.[12] Jefferson's tone gives us a clue as to his general attitude toward the importance of data: "It does not appear that Messrs. De Buffon and D'Aubenton have measured, weighed or seen those [animals] of America. It is said of some of them, by some travelers, that they are smaller than the European. But who were those travelers? . . . Was natural history the object of their travels? Did they measure or weigh the animals they speak of? Or did they not judge of them by sight, or perhaps even from report only?"[13] Nonetheless, he acknowledges that Buffon subsequently withdrew some of his statements.

Besides the comments in the *Notes,* Jefferson also sent Buffon an elk and bones of the mastodon. His enthusiasm for paleontology was such that he spread the bones of an extinct mammoth on the floor of the White House while piecing them together.[14] Jefferson was elected president of the American Philosophical Society in 1797 and was a regular correspondent of major European natural historians, including Humboldt, who, as we have already seen, visited him in the White House shortly after Lewis and Clark set out.[15]

In preparing to send out the Corps of Discovery, Jefferson found himself caught between two opposing sets of concerns. Were he to inform the French, Spanish, and British that he was dispatching an exploring team to examine the commercial prospects of the as yet unmapped central portions of the continent, he might attract their interest and queer the deal that he had just concluded with France. However, if he were to announce that the purpose of the expedition was strictly "literary" or scientific, Congress might well say that he had no business using government funds and government troops for a purely intellectual pursuit. Jefferson got around the problem by assuring everyone of what they wanted to hear: Congress was told in secrecy that there would be economic and military advantages to exploring the Northwest, and foreign embassies were asked to provide passports for members of a scientific team. As a result of this diplomacy, or duplicity, Jefferson secured funding for a team of twenty-eight men and one woman (the Indian guide Sacajawea), led by his own private secretary Meriwether Lewis (1774–1809) and William Clark (1770–1838).

Jefferson's desire for the Missouri expedition to incorporate as broad a scientific purpose as possible is clear in his letters. Writing to his regular correspondent Robert Patterson in March 1803, he discusses Lewis:

> If we could have got a person perfectly skilled in botany, natural history, mineralogy, astronomy, with at the same time the necessary firmness of body & mind, habits of living in the woods & familiarity with the Indian character, it would have been better. But I know of no such character who would undertake an enterprise so perilous. . . . Capt. Lewis joins a great stock of accurate observation on the subjects of the three kingdoms which are found in our own country but not according to their scientific nomenclatures. But he will be able to seize for examination & description such things only as he shall meet with new.[16]

It is apparent that the president was somewhat concerned about Lewis's (and presumably Clark's) lack of training in science, and he was anything but hands-off in planning the expedition. The degree of detail in his instructions is remarkable, and one has some sense that he wished that he could have gone himself. Instead, he tried to make sure that he told Lewis precisely what needed doing, with a list of requests that covered as many possibilities as he could think of. He also made it quite clear that some aspects of the mission were confidential, in terms of both Congress and foreign powers: "& such assurances given them as to [the expedition's] objects, as we trust will satisfy them." In terms of natural history, he spells out a list of his hopes:

> Other objects worthy of note will be the soil & face of the country, it's growth & vegetable productions, especially those not of the US. The animals of the country generally & especially those not known in the US. The remains & accounts of any which may be deemed rare or extinct . . . climate, as characterized by the thermometer, by the proportion of rainy, cloudy, & clear days, by lightening, hail, snow, ice, by the access & recess of frost, by the winds prevailing at different seasons, the dates at which particular plants put forth or lose their flower, or leaf, times of appearance of particular birds, reptiles, or insects.[17]

The last part of this excerpt could have come straight out of Gilbert White, and in fact it quite possibly did. We know that Jefferson had a copy of *The Natural History and Antiquities of Selborne*, and his logical mind would have been drawn to the orderly phenologies that White had laid out in his notebooks.[18] All this, and let's not forget backups: "Two copies of your notes at least & as many more as leisure will admit, should be made & confided to the care of the most trusty individuals of your attendants."[19]

One has to admire the "as leisure will admit" and wonder how often Lewis, shivering under two blankets in the heart of the Rockies, wet through from an unforeseen rapid or painfully plucking out cactus spines after a hard portage, thought of where he wanted to tell the president to put those extra two copies. At the same time, we should remember that Henslow made a very similar request to Darwin. Transmission of information was difficult, letters and packages could go astray, and, once lost, notes were irretrievably gone—witness Wallace's loss of most of his South American journals through a chance fire.

The mission of the Corps of Discovery was to move up the Missouri River to its headwaters, cross the Rockies, and then proceed westward in search of a route to the Pacific coast. Jefferson assumed that they would be able to make use of the Missouri for most of the first half of their outward journey, and the unknown Great Western River for the second half. This emphasis on river transport played into the notion of the "economic" role of the Corps' mission and also was intended to minimize the amount of time spent actually marching through strange country.

The Corps departed from an encampment near present-day Hartford, Illinois, in May 1804. They initially traveled the Missouri River in a fifty-five-foot-long "bateau."[20] Like Humboldt in Venezuela, the Corps was equipped with the latest in scientific instruments, including a variety of devices for accurately surveying their route of travel. Following Jefferson's instructions, Lewis and Clark kept detailed journals of their travels, recording their progress, their encounters with Indians, the general shape of the landscape, and descriptions of plants and animals that they encountered along the way.[21] Lewis had taken a crash course in natural history prior to departure, and Jefferson was to say of Lewis after his death that he was "guarded by exact observation of the vegetables and animals of his own country against losing time in the description of objects already possessed."[22]

Among other things, Jefferson was anxious to know if any of the llamas reported from South America were to be found in the western mountains, and he was also probably interested in any new large mammals that could further his disproof of Buffon's claims that American fauna was inferior to that elsewhere. His instruction to Lewis to watch for remains and accounts of any rare or extinct animals reflected his abiding interest in paleontology. Writing to the French natural historian Bernard Lacépède, he says that he has great hopes that the expedition will "give us a general view of the continent's population, natural history, productions, soil, and climate. It is not improbable that this voyage of discovery will procure us further information of the Mammoth & of the Megatherium also."[23]

This last sentence is a forlorn echo of the hopeful "here be dragons" that illustrated so many medieval charts. Enough remains of the Pleistocene megafauna had already been recovered that there was still hope that mastodons, mammoths, and giant sloths might remain in the uncharted western part of the continent. No llamas or mammoths were found during the course of the journey, but the members of the expedition were intrigued by many of the animals that they did see: "Capt. Clark joined us had killed a curious annamil resembling a Goat. Willard brought it on board. . . . Such an anamil was never yet known in U.S. States. The Capt had the Skins of the hair & Goat Stuffed in order to Send back to the city of Washington. The bones and all."[24]

Clark's "annamil" was a pronghorned antelope, one of a variety of new species that the expedition would be able to report on once they returned. During the outward journey, the Corps attempted to maintain at least some connection with home. At one point a small party of men was sent back downriver, taking with them the requested copies of journals and over a hundred specimens of plants and animals for Jefferson's examination.

As the group moved farther upriver, they switched their means of transport to canoes, and eventually they were reduced to walking. There would be no easily navigated river route to the Pacific after all. Lewis made a point of befriending many of the groups of Indians whom they encountered, and, mindful of Jefferson's instructions to get as much detail as possible about local inhabitants, recorded in some detail what he saw of differences and similarities in their manners and customs. He was not always particularly complimentary. Describing one group and their elaborate ornaments, seen once the party had reached the mouth of the Columbia, he says: "Yet all these decorations are unavailing to conceal the deformities of nature and the extravagance of fashion; nor have we seen any more disgusting object than a Chinook or Clatsop beauty in full attire."[25]

He goes on to discuss at some length the prevalence and treatment of venereal disease in different groups and to wax thoroughly disapproving of both what he regards as the Indians' promiscuity and that of his own men who are willing to engage in sexual relations with Indian women. Again, this seems in keeping with Jefferson's detailed list of things he is interested in, which included "the extent and limit of their possessions; their relations with other tribes of nations; their language, traditions, monuments; their ordinary occupations in agriculture, fishing, hunting, war, arts & the implements of these; their food, clothing, & domestic accommodations; the diseases prevalent among them, & the remedies they use; moral & physical circumstances which distinguish them from the tribes we know."[26] The list goes on and on, and again one can imagine poor Lewis grimly ticking off each bullet point while trying to keep his small band fed, housed, and on track.

In contrast to their attitudes toward people, Lewis and Clark are much kinder in their descriptions of some of the animals that they saw; sea otters, for instance, get special praise: "This animal is unrivalled for the beauty, richness, and softness of his fur; the inner part of the fur, when opened, is lighter than the surface in its natural position: there are some black and shining hairs intermixed with the fur, which are rather longer, and add much to its beauty."[27]

One has to also remember that one of the goals of the expedition was to determine the economic potential of the region. Otter skins were already fetching a high price from trade along the Pacific, and Lewis and Clark were following a congressional mandate to look for new sources of income as well as new trading routes. Over the course of the ensuing century, hunters would come close to exterminating the sea otter, just as they had already wiped out Steller's sea cow.

Overall, the journals of the expedition are much drier and more quantitative than those of either Humboldt or Darwin. One gets the sense that Lewis and Clark were very conscious of their duty both as army officers leading a small body of men into unknown and potentially hazardous country, and also as direct envoys of the president, who had made it abundantly clear what he wanted to see in their report once they returned. Humboldt reports his measurements of altitudes, temperatures, and the relative sizes of plants and animals throughout the *Personal Narrative* (Darwin, by contrast, never seems quite comfortable with quantification), but Humboldt is also free to wax lyrical about what he sees or to go off on tangents about philosophy, politics, or whatever else takes his fancy. Lewis and Clark had a job to do.

Humboldt, Darwin, and even Wallace were coming out of a privileged background within which they were traveling by choice and not from duty. In addition, the European natural historians (unlike the colonial administrators or colonists who were another element of European expansion) were not planning on remaining in any of the countries they visited. They were guests passing through. By contrast, Lewis and Clark and the Corps were soldiers, quite literally the thin end of the spearpoint of American imperial destiny, moving into lands that soon would be incorporated into the United States. Within fifty years of Lewis and Clark's passage through the High Plains, many of the Indian groups whom they met would be devastated by cholera and smallpox brought in by European settlers.

The mood of the small party was probably profoundly affected by their sense of isolation. Darwin and Wallace regularly put in at ports and towns built by fellow Europeans. Even during his longest stint overseas, Wallace could take Christmas with the white rajah in Sarawak. Lewis and Clark and their companions must have felt extremely alone, off in a new part of the world, surrounded by peoples who were alien and potentially hostile to everything that they were familiar with. There were no pleasant towns, no familiar foods or letters from home awaiting them around the next bend or over the next ridge. It was possible that they might encounter Europeans once they reached the Pacific coast, but they realized soon enough on their journey that distances were deceptive: there was a long way to go to reach the coast, and the coast itself was probably much longer and more desolate than they had imagined.

As they moved into the headwaters of the Missouri in their first year away, the traveling season was coming to an end. The Corps passed into the High Plains, spending their first winter with the Mandans near modern-day Washburn, North Dakota. By April 1805, they were ready to continue up the remaining Missouri waterway. They portaged their canoes around the worst rapids, paddled until they ran out of river, and then went into and through the Rocky Mountains and the Bitterroot Range on horseback and on foot. Instead of a relatively narrow chain of mountains that could be crossed easily, the expedition found themselves in a confusing maze of ranges, none of which seemed to be *the* single Continental Divide that they had been expecting. This portion of the journey was extremely difficult, requiring the traverse of rugged country of great beauty to today's traveler, who arrives with a good map and the near certainty of rescue if things get too tough. In the early nineteenth century, with no clear pathway to follow other than the river and only limited information from local Indians, it was a damp, cold slog to the Corps. They recorded in their journal: "Proceded thro' thickets in which we were obliged to Cut a road, over rockey hill Sides where our horses were in pitial danger of Slipping to Ther certain distruction & up & Down Steep hills, where Several horses fell. . . . we call this place dismal Swamp. . . . this is a verry lonesome place. Horrid bad going."[28]

Sometimes together, sometimes dividing the party in order to better map tributaries of the river, Lewis and Clark kept moving west and moving up through range upon range. Their logic was impeccable: follow the branching river to its source, and from that source there must be only a short portage over the Continental Divide to the sources of the Great Western River system that would lead them to the sea. Their biggest advantage proved to be good relations with the Indians, relations that were facilitated in large part by Sacajawea and her French-Canadian husband, who could help with translations as well as guiding the group through areas with which the pair were already familiar.

Finally, after descending a long ridge toward the Lemhi River, Lewis encountered a group of Indians who were interested in trading supplies. To his great delight, one of the foodstuffs offered in trade proved to be salmon, and from his knowledge of that fish's anadromous life history, Lewis knew that he must at last be at the edge of the western watershed. The Lemhi does indeed feed into the Salmon, and the Salmon into the Snake, and the Snake into the Columbia, the Great Western River that would take the Corps to the sea. There was no possibility of a return by sea, as the coast was bare of trading ships, so the Corps built a fort on the south side of the Columbia and prepared to winter over.

The winter of 1805–06 was cold, wet, and dispiriting. Many of the men fell sick, and game was scarcer than they had expected. Nonetheless, Lewis's journal entry for March 20, 1806, reads: "Altho' we have not fared sumptuously this winter and spring at Fort Clatsop, we have lived quite as comfortably as we had any reason to expect we should; and have accomplished every object which induced our remaining at this place."[29] There is an addendum by another member of the party: "I made a calculation of the number of elk and deer killed by the party from the 1st of Dec 1805 to the 20th March 1806, which gave 131 elk, and 20 deer."[30] More than an animal a day seems pretty good hunting, but for a large group that was not only subsisting in place, but also trying to store up rations for a long march home, every elk mattered.

The return journey began in pouring rain on March 23, 1806. The party canoed up the Columbia, stopping periodically to hunt and trade with Indian encampments as they went. One intriguing note is that several members of the Corps seem to have been convinced that the Indians between the mountains and the sea must be the legendary "Welsh Indians"—descendants of the Welsh prince Madoc ab Owain Gwynedd, who according to legend had fled to America in the twelfth century. The English claim to America in the sixteenth century was based on this notion: if the Welsh, subjects of the English crown, had "discovered" America first, the Spanish rights obtained by Columbus's voyage would be annulled. It is interesting to find this story still active hundreds of years later.

The party briefly split up after crossing the Divide in early July, as Lewis was anxious to explore as much as possible on the return journey. This separation was unfortunate in that Lewis and his party were small enough to be a tempting target for thieves, and in one attempted raid two Indians were killed—the only known Indian casualties of the whole journey. Once Lewis reached the junction of the Yellowstone and the Missouri, he rejoined the main party, and together they canoed down the Missouri without further incident, arriving in St. Louis in late September 1806.

Lewis's reward for his part in leading the expedition was to be made governor of the new territory. He seems to have been less successful as a static politician than he had been as a leader in the field. In 1809, he was still working on writing up the results of the expedition when he was found dying of gunshot wounds while on his way to Washington. It is still debated whether his death was murder or suicide. Clark lived for more than thirty years after the return of the Corps of Discovery. He served in the War of 1812, was married twice, had eight children, and was both governor of the Missouri Territory and the first superintendent of Indian affairs, a position he held until his death in St. Louis in 1838.

The Corps of Discovery contributed significant cartographic information about the nature of the vast drainages of the Missouri and Columbia rivers, as well as sending back to Washington specimens of over 100 plants and 250 animals, many of them new to eastern naturalists.[31] While this total seems small in contrast to the thousands preserved by Bates and Wallace in the tropics, it must be put into both taxonomic and regional perspective. Wallace and Bates were collecting across a much broader scale of organisms, and the regions in which they were collecting were and are major biological hot spots, with a vast number of unknown species even in the present day. They were also making multiple out-and-back forays from a centralized base that allowed them to ship successive loads of samples home. Beyond this—and it is hard to know just how to phrase this tactfully—Wallace and Bates and many of their intellectual kin were somewhat fanatical about finding and collecting interesting rarities. Lewis and Clark were operating in a much less biologically diverse environment, were limiting their collections to vascular plants and vertebrates, and, once they headed into the Rockies, had to carry everything that they wanted to keep as part of the expedition's baggage. Neither Lewis nor Clark were trained naturalists, and they lacked some of the singlemindedness necessary for the really passionate collector. Yet overall, the Corps of Discovery succeeded remarkably well, both in terms of new organisms discovered and in setting a tone for subsequent expeditions. They established a precedent for federal support of expeditions into the West that would be followed up by subsequent generations of explorers.

After the return of Lewis and Clark, there was something of a hiatus in terms of government sponsorship of exploration while Lewis struggled to write up the results of the expedition. Concern about the trans-Mississippi West did not abate, however, and the federal government saw a growing need to obtain further information about the landscape and its resources, as well as the population, cultures, and sympathies of the Indian nations.[32]

On the nongovernmental side of natural history, Charles Peale is worthy of mention. He was born in Maryland in 1741 in an impoverished genteel setting, which required him to apprentice himself to a saddlemaker.[33] Peale did well in the business and was eventually able to open his own shop, which gave him sufficient time and funds to pursue his passion for portrait painting. Support from friends allowed him to visit Britain and study with leading painters in the capital before returning to America. Upon his return, he became embroiled in revolutionary politics, which cost him his business but gained him notice from Jefferson and Washington. After the end of the war, he founded the first public museum of science in the new United States. This museum was an interesting mixture of natural history, art, and, for want of a better word, "curiosities." Peale lacked formal training in science, but he believed passionately in public education, and his museum contained a large collection of stuffed birds and mammals organized in a Linnaean format, as well as the bones of the first mastodon skeleton to be unearthed in America. Peale's Museum foreshadowed the Smithsonian, and his son Titian—also a painter—accompanied some of the next generation of explorers of western North America, recording the new landscapes they passed through.

One of the most colorful explorer-naturalists of the nineteenth century American West was John Frémont (1813–90). Frémont was the product of a romance between an impoverished French émigré and the wife of a wealthy southern landowner. Frémont's mother had been married off to a man three times her age after the death of her parents, and she proceeded to have an affair with her tutor, Frémont's father. Upon the discovery of the affair, the couple ran off together and had several children, of whom John was the eldest boy.[34] Frémont seems to have been gifted in mathematics from an early age, and enrolled in Charleston College at sixteen, where he initially impressed his teachers with his great ability. Unfortunately, he soon took up with "a young West Indian girl, whose raven hair and soft black eyes interfered sadly with his studies."[35]

Interfere they clearly did, and young John was expelled from Charleston. What became of the "West Indian girl" is not known, but John joined the navy, and after a two-year cruise, returned to Charleston, where the college awarded him a BA and an MA in mathematics. With his degrees in hand, Frémont applied for and received the position of professor of mathematics in the navy.

Frémont soon tired of the navy and joined a railroad survey in western Georgia. From this he obtained skills and experience that allowed him to go to the upper Mississippi to assist the French geographer Joseph Nicolas Nicollet in a survey between the Mississippi and Missouri rivers. Upon the return of this expedition, Frémont assisted Nicollet in preparing the resulting maps and was tutored in natural science. Besides studying science and cartography, Frémont was very much attracted to the fifteen-year-old daughter of Senator Thomas Benton of Missouri. Jessie Benton was equally interested in young John Frémont, and it is perhaps no surprise that her influential father arranged to have John shipped off to Iowa on an army mission. In this case, parental scheming was to no avail: Frémont finished the Iowa mission in record time and returned to Missouri, at which point the Bentons allowed the couple to marry.

Benton was a leading Democrat of the period and also a dedicated expansionist who actively supported efforts to advance the frontier of the United States to the Pacific coast. Benton may have been concerned about his daughter's choice of husband, but having bowed to the inevitable, he made sure that Frémont would get the benefit of his influence in Washington in terms of future employment. In

1842, Frémont was ordered to explore and map the western portion of the Oregon Trail, or, more explicitly, "the country between the frontiers of Missouri and the South Pass in the Rocky mountains, and on the line of the Kansas and Great Plains Rivers."[36] Frémont was accompanied by a party of twenty-one men, including his twelve-year-old brother-in-law "for the development of mind and body which such an expedition would give," and the famous (or infamous) scout Christopher "Kit" Carson as chief guide.

Frémont's account of his expeditions is in the best tradition of travel writing, and frankly is much better reading than some of the adoring biographies that started being produced as soon as his subsequent career in politics was established. Frémont had an excellent eye for country, and made a point of collecting plants at each stopping place, which he subsequently submitted to John Torrey (1796–1873), Asa Gray's teacher and the author of an early flora of North America, for classification. He also took note of geology, including a variety of fossils, and recorded patterns of climate. Some aspects of the first expedition, such as planting an improvised Eagle Flag on the highest point that the party ascended in the Rockies, were little more than publicity stunts, but his surveyed route filled in some of the blank space on Humboldt's map of western North America, and his observations of flora and fauna qualify him for space in the roll of natural historians.

On his second expedition, also guided by Carson, Frémont was instructed to follow the Oregon Trail to Fort Vancouver on the Columbia and to link his line of survey with that of the Wilkes Expedition, which was also mapping the mouth of the river.[37] An anomalous element of this journey was Frémont's insistence on taking with him a number of additional rifles and a mountain howitzer—not the sort of equipment that one would expect on a scientific expedition. The peculiarity of his armament alarmed his superiors, who were justifiably nervous about how the Spanish and British authorities on the West Coast might view what seemed to be a military mission, and orders were sent demanding that Frémont return for further instructions. The letter ordering the recall was intercepted by Frémont's wife, Jessie. Jessie shared her father's and husband's expansionist views, and instead of forwarding the orders, she sent Frémont a note telling him to leave St. Louis quickly, without permitting any delays. Frémont headed west immediately, taking the howitzer with him.

The expedition's route passed the north end of the Great Salt Lake, which Frémont mapped in much greater detail than had previous explorers, as well as conducting some chemical analyses on the lake water and nearby hot springs. From Fort Vancouver, Frémont returned eastward up the Columbia before cutting

FIGURE 16. Frémont's Pyramid, Nevada, from Frémont's *Report of the Exploring Expedition to the Rocky Mountains*, 1845. Looking closely, one can see the cannon that Frémont's party transported with them on their expedition. (Author's collection.)

south along the western edge of the Great Basin. Much of the party's travel was over extremely difficult country, including portions of the Black Rock Desert, and they might well have died in the basin had they not stumbled on Pyramid Lake, in modern Nevada, whose discovery Frémont describes in somewhat lyrical prose: "Beyond, a defile in the mountains descended rapidly about two thousand feet, and filling up all the lower space was a sheet of green water, some twenty miles broad. It broke upon our eyes like the ocean. . . . The waves were curling in the breeze, and their dark-green color showed it to be a body of deep water. For a long time we sat enjoying the view, for we had become fatigued with mountains."[38]

At Pyramid Lake they were fed the endemic Lahontan cutthroat trout by the Paiutes, but Frémont decided that the party lacked sufficient supplies to return directly to St. Louis, so he decided instead to head across the Sierra Nevada to reach Sutter's Fort in California. Ascending the Sierra in midwinter proved an almost impossible task. Many of their pack animals died, and the men lived on what they could find, including the expedition's dogs, but after five weeks they reached the summit and became the first Europeans to see Lake Tahoe, on the crest of the Sierra. They had thus, unknowingly, seen both the source and the end of the Truckee River, one of the major rivers that flow into the Great Basin. From the crest of the mountains, they descended to Sutter's trading post in the Sierra foothills, where they rested and were resupplied before continuing their travels.

Frémont's later journeys were more explicitly political than scientific in nature. After instigating a revolt against the Mexican authorities in 1846, he was briefly appointed governor of the new California Territory, but was court-martialed after refusing to relinquish the position to a higher-ranking officer. The rest of his career is political in nature and of little interest to natural history. It must be noted, however, that Humboldt had nothing but praise for Frémont's abilities as a cartographer and naturalist, saying: "The physical and geognostical views entertained respecting the western part of North America have been rectified in many respects by the adventurous journey of Major Long, the excellent writings of his companion Edwin James, and more especially by the comprehensive observations of Captain Frémont."[39]

Following Frémont, the most successful western expeditions, in terms of both natural history and of connecting the central part of the continent to the United States, were without question the Pacific Railroad Expeditions of 1853–54. With California ascending in both population and importance, it was essential to establish easy lines of communication from the eastern seaboard to the West Coast. Railroads had developed to a point where the need could be met if an appropriate route across the continent could be established. The Department of War, under the guidance of Jefferson Davis (to become better known as the president of the Southern Confederacy seven years later), set out on a massive effort to not only determine the ideal route for a railroad, but also to use the opportunity to catalogue as much of the natural history of the continent as possible.

Davis's instructions to the surveying teams were quite specific:

> As in the prosecution of this exploration and survey it will be necessary to explore the passes of the Cascade range and of the Rocky mountains from the 49th parallel to the head-waters of the Missouri river, and to determine the capacity of the adjacent country to supply, and of the Columbia and Missouri rivers and their tributaries to transport, materials for the construction of the road, great attention will be given to the geography and meteorology, generally, of the whole intermediate region, the seasons and character of its freshets, the quantities and continuance of its rains and snows, especially in the mountain ranges; to its geology in arid regions . . . its botany, natural history, agricultural and mineral resources, the location, numbers, history, traditions, and customs of its Indian tribes, and such other facts as shall tend to develop the character of that portion of our national domain.[40]

The overall plan of the survey involved a multipronged approach, sending out independent parties to follow as closely as possible lines along the 32nd, 35th, 38th, and 47th parallels of north latitude, with return parties scheduled to cover possible alternate routes. The northernmost survey actually consisted of two parties, one moving from the West Coast eastward, and the other from the East to the West in order to maximize the likelihood of a completed survey in the limited time available before the onset of the northern winter. The southernmost survey was done with the permission of the Mexican government, as some of its route passed through what at the time was Mexican territory.

Davis proposed an interesting innovation for the southern survey: the purchase and importation of camels and dromedaries, which he believed would be best suited for desert conditions. Davis eventually persuaded the War Department to try the experiment, but it was too late for the Railroad Survey. The first camels were imported in 1855, and they proved to be hardy and capable beasts of burden.[41] One group was ridden up the Colorado to California and was stationed for several years near Benicia. Unfortunately, the camels induced panic in any horses they encountered, resulting in stampedes and pile-ups on the wagon trails reminiscent of the ancient British cavalry's response to Claudius's camels nearly two millennia earlier. The soldiers found the camels bad-tempered and smelly, and the experiment was abandoned by the outbreak of the Civil War. A number of animals were turned loose in the Southwest, and there were reports of roaming camels there as late as the early 1900s.

The results of the Railroad Surveys were presented in a massive thirteen-volume series, consisting of over seven thousand pages of text as well as illustrations, maps, and figures.[42] The naturalists assigned to each surveying party had been selected on the advice of Spencer Fullerton Baird, the assistant secretary of the Smithsonian Institution. The naturalists presented the Smithsonian with specimens or descriptions of 256 species of mammals, 52 of which had never been previously classified. Each species was presented with a synonymy, a description of geographical variation (if any), and also as much of a geographical distribution as was possible at the time. In addition to the mammals, subsequent volumes presented descriptions of 716 species of birds, reptiles, and amphibians, and a remarkable 289 species of fish found west of the Mississippi.

The actual contents of the survey reports is natural history in the classical sense—there is little, if any, theorizing or suggested explanations for distribution or synthesis of patterns. The style is essentially "We found *this, here, then,*" and occasionally a note on particular behaviors. As such, the reports served as a remarkable starting point for future students of natural history (and, eventually, ecology and biogeography) rather than being absolute ends in themselves.

Before leaving the West, it would perhaps be remiss not to mention one final pioneering naturalist-explorer, although, as with Lewis and Clark, John Wesley Powell (1834–1902) has been fortunate in his biographers.[43] Powell is the sort of man around whom mythology is likely to gather, although Wallace Stegner says of him that he "was as practical as a plane table."[44] He was attracted to both natural history and adventure from childhood, and long before the expeditions on the Colorado that would make him famous, he had already singlehandedly rowed most of the length of the Mississippi River and also the Ohio River from Pittsburg to its mouth. In 1859, he was elected secretary of the Illinois Natural History Society, an organization to which he contributed for much of his career.[45] Powell attended college somewhat sporadically, focusing on the classics as well as geology and natural history. Powell came from a relatively impoverished background, and supported himself by giving lectures on natural history.[46] The outbreak of the Civil War led him to enlist in a volunteer regiment as a military engineer. He was seriously wounded at the Battle of Shiloh, losing his right arm to a Minié ball. In spite of this wound, he continued in the army, leading a division of artillery at Vicksburg and continuing down the river to Natchez and New Orleans. During the course of all this, he married his cousin Emma Dean, who promptly volunteered as a nurse so that she could accompany her husband to the front.

As soon as the Civil War was over, Powell resigned from the army and returned to his career as a lecturer in natural history. He was appointed professor of geology and museum curator at Illinois Wesleyan University. In what has to be one of the pioneering moments in natural history education, Powell took a class of sixteen students on an extended field trip to the Rockies in the summers of 1867 and 1868. These field trips are worth noting if only as a way to mark the rapid pace of change in the West. Twenty years earlier, most of Colorado had been wild, unexplored country; by 1867, it was suitable for college field trips. One assumes that Powell's idea of a field trip was probably much more rugged than that of most of his twenty-first-century successors, but, oh, to have been able to say, "Mom, Dad, Major Powell is taking the whole class to Colorado this summer. May I go?"

It was probably on one of these trips that Powell decided on the expeditions that were to place his name among the great heroes of exploration and natural history: his passages through the Grand Canyon. In May 1869, Powell and a party of nine other men left the Green River Junction with the Colorado and disappeared downriver for three months. Many people assumed that the canyonlands of the

Colorado would be completely unnavigable and the steepness of the canyon sides would prevent any escape once the party realized the folly of their journey. Powell had calculated the necessary fall of the river over the course of the thousand miles that separated Green River Junction from the sea and figured that although there would indeed be rapids, these would be manageable with skill and luck. The team collected geological specimens as they went and recorded both the physical and the biological landscape of the river margins. On several occasions they suffered capsizes, loss of supplies, and near disaster, but it is a testimony to Powell's abilities as both an explorer and a leader that they made it to within two days of the end of the canyon without a single casualty. Sadly, at this point, three members of the party mutinied and set off up the side of the canyon, never to be seen again. Not knowing their fate, Powell left one of the expedition's boats at their point of departure in case they changed their minds, and proceeded downstream, arriving at the end of the journey in August 1869.

One additional unfortunate consequence of the desertion of the three men on the first expedition was that Powell was compelled to leave behind in the canyon all of the geology specimens that had been collected, as there was no room in the remaining boats. As a result, he determined to repeat the voyage in order to recollect specimens and also to conduct a more detailed geographic survey of the canyon. The second voyage was sponsored by the federal government and took place between 1871 and 1872. This time the trip—while still hazardous—was accomplished without casualties.

The results of the second expedition were presented in a series of official reports as well as a number of technical papers by Powell, who used his experience to develop a new system of nomenclature to describe river systems and regional geological structures. Powell became director of the Geological Survey and also head of the Ethnological Bureau, positions that allowed him to train the next generation of geologists and anthropologists who would begin the radical transformation of the landscape that he had first mapped under the guise of "reclamation." Much of the river that Powell traveled down 150 years ago is now buried under reservoirs or controlled through an intricate system of spillways and floodgates. One has to wonder how much he would have approved of the lake that now bears his name.[47]

THIRTEEN . Breadfruit and Icebergs

At sea, too, the course of empire was continuing the tradition of exploration in natural history. We have already discussed James Cook's First Voyage in relation to Joseph Banks, but in his role as a global explorer and navigator of great skill, Cook was of importance to several other people involved in natural history. Cook was born the son of a farmhand on October 27, 1728.[1] There was no immediate nautical tradition in his family, but Cook was fascinated by the sea from an early age. In 1742, at the age of fourteen, Cook literally ran away to sea, signing on with a collier on which he served for thirteen years, learning all he could about sailing and navigation. In 1755, the outbreak of the Seven Years' War with France led to active recruitment of able-bodied seamen, and Cook joined the navy. He was quickly identified as a man of great promise and sent to the North American Station to aid in the siege of Québec.[2]

Successful service on the North American station, including several stints as a cartographer, led to Cook's rapid promotion and selection as commander of the circumnavigation that included the observation of the Transit of Venus in Tahiti. Although Cook's major interests were mathematical and astronomical, he was sensitive to other demands of natural history, and gave Joseph Banks room and time to collect species of plants as they traveled. Of particular note in light of subsequent maritime history was Banks's acquaintance in Tahiti with the breadfruit *(Artocarpus altilis)*, which I discuss later.

In 1775, Cook completed a successful second circumnavigation, which took ship and crew to higher southern latitudes than had ever before been attempted, and their track demonstrated the absence of any significant land mass north of the ice pack (Cook got almost far enough south to spot Antarctica, but weather and floating sea ice prevented an approach). In his third and final voyage, he was reappointed captain of *Resolution*, and, along with a second ship, the *Discovery*, he returned to the Pacific for further exploration. After cartographic work in Tasmania and New Zealand, the flotilla steered north in search of a Northwest Passage. During the course of this leg of the voyage, Cook discovered Hawaii, which he named the Sandwich Islands, after Lord Sandwich, who had been such a supporter of Joseph Banks.[3] After a foray along the coast of Alaska, Cook returned to Hawaii, where, sadly, he was set upon and killed by natives.[4]

The British West Indies had suffered a series of famines as a result of hurricane damage to the islands' crops and poor planning by colonial administrators.[5] Joseph Banks, by this time well established as president of the Royal Society, remembered his experience with breadfruit in Tahiti and realized that Jamaica and other islands in the Caribbean are at approximately the same latitude north of the equator as Tahiti is south of it, and hence the islands might share a common climate and be able to support the same sorts of vegetation. He used his connections within the government to get the Royal Navy to sponsor the transport of breadfruit seedlings to Jamaica, primarily to serve as a food source for the slaves employed on the sugar and coffee plantations.

William Bligh (1754–1817) had served as master of the *Resolution* under Cook and was familiar with tropical seas. The admiralty appointed Bligh as the commander of HMS *Bounty* with explicit instructions from Banks to travel to Tahiti and ensure the selection and care of breadfruit trees suitable for transplantation in Jamaica. Bligh and the *Bounty* had a very rough journey to the Pacific. Contrary winds kept them from rounding Cape Horn, and eventually Bligh turned around and headed east via the Cape of Good Hope. This difficulty added several months to the voyage and also exhausted the crew, who had hoped for a speedy passage. Once they finally reached Tahiti, they had to wait several months for the breadfruit to be suitable for transport, and a number of the crew, including the first mate, Fletcher Christian, spent much of their time enjoying the island and frolicking with the Tahitians.

When the *Bounty* finally sailed, in April 1789, many of the crew were unhappy to leave Tahiti. Within a few days, Christian led a mutiny. Bligh and sailors loyal to him were cast adrift in an open boat without charts or compass. In a miraculous piece of seamanship, Bligh managed to sail over thirty-five hundred miles in forty-seven days and land successfully on the island of Timor, losing only a single sailor during this epic journey.

Bligh returned to England in 1791, where he was acquitted by a court martial for the loss of the *Bounty*. Banks was still keen on bringing breadfruit to Jamaica and convinced the admiralty to fund a second expedition, with Bligh again in command. This time two ships were sent out, along with two botanist-gardeners, whose job was both to look after the breadfruit and to collect any other useful or interesting plants that could be brought back for the Royal Gardens at Kew.[6] Banks also gave them £10.10s (about two thousand dollars in contemporary currency) in advance for any interesting specimens, including birds, insects, and so on, that they might bring back. They took with them a number of European plants that were intended to become "naturalized" in Tahiti and Tasmania. The ships reached Tahiti without incident, and in the course of two months the captain and crew collected over two thousand breadfruit trees, which they stored in pots in greenhouses onboard.

The flotilla proceeded to St. Vincent, in the West Indies, where half the cargo was unloaded and local species destined for Kew were brought onboard before Bligh resumed the journey to Jamaica. There the remaining plants were put in a nursery, and the botanists elected to remain on the island as caretakers on government salary. In Jamaica, Bligh also picked up several hundred additional species of plants for Kew Gardens, but his departure was delayed by the outbreak of war with France. He was finally able to return home in August 1793, having been out more than two years. The collections of plants from Tahiti and other Pacific islands, as well as those from the West Indies, delighted Banks and greatly expanded the collections in the Botanical Gardens.

British dominance of oceanic ventures, whether for cartography, general exploration and acquisition, or scientific study, continued for much of the eighteenth and nineteenth centuries. If the United States was to compete successfully with its rivals, it would need better charts and a better understanding of the natural history of the oceanic areas so important to the whaling and seal-hunting trades. But, as Jefferson had discovered with the Lewis and Clark Expedition, Congress was not a natural supporter of science. Unlike in Britain, where royal patronage of learned societies had long been the rule, the federal government tended to shy away from research unless some clear benefit to the body politic could be demonstrated.

The full story of the Wilkes Expedition, or the United States Exploring Expedition of 1838–42, as it is otherwise known, has been beautifully told by William Stanton, but it is worth a brief summary here.[7] Extended lobbying for a major maritime expedition over the course of two decades was spearheaded by Jeremiah Reynolds (1799–1858), a notorious enthusiast of the hollow earth theory.[8] Reynolds's efforts eventually led the United States Navy to commission six vessels, including two schooners and a supply ship, to explore the southern ocean and to map the islands of the Pacific.

The Exploring Expedition was intended to demonstrate the United States' standing in the world of science and to divorce it from dependence on Britain for cartographic information. Navy crews were supplemented by a corps of scientists, including James Dwight Dana (1813–95), the leading American-born geologist of the nineteenth century. Titian Peale (1799–1885), the son of Charles Peale, who, as mentioned earlier, already had gained experience in fieldwork on expeditions to Florida and the Rockies, was recruited as expedition painter and naturalist. Asa Gray (1810–88), the man to whom Darwin was to confide his views on natural selection fifteen years after the expedition, was invited but declined.[9]

After the original commander resigned, Charles Wilkes (1798–1877) was selected to lead the expedition. Wilkes was no Fitzroy; he was a very junior lieutenant whose experience of long ocean voyages consisted of one cruise to the Mediterranean. Wilkes was also unused to command and seems to have allowed his mercurial personality to get in the way of sensible decision-making and discipline. During the expedition he became notorious for flogging, and also made a point of constantly switching officers among ships in order to block plots real or imagined.

The expedition finally got underway in August 1838. The little fleet sailed south to the Cape Verde islands before turning west to Rio de Janeiro, arriving in Brazil in late November. From Rio, they steered south along more or less the same track that the *Beagle* had followed a few years earlier, visiting Buenos Aires and Tierra del Fuego, where they encountered Fuegians, whom they described much as Darwin and Fitzroy had in their accounts. Rounding up for the west coast of South America, the squadron ran into a series of gales, and one of the schooners, the *Sea Gull,* was lost with all hands. In the harbor of Callao, Peru, several of the ships proceeded to ram one another or to collide with other ships in the anchorage: in all, not a very happy demonstration of seamanship.

Once they cleared the coast of Peru, the expedition sailed southwest across the Pacific to the Tuamotu Archipelago. Their ultimate goal included determining the extent of land in the extreme south. Besides developing better charts of the southern ocean, one mission of the expedition was to bring home better collections of the plants and animals of the Pacific region. The islands of the South

Pacific and the continent of Australia had presented both an enormous attraction and a real intellectual challenge since before Cook's voyages. Medieval natural history assumed that the Antipodes would be a land of monstrous forms—a sort of reversed Northern Hemisphere that would contain many of the fantastical missing elements of the *scala naturae*.[10] The actual encounter with Southern Hemisphere flora and fauna was a traumatic shock that proved to be much broader and more long-lasting than one might have expected. There were indeed strange organisms that stubbornly refused to fit into tidy northern classification schemes, but their strangeness also failed to fill any gaps in a linear organization of life.

At first scientists to the north were tempted to reject accounts of marsupials and monotremes as little more than wild stories told by fanciful sailors. When the platypus was first discovered, it was assumed by many naturalists to be a taxidermist's forgery, or, in more gentle tones: "It was difficult to preserve the mind from entertaining some doubts as to its genuine nature, and from surmising that some sort of deception in its structure might have been practiced."[11]

Kangaroos, wallabies, koalas, and Tasmanian devils seemed to break up the whole idea of an ordered and structured nature and did not present a mirror image of the nature to the north. Only with further collection could some sort of system be restored. Equally threatening were ideas about the human inhabitants of the Pacific islands. Accounts ran from the extremes of lands of lotus-eaters—paradises of free love and communal living—to those of brutal savagery and cannibalism. In all, the south represented a great strangeness to nineteenth-century American beliefs, and it was southward that Wilkes and his ships were sailing.

Wilkes put in at Sydney before steering for the ice. The actual "discovery" of Antarctica is an event surrounded in controversy. Cook had sailed to higher southern latitudes than anyone before him, but it is unclear if he actually sighted land or simply the ice shelf. Russian and British sailors had definitely recorded some sort of land mass by 1820, but they were unsure of its extent. Due to sloppy recordkeeping and in spite of subsequent wrangling, it is unclear just who first approached the Antarctic continent, but the first American ship almost certainly sighted land on January 16, 1840.[12]

The coastline of the new continent—for such it proved to be—was guarded with a barrier of ice that took a toll on the poorly protected ships of the flotilla. One had its rudder knocked away almost at once and was nearly wrecked on an iceberg before limping back to Sydney. Closing with the barrier, Wilkes was able to recover samples of earth and rock from a calved iceberg some distance from the land mass. His soundings and periodic sightings of land over a course of more than eight hundred miles of standing on and off the barrier determined that they had discovered more than just an island.

After returning to Sydney for repairs, the expedition headed for Tonga. Passing through the South Seas, Dana collected coral fragments and made soundings that later allowed him to confirm Darwin's theory that coral atolls were the sunken crests of old volcanoes. From Tonga, Wilkes sailed to Fiji, an archipelago notorious for its reefs and cannibals. Arriving there in July 1840, the crew set about surveying the archipelago, using the remaining schooner and the small boats to move among the fringing coral reefs and outcrops. The scientific party set up a base on the islands and collected specimens of plants and animals for later classification.

Although initially the Americans had good success with the natives, there seems to have been a degree of disorder and confusion among the different ships' crews, both in terms of actual survey work and in interactions with the Fijians. Eventually one party ran afoul of the islanders and lost a boat to a group of natives. Wilkes responded by sending in armed sailors, and, after securing the boat, they burned the village. This served only to heighten tensions, and in a brief brawl two of the American crew, including Wilkes's nephew, were killed. The response was quick and brutal. Wilkes landed a heavily armed force that burned a fortified village to the ground and killed at least eighty-seven Fijians.

The savagery of the expedition's response was subsequently justified on the grounds that the Fijians had attacked first and, besides, they were cannibals (there is a gruesome account of one native arriving alongside the expedition ships happily munching on a human head).[13] James Dana, in a letter written after his return, goes into some detail about the cannibalism of the Fijians, although one suspects that he is playing somewhat to his Sunday-school audience.[14] In any case, the slaughter of the Fijians made further surveys impractical.

Departing Fiji, the expedition headed for the Sandwich Islands (Hawaii), where they ascended Mauna Loa and established a camp on the edge of the volcanic crater. There they remained for several weeks, surveying the surrounding area, estimating the depth of the crater, and collecting samples. By this point many of the sailors were tired of the expedition (Wilkes had consistently lied to everyone about how long they would be gone). A number deserted before Wilkes gave orders to sail for the West Coast of North America. Sailing northeast, they made landfall north of modern Seattle and gradually worked their way along the coast, exploring the Strait of Juan de Fuca and Puget Sound. They arrived at the Columbia River in July 1841, where their second schooner was lost in an ill-advised attempt to sail across the bar at the river's mouth. Fortunately no sailors drowned, but many valuable specimens went down with the ship, and the event points to an overall lack of care and competence among the crews, who were increasingly unsure of what they were doing and why they were doing it.

Wilkes ordered a party ashore to map the lower reaches of the Columbia and, ideally, to link their survey with that of Frémont's party, which, as we saw in the previous chapter, was then coming overland from the Mississippi. No link-up was achieved, and Frémont subsequently challenged the accuracy of Wilkes's surveying, a charge that led to a long-term quarrel between the two leaders. The remaining ships, in the meantime, sailed down the coast, meeting up with the shore party in San Francisco Bay. Now it was clearly time to head home. Wilkes and his men departed the West Coast, sailing to the Philippines and Singapore, across the Indian Ocean, around the Cape of Good Hope, and so back to the United States in June 1842.

Following the explorers' return, the animosity and bickering that had dogged them throughout the voyage burst into full bloom and delayed publication of results for years. In spite of this, the expedition achieved some tangible results. Dana's career was set up by his publications stemming from the expedition, and he spent the rest of his life as a professor at Yale, refining his ideas about geology and mountain building—and attempting to reconcile the new discoveries with a biblical notion of creation. The vast collections of specimens from islands across the Pacific were eventually gathered together to form a major portion of the initial holdings of a new institution of research and public display: the Smithsonian Institution. The Smithsonian is a uniquely American institution. It has maintained and expanded on its original benefactor's idea of a research center, and the Smithsonian's Tropical Research Institute in Panama has trained generations of young ecologists, many of whom now play a major role in conservation efforts throughout the tropics.

Beyond housing the products of the Wilkes Expedition, the Smithsonian received important collections from the Hudson's Bay Company and also acted as a repository for many of the exploration parties involved in mapping and sampling the West. With the American Museum of Natural History in New York, the Field Museum in Chicago, the Museum of Comparative Zoology in Cambridge, Massachusetts, and the Museum of Vertebrate Zoology in Berkeley, the Smithsonian is part of the lasting legacy of natural history collections in the United States.[15]

While the United States sent out the Wilkes Expedition, the British government had by no means been idle in its examinations of the Antarctic. In 1839, the Royal Navy instructed James Ross (1800–62) to take two ships, HMS *Erebus* and HMS

Terror, to proceed to the Antarctic and map whatever they might find.[16] Ross was an experienced sailor who had served in the navy since the age of twelve, and had accompanied his uncle on an Arctic voyage in search of the Northwest Passage in 1818, as well as completing four other voyages to the Arctic prior to commanding *Erebus* and *Terror.*

Of greatest importance to natural history was the presence among the ships' company of Joseph Dalton Hooker (1817–1911), whom we have already met briefly in earlier chapters. Hooker was the son of William Jackson Hooker, and like his father spent the most important years of his career as director of Kew Gardens. During Joseph's childhood, William Hooker was Regius Professor of botany at the University of Glasgow, and young Joseph exhibited a desire to follow in his father's footsteps from an early age.[17] Even in the first quarter of the nineteenth century, botany was not regarded as a "profession" in any meaningful sense; rather, botanists either had independent means (Sir Joseph Banks comes to mind) or did something else to earn their keep and practiced botany on the side. In Joseph Hooker's case, the something else was medicine, and he trained as a surgeon at the University of Glasgow.

As Huxley has pointed out, in the nineteenth century the distance between medicine and botany—and perhaps particularly tropical botany—was not as great as one might expect.[18] The British Empire was expanding into all sorts of new environments, travel was still slow, and a doctor in the colonies would probably have to manufacture at least some of his medicines from local plants. Many of William Hooker's students at Glasgow had been doctors in training, readying themselves for overseas postings, and lessons on plant taxonomy and at least an outline of biogeography would have made perfect sense.

Joseph Hooker's chief interest in botany lay in biogeography, which required extensive travel. This wanderlust was further encouraged when a friend gave him a prepublication draft of Darwin's *Journal of Researches* (the original version of *Voyage of the* Beagle). Hooker literally slept with the *Journal* under his pillow, and he met Darwin himself quite by chance as he was walking in London just before the *Erebus* and *Terror* sailed. We can see in these circumstances a delightful chain of influence that drove so much of nineteenth-century natural history. Humboldt was intrigued by early descriptions of the New World and arranged to come to America. Humboldt's *Personal Narrative* inspired Darwin to accept Henslow's suggestion that he sail on the *Beagle*. Darwin's *Journal of Researches* inspired Hooker to go to Antarctica, and Hooker returned to become Darwin's most steadfast supporter in the evolution debate.

Hooker's position on *Erebus* was significantly different from Darwin's on the *Beagle*. Darwin was a supernumerary, with no duties except to entertain the captain when needed. He could go ashore whenever the *Beagle* touched land and stay ashore as long as he wanted (he could even have left the voyage permanently at any point if he so wished). By contrast, Hooker was officially the assistant surgeon onboard *Erebus*. As such, he had specific duties to the ship and crew, answered to naval discipline, and was expected to be present not only when the ship was under sail, but also for as much time in port as was needed to discharge his medical responsibilities.

Hooker was not the only naturalist onboard. Ross was actually a trained scientist, a fellow of the Royal Society, and fully intended to be an active participant in any zoological studies performed.[19] In addition to Ross, the official naturalist for the voyage was Robert McCormick (1800–90), who had also been appointed to the *Beagle* on Darwin's voyage, but had left that vessel in Rio in a fit of temper over what he saw as Fitzroy's preference for Darwin.[20] Poor McCormick; from his writing fifty years later, it is clear that his bitterness lasted. His only mention in his autobiography of his part in the *Beagle* voyage is two pages, ending as follows: "Having found myself in a false position on board a small and very uncomfortable vessel, and very much disappointed in my expectations of carrying out my natural history pursuits, every obstacle having been placed in the way of my getting on shore and making collections, I got permission from the admiral in command of the station here to be superseded and allowed a passage home in H.M.S. *Tyne*."[21] Neither "*Beagle*" nor "Darwin" appears anywhere in the more than eight hundred pages of McCormick's accounts. Poor, poor Robert McCormick; one can almost hear the whistle of fate's wings passing him by. The "small and very uncomfortable vessel" had carried Darwin to immortality. In contrast, by the time McCormick's *Voyages* came out, the general public had long since forgotten him.

Hooker pulled every string available to ensure himself a place among the scientific detachment of the crew. Ross, who seems to have been a very tolerant man, understood Hooker's strengths as well as his ambition, and tactfully appointed him "expedition botanist," promising to allow him as much shore time as possible. Although this was not the ideal situation for an aspiring naturalist, it was certainly the best offer that Hooker could hope to get, and he somewhat grudgingly accepted the appointment and settled into his quarters on *Erebus*. Hooker had every reason to be grateful to Ross for any concessions to general natural history—the official purpose of the voyage had very little to do with plants and animals. Instead *Erebus* and *Terror* were tasked with measuring local magnetic variations at high southern latitudes in order to improve navigation.

The ships reached the Kerguelen Islands on May 12, 1840. These proved to be among the most biologically interesting islands of the first part of the voyage. The main island was also something of a homecoming for Hooker. Cook had visited the island on one of his circumnavigations, and Hooker says in his autobiography, "When still a child I was very fond of Voyages and Travels; and my great delight was to sit on my grandfather's knee and look at the pictures in Cook's 'Voyages.' The one that took my fancy most was the plate of Christmas Harbour, Kerguelen Land, with the arched rock standing out to sea and the sailors killing penguins, and I thought I should be the happiest boy alive if ever I would see that wonderful arched rock, and knock penguins on the head."[22] Hooker had finally gotten to Kerguelen, but he was much more interested in the island's vegetation than in clubbing penguins. McCormick shot plenty of birds and waxed lyrical over the fossil trees that he found on the upper slopes, but he sneered at the island's lack of living trees and shrubs. Hooker worked away quietly, increasing the island's flora by nearly an order of magnitude over Cook's records.

Overall, the voyagers spent three months on the main island of Kerguelen before proceeding to Tasmania, where Ross received a letter and sketch from Wilkes describing his estimates of the coastline of Antarctica.[23] Ross was remarkably unimpressed and indeed expressed a degree of pique that the Yankees had sailed in waters that he was planning to explore. *Erebus* and *Terror* scored a coup in the beginning of 1841, when, passing to the east of Wilkes's route, they managed to break through the ice pack into the open waters of the Ross Sea. On January 11, they sighted a range of mountains to the south, which Ross named the Admiralties; shortly thereafter, they spotted two volcanoes, one active and one dormant: these were named Mt. Erebus and Mt. Terror in honor of the ships. Mindful of the importance of pleasing patrons, a nearby island was named Beaufort, after the royal hydrographer (and friend of Fitzroy) Captain Francis Beaufort (1774–1857).

After extending their cruise farther south than had ever previously been recorded (and finding no trace of land in areas marked by Wilkes as parts of Antarctica), the *Erebus* and *Terror* returned to Tasmania and eventually to the North Island of New Zealand to wait out the southern winter. The next season, they proceeded south again, pushing their latitudinal record to 78 degrees, 10 minutes, south, a figure that would stand as a record for the rest of the nineteenth century. The second southern cruise almost led to the loss of both ships and everyone onboard. Moving through an area rich in icebergs, the ships lost sight of each other. McCormick describes what happened next: "On gaining the deck what a scene met the eye! First, the massive hull of the *Terror* surging heavily in the swell

FIGURE 17. The arched rock on Kerguelen, with James Cook's sailors clubbing penguins, an early-nineteenth-century reproduction of an illustration in *Cook's Voyages*. This image inspired Joseph Hooker's travels. (Author's collection.)

on our starboard-bow, carrying away our bowsprit, and with it our fore-topmast; whilst, above all, towered through the mist of a dark gloomy night, the tremendous form of an enormous iceberg."[24] The *Terror* was relatively undamaged by the collision, but *Erebus* lost not just her bowsprit, but with it her foresails and most of her ability to maneuver. With remarkable coolness, Ross managed to steer the ship between two converging icebergs and into clearer water beyond. A jury-rig got them underway once more, and the crew spent the next few weeks repairing what damage they could.

The flotilla then sailed to the Falkland Islands, where McCormick lamented that the midshipmen "thoughtlessly" shot two horses for meat, an event that he describes as "so wanton an act of cruelty" and quite unnecessary, as "I had, with my own gun, alone, contributed no less than four dozen upland geese, forty brace of snipe, two dozen rabbits, besides two dozen and a half of the Antarctic geese, and other edible birds, teal, plover, and grey ducks, without limit to our mess."[25] Once again, it is interesting to consider different mores between the nineteenth and twenty-first centuries. The birds were natives and would probably now enjoy a high degree of protection; then they were simply game. The horses would now be regarded as introduced exotics; then they were "noble animals in the wilds of nature."[26]

The ships sailed on to Tierra del Fuego, having the seemingly obligatory interaction with Fuegians while they paused to collect plant and animal specimens. Hooker was enthralled with the botany of the region. From a biogeographical point of view, the expedition could not have been more interesting, constituting a grand transect around a great arc of the Southern Hemisphere. Hooker was fascinated by the similarities and discontinuities that he saw in the floras of the various islands and archipelagos. Well before Wallace's magisterial work on zoogeography, Hooker was taking Humboldt's ideas of elevation in relation to plant distributions and expanding on them laterally—why did some regions seem to have so much more in common in terms of plant forms than others? What effect could wind and weather impose on plant "migration"? Why were some floras seemingly continuous across broad arcs of longitude, while others appeared so disjunctive?

The voyage was a major success for both Ross (who was knighted for his endeavors) and Hooker, who immediately set to publishing an important account of the flora of Antarctic islands.[27] This work took him the next four years to complete and marked the beginning of his rise in the scientific world. Sadly, *Erebus* and *Terror* and many shipmates would not survive long enough to see the work in print. Both ships and their crews were lost in the search for the Northwest Passage. After no word had been heard for some years, Robert McCormick pushed for a relief expedition, and piloted an open boat, aptly named the *Forlorn Hope*, through some of the trickiest straits in the western Arctic in hopes of finding his lost fellows. He may have been a bad writer and a poor naturalist, but he was a brave and determined man. In spite of his efforts and those of numerous other would-be rescuers, no survivors were ever found.

Hooker flourished. The first letter from Darwin arrived in November 1843, encouraging Hooker to publish his results as a clear and separate flora rather than letting them get lost in more general reports.[28] Darwin had been aware of Hooker's progress through letters from and to Sir Charles Lyell, and may have already seen in Hooker a botanical counterpart to his zoological focus.[29] Darwin had done little as yet with his botanical collections from the *Beagle* voyage, and was delighted that Hooker could put them to use once he was safely back. Hooker replied almost at once in a two-page letter thanking Darwin for his offer of specimens and elaborating on some of his own observations.[30] Thus began one of the most remarkable and long-running communications in the history of science. To begin with, the pair were very formal with each other, beginning each letter with "Dear Sir" and ending "very truly your's" *(sic)* or some variation on the theme. Darwin was itching for someone to confide in, and on January 11, 1844, there is the famous letter that starts off with the usual series of questions about distributions and then dives into the heart of the matter. I quote it here at some length because it also gives a good sense of Darwin's overall methodology:

> Besides a general interest about the Southern lands, I have been now ever since my return engaged in a very presumptuous work & which I know no one individual who wd not say a very foolish one.—I was so struck with distribution of Galapagos organisms &c &c & with the character of the American fossil mammifers &c &c that I determined to collect blindly every sort of fact, which cd bear any way on what are species.—I have read heaps of agricultural & horticultural books, & have never ceased collecting facts—At last gleams of light have come, & I am almost convinced (quite contrary to opinion I started with) that species are not (it is like confessing a murder) immutable. Heaven forfend me from Lamarck nonsense. . . . I think I have found out (here's presumption!) the simple way by which species become exquisitely adapted to various ends.[31]

One can imagine how Darwin felt posting the letter and awaiting a reply—he was sending very strong hints of the way that his mind was working, and Hooker was one of the first people who had the intellectual horsepower to wrestle with the ideas. Hooker's responses are at first glance noncommittal—he doesn't bite at the "murder" reference, but he is clearly interested. Careful reading suggests caution, both on Hooker's part and perhaps in a suggestion of caution to Darwin, but there is also encouragement:

> Vegetation was doubtless once very different on the same spot to what it is now. Nor do I see that we have any chance of solving the question that relates to the existence of certain plants on islands created, (we suppose,) before the time of man. That there was a beginning to the creation of plants on our globe is very true, we can hardly suppose that we have now only the remains of that original stock. . . . There may in my opinion have been a series of productions on different spots, & also a gradual change of species. I shall be delighted to hear how you think this change may have taken place, as no presently conceived opinions satisfy me on the subject.[32]

Then it is immediately back to distribution and abundance.

One suspects that this is exactly what Darwin hoped for—he had found a friend whom he could use as a sounding board for ideas and who could also throw back at him information and new concepts as fast as Darwin could bring them up. In a quick note in 1847, Hooker sums things up very nicely: "All this will do better for a palaver, it is easier to me than migration. Your Gnats you know are my Camels & vice versa exactly."[33] Long before this, the two had become friends. By February 23, 1844, Darwin had switched to the informal "Dear Hooker" (with an apology for "my freedom of address"), and so it was to remain for the literally hundreds and hundreds of letters that would flow back and forth until Darwin's death.[34]

Hooker must have been delighted to have his erstwhile hero so swiftly welcome him as a friend and colleague, but he still had the problem of making a living. There was also the matter of a personal life—he had become engaged to Frances Henslow, Darwin's teacher John Henslow's daughter. He hoped for a university position and applied (with Darwin's endorsement) for a job in Edinburgh that also would have put him in charge of the Botanic Garden. Much to both his and Darwin's surprise, he was turned down for the position. His father's directorship of Kew Gardens gave Joseph excellent contacts, but the gardens could not support him; he needed to go back into the field. Having published his Antarctic flora, he headed off on another expedition, this time to the Himalaya, arriving in India in April 1848 and basing himself in the hill station of Darjeeling.[35]

Hooker's letters to Darwin from India could be the subject of a chapter in and of themselves. His excitement is palpable as he explores the high country in northern India, going into Sikkim and Nepal to collect, recording geological and zoological information for his friend at home, and employing an army of collectors to further his own botanical dreams. It is amusing to note him gently teasing Darwin about "the old fable of the geese" in relation to Darwin's work on barnacles.[36] He also asks Darwin to keep his letters as a sort of backup because "I seldom venture to speculate, except in letters to friends & my spects. are very transient—after we have talked over each at Down they may all go into the fire."[37]

Upon his appointment as director of Kew Gardens after the death of his father in 1865, Hooker was in a position to expand the reach of the Royal Botanic Gardens by encouraging satellite botanic gardens overseas that could send live specimens to be grown at Kew. The result of his work in India and the subsequent collections that he had sent to him later was a near-definitive flora of India, which he kept working on in different drafts for more than fifty years.

After his time in India, Hooker returned to Britain to write up his results, a project that required several years of concentrated study. He also married Frances Henslow, and together they had seven children, five of whom survived into adulthood. When Frances died, in 1874, he went through two years of quiet mourning before marrying the widow of William Jardine. Jardine had published an impor-

FIGURE 18. Hummingbird, from William Jardine's *Natural History*. (Author's collection.)

tant popular series of illustrated natural history texts in the 1830s that had done much to stimulate interest in the fauna of Great Britain, so his widow was doubtless familiar with the behavior of naturalists.

The next year, Hooker visited the United States as the guest of Asa Gray, who shared his support for Darwinism (remember that it had been Darwin's letter to Asa Gray that was read at the Linnean Society in 1858 and that confirmed his priority in developing the idea of natural selection). Gray was also a keen student of plant geography, and together they traveled to the western United States, visiting many of the areas that Frémont had struggled to reach just a generation earlier. After crossing the Great Basin, they ascended the Sierra Nevada, crossing into California in ten days (it had taken Frémont five weeks to make the same journey). Once in California, they visited Yosemite and San Francisco and met John Muir before Hooker returned to Britain with a new trove of specimens. Unlike Darwin, Hooker never came out with a truly original theoretical synthesis of his work. To him, it would seem that the teasing out of facts in the form of classification and distribution of individual species was what really mattered. He never really retired; instead he went on working on his beloved plants until his death, two years before that of the other last of the great Victorians, Alfred Russel Wallace.

FOURTEEN · Naturalists in New England

Thoreau, Agassiz, and Gray

In July 1896, the following paragraph appeared in *Science*, the journal of the American Association for the Advancement of Science:

> After having published some fifty volumes in the series of "Classics for Children," it is time that Ginn & Co. should include a scientific selection. They have done well in choosing Gilbert White's *Natural History of Selbourne* [*sic*]. . . . It would not be possible to place a better book in the hands of a boy of fourteen. Observers of nature, such as White, Thoreau, and Audubon, seem to be lacking at the present time. Biology has perhaps become so extended and complex that the amateur is discouraged, but, as has recently been suggested . . . boys do not now take an interest in nature, and there is no large class from which naturalists may be supplied.[1]

There is something eerily modern about the sentiments expressed here, and the writer goes on to say: "The growth of cities, the preponderating interest in athletic sports, and the study of biology in the laboratory, have led the schoolboy away from contact with nature . . . collecting still goes on, but stamps are a poor substitute for birds' eggs, butterflies, shells and the like. Under these conditions nothing could be more useful than a copy of *The Natural History of Selbourne* in every school and in every home."[2]

My daughter, who has grown tired of being told how much more in tune with nature previous generations were, especially when compared to hers, responded to this with "Hah! So much for 'When *I* was a boy!'" Darwin was only fourteen years dead and Hooker still had fifteen years of botanizing ahead of him, yet science had shifted dramatically away from the sort of studies that had characterized the eighteenth and nineteenth centuries. The exact date when natural history began to decline is impossible to pin down, but it is clear that the slide was underway by the 1890s. Why this might have happened, whether this shift was inevitable, and whether it was a bad or a good thing are the subjects of the last three chapters of this book.

In seeking possible causes for the decline of natural history, it seems worthwhile to examine some of the important figures within both the popular and scientific culture of nineteenth-century America. Ironically, it may be that by bringing aspects of natural history to the attention of the general public, these writers might have hastened the dismissal of natural history within the scientific community.

Henry David Thoreau (1817–62) holds an iconic place in the realm of American nature writers. Generations of students have been exposed to fragments of his writings, and more than a handful of us have been inspired by this statement: "I went to the woods because I wished to live deliberately, to front only the essential facts of life, and see if I could not learn what it had to teach, and not, when I came to die, discover that I had not lived."[3]

Thoreau is something of a puzzle in terms of a history of natural history. It is obvious throughout his writings that he had read deeply—he was familiar with Gilbert White, Humboldt, and the Bartrams.[4] He read *Origin of Species* within a short time of its publication in the United States.[5] During his time at Harvard, he took courses in the sciences. One might have assumed that he would have become a leader in American field biology. In spite of all this, there is a hint of trouble in his focus—or perhaps in his lack of focus, which might have given "serious" naturalists some pause. In his essay "Natural History of Massachusetts," he cannot resist: "Nature is mythical and mystical always, and works with the license and extravagance of genius. She has her luxurious and florid style as well as art. Having a pilgrims' cup to make, she gives to the whole, stem, bowl, handle, and nose, some fantastic shape, as if it were to be the car of some fabulous marine deity, a Nereus or Triton."[6]

I am probably being unkind, but at this point I imagine Darwin or Hooker gently laying the book to one side and saying something like, "Well, I must get back to my work." One can feel the frustration even in Thoreau's contemporaries. Ralph Waldo Emerson says of him in a posthumous sketch: "He resumed his endless walks and miscellaneous studies, making every day some new acquaintance with Nature, though as yet never speaking of zoology or botany, since, though very studious of natural facts, he was incurious of technical and textual sciences."[7] Emerson suggests that Thoreau was at least as knowledgeable of the natural history of Massachusetts as the official state naturalists were, but that he refused to behave as his friends felt a naturalist *ought* to behave, and in this lay the problem.

At the end of the "Natural History of Massachusetts," Thoreau is as clear as he can be in his intentions: "Let us not underrate the value of a fact; it will one day flower in a truth. It is astonishing how few facts of importance are added in a century to the natural history of any animal. . . . Wisdom does not inspect but behold. We must look a long time before we can see . . . —we cannot know truth by contrivance and method."[8] To a very great degree, this is the problem with Thoreau: he *has* "look[ed] for a long time," and we sense that he has all sorts of interesting things to tell us, but he chooses not to—he abjures both "contrivance and method." It is up to us to go see for ourselves.

Thoreau was familiar with the events of the scientific world around him, including many of the ones that we have examined here, but he drew his own conclusions from them. Speaking of the Wilkes Expedition, he says: "What was the meaning of that South-Sea Exploring Expedition, with all its parade and expense, but an indirect recognition of the fact that there are continents and seas in the moral world, to which every man is an isthmus or an inlet, yet unexplored by him, but it is easier to sail many thousand miles through cold and storm and cannibals, in a government ship, with five hundred men and boys to assist one, than it is to explore the private sea, the Atlantic and Pacific Ocean of one's being alone."[9] Wilkes would probably have been completely confused by any suggestion that his expedition had anything to do with any sort of "private sea," in spite of the many explicitly moral criticisms that the accounts of the voyage heaped on Fuegians and Fijians alike.

I believe that Thoreau and his writings both represent and encourage a divorce between natural history with its naturalists on one side and biology/ecology and their scientists on the other.[10] At its best, science obviates the need for direct experience by its readers. A good scientist presents her or his evidence and argument in such a way that readers are convinced that they would have seen or otherwise sensed the same information and reached the same conclusion had they been the ones doing the observing or conducting the experiment. At the same time, science is ultimately about doubt.

Thoreau never seems to have settled in his own mind the question of methodology. He was not interested in collecting for collection's sake. In *A Week on the*

Concord and Merrimack Rivers, he says: "The process of discovery is very simple. An unwearied and systematic application of known laws to nature causes the unknown to reveal themselves. Almost any mode of observation will be successful at last, for what is most wanted is method. Only let something be determined and fixed around which observation may rally."[11]

In this work (published in 1849, while he was busy on *Walden*), Thoreau offers advice that any scientist might approve of in an ideal sense. Darwin might have been enthusiastic about piling fact on fact in the "long argument" that would become the *Origin of Species,* but he did not collect facts blindly; instead he had initial, tentative hypotheses that he refined as information led him to new insight: "In July I opened my first note-book for facts in relation to the *Origin of Species,* about which I had long reflected, and never ceased working for the next twenty years."[12] Yet it is important to also note a somewhat later comment that Darwin makes about an earlier geological paper: "Because no other explanation was possible under our then state of knowledge, I argued in favor of sea-action, and my error has been a good lesson to me never to trust in science to the principle of exclusion."[13] In other words, Darwin recognized both the importance of data collection and analysis in light of hypothesis formation and the danger of becoming too wedded to a hypothesis or "law" around which facts might sometimes be erroneously ordered.

Thirty-five years after Thoreau's death, the geologist T. C. Chamberlin published what should be required reading for every graduate student, in which he cautions against excessive reliance on theory.[14] Prior to the late nineteenth century, natural historians accumulated facts, in many cases in the concrete form of specimens. The specimen was *there,* it was shaped *thus,* and it possessed a particular reality. From a sufficient array of facts, a Darwin could draw out patterns and processes that provided deeper or more general insights. There was always the risk of hypothesis slipping into law, and blinding naturalists with a particular typology that prevented them from seeing what was actually in front of them. One could also be so enamored of a particular theory that one ignored any evidence that might refute one's beliefs. Chamberlin encourages the use of the term *working hypotheses* and insists on the addition of *multiple* so that the process of testing could be made explicit and continuous.

Thoreau was a wonderful observer, and his writing is periodically illuminated by flashes of brilliance, but his mysticism was both contagious and in a sense damning to perceptions of natural history. The florid nature of his language could not but encourage serious scientists to dismiss more and more of natural history as being too vague and too philosophical to be worthy of attention.

During the final years of Thoreau's all-too-brief career, New England was the scene of a major campaign in the nineteenth-century war over science in general and Darwinism in particular. This war was at times remarkably bitter, and it played out at both a local and a national scale. Thoreau surely was affected by the images of squabbling academicians, and some of his ambivalence about science may be explained by the bitterness and, at times, pettiness of this campaign. For someone wishing simply to understand the plants and animals around him, the degree of meanness displayed by people whom one was supposed to look up to would have been decidedly off-putting.

To understand the nature of the evolution debate in nineteenth-century America, we have to go back in time, and take something of a detour into the lives of its most important participants: Asa Gray, whom we have already met in passing, and Louis Agassiz (1807–73).[15] We know that Thoreau was familiar with the work of both men, and he periodically cites particular pieces by each in his own writing. As Thoreau's interest in botany and zoology increased, he likely was exposed to the fallout of the debate between the schools of thought represented by the two men, and particularly during the last few years of his life, as he became aware of Darwinian concepts of change, he must have been drawn to examine in more detail the differences of opinion that led to so much bitterness.

Agassiz is one of the most complex people in this whole story. In many respects he defies classification. Personally and professionally he was a hero and a knave, a brilliant scientist, and yet also someone who was blinded by his religious faith. He was a wonderful lecturer and teacher, yet he could be remarkably cruel to his immediate family; he was an original thinker, but one who also openly stole from his students.

He was born in Switzerland and grew up in an environment of high mountains sheathed in snow and ice, so it is perhaps no wonder that he was intrigued by the interactions of ice and rock throughout his career. Agassiz' greatest lasting intellectual contribution to science is probably the notion of ice ages. He also was trained in zoology, however, and in many respects it is his teaching and enthusiasm for zoological topics that he might have thought of as his legacy.[16] He obtained his PhD in 1829 from the University of Munich with a dissertation on Brazilian fish, which he dedicated to Georges Cuvier, and a subsequent volume on fossil fish, which was justly celebrated as a groundbreaking piece of work.[17] In 1830, Agassiz received his MD and traveled to Paris to study with Cuvier, who had doubtless been flattered by the book dedication. There Agassiz also met Humboldt, who, as mentioned in an earlier chapter, supported him in his studies and also helped him stay in Paris after Cuvier's death.

It seems likely that Agassiz' time in Paris gave him the first taste of high society, which would become an important element of his later years. Contact with Humboldt also ensured the advance of his career. At that moment in history, Prussia had significant sway over much of Switzerland. Humboldt, as we saw earlier, was on excellent terms with the king of Prussia, and through this connection Agassiz was able to secure a professorship at the University of Neuchâtel in 1832. He soon came to be regarded as a brilliant lecturer and innovative teacher. He formed a natural history club, and encouraged students and townspeople to actively engage in fieldwork. At the same time, Agassiz also married his first wife, Cécile Braun, daughter of a German postmaster-general and geologist and herself a talented artist who drew the plates for several of Agassiz' early books.[18]

Agassiz continued to work on fossil fish, work that quickly drew the attention of Adam Sedgwick and Charles Lyell in Britain, as well as praise from Humboldt. Although Sedgwick was impressed with Agassiz' fish, he was less so with some of his geology, writing Lyell in September 1835: "Agassiz joined us at Dublin, and read a long paper at our section. But what think you? Instead of teaching us what we wanted to know, and giving us of the overflowing of his abundant icthyological wealth, he read a long stupid hypothetical dissertation on geology, drawn from the depths of his ignorance."[19]

In describing his fossilized fish, Agassiz developed a new system of classification based on structures commonly preserved in the process of petrification. From the first, it seems that Agassiz' deep-seated Protestantism played a distinct role in the development of his scientific concepts.[20] He seems to have had little, if any, doubt as to the idea of Creation, and he structured his taxonomy—and indeed much of his thought—on the idea of the immutability of species. Within this assumption, species had been explicitly introduced by a Creator, had flourished for a period of time, and then disappeared, leaving no connection to modern forms. Over time, the ice age that he had first described in the Swiss Alps assumed an increasingly global dimension in his mind, and it marked a clear break between the fossilized forms of the past and modern plants and animals. In this sense, Agassiz was a consistent "catastrophist" for his entire career—the geological and biological histories of the world consisted of distinct moments of creation, dispersal, and then abrupt termination under universal ice, after which a new Creation started things over again.

Agassiz' attitude about the relationship between religion and science is very different from what we see in the work of Gilbert White. At first blush, one might assume that White, as an ordained cleric, would be much more concerned about using study of the Creation to illustrate the intent and nature of the Creator. Unlike Agassiz, White seems to have been perfectly comfortable simply recording his information, speculating on ideas of migration or hibernation, and living a life of science comfortably alongside, but in many respects separate from, his duties as a curate. Agassiz' more explicit (and more confrontational) mingling of religion and science harkened back to John Ray's attempt to reconcile natural history with theology.

Neither Agassiz nor Sedgwick was a biblical literalist in the sense that he believed that every word in the Bible was unquestionable truth—both had seen enough geological evidence to abandon any literal "six days of Creation," and they were also convinced of a vastly greater antiquity of the earth than was accepted by fundamentalists. It was in their biology, rather than their geology, that they most immediately conflicted with Darwin. Sedgwick's abandonment of catastrophism and his support of Lyell's more gradual and developmental approach to geology certainly helped the rise of Darwinian thought.

Soon after their marriage, Louis and Cécile began visiting Jean de Charpentier, a well-known Swiss geologist who lived in the Alps near Bex.[21] De Charpentier had spent a great deal of time examining the glacial moraines and erratic boulders moved by high alpine glaciers, and had come to the conclusion that at some point in the past there had been more extensive glaciation than presently existed. An engineering friend, Ignatz Venetz, had confirmed and elaborated on these ideas—he had seen signs of glacial carving on rocks at quite low elevations. Agassiz was intrigued with the concept, and in 1837, at the annual meeting of the Natural History Club of Neuchâtel, he gave a presidential address in which he outlined a theory of universal glaciation. Sedgwick responded cautiously but favorably to initial reports, but he pointed out that whereas Darwin had seen plenty of evidence of glacial action in the higher latitudes of South America, he had seen none in the tropics of Brazil.

Agassiz' visit to Britain in 1835 gave him access to large collections of fossil fish around which he could build his zoological reputation. At home, Agassiz' time at Neuchâtel was marred in part by increasing feuds with erstwhile collaborators, including de Charpentier, who felt that they had received insufficient credit for their contributions to ideas that Agassiz publicized. Some of these accusations were overblown or downright false, but they suggested what was to become a lifelong issue: Agassiz liked to be the lead dog in any pack. Agassiz' obsession with his work, and his insistence on spending large amounts of money on illustrations for his books, also led to estrangement from his wife. Cécile felt increasingly uncomfortable in Switzerland. She had most of the responsibility for raising the couple's three children, and her health began to collapse. She had contracted tuberculosis, and the infection was gradually killing her.

In 1845, Agassiz arranged to tour the eastern United States for a combination of lecturing and studies in geology under the patronage of the king of Prussia. Through his connections with Lyell, Agassiz arranged an invitation to the Lowell Institute in Boston, where he was to deliver a series of lectures, "The Plan of Creation as Shown in the Animal Kingdom," as well as lectures on ichthyology and embryology. In Europe, Agassiz would always have to contend with long-standing institutions of science. In America, he would have the opportunity to shape the very structure of science itself.

Agassiz' arrival in the United States was greeted with great enthusiasm. The American public was impressed with his looks, his humor, his intelligence, and his dynamic lecturing style. His lectures sold out, and Agassiz was asked to repeat each one the following day in order to satisfy the demand for tickets. Agassiz, in turn, was thrilled with America. His sponsor, John Amory Lowell, was a wealthy mill owner who devoted a substantial portion of his fortune to supporting the sciences. Luring Agassiz to America was a major coup, and he made sure that his guest was treated to any comforts he might demand. As soon as the Lowell lecture series had been completed, additional offers poured in, including a request for a series on natural history.[22]

In 1847, Agassiz was offered a newly created professorship in geology at Harvard, in spite of the position's original focus on purely practical hard-rock geology, and he turned his back on Europe once and for all. The new position was a perfect springboard for general studies in natural history once it had been rewritten to allow Agassiz to pursue further work on glaciation, marine biology, ichthyology, and classification. Agassiz at last had a secure financial and political base from which, he felt, he could create an American science that could equal or surpass anything that Europe had to offer.

Whether Thoreau actually attended Agassiz' public lectures I do not know—he would have been in the middle of his Walden experiment at the time—but he was certainly aware of the new academic superstar who had arrived on the Harvard scene. In his first year at Walden Pond, Thoreau volunteered to collect specimens of fish and reptiles for Agassiz, sending him at least two snapping turtles. Agassiz' emphasis on field trips probably would have been very appealing to at least some parts of Thoreau's philosophy, but his increasing emphasis on quantification, measurement, and specimen collecting would have been repugnant to the free spirit in Thoreau. The two met at Emerson's for dinner in March 1857, but the terse entry in the *Journals* does not suggest any great liking or agreement.[23]

Agassiz loved an audience, and his audiences loved him.[24] Part of this adoration came from his somewhat unconventional style of teaching: he enjoyed lecturing, but he also believed in direct observation and illustration of whatever was under discussion. He started taking large parties into the field, both in the immediate vicinity of Cambridge and farther afield to the Great Lakes and Cape Cod (later, his summer courses in marine biology at Penikese Island would be generally credited with playing a major role in the genesis of the Woods Hole Oceanographic Research Center). Thoreau would have enjoyed the destinations of the field trips, but the idea of traveling as part of a large "eco-tour" would have been anathema to his solitary method of study. Thoreau might have contributed to Agassiz' collections, and he read some of what Agassiz wrote, but philosophically and ideologically there was a significant gap between them.

Agassiz' personal life was also more complex than Thoreau's. Thoreau never married and never had children. Agassiz had essentially abandoned his family, including his dying wife, to come to America. Cécile died in 1848, and Agassiz almost at once began seriously courting Elizabeth Cabot Cary, the daughter of a wealthy Bostonian and cousin to the Cabots—one of the most prominent families in New England. The couple married in April 1850, less than two years after Cécile's death. The children were soon brought over from Switzerland, and Agassiz continued his ascent in Boston society.

What Agassiz really wanted was a lasting memorial to his type of natural history. This monument was to take two forms, the first the Museum of Comparative Zoology (MCZ) at Harvard, and the second the National Academy of Sciences, the members of which Agassiz felt uniquely capable of selecting. With his general popularity, social connections, and widespread recognition as a leading scientist of his age, Agassiz must have felt certain that both goals were easily within his grasp.

The MCZ is arguably one of the great museums of North America, and unlike the Museum of Vertebrate Zoology, which we discuss in the next chapter, it has from an early age catered to both the research community and the general public. For both functions, we have Agassiz to thank. Ever mindful of the need to keep his audiences happy, Agassiz made a point of ensuring that the MCZ was supported by both the state of Massachusetts and by the elite of Boston as a teaching and research institution. Much of the latter half of Agassiz' life was devoted to securing funding

FIGURE 19. Victorian couple examining the skeleton of a mastodon, from Louis Agassiz, *An Introduction to the Study of Natural History*, 1847. (Author's collection.)

for "his" museum, and also in developing its collections, which were essential tools for the research that he and his students conducted and also a means to educate the public in natural history. The ordering of the displays was in keeping with Agassiz' philosophy, specifically illustrating the range and logic of created design.[25] There is something remarkably nostalgic in this—John Ray, at the end of his life, probably would have felt very much at home with this display of "the Wisdom of God," but the younger Ray might have been somewhat surprised that so much of the idea had persisted, intact, for over 150 years.

Ironically, work on the museum, dedicated to the fixity of species, was begun in 1859—the same year that Darwin finally published *The Origin of Species*, and a year after Darwin's letter to Asa Gray at Harvard had been read at the Linnean Society to establish the priority of the theory of natural selection. Over time, the MCZ moved into increasingly larger quarters, first to a small wood-frame structure on the Harvard campus, and then to several floors of a new building originally intended for the Engineering Department. One real fear was the collection's vulnerability to fire, and it was with great relief that a dedicated brick building was finally constructed specifically to house the museum collections. This building is no grand palace to natural history in the sense of the Natural History Museum in London or the American Museum of Natural History in New York. The façade is much more workmanlike—almost industrial—but the space inside provides the public with an intimate view of particular specimens, and the behind-the-scenes workrooms and storage areas house an enormous collection of organisms. As recently as 2010, the MCZ resisted the trendy tendency to replace actual specimens with realer-than-life digital simulations. It is an old-time museum, in the best sense of that term, and one feels that Agassiz himself would have no trouble moving around in it.

As noted, the second project that Agassiz developed to ensure his lasting impact on American science was the creation of the National Academy of Sciences. The idea grew out of Agassiz' early exposure to learned bodies in Europe, including the Royal Society in the United Kingdom and the Académie des Sciences in Paris, whose role was to advise their governments on matters relating to scientific study and also to serve as arbiters of scientific debate. If a similar institution could be developed on a national scale in the United States, Agassiz reasoned that whoever controlled the academy would be in a position to direct federal support for research and influence selection of faculty at major universities. In essence, this position would dictate the direction that science would take for the foreseeable future.

The United States already had a number of regional institutions of science. The Academy of Natural Sciences in Philadelphia was the oldest specifically scientific institution, dating to 1812, although it was predated by the American Philosophical Society, which had its start in 1743. Boston had the American Academy of Arts and Sciences, from 1780, and the Natural History Society, founded in 1832. Even California had its Academy of Sciences within a few years of its admission to the Union, but none of these organizations was truly national in scope. The Smithsonian was just getting off the ground, and it was unclear which direction it might take. Agassiz' plans were for a much more impressive and powerful institution than any of these, one that would shape policy in Washington. Initially the need for this sort of organization seemed to be met through the formation of the American Association for the Advancement of Science (AAAS) in 1848, but the group was *too* inclusive for the likes of Agassiz. If just about anyone could be a member, where was the power in membership?

The nucleus of an Academy developed among a group of colleagues called the Scientific Lazzaroni, which was formed at the instigation of Agassiz and the engineer Alexander Bache (1806–67), the great-grandson of Benjamin Franklin.[26] Bache had strong connections in Washington, having been appointed head of the United States Coastal Survey—a position that allowed him to provide support for Agassiz and his students in the collection of marine specimens and the examination of coastal geology. The Lazzaroni was an association of friends of Agassiz, originally centered in Boston, but eventually including James Dana at Yale and other influential scientists outside the Boston/Cambridge area. The group met informally starting in 1853.[27] Bache and Agassiz saw the group as a suitable springboard to an independent national institution. With the outbreak of the Civil War, pressure was brought to bear on the federal government to make better use of scientific expertise in the war effort. Agassiz enlisted the support of Massachusetts Senator Henry Wilson, and through him got a bill submitted to Congress authorizing the National Academy.

What followed was an example of Agassiz at his worst. He had come to Washington to take up a post as a trustee of the Smithsonian, and he immediately settled down with Bache and other Lazzaroni and drew up a list of members who met their concept of ideal academicians. They agreed on a list of fifty names, which contained a few people who were not friendly to Agassiz' interests but too prominent to be excluded (including Asa Gray), yet the majority could be counted on to follow where Agassiz and Bache led. The bill itself, which left the organization and future selection of membership entirely in the hands of the academy, was passed on a voice vote without the reading of any of the proposed members, and Lincoln immediately signed it into law. Agassiz had his museum and his academy; it would seem that he was unchallengeable in terms of his position in science.

For much of the 1850s, Thoreau was involved in his own brand of natural history. At the beginning of the decade, he was elected a corresponding member of the Boston Society of Natural History. Nine years later, he was appointed to the Visiting Committee in Natural History at Harvard, which was supposed to review all curricula, and it would, at least on paper, put Thoreau in direct contact with the staff and faculty of the college. He thus had reason to be present in Cambridge at the very moment that Agassiz launched his museum, and as a contributor to Agassiz' collections he may well have had a more than passing interest in it.

It is interesting to note the difference in both content and tone between the very early "Natural History of Massachusetts" (1842) and *Walden* (1854) and *The Succession of Forest Trees* (1860). This last essay is very much in the spirit of what we might call conventional natural history, lacking the high flights of fancy that mark the earlier pieces and containing a great deal of careful observation and thought. David Foster has done an admirable job of setting both the essay within the context of Thoreau's other writing and Thoreau within the rapidly changing landscape around Concord.[28] It is unclear if Thoreau was the first person to use the term *succession* in relation to vegetation change on the landscape, but he does a much better job of discussing the importance of seed dispersal than do many later ecologists with far stricter scientific backgrounds.[29] In the *Succession* essay, when

Thoreau says he "has faith in a seed," he means just that: he is explicitly rejecting metaphor and mysticism for the realities of what he has himself observed in the changing landscape.[30]

Thoreau's health had been failing for some time when he wrote *Succession*, and he died two years later. It is unlikely that Thoreau attended the opening or even visited the MCZ, but he was not tone-deaf to academic politics and likely realized the degree of strain among the science faculty members at Harvard. The Lawrence School of Science, headed by Agassiz, was on a collision course with the Natural History Department, over which the Visiting Committee, with Thoreau as a member, was supposed to cast a watchful eye. The latter was under the direction of the botanist Asa Gray, whom we have already met in relation to Darwin and as a nonparticipant in the Wilkes Expedition. If Thoreau played an active role during the two years that he served as a visitor (and his willingness after the first year to be reappointed for a second term suggests that he did), he would have been exposed to the schism within American science firsthand.

Asa Gray was in many ways the anti-Agassiz. Unlike his flamboyant, self-promoting opponent, Gray tended to be much more reserved and focused on practicing his science, and when he engaged in academic politics, he tended to do so from behind the scenes. Gray was born in upstate New York and, like so many of the natural historians whom we have encountered, was originally trained as a doctor. Early in his career he came under the influence of John Torrey (1796–1873), who had written the *Flora of the Northern and Middle Sections of the United States* and was to become the state botanist for New York.[31] Torrey had also trained as a doctor, but had switched to botany, and he encouraged the young Gray to follow his example. Gray was delighted at the prospect of being mentored, and he spent much of the 1830s either corresponding with Torrey or actively assisting him in his botanical work. Gray also published several papers that favorably impressed Joseph Hooker in Britain and in 1836 finished his own book, *Elements of Botany*.[32]

Harvard had established a chair in natural history in 1805 that originally was intended to cover all branches of the natural sciences, but by 1836 the tenor of academic study had become increasingly focused, and there was growing call for greater attention to be paid to the college Botanical Garden.[33] Just how a position in natural history could be configured to concentrate on one branch of the sciences would take some doing; Gray was hardly qualified to meet the combined needs of botany and zoology. Funding was always tight, and there seemed little possibility that he could settle down and concentrate on any long-term plan of research. In 1838, Gray traveled to Britain and Europe. During a stop at Kew Gardens, he was introduced to Charles Darwin, although neither then realized the importance of the friendship that would eventually spring up between them.

Upon returning to the States, Gray was approached by the organizers of the Wilkes Expedition as a possible expedition botanist. Gray was troubled by the chaos surrounding the expedition's planning and eventually rejected the offer of a place on the scientific team. In hindsight, this was a wise decision: in 1841, the Harvard Corporation finally decided that they wished to fill their chair with a botanist. Had Gray been wandering the Pacific, the position would doubtless have gone to someone else. Instead he was ready and available when Harvard called, and he took up the position that would support his life's work in 1842.

The arrival of Agassiz in 1846 initially seemed a pleasant boost to the reputation of Harvard: it would provide an agreeable and energetic colleague who could address questions of zoology while Gray concentrated on botany. There was certainly more than enough of the latter to keep a serious botanist busy. Expeditions into the trans-Mississippi West were bringing back specimens faster than they could be catalogued, and the return of the Wilkes Expedition, with its large store of Pacific plants, required additional attention. In 1848, the newly married Gray traveled to Washington, D.C., to discuss assuming responsibility for the botanical portion of the Wilkes Expedition's collections. Once there, he negotiated an agreement with the government that would fund his return to Europe to use British and European collections to classify Wilkes's specimens.

Gray's second expedition to Europe was the defining moment in his international reputation. He spent time at Kew, working with the Hookers and meeting Darwin again—by this time, each had realized the importance of the other in the new biology that was developing almost overnight. In Britain he also met Huxley, Owen, and the other stars of Victorian natural history and honed his skills as a taxonomist. Gray and his wife were accepted into the inner social circle of Victorian naturalists, and, unlike Agassiz, Gray had a knack for making lifelong friends who could also be supporters and sounding boards for future work.

Write-up of the botany of the Wilkes Expedition proceeded agonizingly slowly, in large part due to endless disputes with Wilkes about both the form and the substance of any reports (the final volume was not completed until 1873). Gray must have periodically wished he had never taken on the task. The Grays returned to Harvard in 1851 to find Agassiz fully ensconced and already drawing the bulk of attention and funding to zoology and geology rather than botany.

Gray's theological beliefs are worth a brief examination. Like Dana and Agassiz, he had been raised a Protestant, and, unlike Darwin, he remained an openly practicing Christian throughout his life. Gray's *Botany for Young People and Common Schools* begins by quoting Matthew 6:28—"Consider the lilies of the field"—and its first paragraph says, "When Christ himself directs us to consider with attention the plants around us,—to notice how they grow—how varied, how numerous, and how elegant they are . . . we shall surely find it profitable and pleasant to learn the lessons which they teach."[34]

There is something rather touching about this view of Jesus Christ as botanist, and Gray has no difficulties with questions of teleology or ultimate design. Unlike Agassiz, he seems to have had no trouble in regarding much of the biblical account of Creation as at most a metaphor. In a series of lectures given at the Yale School of Theology in 1880, Gray presented what by then must have been a long-thought-out statement of principle: "We may take it to be the accepted idea that the Mosaic books were not handed down to us for our instruction in scientific knowledge, and it is our duty to ground our scientific beliefs upon observation and inference, unmixed with considerations of a different order."[35]

As Keeney has pointed out, much of this is in keeping with the overall tenor of mid-nineteenth-century natural theology.[36] Gray was entirely comfortable with the idea that evolution by natural selection provided a mechanism whereby his assumed Creator worked out the Creation.

Against this relaxed theism, Agassiz' strident rejection of evolution, coupled with the Swiss newcomer's grandstanding and appropriation of funds and funders must have been enormously frustrating. In his quiet way, Gray was at least as ambitious as Agassiz, and a Harvard that had a great zoological museum without equivalent attention to botany was no more acceptable than a Harvard that was seen as opposing the rising theoretical framework of the biological world. Gray and Agassiz's conflict smoldered throughout the late 1850s as each jockeyed for position within the framework of science. Gray seems to have had the advantage of Agassiz in that he was capable of developing and maintaining strong personal friendships without hint of appropriation of ideas or credit, whereas Agassiz constantly sought the limelight.

Agassiz' increasingly personal attacks on Darwinism, and the role of the Lazzaroni in the development of the National Academy, brought the underlying hostility between these two powerful personalities into the open in the early 1860s. Agassiz encouraged any assault on what he saw as the dangerous atheism of Darwinian biology, while Gray responded both in public debate and in an important article in the *Atlantic Monthly* that was later widely circulated in Britain and situated him as one of the foremost defenders of Darwinian ideas.[37]

Gray's *Natural Selection* essay specifically named Agassiz as both a leading opponent of Darwinian ideas and also as a representative of old and outdated ideas in science. Things were eventually patched up, with Agassiz apologizing for some particularly harsh counterstatements, but the tide had turned in favor of Gray and the Darwinians. Agassiz was never able to reconcile his theology with his science, and from the 1860s on his star, which had seemed so ascendant with the foundation of the MCZ, began to wane.

Agassiz had envisioned the MCZ as a "scientific factory" that would not only turn out new ideas and explanations of the natural world, but also train the next generation of scientists, who would go on to populate other universities and dominate institutions such as the National Academy. Unfortunately, his extreme jealousy of his students, and his willingness to not only control their work but also to appropriate their writing and research as his own, lost him any hope of a devoted professional following. In an attempt to jumpstart his reputation, he and his wife convinced the railroad baron Nathaniel Thayer to fund an expedition to Brazil to collect freshwater fish and to determine the degree of glaciation that might have occurred in the tropics.

The result was a semipopular book that was met with disbelief by the scientific community.[38] To the surprise of most of his fellow geologists, Agassiz announced the presence of clear signs of recent ice activity in the Amazon basin. Nobody else could see what he saw, and many questioned how he could claim to have found in a matter of a few months what observers such as Bates and Humboldt had not seen in years of travels in the same region.

In 1864, Gray staged what amounted to a palace coup in the National Academy, ensuring the election of Spencer Baird, the assistant secretary of the Smithsonian, to the academy in spite of Agassiz' strong objections. Gray resigned from the academy shortly thereafter, but he seems to have taken a benign view of the institution, making helpful suggestions about restructuring the organization when stroke incapacitated Agassiz in the 1870s.[39] By this stage, it was clear that the future of biology belonged more to Gray than to Agassiz, and Gray could afford to be magnanimous toward an institution of which he had never entirely approved.

In 1871, Agassiz was offered the use of the Coastal Survey vessel *Hassler* for studies of offshore regions. The Coastal Survey had been his friend Bache's organization, and its surviving Lazzaroni remained friendly to Agassiz as a presumed leader in science. Agassiz jumped at the chance to repeat at least some of Darwin's travels around South America, including a visit to the Galápagos and deep-water dredging—a function at which the steam-powered *Hassler* was intended to excel.

Unfortunately, things failed to work out as he had hoped. The *Hassler* broke down repeatedly, and although Agassiz was able to observe glaciation at the southern tip of South America and early dredging efforts produced many new specimens, he gained no really new insights, and the strain of the voyage further weakened his already precarious health. Agassiz returned to Cambridge overland and slipped into the final year of his life. Increasingly, responsibilities for the MCZ devolved on Agassiz' son Alexander, who expanded on his father's work in marine biology, developing a reputation of his own for careful work in ichthyology and oceanography, as well as building a fortune from mining, part of which he used to ensure the long-term endowment of the MCZ.

After Louis Agassiz' death, in 1873, his critics were free to express their displeasure with his general behavior. Agassiz' role as a popularizer of science weighed against his long-term reputation, and his bad treatment of students and colleagues seems to have provoked at least as much relief as sorrow at his departure. Ernst Haeckel refers to Agassiz as "the most ingenious and most active swindler who ever worked in the field of natural history."[40] This was a brutal and perhaps unnecessary epitaph for someone who had by then already slipped off the central stage of science. Gray, by contrast, continued to flourish, teaching and lecturing to an admiring audience of students and successors, and leaving behind him the Gray Herbarium, certainly as worthy a memorial as Agassiz' museum.

What Thoreau thought of all this we shall, of course, never know. By 1860, it seems unlikely that the increasingly elite and academically oriented scientific community would have welcomed much from an amateur, however well informed—so much had already happened in the few short years since the very amateur Darwin had been welcomed home from the *Beagle*.

The nature of science was changing, with an ever-increasing emphasis on controlled experiments, replicable results, and clearly defined hypotheses. These tools worked very well in the physical and applied sciences, where a controlled environment was almost a given. Yet the same tools were not nearly as applicable to field-based natural history, where sample sizes tended to be small, context became critical and often was hard to replicate, and results were frequently subject to interpretation. Thoreau did a tremendous favor to literary enthusiasts with his soaring prose and often elliptical allusions that at once brought in natural themes and obscured them under layers of metaphor. He also set up a possible cartoon of naturalists as odd eccentrics, back-to-the-landers, people who were more interested in questions of communion than in comprehension and communication. Darwin could still get away with seeing "grandeur in this view of life" because he was, well, Darwin, and besides, he backed up all his points with meticulous volumes of information. Scientists began to lose patience with prose, however, relying increasingly on what was measureable and reducible to mathematics, a form that would increasingly come to be regarded as the true language of science.

Gray could remain comfortably Christian and also a botanist to the end of his life. Huxley applied logic to the issue, shrugged, and coined the term *agnostic*. Their successors increasingly would pass any further discussion of the issue to the humanities and get on with what they regarded as the more important issues of their trade. By the end of the century, as we saw in the opening quotations of this chapter, the whole idea of the naturalist already had fallen out of favor. At the same time, the growing human population was creating a new set of issues for scientists and nonscientists alike. For the first time, humans could comprehend the finite nature of the earth at a truly global scale, and this would require new questions—questions of conservation that certainly would have troubled Thoreau, quietly watching the leaves falling on Walden Pond.

FIFTEEN · From Muir and Alexander to Leopold and Carson

In 1869, the German embryologist Ernst Haeckel (1834–1919) wrote that "the body of knowledge concerning the economy of nature—the investigation of the total relations of the animal both to its inorganic and to its organic environment . . . in a word, ecology is the study of all those complex interrelations referred to by Darwin as the conditions for the struggle for existence. . . . The science of ecology, often inaccurately referred to as 'biology' in a narrow sense, has thus far formed the principal component of what is commonly referred to as 'Natural History.'"[1]

Whether Haeckel was the first person to actually use the term *ecology* (or *oecologia*, from the Greek οικος, or "house") is somewhat beside the point. Haeckel both popularized the term and set it firmly within a historical context, tying it to some of the key people in natural history (Darwin explicitly, Linnaeus implicitly through the invocation of the "economy of nature"). In hindsight, the two most important words in Haeckel's definition are perhaps "thus far," implying a significant change in the offing. Darwin had opened up new vistas for study: if God had not made everything as it was and placed it where it was now found, other agencies of causation must be determined, and the relationships between organisms could no longer be simply assigned to a celestial master plan.

Specialization within natural history had become obvious by the 1840s, with naturalists increasingly identifying themselves by the group of organisms that they studied.[2] The ecological or "zoological" approach to the life sciences was a shift in both emphasis and methodology, as was strongly suggested by Karl Semper in his

1877 series of lectures at the Lowell Institute (the same podium occupied earlier by Asa Gray and Louis Agassiz). I quote Semper at some length in the next few pages, not because what he said was unique, but because he said it more clearly than many others and much earlier than we might expect. In the preface to the published version of the lectures, Semper says: "It was Jaeger who once said—but I forget where—that enough had been done in the way of philosophizing by Darwinists, and that the task that now lay before us was to apply the test of exact investigation to the hypotheses we had laid down."[3]

It is interesting to consider again the terminology. Darwin, Hooker, and their allies all would have said that they engaged in "exact investigation," but Semper goes on to make his meaning quite clear: "Zoologists are very badly off—worse off than any other class of scientific enquirers—for until lately they were simply directed to interpret the facts presented to them by nature, without being in a position to formulate their own problems or to force nature by any critical experiments to give a direct answer to them."[4] Semper implies that henceforth there will be a much greater emphasis on experiment and manipulation—the life sciences must emulate the physical sciences if they are to be considered "science" at all. This imposes an interesting burden—how is one to establish relevant context under laboratory conditions for behavior or physiology that has been selected for in the field?—but this is not something that seems to trouble him.

Perhaps even more interesting is the shift in worldview in the following excerpt: "Although it is certainly true that the various animals inhabiting a country are not so intimately interdependent as the organs of the individual, the relations of the two cases may be very directly compared. The normal numerical proportion, mode of life, and distribution of animals would be altered or destroyed by the extermination of one single animal, just as the whole body suffers, with all its organs, if only one of them is destroyed or injured."[5]

This is enormously interesting, not only because of the change in scale, but also because the entire metaphor of study has been altered. Darwin, Wallace, Hooker, and the like studied *organisms*. Darwin was interested in the origin of species, but the unit of study was the individual, to which other individuals were compared. By contrast, in applying his physiological analogy, Semper advocates an approach that resembles the twentieth-century fixation on communities or ecosystems. Later in the text, he presents what is remarkably like an Eltonian Pyramid in addressing trophic structure. It would take another seventy years, but as Semper does his rough calculations of efficiencies and energy transmission from herbivore to carnivore, one can already see a whole new form of field biology on the horizon.

The last quarter of the nineteenth century also saw profound changes in the relationship between settlers and countryside in the United States. The American Indian had been almost completely dispossessed of the remaining lands of the Mississippi drainage. The buffalo, which had roamed the prairie in the millions and provided an entire way of life for Indian and trapper alike, were reduced to a tiny fragment of their former numbers, more a museum piece than an integral part of any natural landscape. Conservation was doubtless on the minds of many people, but it needed a voice. That voice was on its way.

John Muir (1838–1914) was born in Dunbar, thirty miles southeast of Edinburgh, Scotland, the same town where Ray and Willughby had sat down to a dinner of gannet chicks 170 years earlier. His father was a deeply religious man who insisted that his children memorize large portions of the Bible—Muir later said that he knew the whole of the New Testament and three-quarters of the Old by heart. Donald Worster suggests that this early exposure to a fundamentalist form of what he describes as "left-wing Protestantism" profoundly affected Muir's subsequent views of nature and the roles of humans within that nature.[6] When John was eleven, his father decided that the Scottish Church had become too liberal for his tastes, and he moved the entire family to a farm in Wisconsin.

Muir's own description of his childhood, written at the very end of his life, includes passages that are almost idyllic—the farm, ponies, oxen, cows, and draft horses all, one might think, conspiring to teach him.[7] In spite of this, life was hard on what had been the frontier not long before. Muir's formal schooling had ended when he had left Scotland, and was not to be resumed until a stint at the University of Wisconsin. Everyone in the family was responsible for chores, and free time was hard won: "We always had to work hard, but if we worked still harder we were occasionally allowed a little spell in the long summer evenings about sundown to fish, and on Sundays an hour or two to sail quietly without fishing-rod or gun when the lake was calm. Therefore we gradually learned something about its inhabitants,—pickerel, sunfish, black bass, perch, shiners, pumpkin-seeds, ducks, loons, turtles, muskrats, etc."[8]

John was an avid reader in spite of parental disapproval of anything other than the Scriptures, and he writes of stealing time for himself by getting up at one in the morning to read fiction or to work on his many inventions. Muir seems to have been a natural-born engineer. He taught himself mathematics and invented a variety of clocks, thermometers, and machines, some of which are lovingly illustrated in his autobiography. Because he lacked metal, he hand-carved many parts of these gadgets out of wood, and they ranged in size from small shelf models to enormous constructions mounted on the side of the barn. Muir says with great satisfaction that one of his clocks was still "a good time-keeper" fifty years after he assembled it.[9]

One cannot but admire the image of the young John Muir stealing downstairs at one in the morning after a hard day's work in the field to read by candlelight. Whenever my students tell me that they have no time to read these days, I wonder how they (or I, for that matter) would have fared on that farm on the edge of the Wisconsin woods so long ago. Muir read everything that he could lay his hands on—Shakespeare, Milton, Plutarch, and so forth. It is perhaps no surprise that, like Alfred Wallace, thousands of miles away across the Atlantic, he was fascinated by Mungo Park's stories of travels in Africa and Humboldt's writing on the Amazon and Rio Negro.

One of the most comforting things that I have encountered in writing this book is the sense of connectivity among the people whom we call naturalists. In a way that no longer seems possible in our crowded world, they all seem to have known, or known of, one another. They read the same manuscripts, they asked many of the same questions, they suffered similar hardships, and again and again they reached the same joy. It is as if all their stories are in fact one story with many different chapters and plots, linked together across great expanses of time and space. Muir might not have approved of Michael Scot's religious views, but he would have appreciated his inventions (and vice versa), and both would have enjoyed puttering with Aristotle or arguing with Willughby or Frederick over the flight of hawks.

Between 1860 and 1864, Muir attended the University of Wisconsin. He did not take any regular sequence of courses; rather, he sat in on those that interested him and paid his way with odd jobs ranging from teaching to farmwork. He studied chemistry, geology, and botany as the opportunity arose, and he continued to make inventions, including a bed that tipped him upright when it was time to get up in the morning and a desk that pulled out class books in the correct sequence for prescribed study times. He never actually graduated; instead, as he put it: "I wandered away on a glorious botanical and geological excursion, which has lasted nearly fifty years and is not yet completed, always happy and free, poor or rich, without thought of a diploma or of making a name, urged on and on through endless, inspiring, Godful beauty."[10]

Part of his "wander[ing] away" was done to avoid the draft in the final year of the Civil War. Muir crossed into Canada, where he worked in a mill and explored the woods of Ontario before returning to the United States.[11] In 1867, he suffered what could have been a devastating accident: he was struck in the head by a piece of machinery, and for a while feared that he might go blind. After an extended convalescence, his sight was largely restored, but he left the world of machinery and set off on a botanical ramble through Indiana, Illinois, and home to Wisconsin. Muir had been studying maps of South America for some time before his accident, and he had read Humboldt's *Personal Narrative* closely and wanted to see the jungles of South America for himself.

In the autumn of 1867, he set off on foot for Florida, a journey that he recounted in *A Thousand Mile Walk to the Gulf*.[12] Muir at this point in time can perhaps be best described as a hippy, with all the good and bad associated with that term. Badé tells us, in his introduction to the *Thousand Mile Walk*, that Muir inscribed "John Muir, Earth-planet, Universe" as his address on the inside cover of his journal of the trip.[13] While the middle-aged man in me shudders at this silliness, it is a defining moment. Muir cast aside everything that he had been working toward and set off, not wealthy and well prepared as Darwin or Humboldt were, but essentially with what he could carry, what he had learned at university or through his reading, and an open-hearted attitude, seeming to assume that good would always come of good intentions.

Casual accounts of John Muir's life often want to present him as some sort of eccentric hermit who rejected the company of other humans. In fact, the reverse is more accurate: Muir liked human companionship; he loved to talk as well as to listen; and he had the gift of making and keeping friends wherever he went.[14] This was a good thing, for by the time he reached the Gulf Coast of Florida he had contracted malaria and needed to recuperate for an extended period with newfound friends. He rethought his South America plans and instead took ship for San Francisco. Arriving in California in 1868, he worked odd jobs for a while before finding employment as a shepherd in the Sierra Nevada during the summer of 1869.[15] This was the beginning of a love affair with the Range of Light that would last for the rest of Muir's life and would captivate millions of other people.

The Sierra Nevada in the 1860s and 1870s were no longer the rugged rampart that had almost killed Frémont a few years earlier. The foothills were filling up with ranches, railways and stagecoaches were crisscrossing the state, and an insatiable demand for timber was gnawing at the edges of the great pine and redwood forests. Muir entered the Sierra and found both a spiritual and an intellectual home. He had read Emerson and Thoreau and had been intrigued by their ideas of transcendentalism, but he was also deeply immersed in studies of botany and geology. At the time of his arrival in the Yosemite Sierra, conventional wisdom suggested that the great valleys through the mountains were the result of massive prehistoric earthquakes. Muir had read Agassiz and was familiar with the idea that glacial activity could shape whole landscapes. Everywhere he went in Yosemite, he saw marks of ice on the land. He soon became convinced that the valley itself and its great granite domes were the product of erosion, first by glaciers and then by the ensuing rivers.

Muir was an active correspondent with scientists both on the East Coast and at the newly opened University of California. Letters from Muir were read at the Boston Natural History Society, and his theory of a glacial origin for the valley gradually gained wide acceptance. Long after the fact, an Australian geologist commented: "John Muir's note on glacial action is very fine indeed. . . . John Muir evidently was not understood in his generation, but he will surely come into his own now, and he will become one of the 'Immortals.'"[16]

Unlike Thoreau, Muir kept in touch with the scientific community about his own work and was able to speak in a language that they could understand and appreciate. He constantly walked a fine line between popular writing, abstract expressions of feelings and personal thoughts, and "serious" scientific observation.

Muir was also an enthusiastic botanist, communicating with Asa Gray at Harvard and sending him large quantities of specimens to identify and name. Muir's letters to Gray are hardly technical: "I call your attention to the two large yellow & purple plants from the top of Mt. Lyell above all of the pinched & blinking dwarfs that almost justify Darwin's mean ungodly word 'struggle.' . . . They are the noblest plant-mountaineers I ever saw, climbing above the glaciers into the frosty azure & flowering in purple and gold, rich and abundant as ever responded to the thick creamy sungold of the tropics."[17] These letters reveal a real force of personality and learning to which academics and nonacademics responded. Trees and mountains were far more to him than objects of study; instead he seems to have been constantly in search of a broader and more sublime interpretation than could be found by science alone.

To Muir's intense delight, Emerson came to Yosemite in the summer of 1871 in a party of eastern tourists examining the sights of the New West. Muir arranged a meeting, and the two apparently hit it off from the first, wandering through the valley, talking nature and philosophy together for hours. Much to Muir's disappointment, when he took Emerson to see the giant sequoia, Emerson refused to camp out with him under the stars and appreciate the flickering firelight against the great trunks. In his letter to Emerson, written later, Muir makes mention of a sense of loneliness when the visitors rode away, leaving him with his trees. The two remained correspondents, and one cannot but wonder whether the aging Emerson saw in Muir the Thoreau who had never quite come to be.

Asa Gray and Joseph Hooker came to California in 1877, and Muir took them on a botanizing trip to Mount Shasta. Muir and Hooker had exchanged letters, and Muir had visited Kew Gardens on a visit to Britain, but the relationship with Hooker was much more formal than the one with Asa Gray. It seems clear that their mutual interest was botanical rather than philosophical, and Hooker makes no mention of him in his *Life and Letters*.[18]

Another visitor was Theodore Roosevelt. Muir had been gradually transformed from someone for whom the appreciation and study of nature were all important into an activist who was appalled by the destruction of the great forests and the loss of fragile high alpine meadows to grazing sheep (an irony when we remember that it was this very grazing that had given him his first job in the high country). In 1892, he cofounded the Sierra Club, dedicated to the preservation of the remaining wild areas of the Sierra Nevada. Initially this endeavor had a broad base of support, including Gifford Pinchot, the head of the federal Forest Service, but the two parted ways in 1898. Pinchot went on to represent the idea of conservation of resources for later use, whereas Muir stood for the aesthetic of preservation of what existed.

In this day of vast presidential extravaganzas and armies of Secret Service agents, communications experts, aides, and press handlers, it is hard to imagine the president of the United States slipping off with a single private citizen for a long weekend, but in May 1903, that is exactly what happened. Muir had actually intended to leave California for an extended trip to Europe and the Far East, but he agreed to meet Roosevelt in the Mariposa redwoods. In making his excuses to his traveling companion for the delay of their trip, he wrote: "An influential man from Washington wants to make a trip into the Sierra with me, and I might be able to do some forest good in freely talking around the campfire."[19]

Muir and Roosevelt disappeared into the mountains for four days. What talk transpired around the campfire has not been preserved, but both emerged with a deep affection for each other, and Roosevelt became an ally, supporting Muir's campaign for preservation of the high country. By the time Roosevelt left office, the number of national parks had doubled and national forest land had increased by nearly 150 million acres.

John Muir is generally associated with California, and his writings on its mountains are his enduring legacy. He was able to support himself to some extent through publication, but his livelihood was ensured by his marriage in 1878 to

Louisa Strentzel, who owned a small fruit farm in Martinez, just northeast of San Francisco Bay. Louisa must have been a remarkably patient and tolerant woman. Muir never really settled down to domestic life, periodically slipping off to the mountains, sometimes taking one or both of the couple's daughters with him.

Besides his California treks, Muir went to Alaska on several occasions; one trip was sponsored by the railroad magnate Edward Harriman.[20] Harriman had made a vast fortune by cornering a sizable portion of transcontinental rail traffic, and he saw the expedition as an act of patronage that would demonstrate his status as a supporter of the sciences and also provide an entertaining family vacation. The scientific team included Robert Ridgway, the curator of birds at the Smithsonian; William Trelease, director of the Missouri Botanical Gardens; William Ritter, the president of the California Academy of Sciences; and C. Hart Merriam, the director of the U.S. Biological Survey, among nearly two dozen luminaries. The arts were represented by Louis Agassiz Fuertes, whose bird paintings had already made him famous, and by the photographer Edward S. Curtis, who is best known for his exhaustive and moving documentation of American Indians at the close of the frontier period.

The logistics of the expedition were about as different from Muir's earlier wanderings as can be imagined. The party traveled aboard a luxuriously reappointed steamship with plenty of crew and supplies—a far cry from Muir's solitary strolls with a loaf of bread and a bag of tea. The expedition proceeded up the coast of British Columbia and Alaska, stopping periodically to admire the glacial scenery, to botanize, and, to Muir's discomfort, to collect totem poles and other artifacts from abandoned Native villages. These trips led to a number of books and publications, ranging as always from professional geological and botanical works to more popular accounts.

Muir was always a firm believer in bringing notice of wild places to a broad audience—it was a key element of his campaign for preservation. As he aged, his desire to travel only strengthened. In 1903–04, he took off on a "Grand Tour," starting in Europe, crossing Russia via the Trans-Siberian Railway, and visiting Manchuria and Shanghai before doubling back to Egypt. From there he sailed to India, Ceylon (Sri Lanka), and Australia, where he spent some time enjoying the native eucalyptus (by then imported as a familiar exotic in California). He then went on to New Zealand, where he spent six weeks, visiting the hot springs at Rotorua and the lower slopes of Mount Cook on the South Island.[21] Muir loved the Southern Alps, but he was horrified by the rate of deforestation that he witnessed on both the North and South Islands—a degree of human impact that only brought home the similar effects occurring in his adopted California.

In 1911–12, Muir finally got the chance to complete the original goal of his "thousand-mile walk to the Gulf" when he visited South America.[22] This was a truly remarkable journey, involving a series of long sea voyages as well as treks across country. Muir visited the Amazon Basin before heading south to Argentina, Chile, and Uruguay, where a request for a "few brief remarks" to an audience of expatriates turned into a two-hour soliloquy. He then booked ship for south and east Africa, pausing in Tenerife beneath the great peak that Humboldt had climbed a century earlier, before returning to California late in 1912 to resume his battle for the conservation of the High Sierra.

Unfortunately for Muir, his last battle resulted in his greatest defeat. Yosemite itself had been preserved (although its increasing popularity destroyed much of the quiet that he so treasured), but the neighboring Hetch Hetchy Valley was the target of developers anxious to harness the flow of the Tuolumne River. In 1906, after the great fire and earthquake that had leveled much of San Francisco, the push for development gained ground. Muir and the Sierra Club launched a determined campaign to preserve the canyon, but in 1913, Woodrow Wilson signed authorization for the O'Shaughnessy Dam into law. Muir died the following year, one feels of a broken heart.

I have hiked in Hetch Hetchy Valley by the still waters that have built up behind the great dam that flooded Muir's river. I did so with mixed feelings. The valley is still majestic, though it would perhaps be doubly so with a wild river at its heart. It was also quiet in a way that I have never known Yosemite to be except perhaps in the depths of winter. At least then (I am writing of more than thirty years ago), Hetch Hetchy seemed to have been forgotten by the millions of tourists who pour every year into Yosemite and fill the air with the smoke of their campfires and the smog of their autos. There were no RVs or loud stereos, no interpretive tours or tourist mementos, just the mountains and the water. During at least that one backpacking trip, I felt that perhaps I had touched something of the mountains that Muir had felt, and for all my sorrow at what the dam had drowned, I was grateful that it had left me that great silence.

In spite of the increasing shift in what might be considered science, natural history continued to be practiced in the waning days of the nineteenth century. Other patrons besides Harriman were interested in sponsoring the collection and display of natural artifacts, and national governments continued to demand assessments of the wealth of newly acquired territories. In the United States, the Biological Survey under C. Hart Merriam continued and expanded upon the work done by the Railroad Surveys of midcentury. Merriam was born in New

York City in 1855 and studied anatomy and medicine at Yale and Columbia universities. In the late 1880s, the federal government created the Biological Survey within the Department of Agriculture as a complementary organization to the U.S. Geological Survey, and Merriam served as its director between 1885 and 1911.

Merriam was something of a polymath—in some respects, he was more representative of naturalists at the beginning of the nineteenth century than of those at its close. He published widely on birds and mammals and was also intrigued with anthropology, studying the cultures and religious practices of American Indians in the West.[23] His bibliography lists over five hundred articles, notes, books, and reviews published between 1873 and 1934, most of which are in ornithology or mammalogy, but they also include forays into paleontology, herpetology, and history.[24] Merriam is probably best remembered for his biogeographic work, which divides North America into a series of "life zones" based on climate and elevation in a manner very similar to that begun by Humboldt at the start of the century.[25]

Natural history was something of a family business to the Merriams. C. Hart's sister Florence Merriam Bailey (1863–1948) was in many respects a pioneer of ornithology.[26] Florence was born in upstate New York and appears to have been interested in the outdoors from a young age. She was accepted to Smith College as a "special student" because of her lack of high school preparation, and although she spent four years there, she left without being awarded a degree. During her time at Smith, she became actively involved in ornithology and bird protection, writing articles for the new *Audubon Magazine* that she eventually collected into her first book.[27] Sometime in her twenties, Florence contracted tuberculosis, and, as was the custom in the nineteenth century, she was sent to the West Coast, where it was hoped that the dry air of California and Arizona would cure her. This trip allowed her to attend classes at Stanford University and to observe the bird life of California and the Southwest, the subject of her later books. Among these was *Birds of Village and Field: A Bird Book for Beginners*, which is one of the first "popular" bird guides to North American birds and contains illustrations by Louis Agassiz Fuertes (who accompanied Muir and C. Hart Merriam on the Harriman Expedition), Ernest Seton Thompson (the well-known popular writer also known as Ernest Thompson Seton), and John Ridgway.[28]

Bailey's involvement with professional ornithology increased steadily over time, with additional books adding to her reputation. Her *Handbook of Birds of the Western United States*, also illustrated by Louis Agassiz Fuertes, is much more technical than her field guide and is organized taxonomically rather than by bird color.[29] Her intended audience had clearly shifted from the general public to serious ornithologists, but some of Bailey's humor and enthusiasm still shine through in her descriptions. The book also contains basic instructions on specimen collecting, an overview of her brother's system of life zones, and a species list for the birds of Pasadena by one Joseph Grinnell, of whom we soon will hear more. Florence's work was honored by the American Ornithological Union, which made her a fellow in 1929 and awarded her the Brewster Medal in 1931—the first woman to be so honored.

Natural history still had a powerful following in academia, as evidenced by the remarkable team of Annie Montague Alexander, Louise Kellogg (about whom see below), and Grinnell, who had a profound impact on the natural history of the western United States, and whose legacy is detailed in the final chapter of this book. Alexander (1867–1950) was born in Hawaii, the granddaughter of missionaries.[30] Annie's father, Samuel, was born in a grass hut on the island of Kaua'i, but the family relocated to Maui, where Annie's grandfather became headmaster of a mission school.[31] While there, Samuel met Henry Baldwin, the son of another missionary, and the two became fast friends, business partners, and eventually brothers-in-law. The friends' company, Alexander & Baldwin Inc., eventually controlled much of the shipping and sugar cane industries of Hawaii, and Annie grew up outside Honolulu in an atmosphere of carefree wealth and privilege.

It is dangerous to guess how one would react to one's heroes or heroines if one were to meet them in the flesh, but the overwhelming impression that biographers have left us of the young Annie Alexander is that she was *fun*. In an era when, as my grandmother put it, children were "seen and not heard" and young ladies were expected to show a high degree of decorum, Annie preferred to enter her upstairs bedroom through the window rather than bothering to use the stairs. She and her father enjoyed the out-of-doors, and she seems to have taken every opportunity to explore the then relatively unpopulated island of Maui. When her uncle offered her seventy-five cents an avocado plant if she put her botanizing skills to practical use, she showed up with a wheelbarrow full of a hundred plants.

When Annie was fifteen, her father decided that the climate of Hawaii was bad for his health, and the family moved to Oakland, California, joining a neighborhood that already contained the novelist Jack London; Julia Morgan, California's leading architect; and Jane and Peder Sather, who were instrumental in the development and expansion of the University of California in neighboring Berkeley. Another U.C. connection was the family of Charles Kellogg, whose cousin Martin was professor of Latin and Greek and would be president of the university between 1890 and 1899.

Annie attended Oakland public schools for the next four years before being sent to Massachusetts to study at the Lasell Seminary for Young Women. In 1889, Samuel Alexander took his family on a leisurely tour of Europe. When the rest of the family returned to America, Annie remained behind, studying art at the Sorbonne. An unexplained eye condition required her to abandon drawing, and she returned to Oakland to work out what she would do with her life.

During the next several years, Alexander traveled extensively, both with her father in Britain and on the continent and with her brother in Asia and south to New Zealand. The prospect of blindness was a constant concern, and Annie had a series of operations that seem to have preserved her distance vision at some cost to close-up observation. In 1899, Annie and her friend Martha Beckwith made an expedition into southern Oregon, getting as far north as Crater Lake. The pair botanized, observed birds, and talked natural history throughout the trip. Annie thoroughly enjoyed roughing it in what was then still quite wild country. Beckwith was intrigued with paleontology and encouraged Alexander to audit classes in the subject at Berkeley.

By good fortune, John C. Merriam (a cousin of C. Hart and Florence Merriam) was teaching classes in vertebrate paleontology. Annie was fascinated by the material and soon began collecting fossils on her own and also sponsored expeditions by Merriam to rich fossil beds in southern Oregon. Whenever possible, Annie spent time in the field. The social mores of the day made it impossible for a young woman to travel either alone or as the only woman in a company of men, even when she was paying all the bills, so Annie recruited other women to accompany her on these trips. Alexander proved to have an excellent eye for fossils, locating a number of ichthyosaur specimens on journeys to Shasta County in Northern California.

In 1904, Annie and her father went on safari in British East Africa (modern Kenya). After arriving in Mombasa by sea, they took the train inland to Nairobi. From there they trekked more than eight hundred miles, accompanied by porters and beaters, with both father and daughter hunting large mammals and Annie building on her camera skills by photographing plants and wildlife. Unfortunately, as they began their return journey, the pair decided to stop at Victoria Falls on the Zambezi. A falling rock crushed Samuel's left leg and side, and he died the following day. Annie buried her father in Africa and proceeded to Cape Town, where she took ship to Britain and home to the United States.

Integral to what followed was a meeting between Alexander and C. Hart Merriam. Merriam was keen on obtaining additional specimens for the Biological

Survey from the West Coast and Alaska. The California Academy of Sciences, in San Francisco, was notoriously reluctant to lend specimens to other research institutions—and personal examination of specimens was an essential element in taxonomic research. With Merriam's encouragement, Annie began to develop a plan for a West Coast museum of vertebrate biology.

In seeking out potential collaborators, she encountered Joseph Grinnell (1877–1939), then a doctoral student at Stanford, Berkeley's long-time rival.[32] Grinnell had been born in Oklahoma, but his family had moved to California when he was still young, and he had already launched into what would become his lifelong task—collecting and preserving as many specimens of California vertebrates as possible.

Grinnell had visited Alaska on several occasions, including a two-year stint in 1898–99 during which he had snowshoed over a thousand miles in search of specimens, and he had a number of suggestions for suitable collecting sites and desirable specimens.[33] Grinnell's hallmarks were intensive, detailed notetaking and a near-obsessive attention to field technique. He had assembled a remarkable private collection of birds and small mammals, but he lacked the necessary resources to really apply his skills on an appropriate scale. Alexander and Grinnell seem to have immediately sensed their shared enthusiasm, and Grinnell followed up their meeting with a long letter giving additional detailed suggestions for fieldwork in Alaska. Alexander responded by inviting him to visit her in Oakland when she returned from her expedition.

The 1907 field season was a success, even though Alexander had to leave partway through for a family emergency. Before her departure, Annie and her team explored Admiralty Island, just southwest of Juneau, Alaska, as well as a number of other sites along the Chatham Strait. Field conditions were rugged—snow lasted well into the season—and base camp consisted of six tents, three used for sleeping, one set aside as a field lab for specimen preparation, one the cookhouse, and one a supply shed.[34] From this camp, the collectors ventured out to collect a broad range of bird and mammal specimens, including a number of birds' eggs.

Upon her return to the San Francisco Bay Area, Alexander began serious discussions with Grinnell on a future museum of natural history. A major issue at the outset was the actual location of any new museum. Neither Grinnell nor Alexander wanted anything to do with the California Academy of Sciences (whose original building had been destroyed in the 1906 earthquake and fire). Grinnell was anxious to have the new museum housed at Stanford, and wrote to Alexander about all the advantages of a Palo Alto base for the work. Alexander, however, had other plans. She had no connection with Stanford and was concerned that if the museum were located on its campus, she would always feel like an outsider there. She also had no interest in simply being a benefactress who then backed off and let other people have all the fun. She fully intended to be part of whatever research the museum did.

Alexander was willing to guarantee at least seven years of funding for the museum, as well as to donate her personal collection, which by now included over three thousand specimens of vertebrates. When combined with the specimens already under the care of the U.C. Department of Zoology, the new museum would have an excellent start. Furthermore, the destruction of the California Academy had left a major gap in collections of California fauna. After a series of negotiations throughout 1907 and 1908, the University of California agreed to accept Alexander's plan. The museum, initially called the California Museum of Vertebrate Zoology (MVZ), began to take form in Berkeley, with Joseph Grinnell as its first director and Annie Alexander as the force to be reckoned with.

Alexander clearly believed in doing her homework. Before any actual installation was begun in the new museum, she visited the Smithsonian and consulted with C. Hart Merriam (her letters suggest that she had little time for any of the other Smithsonian personnel), and she sent Grinnell back East to tour the major natural history museums for ideas and techniques. Initially there was some thought of a public display area, and some lifelike mounts were even prepared, but Alexander was primarily interested in research, and money spent on dioramas could be better spent on new field expeditions. For most of the twentieth century, the MVZ remained something of a secret gem, known to serious students of vertebrate biology but a mystery to the general public.

Louise Kellogg (1879–1967) was born in Oakland, near the house that Annie Alexander and her family had moved to after leaving Hawaii.[35] Louise was thirteen years younger than Alexander, and it is unlikely that their paths crossed in a meaningful way as each grew up. Louise went to U.C. Berkeley and graduated in 1901 with a degree in classics. Her father was an avid outdoorsman, and Louise learned to hunt and fish in the marshes surrounding San Francisco Bay.

When Alexander returned to Alaska in 1908, she needed a female companion. From the perspective of the early twenty-first century, one can only marvel at a world in which it was acceptable for a woman to travel into the wild to hunt bears but unacceptable for her to travel as a sole woman in the company of men. Such, however, was the world of Alexander and Kellogg, and it was indeed a happy accident that they ran into each other at this important moment. The Alaska trip was a great success, both in terms of collecting and in the formation of a partnership that would last the rest of Annie's life. Kellogg was a crack shot, enjoyed the out-of-doors, and, as one of the other members of the expedition put it in a letter to Grinnell: "Miss Kellogg is apparently the right sort, without any yellow streak or quitting propensities."[36] One could hope for no more generous opinion among this tough crew of serious field biologists.

In 1911, Kellogg and Alexander bought a farm in Suisun Bay, California, initially to raise cattle, but later converting it to vegetable production. For forty years they continued to collect fossils, mammals, and, after Grinnell's death in 1939, plant specimens for the university herbarium. Kellogg continued work in the field after Annie's death, and made her final field expedition to Baja California at the age of eighty.

The relationship of these three remarkable people—Grinnell, Kellogg, and Alexander—was complementary to a level somewhat hard to imagine. Kellogg's presence allowed Alexander the freedom to be in the field. Both were avid collectors, extremely knowledgeable of both the fossil and current fauna of California (Alexander also began an endowment at the Paleontology Department at U.C. Berkeley in 1911 and later supported the creation of the Paleontology Museum, which, long after her death, was moved to be housed in the same building as the MVZ). Neither Kellogg nor Alexander seems to have wanted to publish their work; much of that was left up to Grinnell. Alexander in particular seems to have liked to remain quietly behind the scenes, with minimal publicity. It was only with great reluctance that she allowed a portrait to be made of her for the museum, and then on the condition that it not be displayed there until after her death. She was, however, very much involved both in the day-to-day operations of the museum and in actively obtaining specimens. Alexander and Kellogg obtained over 30,000 specimens for the museum. Grinnell collected approximately 20,000 birds and mammals, as well as writing a remarkable 3,005 pages of detailed field notes between 1908 and his death.[37]

One of the deep and abiding hallmarks of the MVZ was the attention paid to carefully documenting every specimen contained within its collections. Grinnell developed a detailed system both of notetaking and cataloguing everything that was obtained on an expedition. Both he and Alexander felt that field time was too precious ever to be wasted, and that the maximum amount of information must be obtained from every venture into the wild. Part of the reason for this was a mutual concern that many of the species that they observed might soon become extinct. Interestingly, one of the few publications to bear Alexander's name is a comment on the passenger pigeon after its extinction.[38] Kellogg published a total of six papers, including the second refereed paper authored by a woman.[39]

The MVZ grew rapidly, earning a favorable commendation from C. Hart Merriam in 1914.[40] Besides holding a comprehensive collection of specimens for California and other western states, the museum became an important teaching institution, training generations of field biologists in techniques of organismal biology. Grinnell's students went on to establish what amounts to a dynasty of ecologists, each of whom retained a strong sense of natural history in his or her working style. As late as the 1970s, "Zoology 107: Vertebrate Natural History" retained many elements of the courses that Grinnell had taught his students, and those of us lucky enough to take the class with Grinnell's "grand-student" Ned Johnson were exposed to something of the romance of the early days of the "house that Joe and Annie built." Even then, legends of Grinnell persisted: Grinnell, during his work on the birds of California, pursued a bird over the crest of the Sierra in an early automobile, and then slammed on the brakes as the desired specimen crossed into Nevada and no longer qualified as a bird of California.

Grinnell was the first of the three to die, succumbing to a stroke at the age of sixty-two. With him passed a link to an entire era. He had been born in what was then Indian territory (his parents had introduced him to Red Cloud before the family moved to California). By the time he died, the frontier had long been closed, and the great age of natural history was passing. He was succeeded by his student Alden H. Miller, who in turn was responsible for ecologists and taxonomists including Starker Leopold (son of Aldo Leopold, whom we will discuss soon); Ned K. Johnson, who was to become an expert on one of the most difficult groups of North American birds, the *Empidonax* flycatchers; Robert Bowman, who would spend far more time in the Galápagos studying its finches than Darwin ever did; and Frank Pitelka, expert on everything from hummingbirds to Arctic shorebirds and mammals. Alexander went next, in 1950, leaving only Kellogg as a living witness to the enterprise for which the three had been responsible. By the time of her death, in the mid-1960s, field biology had changed out of all recognition.

As the American frontier closed, there was an enormous outpouring of longing and sentimentality for both the wildness and the wilderness that had seemed such an inherent part of the birth of the United States. Much of this longing (as well as a great deal of sentimentality) was captured by writers such as Ernest Thompson Seton (1860–1946), who enthralled generations of increasingly city-bound children with books such as *Lives of the Hunted* and *Wild Animals I Have Known*.[41] These books, filled with charming illustrations, were told using the animals involved both as central characters and as moral illustrations. In his preface to *Lives of the Hunted*, Thompson Seton makes it clear that some of his stories are based on composite observations of several animals while others are about a single individual, but he asserts that everything he writes is "true." This claim of truth infuriated many natural historians, who objected to the liberties that Thompson Seton and other authors were taking with actual animal behavior. They feared—quite rightly—that the excesses of fiction would lead to a much more general dismissal of natural history as being unscientific at the very time that nature writing was capturing the popular imagination.

One of the most outspoken critics of the entire genre was the naturalist John Burroughs, who used the term "nature-fakers" to dismiss what he saw as both excessive anthropomorphizing and outright fantasy being presented as true natural history.[42] Burroughs enlisted Theodore Roosevelt to join the attack. Roosevelt, who had long regarded himself as something of an amateur naturalist as well as a hunter, responded to the request with an article entitled "Nature Fakers," in which he attacks claims of intelligent, individualized behavior by wild animals.[43] The result was a series of savage back-and-forth denunciations and rebuttals that probably did little to hurt sales, but doubtlessly damaged the overall perception of natural history within the academic community.

In contrast to Ernest Thompson Seton, Aldo Leopold (1887–1948) was the sort of scientist who was able to walk on both sides of the divide between popular and academic writing. Leopold was born in the Flint Hills of Iowa to a family of German immigrants, and German remained his language until he began to attend public schools.[44] His parents were first cousins, and the families rode the wave of prosperity as the frontier moved west and faded. Aldo spent as much time as possible in the woods and fields surrounding Burlington, Iowa, where the extended family of Leopolds and Starkers (Aldo's mother's family) had settled, but he was also an excellent student, graduating at the top of his high school class. His childhood reading included Thoreau, Jack London, and Thompson Seton, and doubtless these authors had an impact on his love for the outdoors, but he took his natural history seriously, collecting copious notes on the species that he saw.

Gifford Pinchot, John Muir's great opponent in the battle between conservationists and preservationists, had founded the School of Forestry at Yale University in 1900, with the goal of preparing a new generation of foresters capable of managing timber resources better than had their forebears. Leopold was determined to attend Yale, and at the age of seventeen he traveled to New Jersey to attend college preparatory courses at the Lawrenceville School.

Then as now, the Yale School of Forestry was a graduate program, so Leopold had to attend the Sheffield Scientific School before he could enroll in it. Coursework at Sheffield included surveying, hydraulics, and plant taxonomy. Leopold spent the summer before his senior year at forestry camp in Pennsylvania, learning silviculture, timber cruising, and harvesting techniques. Leopold graduated in 1908 and immediately enrolled in the School of Forestry. There Leopold was an avid cartographer and student of science, but he also read Milton's *Paradise Lost*.[45] Later in life, his most important essay on conservation would begin with a reference to Homer rather than to any scientist, and end with a quote from the poet Edwin Arlington Robinson.

Leopold joined the Forest Service in 1909 and was sent to work in Arizona and New Mexico. By 1910, the National Forest system contained over 200 million acres—land that required survey and management by Pinchot's new generation of professionals. As assistant forester, Leopold's job was in part to scout the area for suitable timber to harvest. He was new on the job and also new to responsibility for a team of workers in the field. His first expedition reads like a chapter of accidents, but it was during this trip that he had an encounter that would become iconic within the environmental movement.[46] While scouting along rimrock, Leopold and one of his companions startled a female wolf with her pups. Leopold describes what happened next: "In a second we were pumping lead into the pack, but with more excitement than accuracy; how to aim a steep downhill shot is always confusing. . . . We reached the old wolf in time to watch a fierce green fire dying in her eyes."[47]

The image and the language are both compelling and haunting and have been echoed in countless book titles, websites, articles, and talks. The story of the wolf illustrates both sides of Leopold's personality—note the technical comment about "how to aim a . . . shot" and then the poetic imagery of the "fierce green fire." Leopold in the Southwest was, as he himself puts it, "young, and full of trigger-itch." He was also gaining a great deal of first-hand knowledge about a broad range of organisms as well as on-the-job training in how to lead a group of people—training that would be invaluable when he became a professor with graduate students. Throughout his career, his writing would mix the technical expertise that kept him clear of charges of nature-faking with a hint of romanticism that at times bordered on Ernest Thompson Seton's.

Leopold spent the next fifteen years in the Southwest, rising steadily through the Forest Service and publishing a number of papers on various aspects of forestry and wildlife management. He also married Estella Bergere, the daughter of a prominent New Mexico family. Estella seems to have been the perfect spouse for Leopold, raising the couple's five children and dealing with Leopold's extended absences in the field and postings to often remote locations.

Leopold's approach to science was very much in keeping with the transition from strictly qualitative natural history to increasingly quantitative ecology. Hints of this are found in "Resolutions of a Ranger," a satirical poem that Leopold contributed to a largely forgotten collection in 1919. Among the "Resolutions" we find:

> 7. I will count all the cones of the trees, and the full measure thereof will I report as the Seed-Crop. Yea though the D.F. command me to collect an thousand pounds and mine hair be made gray and full of pitch, so will I report.[48]

All satire aside, Leopold was developing a science of range management that would appear in many of his professional publications over the rest of his career. He was an astute observer of the land and its contents, but the new emphasis was on counting organisms and modeling why there were more of some things and less of others.

The Kaibab Plateau, in northern Arizona, had been declared a game reserve by Theodore Roosevelt in 1906. Hunting of ungulates was eliminated and a stringent program of predator elimination was instituted. What happened next, and why, has been debated ever since. While in Arizona and New Mexico, Leopold had actively participated in predator control and had encouraged partnerships between livestock owners and the federal government in developing strategies to limit or eliminate predators from many areas.[49] When the Kaibab deer herd was reported to have crashed from overpopulation and overgrazing, Leopold concluded that the elimination of natural control in the form of nonhuman predators had caused a presumed the explosion in deer numbers, and consequent destruction of vegetation.[50] The role of prior human predation does not seem to have been considered.

In both his professional and popular writings, Leopold turns against predator elimination as a suitable form of management, although he was still willing to advocate a bounty on wolves in certain situations as late as the 1940s (interestingly, Meine points out in his biography of Leopold that it was a group led by Joseph Grinnell that first raised serious issue with the federal policy of predator management).[51] In 1929, Leopold began a series of lectures at the University of Wisconsin, Madison, on the subject of game management. His relationship with the university gradually built over the next three years into a professorship in the Department of Agricultural Economics.

During the transition period between the Forest Service and professorship, Leopold had done a variety of consulting jobs and had worked on his major technical text, *Game Management*.[52] In its preface, Leopold stakes out his territory very clearly: "We of the industrial age boast of our control over nature. Plant or animal, star or atom, wind or river—there is no force in earth or sky which we will not shortly harness to build 'the good life' for ourselves. But what is the good life? Is all this glut of power to be used for only bread-and-butter ends? Man cannot live by bread, or Fords, alone."[53]

This book, which once and for all established Leopold as a leading figure in applied ecology, was heavily influenced by a fortunate encounter with the British ecologist Charles Elton, who had been drawing on the records of the Hudson's Bay Company naturalists to map out long-term changes in game populations in the far north. Elton and Leopold seem to have shared both a desire to apply their work and a focus on bringing natural history approaches into line with more contemporary ideas of science.

In his remarkably prescient (and readable) text *Animal Ecology*, Elton presents an interesting definition: "Ecology is a new name for a very old subject. It simply means scientific natural history."[54] But he also comments on the problem of natural history in modern biology:

> The discoveries of Darwin, himself a magnificent field naturalist, had the remarkable effect of sending the whole zoological world flocking indoors, where they remained for fifty years or more, and whence they are now beginning to put forth cautious heads again into the open air. But the open air feels very cold, and it has become such a normal proceeding for a zoologist to take up either a morphological or physiological problem that he finds it a rather disconcerting and disturbing experience to go out of doors and study animals in their natural conditions.[55]

Elton went on to create a most remarkable collection of students, who were not particularly concerned with the coldness of the air or whatever else was needed to study animals in natural conditions.

Leopold must have felt an immediate kinship with someone who could express so clearly a deep sense of what it meant to be an ecologist, yet was firmly fixated on the development of scientific natural history. At the University of Wisconsin,

Leopold would develop his own collection of bright young graduate students (not to mention his own children, each of whom would contribute to our understanding of the out-of-doors). He also had something to say directly about the conflict between natural history and other aspects of science:

> Unfortunately the living animal is virtually eliminated from the present system of zoological education. . . . The reason for this eviction of outdoor studies from the schools goes back into history. Laboratory biology came into existence at about the time when amateur natural history was of the dickey-bird variety, and when professional natural history consisted of labeling species and amassing facts about food habits without interpreting them. In short, a growing and vital laboratory technique was at that time placed in competition with a stagnated outdoor technique.[56]

To Leopold, direct contact with the out-of-doors in an extended and intimate sense was a key element not only of hunting, but also of a form of personal growth and development. The articulation of this philosophy was a lifetime task, but one gets a sense of his goals in the very first line of his *Sand County Almanac:* "There are some who can live without wild things, and some who cannot. These essays are the delights and dilemmas of one who cannot."[57] Leopold's experiences in the forests of the Southwest stuck with him all his life. In a very Thoreauvian sense, he saw in wildness the preservation of an important inner world that was of infinite value.

The twentieth century was marked by a remarkable abundance of writers on nature, some of whom were scientists and some of whom picked and chose pieces of science to reinforce particular ideas. Rachel Carson (1907–64) was born in Springdale, Pennsylvania, far from the sea that she came to love. Springdale is located along the Allegheny River, and Carson was born with the sounds of the river in her background. As with so many of the natural historians whom we have examined, Carson's encounter with the natural world began early, in the form of tutoring in natural history by her mother and long, solitary walks in the surrounding countryside.[58] Her biographer, Linda Lear, cites a potentially apocryphal story that Carson's love of the sea began when she found a fossil shell on one of these walks. Carson was determined to be a writer, and she submitted her first published story to a children's magazine at the age of eleven. The Carson family was rich in land, owning a sizeable tract of farmland on the outskirts of town, but they were poor in terms of actual cash, and this kept Rachel from leaving for boarding school, as many other academically motivated children in Springdale did when they reached high school age. Instead she stayed on, tutored in part by her mother, continuing to write and read at a level probably well beyond that of her peers.

In 1925, Carson finally left to attend the Pennsylvania College for Women (now Chatham College). Although this marked a break from her roots, she never entirely left her family behind—her mother visited her on most weekends and remained a dominant force in Carson's life until she died only six years before Rachel's own death.[59] Carson did well in school, getting freshman honors her first year, and she took her first biology class as a sophomore, already recognized by her teachers and peers as someone to watch academically. In her junior year, Carson changed her major to biology—in this she was fortunate, as the biology professor, Mary Skinker, believed in taking her classes on field trips rather than simply lecturing to them indoors.

Unfortunately for Carson, Skinker left the college at the end of the 1928 academic year to finish a doctorate at Johns Hopkins. Carson applied to follow her mentor and was accepted to the graduate program, but was unable to afford the transfer. Skinker remained in touch, and it seems likely that her excited letters from the Marine Biological Lab at Woods Hole (the descendant of Louis Agassiz' summer program on nearby Penikese Island) further encouraged Carson's interest in saltwater. In 1929, Carson herself attended the lab and finally got a real taste of the sea. The next year, she entered the master's program at Johns Hopkins, graduating in 1932 after writing her thesis on fish development. Although Rachel hoped to go on for a PhD, this became impossible after her father's death in 1935. Instead she took a job with the federal government, working as a professional writer for the Bureau of Fisheries.

At the bureau, Carson had both the time and the incentive to write extensively about marine life and the environment for a broad range of popular magazines. In 1941, she published her first (and to my mind, most appealing) book, *Under the Sea Wind*.[60] This book, told from the point of view of various creatures along an unnamed coast (but clearly that of Maine/New England), runs the risk of charges of nature fakery, and one can almost hear Teddy Roosevelt or John Burroughs harrumphing in the distance. Fortunately both were dead, and although the book did not sell well, it remains a classic, capturing the two chief traits of Carson's writing: a beautiful poetical style and a careful attention to real detail. Throughout her career, Carson always did her homework, as my mentor Bill Drury was wont to say. In some senses, Carson's characters Rhynchops, the skimmer, and Scomber, the mackerel (she used the technical generic names for her characters), are reminiscent of Thompson Seton's animal characters, but Carson was careful never to let imagined personality get in the way of actual fact.

Carson rose steadily in the U.S. Fish and Wildlife Service (as the Bureau of Fisheries had become known), and by 1949 she was chief editor, responsible for overseeing service publications. She had also been at work on her second book, the more technical *The Sea around Us*, which was published in 1951 and became a runaway bestseller.[61] Its success allowed Carson to resign from the Fish and Wildlife Service and take up writing full-time. Her third and final strictly "marine" book, *The Edge of the Sea*, was published in 1955.[62] Carson had been concerned about the effects of pollution for some time, and she began work on a book, tentatively titled *Man against the Earth*, that would address issues of persistent pesticides, including DDT, that were being applied in greater and greater quantities on a global scale.[63]

Again, Carson's writing is characterized by careful homework. Her time with the government, and her experience as a lab researcher, allowed her to address the complex issues of toxicity and dosage, but it was her skill as a writer and her deep understanding of natural history that carried the book—renamed *Silent Spring*—to iconic status.[64] Beginning with quotes from Keats, E.B. White, and Albert Schweitzer, Carson then launches into her unforgettable first lines, reminiscent of Dylan Thomas: "There was once a town in the heart of America where all life seemed to live in harmony with its surroundings. . . . Then foxes barked in the hills and deer silently crossed the fields, half hidden in the mists of the fall morning."[65] This idyllic picture of all the best of her childhood home is swiftly shattered by the poisons that have been broadcast over the landscape. Even for people who do not read the rest of the book, chapter 1 of *Silent Spring* is a potent enough "fable for tomorrow" to sound a clear call to action.

The book was greeted with fury from the chemical industry and growing support from environmentalists. Carson was repeatedly called to Washington to testify on toxins; she became both a lightning rod for every fear that industry had about conservation and a symbol for conservation itself. Sadly, she was not to live long enough to see most of the environmental reforms of the late 1960s and 1970s. She died of cancer in 1964, leaving behind her a legacy of quiet activism and opposition to the poisoning and industrialization of the landscape.

SIXTEEN · The Slow Death (and Resurrection) of Natural History

The transition between field and lab science as a dominant feature in twentieth-century American biology has been discussed in depth by Robert Kohler.[1] His thesis is that the important shift from more traditional natural history to contemporary ecology occurred sometime in the 1930s, with an increasing emphasis on quantitative methodology, hypothesis testing, and attempts at what were referred to as natural experiments. Kohler's examples are compelling, and I agree with his labeling of many forms of study in field biology as "border practices" in the broader scheme of biology. As I discussed in the previous chapter, however, the conflicts and alliances along this border started almost at the moment that *ecology* came into the scientific lexicon.

The development of statistics and quantitative field methodologies allowed ecologists to recapture a degree of legitimacy in the eyes of their lab-based brethren, although these techniques also led to a new set of concerns. Done properly, statistical analysis can push a scientist into formalizing what is often—at least initially—little more than an informed guess. Statistics also allows the detection of patterns that might otherwise escape a less quantified examination. The trouble with statistical analysis, as with any theoretical debate, lies both in its assumptions and in its ability to dictate the form in which research is conducted and what constitutes a successful outcome.[2]

Statistical analyses tend to cluster around forms of means separation. That is to say, the focus in many studies is drawn to some average value of a particular parameter and the determination of whether this average differs significantly from another average. The fact that statistical significance might not be equivalent to biological significance often gets lost in the conversation. The emphasis on central tendencies may also encourage a researcher to discount extremes. Natural historians have often been drawn to outliers, and it is from these outliers that many interesting insights have come. An average value may be an artifact of calculation, shown by no actual organism in no actual environment; an extreme value, on the other hand, is exhibited by at least one individual in one actual environment.

Rachel Carson's death, in 1964, marked an important turning point in both ecology and natural history. Carson had been trained as a scientist, but her love of words had drawn her to a more popular venue for publication than journal articles. The success of *Silent Spring* and the rediscovery of Leopold's *Sand County Almanac* spurred a raft of variants and imitators. Suddenly everyone seemed to be buying used-up farms and writing about them, or finding the latest environmental outrage upon which to base a horrifying fable for tomorrow. Environmental writers might draw selectively on science, but many had more enthusiasm than background for what had become a Cause, and they increasingly forgot Leopold's injunction against "mutter[ing] darkly about impending doom if people don't mend their ways. The doom is impending, all right; no one can be an ecologist, even an amateur one, without seeing it. But do people mend their ways for fear of calamity? I doubt it. They are more likely to do it out of pure curiosity and interest."[3]

Curiosity and interest are the hallmarks of a naturalist, and one of the most prominent theoretical ecologists of the 1960s, Robert MacArthur, used for his famous dissertation on warblers field techniques largely indistinguishable from those used by many nineteenth-century natural historians.[4] The seeming cleanness of his conclusions swamped any doubts about methodology, and there is something charming in the idea of a scientist timing his subjects by counting to himself, "One one thousand, two one thousand . . . " Variations of the paper went on to illustrate countless textbooks for the next fifty years, but MacArthur himself veered into ever more mathematical treatments of ecology that were rich in idealized curves but deemphasized actual variation.[5]

Britain had several advantages over the United States in the preservation and encouragement of natural history. First, it consists of a much smaller area, and this in turn is broken down into relatively tiny political and geographic units. Thus a naturalist could both become an expert on a particular locality or landscape that would be recognized on a national scale and also travel readily from one end of the country to the other in a short time. Second, the tradition of publication by informed amateurs encouraged talented individuals to make contributions upon which later syntheses could be based.[6] Finally, for some reason, Britons have been enthusiastic naturalists and birdwatchers in proportions far exceeding those in many other countries (the Royal Society for the Protection of Birds has over a million members, in a nation of 60 million; by contrast, the National Audubon Society in the United States has approximately 550,000 members, in a country of 308 million).

According to legend, British natural history in the twentieth century was placed on solid ground by a chance meeting in an air-raid shelter during one of the grimmest periods of the Second World War.[7] In this story, the publisher William ("Billy") Collins ran into ornithologist James Fisher while they were seeking shelter from a bombing raid. Fisher initiated the process by remarking, "What this country needs is a good series of books on natural history." The publisher replied, "Quite right. We will need an editorial board. You see to it and I will provide them with tea and cream buns."[8] Whether this is true or not is beside the point. It *ought* to be true. In any case, some sort of encounter between Fisher and Collins led to the *New Naturalist* series of books, one of the more remarkable publishing ventures of all time.

From the beginning, the *New Naturalist* series set out to present serious natural history in a readable form. The books were written for a sort of educated public by a broad range of enthusiasts and experts. Titles ranged from *Moths* to *The Folklore of Birds* to *Man in Britain*. Some volumes focused on particular areas, others on groups of organisms. One of the most charming is entitled *A Country Parish*.[9] When I first saw the book, I assumed that it was some sort of rehash of White's *Selborne*. Happily, it is no such thing. The author is clearly aware of White, but he presents his own parish with a strong emphasis on the people and customs of his day. He lived in the parish for thirty years, and knows it intimately. There are descriptions of buildings, village customs and superstitions, folklore, and place names. Only in the second half does he turn exclusively to the nonhuman landscape, with in-depth accounts of local birds, mammals, and vegetation.

I grew up in houses with various volumes of *The New Naturalist* series stuck away on shelves. It was not until I had the opportunity to revisit Britain several times that I realized how important the series could be in introducing one to a broad spectrum of ideas in natural history. This realization was confirmed years later when I read the collected works of my greatest hero in what I had regarded as purely theoretical or abstract biology, W. D. Hamilton.[10] Hamilton formalized many of the most interesting ideas in behavioral ecology and evolution in a series of papers written from the 1960s through the '90s, and I had always regarded him as an armchair biologist, albeit one with an uncanny understanding of the ways of real creatures. Much to my surprise, I found that he had written a glowing review of the first fifty volumes in the series and a discussion of how important they had been in his development as a biologist. I can think of no better endorsement of the power of natural history than this testimony from a brilliant theoretician whose imagination had been fired by a book on moths that arrived at just the right moment in his development and led him to explore a vast range of forms and ideas. In the final paragraph of the review, Hamilton says, "Naturalists are used to being disbelieved. Nature is so fantastic that it is true that we could, if we wanted to, get away with almost anything, and most people suppose that we do."[11]

In the United States, natural history remained in college curricula at least into the 1980s, and in some respects there was even an upsurge of interest in ecological concepts in schools. Much of what came to be known as environmental studies, however, was very abstract, with emphases being placed on invisible cycles and energy flows in which organisms were generalized into mechanical elements of food webs and food chains, rather than being worthy of study as individuals.

Part of this trend emerged from a genuine desire to achieve a greater societal relevancy in the face of severe pollution and growing loss of species, but there was also a pragmatic element to the change. Increasing fears of litigation, costs, and suburban sprawl made field trips ever more difficult, and teachers retreated into classroom-based studies. In addition, the very nature of what constituted teaching in general science changed as teachers grew more concerned about maintaining control within teaching spaces. Arthur Tansley said in 1923: "Every genuine worker in science is an explorer, who is continuously meeting fresh things and fresh situations, to which he has to adapt his material and mental equipment. . . . To the lover of prescribed routine methods with the certainty of 'safe' results the study of ecology is not to be recommended."[12] To a tired high school teacher faced with multiple classes of thirty-plus teenagers, "safe" results were exactly what *was* wanted, and textbook companies were happy to oblige with simplified diagrams, overheads, lesson plans, and computer games.

The small towns that had produced people such as Rachel Carson and Aldo Leopold faded with the twentieth century (Leopold's Burlington reached its peak population in 1960 and has declined ever since), and with them went a certain set of possible experiences likely to resonate with beginning naturalists. It is much easier to become enthralled with frogs if one encounters them by happenstance by oneself in a pond on a walk between here and somewhere else when young than if the first frog one sees is in a video, in a terrarium at school, or pickled in a jar. The importance of these early encounters with the *real* has been a recurrent theme in all the readings and conversations with naturalists that have led up to this book. E. O. Wilson says it very nicely: "A child comes to the edge of deep water with a mind prepared for wonder. . . . Hands-on experience at the crucial time, not systematic knowledge, is what counts in the making of a naturalist."[13] But what if there is no encounter with deep water, or if the encounter comes too late?

Even in rural areas, the notion of what constitutes science has been transformed. I live and teach on an island. The local high school is literally surrounded by a national park. There is also a genetics research facility on the island. My daughter and her friends were given internships to learn modern genetics techniques at the lab. Yet none of her teachers seemed to consider arranging internships for students with park biologists. At one level, I suppose, I should be thrilled that my child is being exposed to cutting-edge techniques, but these techniques will be hopelessly out of date before she graduates from college. How many teenagers who have run gels in high school will ever run them again, and how many of them could distinguish between a downy and a hairy woodpecker if both were on a branch above their heads? Which experience is more likely to present the possibility of a lifetime of enjoyment and learning? Of perhaps more urgency, what proportion of the next generation will ever need to run gels, and what proportion would be useful in an environmental audit of their community?

When I began to write this book, I decided that the best place to start my thinking was at the place where I first conceived of the possibility that I myself might become a naturalist: Annie Alexander's Museum of Vertebrate Zoology. I have already mentioned Grinnell's "Vertebrate Natural History" course at Berkeley, which was my first exposure to field ecology in an academic setting. During the last part of my time at Berkeley, I served as a rather inept volunteer curatorial assistant at the museum, doing jobs that nobody else had time for. Mostly, I tried to keep out of the way and absorb as much as I could from the people and the place itself.

Coming back more than thirty years later, I was not sure what I would find. From the outside, the Life Sciences Building looked very much as I had always remembered it, although the entrances seemed subtly changed. Inside, everything was new. The old building had been gutted and refinished. The Paleontology Museum had been moved into the Life Sciences Building, next to the MVZ, and the central atrium of the building was now dominated by skeletons that I remembered once being entirely elsewhere on campus. Of all the people whom I remembered from my intellectual childhood, only Jim Patton remained to greet me and usher me into the shiny new spaces that were the modern museum.

Patton was exactly the same as I had remembered him, still energetic and enthusiastic, setting off two days later to pursue rodents in the jungles of Southeast Asia, but willing to take time to catch me up on events since my departure. To my dismay, the course in vertebrate natural history had not fared as well with the passage of time. In the 1970s, it had been a two-term course that allowed students to experience what passed for winter and spring in the California hills. We could see the departure of winter migrants from San Francisco Bay and observe mating newts in vernal pools farther inland. The course itself was well populated, in part because it was a requirement for a variety of degrees, including the premed biology program. When Berkeley switched to a semester system, "Vertebrate Natural History" was reduced to a single semester, limiting a student's ability to fully mark the passing seasons. Enrollment numbers were severely reduced by an increase in the number of lab-based electives that could be taken as alternates to the time-intensive field class. Whereas I had been among more than a hundred students taught by three full professors, the class had dwindled to single sections that could be taught by adjuncts.

At the same time that the natural history course was diminished, similar changes were occurring in the more specialized "-ologies." Some were no longer taught; others were taught on a reduced rotation. Weekend field trips to the university's outstations in the Sierra and Coast ranges were reduced or eliminated. Students were no longer required to prepare study skins that, if up to standard, might even have found a place in the museum. Things could have been much worse. The museum still benefited from Annie Alexander's legacy and a tradition of partial separation from the university's enthusiasms and failings. When the university decided to move the cellular and molecular elements of the life sciences to their own complex, money for the museum's transition came in much faster than did funds for the more modern lab-based sciences.

Happily, there are signs that the educational pendulum may be swinging back in favor of natural history. From a low of thirty-five students in 1999, the vertebrate natural history course inched up to sixty-five students in 2011—still well below the numbers of the 1970s, but the trend is good. Faculty remain committed to field experiences for students, including a legendary field trip to Corral Hollow, a tongue of near-desert habitat on the edge of the Livermore weapons lab, to observe owls, bats, and those reptiles bold enough to slither onto road surfaces to absorb the lingering heat of the spring sun.

Patton's own work has demonstrated the importance of long-baseline studies in natural history. In some respects, he has spent his life doing systematics and ecology in ways that would have been immediately understandable to Grinnell and Alexander—careful notetaking, collection of specimens, analysis of morphological traits—but he has also used the most modern techniques of molecular biology to go further in establishing relationships and variations. His most recent studies involve taking Grinnell's notes from a century before and using them as a guide to study the degree of change that has occurred in bird and mammal populations across California. The Grinnell Resurvey Project is an ambitious effort to resample a series of transects studied by MVZ biologists under Grinnell's direction at the beginning of the twentieth century.[14] The project is very much in keeping with Grinnell's overall idea of science: as he said, "After the lapse of many years, possibly a century, the student of the future will have access to the original record of faunal conditions in California."[15] Now the "student[s] of the future" are Grinnell's intellectual great-grandchildren, and, drawing on his notes, sketch maps, and samples, they are able to literally retrace his steps and see what a century of change has done to the fauna of the state.

Some of Patton's and his associates' findings have been expected. Many species of mammals have extended their ranges and/or moved to higher elevations in the Sierra, possible evidence of the impact of climate change on species behavior. If this is so, there is real cause for concern, as some species may literally run out of mountain as temperatures continue to increase. Of equal interest is the fact that other species have not yet shown much sign of change. As Patton says, not only would we be unaware of either the change or lack of change without the careful records from the previous century, we also will be unable to determine why some species are vulnerable and others more robust without a new round of careful observational natural history that will provide additional insights into species behavior and ecology. Lab techniques can tell us a great deal, but in the final analysis, only the observation of the organism in its environment will tell us what we need to know.

One cannot but feel that Alexander and Grinnell would feel vindicated by the Resurvey Project. In the best traditions of everything that they stood for, the results of their work are being combined with modern skill and technology to provide key pieces of the puzzle of changes across the very lands that they knew so well. The project has been so successful that it is being duplicated in other states, although few other areas have the benefit of such a detailed historical record. At the same time, Patton echoes a concern that I have already mentioned: Unless more attention is paid to training the next generation of field ecologists, there may be no opportunity to establish follow-on studies that will be of value to a round of future students.

Natural history's decline in the academic world has lasted for more than a century, but there is evidence that this trend may be changing. When E. O. Wilson chose *Naturalist* as the title of his autobiography, he was both making a clear statement about the importance of natural history in his personal career and making it respectable once more for other scientists to at least take steps toward acknowledging its importance in their own. The lingering controversies around Wilson's stands on sociobiology and biophilia were a two-edged sword: at one level, his celebrity helped highlight the idea that a holistic and aesthetic approach to science was essential, while at another, this idea may have been hurt by association with Wilson's politically sensitive beliefs.

The loss of natural history courses in college curricula has in part been offset by "short courses," workshops, and field days at nature centers and in environmental education programs.[16] While some of these exercises have distinct political or sociological overtones, we must remember Humboldt's commitment to the human condition, which was at least as important to him as that of any of the other organisms he studied, and it is hard to think of any natural historian of the nineteenth or twentieth centuries who was not also a conservationist in some form or other.

The first decade of the twenty-first century saw a growing call for a renewal of the practice of natural history, as an increasing number of authors pointed out the importance of taxonomy and better understanding of life histories and interspecific interactions, including the critical role of multiple species in the modification and transmission of pathogens.[17] Concerns about loss of biodiversity are only heightened when we acknowledge that the great days of classification may be ahead rather than behind us. My colleague Harry Greene of Cornell University recently pointed out to me that the number of known species of frogs has more than doubled since he started teaching herpetology in 1979. Sadly, as our knowledge of herpetological diversity grows, so does our acknowledgment of high rates of amphibian extinction, but we cannot hope to preserve what we cannot identify.

In 2007, a number of natural history enthusiasts, involved in various branches of education, began a series of conversations about the issue of who might ensure that there will indeed be a next generation of naturalists. These conversations eventually coalesced into the Natural History Network, an experiment in coordinating disparate notions of the study of nature. In the spring of 2009, the network decided to stage a "coming-out party" in the form of a paper session on natural history at the annual meeting of the Ecological Society of America (which I attended).

Much to the surprise and delight of participants, the session and its follow-on workshop played to packed audiences. Graduate students got up and said, "Please tell our professors that this is what we went into ecology to be doing." One federal official said later, "Look, you environmentalists have managed to get all these laws passed that require us to do environmental impact statements. I need fieldworkers who can identify snakes and lizards on the ground. All you academics are turning out are labworkers who wouldn't know one herp from another. Do something about it." In all, a great start-up. Since the 2009 meetings, the Ecological Society of America has recognized a natural history section, and the National Science Foundation—long a bastion of conservative lab science—has funded a series of workshops examining the role of natural history in teaching, research, society, and environmental management.[18]

At the same time that the scientific establishment shows signs of, if not embracing, at least nodding toward natural history, technology is opening up opportunities at a level perhaps not seen since the invention of the hand lens or binoculars. Smartphones can now emit bird calls to attract species and act as geolocated cameras to record their presence. Web groups such as I-Naturalist allow the crowd-sourcing of identification, provide a social network in which amateurs and professionals can meet on an equal footing, and may soon provide techniques for data analysis and synthesis. While it is too early to say that we have turned a corner in the revitalization of natural history, the omens are perhaps better than they have been for some time.

In writing this book, I have had the opportunity to read the words and enjoy the pictures produced by some truly remarkable men and women, whose lives and work span at least three millennia. I have encountered many heroes and the occasional villain, and there are few whom I did not wish to meet, and many with whom I would love to share time with in the field. Cultures, languages, and technologies all change; empires have risen and fallen; entire belief systems have flowered and died, but somehow across all this expanse of time, some commonalities exist. There is something remarkably persistent in the joy of seeing a species for the first time. There is a real shared magic in the still moment when one is witness to a particular behavior, or finds the flower unlooked for beside the spring unexpected. Even in my most disheartened moments, I believe that there will always be naturalists and natural history. We have lost a great deal. None of us will ever again experience the "living storm" that Leopold calls the flights of the passenger pigeon (he himself never saw its glory days), but we can still rejoice in what we have, marvel over what our predecessors did and learned, and strive to make sure that our children will have something of wonder to pass on.

This narrative is inevitably but a small and biased portion of the whole story of natural history. If I have done my work aright, some of you readers will go off into the literature and find all sorts of wonderful people who should have been here but whom I missed. Some of you will become (and some of you already are) the wonderful people who will appear in chapters of future histories. Natural history is neither perfect nor complete, but if nothing else, natural historians would have given Job something for his argument with God. Natural historians know full well "the time when the wild goats of the rock bring forth," and they can "mark when the hinds do calve."

For this and for so many other things, men and women have gone out generation after generation, and each has brought back deep things out of darkness.

NOTES

CHAPTER 1. FROM HUNTER-GATHERERS TO KINGS OF KINGS

1. For a parody of this, see Macauley 1979.

2. Williams and Nesse 1991 and references therein.

3. Boone 2002.

4. Penn 2003; see also Kretch 2000 and Martin 1984.

5. Steadman 1989; see also Pimm, Moulton, and Justice 1994.

6. Steadman 1995.

7. Flannery 2002.

8. See Sanchez 1973 for a fictional account of Washoe hunting practices; see also Clemmer 1991.

9. See Waguespack and Surovell 2003 and Surovell and Waguespack in Haynes, 2009 for discussions of diet choice and the debate over specialization or generalization by hunter-gatherers in the Americas. Waguespack 2007 has a nice summary of much of the debate, and Lyman 2006 and Lyman and Wolverton 2002 are just two examples questioning the impact of pre-European hunting on mammal populations in the United States. Grayson 2001 (which includes rebuttals by John Alroy, and rebuttals of rebuttals) firmly rejects the connection between human hunting and Pleistocene extinctions. See also Barnosky, Koch, Feranec, et al. 2006 for a more general discussion that is supportive of anthropogenic causes for extinction but also explores links to climate change.

10. Waguespeck 2005.

11. See, for example, Alvard and Kuznar 2001.

12. Breasted 1920.

13. On goats, see Zeder and Hesse 2000; on sheep, see Pedrosa, Uzun, Arranz, et al. 2005.

14. Beija-Pereira, Caramelli, Lalueza-Fox, et al. 2006. See also Clutton-Brock 1999 for a more general overview of the process and history of domestication.

15. Outram, Stear, Bendrey, et al. 2009.

16. See Waterfield 1963 for a semipopular biography of Austen Henry Layard, the chief excavator of Nineveh. Layard's own books, including *Nineveh and Babylon: A Narrative of a Second Expedition to Assyria during the Years 1848, 1850, and 1851* (Layard 1867), are exciting accounts of travel and adventure as well as descriptions of the actual archaeological sites. See also Smith 2002 [1875].

17. Oppenheim 1965 and Daley 1993.

18. Walker 1888 gives an overview of Asurbanipal's career and contributions. Porter 1993 discusses some earlier aspects of Assyrian agroecology. Dick 2006 has nice illustrations of some of the reliefs in Asurbanipal's palace and a discussion of possible relationships between Assyrian concepts of the world and later biblical texts.

19. Johnston 1901.

CHAPTER 2. A WONDERFUL MAN

1. Darwin quoted in Heather 1939, 244.

2. Darwin's correspondence is being made available through the Darwin Correspondence Project, www.darwinproject.ac.uk/home. In a letter to Crawley dated 1879, Darwin says specifically that he never read Aristotle.

3. Macgillivray 1834, 64.

4. For example, Aristotle 1984 correctly identifies male and female hyenas (*History of Animals* VI: 32), whereas many later authors mistook the enlarged clitoris of the female spotted hyena for a penis and suggested that in hyenas there was no female! I have used *The Complete Works of Aristotle: The Revised Oxford Translation* as my primary source in exploring what Aristotle said rather than just what was said about him.

5. Macgillivray 1834 is a treasure trove of information.

6. Chroust 1967.

7. See Briant 2002 for an overview of Persian history and culture.

8. See French 1994 for a discussion of Aristotle and the pre-Socratics.

9. Cary 1882, 334.

10. Aristotle, *History of Animals* IX: 1, in Aristotle 1984.

11. Aristotle 2004, 249.

12. Hamilton 1965.

13. Macgillivray 1834, 64.

14. Meyer 1992.

15. Aristotle, *Physics* I: 3, in Aristotle 1984.

16. Tinbergen 1963. Tinbergen suggests that a behavior can be explained in terms of an immediate causation, the ontogeny (development) of the organism, the immediate survival value of the behavior, and the evolutionary (phylogenetic) history of the organism. While these four are not absolutely transposable to Aristotle's quartet, they are clearly derived from it, although Tinbergen does not cite Aristotle, either because he felt it unnecessary or because, like Darwin, he may not have read the original.

17. Aristotle, *Parts of Animals* I: 22 and I: 28, in Aristotle 1984, 997: "For it is not enough to say what are the stuffs out of which an animal is formed. . . . For the formal nature is of greater importance than the material nature." Aristotle goes on to point out that a dead body may have the form of a man but is not a man, and therefore the natural historian must study the soul, or whatever leaves the animal at death and renders what was an animal a body.

18. For example, see Aristotle for Nichomachean ethics for love. See *Parts of Animals* III: 4–7, in Aristotle 1984, 1037–40, for livers.

19. Aristotle, *Parts of Animals,* II: 12.

20. Diogenes Laertius 1853, 187, contains accounts written approximately four hundred years after the fact but drawing on sources now unavailable.

21. See Weher, van der Werf, Thompson, et al. 1999 on how these ideas have morphed in recent times.

22. French 1994. See especially the first part of chapter 2 for differences between Aristotle and Theophrastus.

CHAPTER 3. THE SPOILS OF AN EMPIRE

1. Erskine 1995.

2. Delia 1992.

3. See Henrichs 1995 and references therein for a discussion particularly of Cato the Elder's intense dislike of all things Greek.

4. Thiem 1979.

5. Macgillivray 1834.

6. Ibid., 75.

7. Ibid., 77.

8. Nicholson 1886 is somewhat dismissive, but Macgillivray 1834 is downright mean in his assessment of the value of Pliny's work.

9. Letter from Pliny the Younger to Tacitus, quoted at length in Browne 1857, 419.

10. Sarton 1924, 75.

11. Thorndike 1922.

12. Arber 1912.

13. Ibid.; Arber says that some authors have listed Dioscorides as the physician to Antony and Cleopatra, but the tragic pair were dead long before Dioscorides was born.

14. Riddle 1984.

15. Egerton 2001.

16. Galen quoted in Thorndike 1922, 126.

17. Galen 1985, 14.

18. Perry 1977.

19. Thiem cited in Macgillivray 1834.

20. The caliph Omar, accused of the final destruction of the Alexandrine Library, is said to have remarked, in effect, that if the books were in accord with the word of God, there was no need for them, and if they were not in accord with the word of God, they were blasphemous, and again there was no need for them, The story is repeated as recently as Macleod 2004, 10, but this story is now regarded by most scholars as apocryphal.

21. See Walzer 1953, Ivry 2001, and Haskins 1925.

CHAPTER 4. AN EMPEROR AND HIS DESCENDANTS

1. Huxley 2007, 45.

2. Nicholson 1886, 18.

3. Arber 1912.

4. Creasey 1851: an admittedly biased account written at the height of Victorian Britain.

5. See Trompf 1973 and the extensive references therein.

6. Hartwich 1882.

7. Ibid., 527.

8. Lovejoy 1936.

9. Maddock 2001.

10. Baas 1889.

11. See Sacks 1999; for an earlier discussion of Hildegard's symptoms, see Singer 1958.

12. Newman 1985.

13. Kington 1862 is an excellent source on both the emperor and his times. See also the introduction to Wood and Fyfe 1943.

14. Busk 1855, 364.

15. Voltaire 1756, chapter 70, quoted in Gould 1992, 79.

16. Kington 1862.

17. See Haskins 1911, White 1936, and Gabrieli 1964.

18. Kington 1862. Early accounts all seem remarkably high both as to the size of the armies and the casualties suffered.

19. A major source on Scot's life is Brown 1897, which treats Scot specifically as an historical figure. Haskins 1921 rejects much of Brown's chronology, especially his suggestion that the young Frederick was tutored by Scot prior to the latter's time in Toledo. Kington 1862 places the arrival of Scot squarely at the door of Pope Gregory; other authors merely say that Scot joined the court of Frederick at some point in the 1220s.

20. Dante 1871, 1: Canto XX.

21. Haskins 1921.

22. Ibid.

23. I am drawing throughout on Wood and Fyfe's (1943) wonderful edition of *The Art of Falconry*.

24. Wood and Fyfe 1943, 4.

25. See, for instance, Jeffrey 1857.

26. For a version of this story, see Pattingill 1901.

27. Thorndike 1914; on his dabblings in alchemy, see Singer 1932.

28. Lockyer 1873.

29. Thorndike 1916.

30. Stevens 1852; see also Lockyer 1873.

31. Arber 1912.

32. Aiken 1947.

33. Sprague 1933.

34. Lockyer 1873.

35. Thorndike 1923.

36. Sarton 1924 is particularly opposed to this notion. His rather savage review makes many good points, but it is interesting to note that he concludes by stressing the overall value of Thorndike's book.

37. Debus 1978.

38. See Wittkower 1942. The *Buch* was repeatedly republished throughout the fifteenth century. See also Arber 1912.

39. Locy 1921.

CHAPTER 5. NEW WORLDS

1. Diller 1940.

2. Lewis 1999.

3. Perry 1981.

4. See, for example, ibid., figure 3, for a reproduction of Pierre Desceliers's map of the world from 1553.

5. Butzer 1992.

6. Crosby 1986, 146.

7. Rohde 1922.

8. Ollivander and Thomas 2008.

9. Rohde 1922.

10. All quotations from Gerard are from Ollivander and Thomas 2008 unless otherwise noted. Page numbers are cited parenthetically in the text.

11. Lankester 1915.

12. Ibid. Lankester devotes two chapters to the topic of barnacles and geese and cites Sir Robert Moray, the first president of the Royal Society, as supporting the idea of geese coming from barnacles. He also includes a wonderful series of diagrams illustrating how artistic interpretation encouraged the belief.

13. Turner 1903 [1544]. This edition contains a nice introduction to Turner's life.

14. Ibid., 128.

15. Turner quoted in Lee 1899, 364.

16. Macgillivray 1834 is as dismissive of Gesner as he is of most pre-seventeenth-century naturalists, but he gives him several pages, from which much of what follows is drawn. Page numbers are cited parenthetically in the text.

17. Ogilvie 2003.

18. Rohde 1922, 204–14. Rohde also provides us with an annotated bibliography of earlier and later herbals from both the United Kingdom and abroad.

19. Maplet 1930 [1567].

20. Ibid., 149.

21. www.abdn.ac.uk/bestiary/comment/65velep.hti (accessed September 11, 2011).

22. Cronin 1942. Beebee 1944 has a translation of Pliny that closely matches the text in Maplet, and, read in its entirety, it strongly suggests that the "dragons" are in fact some sort of python.

23. Stothers 2004.

24. De Asua and French 2005.

25. Dempsey 2000 [1637].

26. Josselyn 1672. Page numbers for quotes from this source are cited parenthetically in the text.

27. Wood 1634. Page numbers for quotes from this source are cited parenthetically in the text.

CHAPTER 6. RAY, LINNAEUS, AND THE ORDERING OF THE WORLD

1. The book was still in print as recently as 2010 in the form of a high-resolution CD-ROM published by Octavo.

2. Grew 1682.

3. Nicholson 1886.

4. Ray 1660.

5. De Beer 1950. Willughby was elected a fellow in 1661 (the society had received its charter the previous year). Ray was elected a fellow in 1667. It seems possible that Ray's status as a dissenter made him seem initially an unsuitable candidate.

6. Ray quoted in Lankester 1847, 153.

7. Ray quoted in ibid., 155.

8. Ray quoted in ibid., 178.

9. See McMahon 2000 for a very thorough examination of Ray's reasons for refusing to subscribe to the act. Essentially, McMahon argues that Ray was already dissatisfied with the political climate at Cambridge, was fed up with what he saw as a succession of oaths demanded of fellows, and saw the opportunity to travel with Willughby as more attractive and probably more productive than remaining at a Cambridge that seemed to be turning back toward less experimental methodologies in the sciences.

10. Lankester 1847.

11. Lankester 1848.

12. Ray 1673.

13. Willughby quoted in Lankester 1848, 7.

14. Ray 1732, iv.

15. For the former suggestion, see Macgillivray 1834, who seldom spares an opportunity to belittle the work of someone else; his comments, while often insightful, should probably be taken with a grain of salt. For the latter suggestion, see, for instance, Wood 1834, who says that "we find it our duty to say that the amiable and gentle Ray, whatever he might be in Botany, had very little merit as an Ornithologist, the whole of his system, and also the names of birds used in his works, being the production of his friend Willughby" (4). See also Stresemann 1975 for a discussion of Ray and Willughby's contributions.

16. Miall 1912.

17. Willughby 1686. Poor Ray; Sheringham 1902 is by no means alone in attributing the book entirely to Willughby, "with a preface by Ray." The book was nicely illustrated, with the cost of the illustrations paid for by members of the Royal Society. Samuel Pepys, the diarist and also at the time president of the society, was a major contributor.

18. Ray 1686.

19. Ray 1882 [1682].

20. Ray 1686, 1693, 1704.

21. Privately released in 1691, it was republished as Ray 1714. The length of the title is important in and of itself, in that it gives a sense of the scope of Ray's inquiries and his attempts to reconcile dogma with observation. For a review of an earlier edition, see Anonymous 1803.

22. Paley 1813.

23. Werf 1992 provides a review and critique. It is perhaps worth noting that apart

from being one of the foremost ornithologists of the twentieth century, Lack was also a devout Anglican and author of a work (Lack 1957) in which he tries to reconcile his role as a leading Darwinian with his religious faith.

24. Ray 1692.

25. Macgillivray 1834, 165.

26. Birkhead 2010, 79.

27. Macgillivray 1834 devotes the largest part of his text to Linnaeus in a somewhat hagiographic (especially for this usually dour or even snide author) series of chapters. Stoever 1794 is a somewhat oddly anglicized but still informative source.

28. Celsius was the uncle of the astronomer Anders Celsius (1701–44), who invented the Centigrade thermometer. The elder Celsius published an important reference book, the *Hierobotanicum*, that catalogues the plants of the Bible (see Balfour 1885). See also Anonymous 1863.

29. Linnaeus 1811.

30. Ibid., 1.

31. Macgillivray 1834, 216.

32. Gourlie 1953; for the opposing view, see, for instance, Koerner 2001 and Blunt 1971.

33. Linnaeus 1811, 114.

34. Ibid.

35. Farber 2000.

36. Stoever 1794.

37. Dillenius quoted in Brightwell 1858, 8.

38. Details of this as well as Linnaeus's own commentary on his early life can be found in a letter dated September 12, 1739, to Albert Haller (1708–77), a noted scientist and sometime critic of Linnaeus. This letter, along with several others, was published by Haller nearly a quarter of a century later. The publication of what had been a private correspondence caused Linnaeus a great deal of distress, and is credited by some biographers as causing his first stroke. The complete letter is in Macgillivray 1834 and provides some insight into Linnaeus's version of his travels abroad.

39. Robbins 2007.

40. Trotter 1903.

41. Haller quoted in Stoever 1794, 118. Stoever includes fascinating chapters on both the opponents and the defenders of Linnaeus's system, complete with a variety of contemporary quotes that give a sense of the level of debate.

42. Smith 2005.

43. Blunt 1971, 240. Blunt lists the complete treasure trove, which consisted of 19,000 sheets of pressed plants, 1,500 shells, 3,200 insects, 3,000 books, and 3,000 letters.

44. Yoon 2009, 187.

45. Nabokov 2000.

46. Vila, Bell, Macniven, Goldman-Huertas, et al., 2011.

CHAPTER 7. JOURNEYS NEAR AND FAR

1. Schmidt-Loske 2009.

2. See Allen 1937 for much of what follows. All biographers agree that the details of Catesby's life are vague, but Allen does better than most at finding original sources. See also Boulger 1904.

3. Allen 1937, 350, has him baptized in Castle Hedingham in Essex.

4. Ibid.

5. Catesby 1754 [1731], viii.

6. Catesby 1747a, viii.

7. Catesby 1747b.

8. Mabey 2006 is a very nice, concise depiction of both White and his environment.

9. White 1911 [1788].

10. Quoted in Holt-White 1901, 191.

11. May 1999, 1951. May is responsible for much of the theoretical underpinnings that attach chaos theory to population biology. He has also done extensive research in epidemiology and the structure of model ecosystems.

12. See Anonymous 1899. Dadswell 2003 has many interesting insights on White's views on ecology and animal behavior, as well as a number of illustrations including facsimiles of pages from White's notebooks and letters.

13. Timothy survived White by a year and is the subject of a book of her ("he" turned out to have been a "she") own: Warner 1982 [1946]. This is a great "one-stop shopping" source regarding Timothy, and it includes a complete table of tortoise weights, as requested by White's correspondent Daines Barrington.

14. A number of these letters are in the keeping of the Linnean Society of London. White's handwriting is little short of remarkable, clearly legible even more than 250 years later.

15. Two sermons attributed to White are held in trust for the Selborne Society in the archives of the Linnean Society of London. Neither has anything to do with natural history, and one is almost certainly not by White—it is written in an entirely different handwriting and uses the full word "and," whereas the second sermon, in White's remarkably clear script, always abbreviates it to "&." Each sermon includes a list of places and dates where it was read, and it is striking that the first sermon lists dates and places where White was not a curate in a different handwriting, and then it switches to White's handwriting for the last few entries. One can assume that sermons were probably traded among busy curates wishing to minimize their "homework." The second sermon, which *is* entirely in White's hand, is a charming discourse on

the shortest verse in the Bible: John 11:35, "Jesus wept." White builds from these two words an entire picture of Jesus as a very human savior, "with all the passions known to us." Again, this gives us no information on natural history, but it is a wonderful insight into White's own belief structure. He embraces his own humanity with enthusiasm and gusto. One is left with the feeling that here was a genuinely *nice* person with whom one would have liked to spend time.

16. White 1986, 40.

17. Ibid.

18. He later became very enthusiastic about the Linnaean system, writing to his brother John, "I am glad that you begin to relish Linn: There is nothing to be done in the whole boundless field of natural History without system" (letter to J. White, May 16, 1770, archives of Linnean Society of London).

19. White 1986, 192.

20. Ibid.

21. Jardine 1849 contains copies of three letters from Linnaeus to John White, and there is evidence that the two had been writing to each other for some time. Interestingly, Gilbert and Linnaeus do not seem to have corresponded.

22. One of the most fascinating letters to Gilbert White, held in the care of the Linnean Society of London, is a very detailed account of the siege of Québec in 1759, written by a James Gibson, who served on one of the bombarding fleet. The letter starts off on July 8, 1759, and is completed only on September 21, after the city has fallen. While this has nothing to do with natural history, it is a moving account of a major historical event as it is happening, a world away from peaceful Selborne.

23. Pennant 1793.

24. Foster 1986.

25. He was eventually given an honorary degree. Davis 1976 says that Pennant was elected to the Royal Society of Uppsala "at Linnaeus' insistence" (184). It should be noted, however, that in his two-sentence biography in her article, she also says that "he was a correspondent of Gilbert White" (184). One has to wonder which was the greater honor.

See also Pennant 1781. This multivolume series was intended to be an improvement on Ray. Pennant rejects portions of Linnaeus, in part because he feels that Linnaeus's system is too unstable and too frequently undated to be of much use, and in part because he refuses to agree with Linnaeus in placing humans in the same group as other primates. Pennant also published a number of travelogues of trips he had made within the British Isles and various contributions to the *Philosophical Transactions of the Royal Society*.

26. Lysaght 1971, 36.

27. One of Barrington's more intriguing notes is Barrington 1770, in which he

describes meeting and studying the then eight-year-old Mozart. Barrington also wrote on the singing of birds and so forth.

28. Anonymous 1913 describes Pennant as "one of the best known naturalists of his day" (405).

29. Discussion of the actual structure of the notebooks varies among commentators. Greenoak (coeditor of White 1986) says there were nine columns. Foster 1986 says eleven, but reproduces an actual page of the original that has thirteen if you count "Year"—which White also used to record "Date"—and "Place" in the total.

30. *The Journals of Gilbert White* were published in a multivolume series (White 1986).

31. For example, White 1774. It is interesting that Gilbert White never seems to have been considered for membership in the Royal Society. His brother Thomas was elected a fellow: see Benton 1867, which briefly mentions Thomas, who is described as "for many years a Fellow of the Royal Society, and was an excellent classical scholar, botanist, chemist, and electrician, as far as electricity was understood in those days. He contributed materially to his brother the Rev. Gilbert White's natural history of Selborne" (262). Gilbert White himself was periodically in London, had papers read to the society, and seems to have been eminently well connected to become a fellow, but this did not occur.

32. On the hibernation concept, see White 1774. This is not as silly as it seems. When I was young, my mother was involved in wildlife rehabilitation. During a particularly hard freeze one late California winter, dozens of hummingbirds were picked up, inert, having fallen off their perches in the cold. Treatment consisted of putting them in the oven on warm, and in a few minutes they revived and began to fly about.

33. Lowell 1871, 6.

34. White 1986, 286.

35. Smith 1911.

36. Lysaght 1971, 44.

37. Carter 1995 does not believe that Sandwich, then out of power, would have had much sway in getting Banks a berth on *Endeavor* (see later in the chapter) and points out Banks's own energy and initiative in encouraging the voyage.

38. See, for instance, Thomas 2003 and also Anonymous 2008. Complete "secret instructions" for Cook's later voyages can be found in Anonymous 1893, 398–402.

39. Sadly, Parkinson was not to survive the voyage. He contracted dysentery in the East Indies and was buried at sea. His artwork survives and provides interesting insights into Australia at the dawn of colonization.

40. Smith 1911 is inclined to blame everything on the admiralty, but he seems almost incapable of finding fault with Banks at any turn. Lysaght 1971 is less inclined to let Banks off the hook, and indeed it would seem that Banks behaved badly and perhaps had allowed the praise that he had received for his back-to-back successes in Lab-

rador and the circumnavigation to go to his head. Cook seems to have been concerned about being drawn into the fight, and wrote placatory letters once he was underway.

41. The Hellfire Club was essentially a drinking society for the more debauched members of the eighteenth-century aristocracy. It adopted various pseudo-pagan rituals, but these seem to have been more of an excuse for general drunkenness and wenching than any serious revival of early religious beliefs. Needless to say, the popular press had a great deal of fun with the organization, and one suspects that many of its exploits were more rumor than fact. The club lost popularity under the straight-laced rule of George III, but may have staged a bit of a comeback under the more dissolute Prince Regent.

42. Middleton 1925, 193.

43. Darlington 1849, 324.

44. Van Horne and Hoffman 2004.

45. Bartram sent preserved specimens to England, and his letters (Darlington 1849) indicate that he also on occasion sent over live animals, including bullfrogs, which survived their Atlantic passage but were not, as was intended, presented to King George.

46. Quoted in Wilson 1978, 105.

47. Darlington 1849, 340. John Fothergill (1712–80) was a wealthy physician and amateur natural historian from Yorkshire. He got his medical degree in Edinburgh and practiced for most of his life in London. He helped pay for the publication of Sydney Parkinson's memoir of Cook's First Voyage. Fothergill was an insatiable seeker of information on America, and his letters to Bartram would cause most of us to roll our eyes at the long lists of questions and desired samples contained in each.

48. Middleton 1925, 201.

49. Quoted in Van Horne and Hoffman 2004, 107.

50. Middleton 1925, 213.

51. There seems to have been a remarkable degree of amity between botanists on both sides of the war. Among the letters to the Bartrams is one from a "Captain Fraser" in the Guards, dated December 15, 1777, when the British army was occupying Philadelphia. There is no hint of animosity in the letter, just the captain's desire to get to know the family, to see the botanic garden, and, "on quitting this country, to be assured of a fixed correspondence with you, and a certainty of receiving, yearly, assortments of such seeds as I require" (Darlington 1849, 466). Clearly issues about taxation without representation took a back seat to more important things, such as plant specimens.

52. Cashin 2007.

53. Fothergill had earlier written of William to his father, John, "He draws neatly; has a strong relish for Natural History; and it is a pity that such a genius should sink

under distress. Is he sober and diligent?" (quoted in Darlington 1849, 344). Presumably John answered in the affirmative. See also Silver 1978.

54. The full title (see the references) is both instructive and indicative of the need for abbreviation: Bartram 1791. The spelling is original.

55. Gaudio 2001 has some nice reproductions of several of William's pieces, along with a rather peculiar interpretation of his artistic sensibility and vision. One has to wonder if Gaudio has spent much time alone in the outdoors.

56. Darlington 1849.

CHAPTER 8. BEFORE THE ORIGIN

1. Wallace 1889a.

2. Mayr 1982.

3. Huxley 1900, 176.

4. Eiseley 1961 gives some very interesting portraits of many of the important nineteenth-century scientists who surrounded Darwin, as well as a picture of the world they inhabited. Darwin himself is noticeably absent, which may be explained by Eiseley 1979, a very strange little book that basically accuses Darwin of dishonesty in the development of his ideas. I find Eiseley's arguments deeply unconvincing.

5. There are literally bookshelves full of biographies of Darwin (a quick search of an online bookseller in November 2010 produced over two thousand hits, and while many are duplicates or alternate editions, the sheer volume is staggering), and he has also become the central figure in a popular film (*Creation* [Lionsgate, 2009]) as well as the subject of several television series. Without question, the best biography available is Browne 1995 and 2002. Darwin's own *Autobiography* was edited by his wife, Emma, and later his son Francis. Fortunately his granddaughter Nora Barlow republished the book (Darwin 1958) with the pieces Emma deliberately left out reinserted in a different type, so that one can see some of the places where Emma and Charles must have disagreed. Wallace has not been quite so fortunate in his biographers. Yet his own autobiography (Wallace 1905, 1908) is very readable, and Raby 2001 provides some very useful insights into Wallace's overall career.

6. Drury 1998. Drury believes that human thought patterns are conditioned by early experiences, often at a subconscious level. Thus students who come into science via chemistry or physics have a hard time addressing many biological questions, because the way that they were taught to regard what is "scientific," as well as what is not, was "programmed" at a subconscious level by their encounter with the type of questions and answers used in the physical sciences. Ernst Mayr addresses a somewhat similar concern in Mayr 2007.

7. Buffon 1769.

8. Mayr 1982.

9. Ibid., 331. In spite of this criticism, Mayr is a Buffon enthusiast, calling him "the father of all thought in Natural History in the second half of the 18th century" (332).

10. Buffon 1766 quoted in Mayr 1982, 332.

11. Ibid.

12. Stafleu 1971 contains a variety of biographical sources on Lamarck, from which much of what follows is drawn.

13. By one account (ibid., 399), Lamarck was invalided out of the army because a friend had tried to pick him up by the head. The resulting damage to Lamarck's neck muscles made him ineligible for future military service.

14. In one of the most glaring examples of "judicial murder" on record, Antoine Lavoisier, perhaps the greatest chemist of the eighteenth century, was brought before the Tribunal on charges of "incivility" and adulterating the People's tobacco. He was sentenced to death, the assistant judge declaring, "La République n'a pas besoin de savants; il faut que la justice suive son cours" (The Republic has no need of men of science; justice must take its course) (Ramsey 1896, 102). After Lavoisier's head had been struck off, one observer said that it had "required but a moment to strike off this head, and probably a hundred years will not suffice to reproduce such another" (Thorpe 1894, 89). Lamarck seems to have been a much more able political animal than Lavoisier and so escaped the prejudice against educated and potentially aristocratic scientists that dominated some of the worst periods of the Terror.

15. Stafleu 1971, 401.

16. Lamarck 1802, in Stafleu 1971, 419.

17. An interesting discussion of the consequences of Ussher's chronology on biblical scholarship can be found in Numbers 2000. Additional discussion and science-focused attempts to measure the age of the earth are presented in Knopf 1957. That not all natural historians subscribed to Ussher's dating is indicated by the astronomer Edmund Halley's (1656–1742) suggestion, early in the eighteenth century, that the true age of the earth could be obtained by measuring the change in the saltiness of the sea over the course of centuries (Holmes 1913, 61). Given the lack of geological understanding at the time, this was still an interesting idea, and one may sympathize with Halley when he complains that if only the Greeks and Romans had started this project, he would have already possessed valuable predictive information.

18. Lamarck 1801.

19. Lamarck 1783–89 quoted in Stafleu 1971, 433.

20. The classic study on plant plasticity and response to the environment is Clausen, Keck, and Hiesey 1940. This study involved the careful transplantation of clones to "common gardens" in very different environments across California, and measurement of morphological and chromosomal changes in the resulting plants. The authors were able to show that the environment can indeed change morphology within a generation, but that these changes are not heritable in themselves. Darwin himself falls

back on a more Lamarckian element in later editions of *The Origin of Species*. One feels, however, that this was more because of a lack of understanding of a genetic mechanism for particulate inheritance than because of any strong belief in the reality of Lamarck's ides. Molecular genetics has revealed some interesting possible examples of "neo-Lamarckian" processes, but these seem to be rare exceptions rather than anything that can explain the world.

21. The "Preliminary Notice" in Krause 1880 contains a fairly extensive background by Charles on the earlier history of the family, and some delightful family letters.

22. Matthew 8:32. When Jesus casts out a flock of devils, he sends them into a herd of swine, which throw themselves into the sea.

23. Krause 1880, 20. The final sentence is from Isaiah 40:6. It is *very* clear throughout that Erasmus is teasing his sister and that Charles wanted to share the joke.

24. C. Darwin in Krause 1880, 20, 26, 27.

25. Uglow 2002, in her otherwise remarkably readable and informative book, also cites excerpts from this letter and suggests that Erasmus Darwin "panicked" just before his marriage and fussed over the availability of a marriage license. Another reading of the letter suggests the opposite. Erasmus was writing to reassure his young fiancée (she was only seventeen at the time) about their marriage and didn't want to be the subject of gossip or for her to suffer from whatever wild stories locals might want to tell a young bride. The Darwins seem to have married for love and adored their wives and children, feelings that largely were returned.

26. Darwin 1785.

27. Darwin 1806.

28. Darwin 1806, 11.

29. Darwin 1794.

30. Krause 1880, 102.

31. Darwin 1794, ix.

32. Darwin 1804.

33. Krause 1880, 95. Erasmus's poetry was mocked in an anonymous parody, *The Loves of Triangles*, attributed to Canning, Frere, Ellis, and Gifford 1801. Its particularly unpleasant (but admittedly funny) final lines include:

Twas thine alone, O youth of giant frame,
Isosceles! That rebel heart to tame!
In vain coy Mathesis thy presence flies:
Still turn her fond hallucinating eyes;
Thrills with Galvanic fires each tortuous nerve,
Throb her blue veins, and dies her cold reserve. (134)

It ends on an even nastier note, depicting William Pitt the Younger, the Tory prime minister under George III, being guillotined. The parody was sufficiently apt to render Erasmus's writing a source of sniggers for at least a generation.

34. Darwin 1806, 54.

35. Darwin 1804, 3.

36. Hussakof 1916. Erasmus was intrigued with the structure of speech and language. Like the medieval natural historians whom we encountered in earlier chapters, he constructed a brazen head—except that his actually worked, through a mechanical system. According to Charles Darwin, the head was able to say "mama" and "papa" and other simple words. One of Erasmus's friends in the Lunar Society offered him a thousand pounds if he could produce a head capable of reciting the Lord's Prayer. Erasmus never collected (Krause 1880, 121).

37. King-Hele 1998. For a more detailed discussion of the "Lunatics" and their period, see Uglow 2002, who does a wonderful job of capturing both their intellectual and social environment, and their impact on the birth of the Industrial Revolution. See also Schofield 1966.

38. Ten of the other thirteen members of the Lunar Society were or became fellows of the Royal Society.

39. In a sad irony, the Wedgewood sons provided Samuel Coleridge a pension of 150 pounds to free him to write poetry. Coleridge was one of the cruelest critics of Erasmus Darwin's poetry, saying that Erasmus's writing "nauseated" him (Coleridge 1895, vol. 1, 164).

CHAPTER 9. FORMS MOST BEAUTIFUL

1. Darwin 1958. Several editions of *The Autobiography of Charles Darwin 1809–1882* exist, including one titled *Life and Letters* and edited by his son Francis (Darwin 1887).

But Nora Barlow's edition (Darwin 1958) is the only one that contains the complete text as originally written by Darwin for his children; the following quotations from Darwin are from this source unless otherwise noted. Page numbers are cited parenthetically in the text.

2. Perhaps Clarke 1821. Many "wonders"-type books came out in the nineteenth century, but this seems a likely candidate, in terms of both date (1821 was a later American edition) and overall focus. Several of the places Darwin was later to see on the *Beagle* are shown in this work.

3. The Wernerian Society was also founded by Jameson. It was named after the German geologist Abraham Werner, who believed that all sedimentary strata could be explained by a universal primordial ocean, out of which different mineral forms had precipitated. The society seems to have been a "graduate" version of the Plinian Society. It disappeared shortly after Jameson's death.

4. Darwin 1902, 178.

5. See Desmond and Moore 2009 for a recent discussion of Darwin's attitudes on race and slavery.

6. In a memorable moment in Brazil, when Darwin and Robert Fitzroy were debating slavery, Fitzroy called over a slave and asked him if he minded his condition. The slave assured him that he did not, and Fitzroy turned to Darwin for his reaction. Darwin tactlessly said that perhaps the slave would have spoken differently if the overseer weren't standing next to him. Fitzroy was furious and stormed back to the ship, and the two were not on speaking terms for some time afterward. Darwin 1887, 61.

7. Charles Waterton (1782–1865) was a Yorkshire squire who traveled widely in South America, spending time with Indian tribes, from whom he learned the uses of curare and other poisons. He was also an enthusiastic taxidermist, conservationist, and ornithologist. He argued bitterly with Audubon on the role of scent in vultures. There are a number of biographies available; see, for instance, Hobson 1866 for a contemporary (if almost unreadable) volume. More recent biographies exist, but Waterton seems to have attracted eccentrics as well as being one. See also Darwin 1958.

8. Darwin 1985.

9. Browne 2002.

10. He writes, "From reading White's 'Selborne,' I took much pleasure in watching the habits of birds, and even made notes on the subject" (Darwin 1897, 45).

11. Letter from Charles Darwin to Caroline Darwin, April 25–26, 1832, in Darwin 1985, 227. There are similar references scattered through the correspondence.

12. Paley 1813. Interestingly enough, the book is dedicated to Shute Barrington, the bishop of Durham and younger brother of Daines Barrington, Gilbert White's correspondent.

13. Barlow 1967.

14. Francis Darwin notes in the *Autobiography* (Darwin 1958) that when Henslow moved from Cambridge, the gap in the university social and intellectual scene was so severe that it led to the creation of the Cambridge Ray Society, named, of course, after John Ray.

15. Desmond and Moore 1991, v.

16. Barlow 1967, 28.

17. Walters and Stow 2001.

18. Letter from George Peacock to J. S. Henslow, sometime before August 24, 1831, in Barlow 1967, 28. Peacock was a fellow Cambridge don, a friend of Francis Beaufort, the hydrographer to the navy and the inventor of the Beaufort Scale.

19. Letter from J. S. Henslow to C. Darwin, August 24, 1831, in Barlow 1967, 29.

20. Litchfield 1915, 7.

21. Letter from C. Darwin to R. Darwin, August 31, 1831, in Barlow 1967, 34.

The phrasing "all the Wedgewoods" is particularly interesting, knowing as we do that Emma would eventually marry Charles.

22. Letter from J. Wedgewood to R. Darwin, August 31, 1831, in ibid.

23. Parker King 1839.

24. Nichols 2003.

25. Fitzroy's log from May 1829 quoted in Parker King 1839. The weather could change at a moment's notice. In the next entry, Fitzroy talks of it being "fine" and of going swimming in water not "colder than I have felt it in autumn on the English coast" (225).

26. Nichols 2003.

27. Gribbin and Gribbin 2004.

28. She had rendezvoused with the *Adventure* near Cape Horn in April 1829. One cannot but admire the ships and crew of this entire enterprise—deliberately lingering in areas that other mariners fled through as quickly as possible.

29. Letter 16, from C. Darwin to J.S. Henslow, November 15, 1831, in Darwin 1897, 188.

30. A further hint of Fitzroy's insistence on both precision and accuracy can be found in Raper and Fitzroy 1854.

31. This popular nineteenth-century pseudoscience suggested that the precise configuration of the skull and face could provide clues to mental ability and personality. Alfred Russel Wallace was a strong believer, and in his final book, *The Wonderful Century* (Wallace 1899), he lists phrenology as one of the ten things that he expects will be a dominant feature of science in the twentieth century.

32. Letter 9, C. Darwin to J.S. Henslow, in Darwin 1897, 178.

33. Lyell 1831.

34. Railing 1979.

35. Darwin 2009, 43.

36. Ibid., 44. The Bay of Biscay is notorious for its weather. More than 150 years later, the songwriter Gordon Bok—who knew of what he spoke—sang in "Hills of Isle au Haut, "and those Bay of Biscay swells / will roll your head right off your shoulders." Poor Charles Darwin would have known just what he meant.

37. Darwin 2009, 45.

38. Darwin 1845.

39. Ibid., 207.

40. Darwin 1902, 143.

41. Darwin 1985, 220.

42. The notebooks have been transcribed and edited in a remarkable text: see Chancellor and van Wyhe 2009.

43. Ibid, 35. The punctuation and spelling are as in the original.

44. Darwin 2009, 87.

45. Henslow had given Darwin an earlier translation of Humboldt than the one (Humboldt 1852) generally referenced in this book: the earlier one was published between 1814 and 1825 (see van Whye 2011).

46. Darwin 1958. In the *Autobiography*, one gets a sense of tempered sadness as Darwin reflects on his later strained relationship with Fitzroy. Long gone are the days of Fitzroy as his *beau ideal* captain, but one feels that Darwin deeply regrets any hurt that has passed between them.

47. Darwin 2009, 46.

48. Letter from J.S. Henslow to C. Darwin, January 15, 1832, in Darwin 1985, 293.

49. Ibid.

50. He has nothing pleasant to say about the Falklands in his letters home. The islands were then exchanging hands from Argentina to Britain, and several Englishmen recently had been murdered. In a letter to Edward Lamb, dated March 30, 1834, he refers to the islands as "this seat of discord for the elements, as well as for Human affairs" (Darwin 1985, 378).

51. Letter from Charles Darwin to Caroline Darwin, March 30, 1833, in ibid., 302.

52. In the same letter, Darwin writes disapprovingly of the Fuegians as cannibals, saying that a young boy had informed them that the Fuegian men ate the women in winter. When asked why they did not eat their dogs instead, the boy explained, "Dog catch otter." Darwin goes on to comment that Fuegian women "are in small proportion" (ibid., 303).

53. Darwin's journal entry for August 17, 1833, in Rawling 1979, 117.

54. There has been endless speculation about Darwin's illness, ranging from diagnoses of psychosomatic maladies brought on by concern about the later impact of his "heretical" thinking on his wife, Emma, to Chagas' disease. Woodruff 1965 goes over some diagnoses and rejects Chagas' disease on the basis that Darwin exhibited some symptoms of ill health before he went to South America (long before his thinking was other than orthodox). By contrast, Young 1997 favors a diagnosis of lupus.

55. Darwin's journal entry for September 16, 1835, in Darwin 2009, 309.

56. Darwin's note for September 21 (?), 1835, in Chancellor and van Wyhe 2009, 418.

57. Barlow 1963, 262.

58. Darwin 1851.

59. In what can be regarded only as typical Darwin, Charles had prepared a list of the pros and cons of married life, which he left among his other writings. I think it is perhaps the strongest indication imaginable of Emma's feeling for her husband that she did not toss the list into the fire when she was arranging his papers after his death. The delightful internal debate is available as an appendix to Darwin 1958. Among the arguments in favor of marriage are "constant companion, (& friend in old age) who

will feel interested in one—Object to be beloved & played with—better than a dog anyhow. . . . Charms of music & female chit-chat. These things good for one's health, *but terrible loss of time*" (232). Against marriage was (among many others) the fear that "perhaps my wife won't like London; then the sentence is banishment & degradation with indolent, idle fool—" (233). The conclusion of his argument with himself is "marry, marry, marry," and so he did. While Emma must indeed have been "an angel" to put up with his endless illness and to keep him "industrious," he was correct on several points. He never did "go up in a balloon" or visit America or Europe, but one thinks that the overall result was better than he could have possibly imagined (233).

60. Letters from R. Fitzroy to C. Darwin, November 15 and 16, 1837, in Burkhardt and Smith 1986. The original draft of the preface and Darwin's replies, if any, have not been preserved.

61. Raverat 1953.

62. Much has been made of the death of Anne Darwin, her father's acknowledged favorite, in 1851 at the age of ten. Randall Keynes, Darwin's great-great-grandson, wrote a very moving book about the impact of Annie's death on Charles and the family (Keynes 2001). The book served as a basis for a 2009 fictional film, *Creation*.

63. Litchfield 1915, 2: 75.

64. Darwin mentions Gilbert White briefly and somewhat disparagingly in his discussion of the formation of vegetable mold by earthworms (see Darwin 1896). As we know, he had read White early on, and it appears that as with Erasmus Darwin, Charles had no patience with hypothesizing from limited observations.

65. Bell quoted in Browne 2002, 42.

66. Darwin 1859.

67. Litchfield 1915, 2: 253.

68. Darwin 1859, 490.

CHAPTER 10. THE GEOGRAPHY OF NATURE

1. Humboldt 1852, 1: ix.

2. Letter from C. Darwin to A. von Humboldt, November 1, 1839, in Darwin 1986, 240.

3. Schlesier 1853.

4. Humboldt 1852, 1: 1.

5. My father told me a delightful story of the great British archaeologist Sir Arthur Evans, who made the mistake of traveling in the Balkans in the 1870s without a passport. When Sir Arthur attempted to cross one frontier, an official demanded to see his papers. In desperation, Sir Arthur pulled out a five-pound note and handed it over as an intended bribe. The official solemnly turned it over, stamped it, and handed it back. "Of course," my father said, "in those days a five-pound note was really something."

6. Anglo-Spanish relations were often extremely complex. Spain had originally sided with Britain against France, but switched sides after the defeat of the First Coalition. Britain imposed a blockade of the Spanish coast in 1797, seriously inhibiting Spanish contact with and control of its Latin American colonies. This probably led to the heightened suspicion that made the granting of a passport to Humboldt a welcome surprise. The Spanish eventually switched sides again late in the Napoleonic wars, and Britain officially supported her ally while at the same time undermining Spanish control in the Americas—by the time Darwin arrived in South America, many of the old Spanish possessions had achieved independence.

7. Humboldt 1852, 1: 81.

8. Ibid., 1: 88.

9. Ibid., 1: 151.

10. Ibid., 1: 165.

11. Vuilleumier 2003.

12. Griffin 1953 describes echolocation in the oilbird, probably the only example of such in the avian world.

13. Humboldt 1852, 1: 295.

14. Sandwith 1925.

15. Humboldt 1852, 1: 474.

16. Ibid., 2: 133.

17. Ibid., 2: 152.

18. Ibid., 2: 155.

19. Ibid., 2: 184.

20. Ibid., 2: 195.

21. Walls 2009.

22. Humboldt 1852, 2: 213.

23. Ibid., 2: 406.

24. Humboldt 1885, 90.

25. A French naval squadron got through the blockade, and Humboldt arranged for the birds and monkeys from the Orinoco to be sent back to France via Guadeloupe. Sadly, all the animals died on the voyage, and only their skins reached the Jardin des Plantes.

26. Walls 2009 suggests that the later volumes may have been written but were suppressed by Humboldt, perhaps because they contained material of too political or personal a nature. The whole of Spanish South America was about to boil over in revolution, and Humboldt makes it clear that he has no love for authoritarian states, especially if they also permit slaveholding (he is clearly pleased with the revolt in Haiti), and he may have decided that there were too many vulnerable names in his writing.

27. Chimborazo is just over 6,200 meters (20,560 feet) high. By contrast, the summit of Mt. Everest is 8,848 meters (29,029 feet) high. Because Chimborazo sits nearly

on the equator, whereas Everest is significantly farther north, one is farther from the center of the earth on the summit of Chimborazo than anywhere else on the planet.

28. Humboldt and Bonpland 2009 [1807]. Stephen Jackson and Sylvie Romanowski, in this work, have done the English-speaking world an enormous favor by presenting a clear translation accompanied by an interesting and highly informative introduction to the essay. Their beautiful reproduction of the *Tableau physique* makes this text a must-have for biogeographers.

29. Humboldt 1814.

30. A *laisser passer*, or literally "let pass," was a formal letter from a government official asking that the bearer be allowed to travel across frontiers or within a war zone.

31. Napoleon was not a supporter of Humboldt: "You are interested in Botany? My wife also studies it" was all that the emperor had to say when Humboldt was presented in court (Bruhns et al. 1873, 344).

32. Ibid.

33. Stoddard 1859, 305.

CHAPTER 11. HEARTS OF LIGHT

1. Wallace 1899.

2. Ibid., 378.

3. Williams-Ellis 1966.

4. Wallace 1905.

5. Mungo Park (1771–1806) was a Scottish explorer who spent several years in Africa. He was killed in a return trip to the Niger River, but his book (Park 1816) remained popular throughout much of the Victorian era. Humboldt, Wallace, Darwin, and John Muir all read him.

6. Malthus (1766–1834) was an English economist and historian who was actively opposed to many of the negative effects of increased industrialization on the working classes. Like Wallace, Darwin also cites Malthus's *Essay on the Principle of Population* as providing an essential clue to the idea of natural selection.

7. Chambers 1845. *Vestiges of the Natural History of Creation* was originally published anonymously in 1844 and created quite a stir, both for its then heretical evolutionary implications and for the mystery surrounding its authorship. Chambers ended speculation as to the latter with the second edition.

8. The canal network, upon which the Darwin-Wedgewood fortunes had been built, was giving way to an even more comprehensive system of railways. The Darwins invested at just the right moment, and as a result Charles's fortune was assured. Other investors were less lucky. Many of the railroads proposed in 1846 were duplicate lines by rival companies, and were either never built or operated at a loss.

9. Wallace 1915, 256.

10. Edwards 1847.

11. Woodcock 1969.

12. Raby 2001.

13. Wallace 1853.

14. Ibid., iii.

15. Ibid., 11.

16. Beddall 1969, 38.

17. Anonymous 1972 (includes facsimile reprint of the original book).

18. Wallace 1889b [1853]. The book was originally published in 1853, shortly after Wallace's return from Brazil and Venezuela.

19. Ibid., 113.

20. Ibid., 122.

21. Ibid., 149.

22. Ibid., 152.

23. Wallace 1889a, 271.

24. Darwin 1921.

25. Bates 1863. There are a number of editions of the book; unfortunately, the most commonly available is the abridged version, which lacks many of the more interesting descriptions of organisms and locations. See also letter from C. Darwin to H. W. Bates, April 18, 1863, in Darwin 1999, 322.

26. Bates 1863, 27.

27. Letter from C. Darwin to H. W. Bates, January 13, 1862, in Darwin Correspondence Project Database, www.darwinproject.ac.uk/entry-3382/, letter no. 3382 (accessed December 5, 2010).

28. Wallace 1905, 327.

29. Ibid.

30. Wallace 1869.

31. It is interesting to note Wallace's choice of words here. The orang is being *attacked* by the natives, not *attacking*, even though it looks like the orang is winning.

32. Wallace 1869, iv.

33. Brooke had succeeded in forcing the sultan of Brunei to grant him control over the northwest coast of Borneo in 1841. Brooke and his heirs ruled the country as autocratic monarchs until 1946, when the last rajah ceded the territory to the British Crown. The region joined the Malaysian federation in 1963.

34. Wallace 1869, 85.

35. Ibid., 36.

36. I am grateful to Professor Charles Smith for drawing my attention to the reproduction of Wallace's watercolor of the flying frog that can be found in Smith and Beccaloni 2008.

37. Wallace 1869, 39.

38. Ibid., 42–46.

39. Wallace 1855.

40. Wallace 1869, 67.

41. Ibid., 74. The durian is notorious for having the "smell of hell and the taste of heaven." Some localities forbid bringing durian indoors in public places because of its smell, which Wallace describes as "cream cheese, onion-sauce, brown sherry and other incongruities" (ibid., 75); other people have likened it to very decayed meat. Its taste, on the other hand, seems to get widespread approval.

42. Ibid., 75.

43. Wallace 1858, Wallace's portion of the joint Darwin-Wallace publication.

44. There is a series of Darwin-Wallace letters over the years in which each seems to try to sound sicker than the other. This is perhaps funny for people who believe that Darwin was a hypochondriac, but it is also perhaps a commentary on the effects of Victorian tropical travel and medical care.

45. Wallace 1905. Raby 2001 identifies the young lady as a Marion Leslie, and points out that Wallace devotes considerably more space to this failed courtship than he does to his successful courtship of and marriage to his wife, Annie.

46. Wallace 1869, 596. The first sentence also has a page-long footnote in which he explains what he means by "barbarism" in some detail.

47. Letter from C. Darwin to A. R. Wallace, March 27, 1869, in Wallace 1915, 197.

48. Wallace 1876.

49. Ibid., v.

50. Wallace 1905, 255.

51. Wallace 1880.

52. Wallace 1907.

53. Huxley 1942. Julian Huxley was the grandson of Darwin's friend and defender Thomas Huxley, who also coined the term *agnostic*. Toward the end of his life, Julian drifted into a flirtation with spiritualism reminiscent of Wallace's, supporting Pierre Teilhard de Chardin's notions of the evolution of mind.

54. Wallace 1905, 202.

CHAPTER 12. SPOILS OF OTHER EMPIRES

1. James 1997.

2. Cabeza de Vaca 1983 [1542].

3. Houston, Ball, and Houston 2003 is a beautifully illustrated, carefully researched account of the history and people involved in the Hudson's Bay Company's efforts in natural history, climatology, and general study of the far north.

4. Rich 1954.

5. Pennant 1784.

6. Elton 1942.

7. One charge levied against George III in the Declaration of Independence is that "he . . . has endeavored to bring on the inhabitants of our frontiers, the merciless Indian savages, whose known rule of warfare, is undistinguished destruction of all ages, sexes, and conditions." I was taught that what this actually means is that poor King George attempted to honor his treaties with the Indians that limited western expansion of the colonies, and the Boston merchants resented what they saw as the deprivation of rich bottomland for farming along the Ohio. An examination of the treatment of Indians in the independent United States and British North America would be instructive.

8. Smith 1904 says quite accurately of the Mississippi drainage that "the Spanish discovered it, the French explored it and conceived the idea of constructing therein a great empire, and the Anglo-Saxons settled it and developed resources and a population beyond anything of which the boldest French pioneer ever dreamed" (3).

9. See, for instance, Humboldt 1812. Allen 1991 is an excellently written book containing many reproductions of period maps as well as an intriguing discussion of the ideas and misconceptions that went into (and came out of) the journey of the Corps of Discovery.

10. Thomas 1996.

11. John Kennedy is reported to have told a gathering of Nobel laureates that "I think this is the most extraordinary collection of talent and of human knowledge that has ever been gathered together at the White House—with the possible exception of when Thomas Jefferson dined alone" (Gross 2006, 10).

12. Jefferson 1998 [1785].

13. Ibid., 56.

14. Evans 1993.

15. Patton 1919.

16. Jackson 1978, 21.

17. This and the following excerpts are from Jefferson's confidential letter to Lewis dated June 20, 1803. The full text can be found in Jackson 1978, 61–63.

18. Jefferson 1998 [1785]. Jefferson also had copies of publications by White's two primary correspondents, Thomas Pennant and Daines Barrington, as well as by Mark Catesby, Peter Kalm, and others in his library. I wonder whether any president in the past hundred years or more (with the possible exception of Theodore Roosevelt) had anything like Jefferson's familiarity with plants and animals.

19. Jackson 1978, 63.

20. Botkin 1995.

21. Lewis and Clark 2002 [1904].

22. Patton 1919, 3.

23. Quoted in Jackson 1978, 21.

24. Quoted in Moulton 2003, 53. I have preserved the spelling and grammar directly from Moulton's transcription.

25. Lewis and Clark 1902 [1814], 332.

26. Jackson 1962, 1: 59; Jefferson 1998 [1785].

27. Ibid., 375.

28. Quoted in Moulton 2003, 239.

29. Ibid., 344.

30. Ibid.

31. Thomas 1996.

32. Goetzmann 1967.

33. Sellers 1980.

34. Bigelow 1856 is the "authorized biography," published when Frémont was a candidate for president of the United States. The book borders on a hagiography, and conveniently leaves out any suggestion that Frémont's parents were not married. Interestingly, it includes Frémont's expulsion from Charleston and its cause. Such were the moral expectations of the day.

35. Ibid., 28.

36. Frémont 1845, 9.

37. Rolle 1991.

38. Frémont 1845, 216. Frémont and his men had arrived on the northeast shore of the lake. The next day, they moved south along the lake's edge and were the first Europeans to describe Frémont's Pyramid, a unique rock formation from which the lake gets its name.

39. Humboldt 1849, 37.

40. Davis 1853, 55.

41. Perrine 1926.

42. Moore 1986; see also Anonymous 1855–61.

43. Stegner 1992 is but one of many interesting biographies available. See also Worster 2001.

44. Ibid., i.

45. The Illinois Natural History Society morphed into the Illinois Natural History Survey, one of the oldest and most influential examples of its type in North America. Besides Powell, its most significant member was probably Stephen Forbes, the pioneering limnologist and ecologist, whose paper "The Lake as a Microcosm" (Forbes 1887) is justifiably regarded as a foundation for contemporary notions of ecosystem studies. See Ayers 1958 for a brief background.

46. Hobbs 1934.

47. One of the best books on the reclaiming of the rivers of the West is Reisner 1993.

CHAPTER 13. BREADFRUIT AND ICEBERGS

1. Synge 1897.

2. There is something remarkable in thinking that Cook, aboard HMS *Mercury*, would have been part of the same force as Gilbert White's friend James Gibson, who wrote White a detailed account of the siege from the vantage point of a naval ship anchored off the city.

3. Newbolt 1929.

4. In a somewhat gruesome postscript, Hooper (2003a, 76) reports that a walking stick supposedly made of "the spear that killed James Cook" was auctioned for over £150,000 ($236,000) in 2003.

5. Powell 1977.

6. Ibid.

7. Stanton 1975.

8. This was a notion popularized in the United States by John Cleves Symmes Jr., an associate of Reynolds (see Clark 1873). Symmes proposed that the earth consisted of a series of concentric shells, each of which might contain habitable spaces that would be accessible via holes at the North and South Poles. The idea was ignored or ridiculed by contemporary scientists, but persisted into the twentieth and twenty-first centuries among such diverse fringe groups as Nazis, flying saucer enthusiasts, and so forth.

9. One cannot but wonder what the consequences might have been had Gray agreed to accompany Dana as part of the scientific corps of the expedition. As we will see later, Gray became the leader of the opponents to Agassiz's Lazzaroni (the name is a self-mocking allusion to Neapolitan beggars), of which Dana was an important member. Gray was an ardent Darwinist, Dana a reluctant creationist. Had the two spent years together circumnavigating the world, the experience, one would like to think, could have led to a more solid relationship than the Dana-Agassiz alliance, and, as a result, mid-nineteenth-century American science might have avoided some of its more unpleasant quarrels and Darwinian ideas might have had greater and more speedy acceptance.

10. Lansdown 2006.

11. Goldsmith 1822, 402.

12. Wilkes was in this, as in so much else, his own worst enemy. He seems to have initially dismissed reports by his sailors of land to the south, and only after the significance of the observations became obvious (and once he was confronted with French claims of priority) did he go back to alter his logs and write in the missing observations. This sort of behavior is a cardinal sin in seamanship, but seems typical of Wilkes throughout his career.

13. The extent to which nonwestern humans were cannibals has been the subject of enormous amounts of debate in recent years, in large part due to the strong element

of postmodernist critique in American cultural anthropology. The debate seems to run the gamut from "Yes, they were cannibals; their descendants say they were, and denying this is another example of obliterating cultures that we don't approve of" to "It was all a cruel fantasy of the colonialist mentality, and nineteenth-century accounts are either delusional, misinterpretations of mortuary rites, or outright lies." See Hooper 2003b (and subsequent responses to his response in the same issue of *Anthropology Today*) for a flavor of the debate.

14. Gilman 1899.

15. Rader and Cain 2008 contains an interesting discussion of the changing emphasis in exhibits and formats in U.S. museums and the abandonment of dioramas and taxidermy-based displays for other, more "interactive" formats during the 1950s and 1960s.

16. Balch 1901.

17. Enderby 2008.

18. Huxley 1918.

19. McCalman 2009.

20. Darwin was very unkind about McCormick, writing to Henslow on October 30, 1831: "My friend the Doctor is an ass, but we jog on very amiably: at present he is in great tribulation, whether his cabin shall be painted French Grey or a dead white—I hear little excepting this subject from him" (Darwin Correspondence Project Database, www.darwinproject.ac.uk/entry-144/, letter no. 144 [accessed December 17, 2010]). In spite of this assessment, it is worth noting that Hooker was with McCormick when the two of them ran into Darwin in London, and—at least in his reminiscences years later—Hooker was taken by the ease and cordiality between the two men.

21. McCormick 1884, 222.

22. Huxley 1918, 6.

23. Stanton 1975.

24. McCormick 1884, 274.

25. Ibid., 333.

26. Ibid.

27. Hooker 1847.

28. Letter from C. Darwin to J. Hooker, November 13 or 20, 1843, in Darwin 1986.

29. Letter from C. Darwin to J. Hooker, March 12, 1843, in ibid.

30. Letter from J. Hooker to C. Darwin, November 28, 1843, in ibid.

31. Darwin Correspondence Project Database, www.darwinproject.ac.uk/entry-729/, letter no. 729 (accessed December 18, 2010).

32. Ibid., www.darwinproject.ac.uk/entry-734/, letter no. 734 (accessed December 18, 2010).

33. Ibid., www.darwinproject.ac.uk/entry-1067/, letter no. 1067 (accessed December 18, 2010).

34. Ibid., www.darwinproject.ac.uk/entry-736/, letter no. 736 (accessed December 18, 2010).

35. For much of the British Raj, it was traditional to move government and administrative offices from the hot southern lowlands to the cool mountain slopes to avoid the worst of the summer weather. Some of these hill stations became famous, both as convenient entry points into the High Hills and also for a degree of social intrigue. In the late nineteenth and early twentieth centuries, many *memsahibs*, separated from their husbands for extended periods due to the demands of government work, took up painting and amateur natural history. Some very beautiful depictions of the flora and fauna around the stations have come down to us.

36. Darwin Correspondence Project Database, www.darwinproject.ac.uk/entry-1220/, letter no. 1220 (accessed December 18, 2010).

37. Ibid.

CHAPTER 14. NATURALISTS IN NEW ENGLAND

1. Anonymous 1896, 113.

2. Ibid.

3. Thoreau 1993 [1854], 72.

4. He translated portions of Humboldt's *Personal Narrative* even before the English edition came out; he also read *Aspects of Nature* and *Cosmos*.

5. Richardson 1992, in Scholnick 1992.

6. Thoreau 1883 [1863], 65.

7. Ibid.; biographical introduction by R. W. Emerson, 8.

8. Ibid., 71.

9. Thoreau 1910 [1854], 259.

10. Egerton 1983 has commented on this too, and tends to put Thoreau at the periphery of the development of the science of ecology, suggesting that his focus was more that of a "social critic and philosopher than a scientist" (273).

11. Thoreau 1873 [1849], 384.

12. Darwin 1958, 83.

13. Ibid., 84.

14. Chamberlin 1897.

15. Lurie 1988.

16. Aylesworth 1965.

17. Macdougal 2004.

18. Mater 1911.

19. Clark and Hughes 1890, 447.

20. Lurie 1988.

21. Macdougal 2004.

22. Agassiz 1847.

23. Thoreau 1907, 9: 298–99. McCullough 1992 repeats a story originally told by the entomologist Samuel Scudder in which Agassiz presented him with a fish pickled in formaldehyde and told him to describe it. Scudder attempted to do a quick sketch; Agassiz told him to go on looking. Scudder studied his fish for hours and then for days. Each time he presented his results to Agassiz, the professor insisted that he look again. Finally, after four weeks, the fish had rotted, but Agassiz was satisfied that Scudder had started to "see" the fish.

24. Adams 2010 [1906] contains this somewhat amusing commentary on Agassiz as a professor at Harvard: "The only teaching that appealed to his [Adams's] imagination was a course of lectures by Louis Agassiz on the Glacial Period and Palaeontology, which had more influence on his curiosity than the rest of the college instruction altogether" (50).

25. Winsor 1991.

26. Lurie 1988; see also Anonymous 1956 and Dupree 1959, particularly for an account of the opposition to the Lazzaroni.

27. Cochrane 1978.

28. Foster 1999.

29. Consider, for instance, the almost mystical structuring of landscape suggested by Frederick Clements in the 1920s and '30s and the downright mystical "superorganism" of his disciple John Phillips, which led Sir Arthur Tansley to eventually propose the idea of an "ecosystem."

30. Thoreau 1887 [1860], 51.

31. Torrey 1824.

32. Gray 1836.

33. Dupree 1959.

34. Gray 1863, 1.

35. Gray 1880, 8.

36. Keeney 1992.

37. Gray 1861.

38. Agassiz and Hartt 1870.

39. Cochrane 1978.

40. Haeckel quoted in Winsor 1991, 54.

CHAPTER 15. FROM MUIR AND ALEXANDER TO LEOPOLD AND CARSON

1. Keller and Golley, 9.

2. Farber 1997.

3. Semper 1881, v.

4. Ibid., 3.

5. Ibid., 29.

6. Worster 1993, 6.

7. Muir 1913.

8. Ibid., 116.

9. Muir 1913, 130.

10. Ibid., 286.

11. Holmes 1999.

12. Muir 1916.

13. Muir 1916, ix.

14. Worster 2008 says of Muir: "Throughout his life he liked to gab only a little less than he liked to hike. Wherever he went, he started a conversation, and typically it went on and on, Muir doing most of the talking" (3).

15. Muir 1911.

16. Badé 1924, 163. The extract is from a portion of a letter from E. C. Andrews of the Geological Survey of Australia to the secretary of the Sierra Club.

17. Letter from J. Muir to A. Gray, February 22, 1873, http://digitalcollections.pacific.edu/u?/muirletters,18906 (accessed January 8, 2011).

18. Huxley 1918.

19. Badé 1924, 358.

20. Goetzmann and Sloan 1982.

21. Hall 1987.

22. Branch 2001.

23. Merriam 2008 [1910].

24. Grinnell 1943.

25. Merriam and Steineger 1890; see also Merriam 1898.

26. Oehser 1952.

27. Bailey 1889.

28. Bailey 1898.

29. Bailey 1902.

30. Stein 2001.

31. Williams 1994.

32. Hall 1939 and Grinnell 1940. E. Raymond Hall was one of Grinnell's first graduate students and went on to become one of the foremost mammalogists in North America. Hilda W. Grinnell, author of the latter work, was Joseph's widow.

33. On Grinnell's first trip to Alaska, he wrote home, "I was never so well and happy in my life. Think of it! In a new country, collecting new birds every day. It's my ideal of a good time. Fishing, boating, all I want, with lots of adventures" (quoted in Grinnell 1940, 5).

34. Much of the detail here on Alexander's life is from B. Stein's (2001) excellent biography, which draws on documents and letters now housed in the Museum of Vertebrate Zoology.

35. Ibid.

36. Letter from E. Heller to J. Grinnell, May 29, 1908, quoted in Stein 2001, 102.

37. Hall 1939.

38. Alexander 1927.

39. Kellogg 1910.

40. Merriam 1914.

41. Seton 1898 and Thompson 1901. Thompson Seton originally published *Lives of the Hunted* under the name Seton-Thompson and *Wild Animals I Have Known* as Thompson Seton (reversed, and no hyphen). He was actually born Ernest Thompson.

42. Burroughs 1908.

43. Roosevelt 1920.

44. Meine 1988.

45. Ibid.

46. Ibid.

47. Leopold 1968, 130.

48. Guthrie 1919, 54.

49. Young 2002.

50. The Kaibab deer went on to become an iconic topic in game-management discussions for over forty years. New Zealand wildlife biologist Graeme Caughley (1970) reexamined the evidence and suggests that there was little support for either predators controlling prey or even of the "eruption" of deer in this instance.

51. Meine 1988.

52. Leopold 1933.

53. Ibid., xxxi.

54. Elton 1927, 1.

55. Ibid., 3.

56. Leopold 1953, 61.

57. Leopold 1968, vii.

58. Lear 1997.

59. Lytle 2007.

60. Carson 1941.

61. Carson 1951.

62. Carson 1955.

63. Lear 1997.

64. Carson 1962.

65. Ibid., 1.

CHAPTER 16. THE SLOW DEATH (AND RESURRECTION) OF NATURAL HISTORY

1. Kohler 2002.

2. Ernst Mayr once told me an interesting story of attending a lecture by R.A. Fisher, the great British geneticist and statistician, in which someone in the audience had the temerity to raise his hand and point out that Fisher assumed an equilibrium in all his models. Fisher's response was to the effect of "That is correct. Unless I assume equilibrium, the math doesn't work." Mayr said that the truly frightening thing was that the answer was considered entirely sufficient.

3. Leopold 1953, 64.

4. MacArthur 1958.

5. Stilling 2012 is among the latest in a long line of pretty texts that replace MacArthur's perfectly triangular "spruce" diagrams with much prettier tree pictures. Professor Stilling might be horrified to see the real spruce that MacArthur worked under, located a convenient fifteen miles from where I type this text. The trees are older and have lost many branches. Few resemble either Stilling's pictures or MacArthur's diagrams, but they have the advantage of being real.

6. Stevenson 1866 runs to three volumes and over 1,300 pages, though Norfolk, whose avifauna he covers in this work, has an area of just over 2,000 square miles. By contrast, Sprunt 1954 has 527 pages to deal with the birdlife of Florida, an area of over 65,700 square miles. A fairer comparison might be Dawson's (1923) magisterial four-volume set on California birds, which tops 2,000 pages. California, however, has an area of 163,696 square miles.

7. Marren 2005.

8. Ibid., 26.

9. Boyd 1951.

10. Hamilton 2005.

11. Ibid., 187.

12. Tansley 1923, 97, quoted in Elton 1927, 3. It is perhaps equally significant to the theme of the present book that Elton starts his text with a quote from Gilbert White, which reads in part "but the investigation of the life and conversation of animals, is a concern of much more trouble and difficulty, and is not to be obtained but by the active and inquisitive, and by those that reside much in the country" (White 1911 [1788], 125).

13. Wilson 1994, 11.

14. http://mvz.berkeley.edu/Grinnell/index.html (accessed January 28, 2011).

15. Ibid.

16. A computer search revealed over 250 natural history museums or institutions featuring natural history as part of their profile in the United States alone: http://

en.wikipedia.org/wiki/List_of_natural_history_museums (accessed December 22, 2011).

17. Fleischner 2005, Greene 2005, and Schmidly 2005 are just a few examples.

18. Hampton and Wheeler 2011.

REFERENCES

Adams, H. 2010 [1906]. *The Education of Henry Adams: An Autobiography*. New York: Forgotten Books.

Agassiz, L. 1847. *An Introduction to the Study of Natural History*. New York: Greeley & McElrath.

Agassiz, L., and C. F. Hartt. 1870. *Scientific Results of a Journey in Brazil: Geology and Physical Geography of Brazil*. Boston: Fields Osgood & Co.

Aiken, P. 1947. The Animal History of Albertus Magnus and Thomas of Cantimprè. *Speculum* 22: 205–25.

Alexander, A. 1927. A Further Chronicle of the Passenger Pigeon and of Methods Employed in Hunting It. *Condor* 29: 273.

Aligheri, Dante. 1871. *Divine Comedy*. Vol. 1 of 3. Boston: Fields Osgood and Co.

Allen, E. G. 1937. New Light on Mark Catesby. *Auk* 54: 349–63.

Allen, J. L. 1991. *Lewis and Clark and the Image of the American Northwest*. Mineola, NY: Dover.

Alvard, M. S., and L. Kuznar. 2001. Deferred Harvests: The Transition from Hunting to Animal Husbandry. *American Anthropologist* 103: 295–311.

Anonymous. 1803. Review of John Ray's *The Wisdom of God Manifested in the Works of the Creation. Philosophical Transactions of the Royal Society of London Abridged: 1683–1694* 3: 492–95.

Anonymous. 1855–61. *Reports of Explorations to Ascertain the Most Practicable and Economical Route for a Railroad from the Mississippi River to the Pacific Ocean, Made under the Direction of the Secretary of War, in 1853–4*. 13 vols. Washington, DC: Government Printing Office.

Anonymous. 1863. Olaus Celsius. *Notes and Queries: A Medium of Intercommunication for Literary Men, General Readers, Etc*. 3rd ser., vol. 4., 170.

Anonymous. 1893. Cook: 1762–1780. *Historical Records of New South Wales*. Vol. 1, pt. 1. Canberra: National Library of Australia.

Anonymous. 1896. Scientific News and Notes. *Science* 4: 109–15.

Anonymous. 1899. Gilbert White of Selborne. Private reprint of a proof for the *Dictionary of National Biography*. Vol. 61. Cambridge, MA: Samuel Henshaw Collection, Harvard University Library.

Anonymous. 1913. The Thomas Pennant Collection. *Science N.S*. 37: 404–05.

Anonymous. 1956. National Academy Began as Social Club. *Science Newsletter* (November 24, 1956): 322.

Anonymous. 1972. Review: Wallace's Palm Trees of the Amazon. *Taxon* 21: 521–22.

Anonymous. 2008. *Cook's Endeavor Journal: The Inside Story*. Canberra: National Library of Australia.

Arber, A. 1912. *Herbals, Their Origin and Evolution: A Chapter in the History of Botany, 1470–1670*. Cambridge: Cambridge University Press.

Aristotle. 1984. *The Complete Works of Aristotle: The Revised Oxford Translation*. Ed. J. Barnes. Princeton, NJ: Princeton Bolingen Series XXI.

———. 2004. *History of Animals*. New York: Kessinger Publications.

Ayers, J. B. 1958. Illinois State Natural History Survey. *AIBS Bulletin* 8: 26.

Aylesworth, T. G. 1965. The Heritage of Louis Agassiz. *American Biology Teacher* 27: 597–99.

Baas, J. H. 1889. *Outlines of the History of Medicine and the Medical Profession*. New York: J. H. Vail and Co.

Badé, W. F. 1924. *The Life and Letters of John Muir*. New York: Houghton Mifflin & Co.

Bailey, F. M. 1889. *Birds through an Opera Glass*. New York: Houghton Mifflin & Co.

———. 1898. *Birds of Village and Field: A Bird Book for Beginners*. New York: Houghton Mifflin & Co.

———. 1902. *Handbook of Birds of the Western United States Including the Great Plains, Great Basin, Pacific Slope, and Lower Rio Grande Valley*. New York: Houghton Mifflin & Co.

Balch, E. S. 1901. Antarctica: A History of Antarctic Discovery. *Journal of the Franklin Institute* 152: 26–45.

Balfour, J. H. 1885. *The Plants of the Bible*. Edinburgh: T. Nelson and Sons.

Bandelier, A. F. 1905. *The Journey of Alvar Nunez Cabeza de Vaca and His Companions from Florida to the Pacific 1528–1536. Translated from His Own Narrative by Fanny Bandelier.* New York: A. S. Barnes and Co.

Barlow, N., ed. 1963. Darwin's Ornithological Notes. *Bulletin of the British Museum (Natural History). Historical Series* 2, no. 7: 201–28.

———. 1967. *Darwin and Henslow: The Growth of an Idea: Letters, 1831–1860.* Berkeley and Los Angeles: University of California Press.

Barnosky, A. D., P. L. Koch, R. S. Feranec, S. L. Wing, and A. B. Shabel. 2006. Assessing the Causes of Late Pleistocene Extinctions on the Continents. *Science* 306: 70–75.

Barrington, D. 1770. Account of a Very Remarkable Young Musician. In a Letter from the Honourable Daines Barrington, F.R.S., to Mathew Maty, M.D. Sec. R.S. *Philosophical Transactions of the Royal Society* 57: 204–14.

Bartram, W. 1791. *Travels through North and South Carolina, Georgia, East and West Florida, the Cherokee Country, the Extensive Territories of the Muscogulges, or Creek Confederacy, and the Country of the Chactaws; Containing an Account of the Soil and Natural Productions of Those Regions, Together with Observations on the Manners of the Indians.* Philadelphia: James and Johnson.

Bates, H. W. 1863. *The Naturalist on the River Amazons: A Record of Adventures, Habits of Animals, Sketches of Brazilian and Indian Life, and Aspects of Nature under the Equator, during Eleven Years of Travel.* 2 vols. London: John Murray.

Beddall, B. G., ed. 1969. *Wallace and Bates in the Tropics: An Introduction to the Theory of Natural Selection.* London: Macmillan.

Beebee, W. 1944. *The Book of Naturalists: An Anthology of the Best Natural History.* New York: Knopf.

Beija-Pereira, A., D. Caramelli, C. Lalueza-Fox, C. Vernesi, et al. 2006. The Origin of European Cattle: Evidence from Modern and Ancient DNA. *Proceedings of the National Academy of Sciences* 103: 8113–18.

Benton, P. 1867. *The History of the Rochford Hundred.* New York: A. Harrington.

Bigelow, J. 1856. *Memoir of the Life and Public Services of John Charles Fremont.* New York: Derby and Jackson.

Birkhead, T. 2010. How Stupid Not to Have Thought of That: Post-Copulatory Sexual Selection. *Journal of Zoology* 281: 79–93.

Blunt, W. 1971. *Linnaeus: The Compleat Naturalist.* Princeton, NJ: Princeton University Press.

Bonta, M. 1995. *American Women Afield: Writings by Pioneering Women Naturalists.* College Station, TX: Texas A&M University Consortium Press.

Boone, J.L. 2002. Subsistence Strategies and Early Human Population History: An Evolutionary Ecological Perspective. *World Archaeology* 34, no. 1: 6–25.

Botkin, D.B. 1995. *Our Natural History: The Lessons of Lewis and Clark*. New York: Putnam.

Boulger, G.S. 1904. Catesby and the Catalpa. *Nature Notes* 15: 248–49.

Boyd, A.W. 1951. *A Country Parish*. London: Collins.

Branch, M.P. 2001. *John Muir's Last Journey: South to the Amazon and East to Africa*. Washington, DC: Island Press.

Breasted, J.H. 1920. The Origins of Civilization. *Scientific Monthly* 10: 182–209.

Briant, P. 2002. *History of the Persian Empire: From Cyrus to Alexander*. Trans. Peter Daniels. Winona Lake, IN: Eisenbrauns. (Originally published Paris: Fayard.)

Brightwell, C.L. 1858. *The Life of Linnaeus*. London: John VanVoorst.

Brown, J.W. 1897. *An Enquiry into the Life and Legend of Michael Scot*. Edinburgh: David Douglas.

Browne, J. 1995. *Charles Darwin: A Biography*. Vol. 1 of 2. *Voyaging*. Princeton, NJ: Princeton University Press.

———. 2002. *Charles Darwin: A Biography*. Vol. 2 of 2. *The Power of Place*. Princeton, NJ: Princeton University Press.

Browne, R.W. 1857. *A History of Roman Classical Literature*. Philadelphia: Blanchard and Lea.

Bruhns, C., J. Lowenberg, R. Avé-Lallemant, A. Dove, and J. Lassell. 1873. *Life of Alexander von Humboldt*. Vol. 1 of 2. London: Longmans, Green and Co.

Buffon, G.L. 1769. *Histoire naturelle générale et particuliére*. Paris: Royal Press. (Later translated into English by William Smellie: Buffon, G.L. 1791. *Natural History General and Particular by the Count du Buffon*. London: Strahan and Cadell.)

———. 1857. *Buffon's Natural History of Man, the Globe, and of Quadrupeds, with Additions from Cuvier, Lacepede, and Other Eminent Naturalists*. New York: Leavitt and Allen.

Burkhardt, F., ed. 1999. *The Correspondence of Charles Darwin*. Vol. 11. *1863*. Cambridge: Cambridge University Press.

Burkhardt, F., and S. Smith, eds. 1986. *The Correspondence of Charles Darwin*. Vol. 2. *1837–1843*. Cambridge: Cambridge University Press.

Burroughs, J. 1908. Seeing Straight. *The Independent* 64: 34–36.

Busk, W. 1855. *Mediaeval Popes, Emperors, Kings and Crusaders: Or Germany, Italy and Palestine from A.D. 1125 to A.D. 1268*. Vol. 2 of 4. London: Hookam and Sons.

Butzer, K.W. 1992. From Columbus to Acosta: Science, Geography and the New World. *Annals of the Association of American Geographers* 82: 543–65.

Cabeza de Vaca, A. 1983 [1542]. *Cabeza de Vaca's Adventures in the Unknown Interior of America*. Trans. C. Covey. Albuquerque: University of New Mexico Press.

Canning, G., J. Frere, G. Ellis, and W. Gifford. 1801. *Poetry of the Anti-Jacobin*. 4th ed. London: J. Wright.

Carson, R. 1941. *Under the Sea Wind*. New York: Simon & Schuster.

———. 1951. *The Sea around Us*. Oxford: Oxford University Press.

———. 1955. *The Edge of the Sea*. New York: Houghton Mifflin & Co.

———. 1962. *Silent Spring*. New York: Houghton Mifflin & Co.

Carter, H. B. 1995. The Royal Society and the Voyage of HMS "Endeavor." *Notes and Records of the Royal Society of London* 49: 245–60.

Cary, H. 1882. *Select Dialogs of Plato: A New and Literal Version*. New York: Harper Bros.

Cashin, E. J. 2007. *William Bartram and the American Revolution on the Southern Frontier*. Columbia: University of South Carolina Press.

Catesby, M. 1747a. Of Birds of Passage, by Mr. Mark Catesby, F.R.S. *Philosophical Transactions of the Royal Society of London* 44: 435–44.

———. 1747b. Of Birds of Passage. *Gentlemen's Magazine* 17: 447–48.

———. 1754 [1731]. *The Natural History of Carolina, Florida, and the Bahama Islands: Containing the Figures of Birds, Beasts, Fishes, Serpents, Insects, and Plants: Particularly the Forest-Trees, Shrubs, and Other Plants, Not Hitherto Described or Very Incorrectly Figured by Authors*. London: Marsh Wilcox and Stitchall.

Caughley, G. 1970. Eruption of Ungulate Populations with Emphasis on Himalayan Thar in New Zealand. *Ecology* 51: 53–72.

Chamberlin, T. C. 1897. The Method of Multiple Working Hypotheses. *Journal of Geology* 5: 837–48.

Chambers, R. 1845. *Vestiges of the Natural History of Creation*. 2nd ed. New York: Wiley and Putnam.

Chancellor, G., and J. van Wyhe, eds. 2009. *Charles Darwin's Notebooks from the Voyage of the* Beagle. Cambridge: Cambridge University Press.

Chroust, A. 1967. Aristotle Leaves the Academy. *Greece and Rome* 14: 39–43.

Clark, P. 1873. The Symmes Theory of the Earth. *Atlantic Monthly* 31: 471–80.

Clark, J. W., and T. Hughes. 1890. *The Life and Letters of the Reverend Adam Sedgwick*. Vol. 1 of 2. Cambridge: Cambridge University Press.

Clarke, C. 1821. *The Hundred Wonders of the World and the Three Kingdoms of Nature Described According to the Latest and Best Authorities and Illustrated by Engravings*. New Haven, CT: John Babcock.

Clausen, J., D. Keck, and W. M. Hiesey. 1940. *Experimental Studies on the Nature of*

Species. I. *Effect of Varied Environments on Western North American Plants*. Washington, DC: Carnegie Institution of Washington.

Clemmer, R. O. 1991. Seed Eaters and Chert Carriers: The Economic Basis for Continuity in Western Shoshone Identities. *Journal of California and Great Basin Archaeology* 13: 3–14.

Clutton-Brock, J. 1999. *A Natural History of Domesticated Mammals*. 2nd ed. Cambridge: Cambridge University Press.

Cochrane, R. C. 1978. *The National Academy of Sciences: The First Hundred Years*. Washington, DC: National Academy of Sciences.

Coleridge, E. H. 1895. *Letters of Samuel Taylor Coleridge*. 2 vols. Boston and New York: Houghton Mifflin.

Creasey, E. S. 1851. *The Fifteen Decisive Battles of the World: From Marathon to Waterloo*. New York: Harper and Bros.

Cronin, G. Jr. 1942. John Mirk on Bonfires, Elephants, and Dragons. *Modern Language Notes* 57: 113–16.

Crosby, A. W. 1986. *Ecological Imperialism: The Biological Expansion of Europe 900–1900*. Cambridge: Cambridge University Press.

Dadswell, T. 2003. *The Selborne Pioneer: Gilbert White as Scientist and Naturalist: A Re-Examination*. Aldershot, UK: Ashgate Publishing Ltd.

Daley, S. 1993. Ancient Mesopotamian Gardens and the Identification of the Hanging Gardens of Babylon Resolved. *Garden History* 21: 1–13.

Darlington, W. 1849. *Memorials of John Bartram and Humphry Marshall with Notices of Their Botanical Contemporaries*. Philadelphia: Lindsay and Blakiston.

Darwin, C. 1845. *Journal of Researches into the Natural History and Geology of the Countries Visited during the Voyage round the World of H.M.S. "Beagle" under the Command of Captain Fitz Roy, R.N.* London: John Murray.

———. 1851. *Geological Observations on Coral Reefs, Volcanic Islands, and South America*. London: Smith, Elder and Co.

———. 1859. *On the Origin of Species by Means of Natural Selection, or the Preservation of Favored Races in the Struggle for Life*. London: John Murray.

———. 1896. *The Formation of Vegetable Mould through the Actions of Worms with Observations on Their Habits*. New York: D. Appleton and Co.

———. 1897. *The Life and Letters of Charles Darwin*. Ed. F. Darwin. New York: D. Appleton and Co.

———. 1902. *Journal of Researches*. New York: American Home Library Co.

———. 1921. An Appreciation. Foreword in H. W. Bates. *A Naturalist on the River Amazons*. New York: E. P. Dutton and Co. Everyman's Library Edition.

———. 1958. *The Autobiography of Charles Darwin 1809–1882. Edited with Appendix and Notes by His Grand-Daughter, Nora Barlow*. 1st complete ed. New York: Harcourt, Brace and Co.

———. 1985. *The Correspondence of Charles Darwin*. Vol. 1 of 19. *1821–1836*. Eds. F. Burkhardt and S. Smith. Cambridge: Cambridge University Press.

———. 1986. *The Correspondence of Charles Darwin*. Vol. 2. *1837–1843*. Eds. F. Burkhardt and S. Smith. Cambridge: Cambridge University Press.

———. 1999. *The Correspondence of Charles Darwin*. Vol. 11. Ed. F. Burkhardt. Cambridge: Cambridge University Press.

———. 2009. *Charles Darwin's* Beagle *Diary (1831–1836)*. Ed. R. Keynes. Cambridge: Cambridge University Press.

Darwin, E. 1785. *The System of Vegetables Translated from the Systema Vegetablium*. London: Ligh and Sotheby.

———. 1794. *Zoonomia, or the Laws of Organic Life*. London: J. Johnson.

———. 1804. *The Temple of Nature or, the Origin of Society, A Poem with Philosophical Notes*. Baltimore: John W. Butler.

———. 1806. *Poetical Works of Erasmus Darwin*. Vol. 2 of 3. *The Loves of Plants*. London: J. Johnson.

Darwin, F., ed. 1887. *The Life and Letters of Charles Darwin, Including an Autobiographical Chapter*. London: John Murray.

Davis, E.B. 1976. A Bicentennial Remembrance: Important Contributors to Mid-Eighteenth Century Biology. *Bios* 47: 178–86.

Davis, J. 1853. *Report of the Secretary of War*. Executive Document 1. House of Representatives, 33rd Cong., 1st sess. Washington, DC: Government Printing Office.

Dawson, W. 1923. *The Birds of California*. 4 vols. San Diego: South Moulton Co.

De Asua, M., and R. French. 2005. *A New World of Animals: Early Modern Europeans on the Creatures of Iberian America*. Aldershot, UK: Ashgate Publishing Ltd.

De Beer, E.S. 1950. The Earliest Fellows of the Royal Society. *Notes and Records of the Royal Society of London* 7: 172–92.

Debus, A.G. 1978. *Man and Nature in the Renaissance*. Cambridge: Cambridge University Press.

Delia, D. 1992. From Romance to Rhetoric: The Alexandrian Library in Classical and Islamic Traditions. *American Historical Review* 97: 1449–67.

Dempsey, J., ed. 2000 [1637]. *New English Canaan by Thomas Morton of "Merrymount": Text and Notes*. Scituate, MA: Digital Scanning Inc.

Desmond, A., and J. Moore. 1991. *Darwin: The Life of a Tormented Evolutionist*. New York: W.W. Norton and Co.

———. 2009. *Darwin's Sacred Cause: How a Hatred of Slavery Shaped Darwin's Views on Human Evolution*. New York: Houghton Mifflin.

Dick, N. B. 2006. The Neo-Assyrian Lion Hunt and Yahweh's Answer to Job. *Journal of Biblical Literature* 125: 243–70.

Diller, A. 1940. The Oldest Manuscripts of Ptolemaic Maps. *Transactions and Proceedings of the American Philological Association* 71: 62–67.

Diogenes Laertius. 1853. *The Lives and Opinions of Eminent Philosophers*. Trans. C. D. Yonge. London: Bohn.

Drury, W. H. Jr. 1998. *Chance and Change: Ecology for Conservationists*. Berkeley and Los Angeles: University of California Press.

Dupree, A. H. 1959. *Asa Gray, 1810–1888*. Cambridge, MA: Harvard University Press.

Edwards, W. H. 1847. *A Voyage on the River Amazon Including a Residence at Pará*. New York: D. Appleton and Co.

Egerton, F. 1983. The History of Ecology Achievements and Opportunities, Part One. *Journal of Historical Biology* 16: 259–310.

———. 2001. A History of the Ecological Sciences. Part 3. Hellenistic Natural History. *Bulletin of the Ecological Society of America* 82: 201–05.

Eiseley, L. 1961. *Darwin's Century: Evolution and the Men Who Discovered It*. New York: Anchor.

———. 1979. *Darwin and the Mysterious Mr. X: New Light on the Evolutionists*. New York: Harcourt.

Elton, C. 1927. *Animal Ecology*. London: Sidgwick and Jackson Ltd.

———. 1942. The Ten-Year Cycle in Numbers of the Lynx in Canada. *Journal of Animal Ecology* 11: 96–126.

Enderby, J. 2008. *Imperial Nature: Joseph Hooker and the Practices of Victorian Science*. Chicago: University of Chicago Press.

Erskine, A. 1995. Culture and Power in Ptolemaic Egypt: The Museum and Library of Alexandria. *Greece & Rome*, 2nd ser., 42: 38–48.

Evans, H. E. 1993. *Pioneer Naturalists*. New York: Henry Holt and Co.

Farber, P. L. 1997. *Discovering Birds: The Emergence of Ornithology as a Scientific Discipline, 1760–1850*. Baltimore: Johns Hopkins University Press.

———. 2000. *Finding Order in Nature: The Naturalist Tradition from Linnaeus to E. O. Wilson*. Baltimore: Johns Hopkins University Press.

Flannery, T. 2002. *The Future Eaters: An Ecological History of the Australasian Lands*. New York: Grove Press.

Fleischner, T. L. 2005. Natural History and the Deep Roots of Resource Management. *Natural Resources Journal* 45: 1–13.

Forbes, S. 1887. The Lake as a Microcosm. Originally published in the *Bulletin of the Illinois Natural History Society*. www.uam.es/personal_pdi/ciencias/scasado/documentos/Forbes.pdf. (Accessed July 4, 2011.)

Foster, D. R. 1999. *Thoreau's Country: Journey through a Transformed Landscape*. Cambridge, MA: Harvard University Press.

Foster, P. G. M. 1986. The Hon. Daines Barrington F.R.S.—Annotations on Two Journals Compiled by Gilbert White. *Notes and Records of the Royal Society of London* 41: 77–93.

Frémont, J. C. 1845. *Report of the Exploring Expedition to the Rocky Mountains*. Washington, DC: Gales and Seaton.

French, R. 1994. *Ancient Natural Histories*. London and New York: Routledge.

Gabrieli, F. 1964. Greeks and Arabs in the Central Mediterranean. *Dumbarton Oaks Papers* 18: 57–65.

Gage, A. T., and W. T. Stearn. 1988. *A Bicentennial History of the Linnean Society*. New York: Academic Press.

Galen. 1985. *Three Treatises on the Nature of Science*. Trans. M. Frede. Indianapolis: Hackett Publishing Co.

Gaudio, M. 2001. Swallowing the Evidence: William Bartram and the Limits of Enlightenment. *Winterthur Portfolio* 36: 1–17.

Gee, W. 1918. South Carolina Botanists: Biography and Bibliography. *Bulletin of the University of South Carolina* 72: 9–13.

Gilman, D. C. 1899. *The Life of James Dwight Dana*. New York: Harper and Bros.

Goetzmann, W. H. 1967. *Exploration and Empire: The Explorer and the Scientist in the Winning of the American West*. New York: Knopf.

Goetzmann, W. H., and K. Sloan. 1982. *Looking Far North: The Harriman Expedition to Alaska, 1899*. Princeton, NJ: Princeton University Press.

Goldsmith, O. 1822. *A History of the Earth and Animated Nature: New Edition, with Corrections and Revisions*. Liverpool: Whyte and Co.

Gould, S. J. 1992. *Ever Since Darwin*. New York: W. W. Norton.

Gourlie, N. 1953. *The Prince of Botanists: Carl Linnaeus*. London: H. F. & G. Witherby.

Gray, A. 1836. *Elements of Botany*. New York: G. & C. Carvill & Co.

———. 1861. *Natural Selection Not Inconsistent with Natural Theology: A Free Examination of Darwin's Treatise on the Origin of Species, and of Its American Reviewers*. London: Trübner and Co. (Reprinted from the *Atlantic Monthly*, July, August, and October 1860.)

———. 1863. *Botany for Young People and Common Schools: How Plants Grow, a Simple Introduction to Structural Botany*. New York: Ivison, Phinney Blakeman & Co.

———. 1880. *Natural Science and Religion: Two Lectures Delivered to the Theological School of Yale College*. New York: Charles Scribner's Sons.

Grayson, D. 2001. Did Human Hunting Cause Mass Extinction? *Science* 294: 1459–62.

Greene, H. W. 2005. Organisms in Nature as a Central Focus for Biology. *Trends in Ecology & Evolution* 20: 23–27.

Grew, N. 1682. *The Anatomy of Plants with an Idea of a Philosophical History of Plants and Several Other Lectures to the Royal Society*. London: W. Rawlins.

Gribbin, J., and M. Gribbin. 2004. *Fitzroy: The Remarkable Story of Darwin's Captain and the Invention of the Weather Forecast*. New Haven, CT: Yale University Press.

Griffin, D. 1953. Acoustic Orientation in the Oil Bird, *Steatornis*. *Proceedings of the National Academy of Sciences* 39: 884–93.

Grinnell, H. W. 1940. Joseph Grinnell 1877–1939. *Condor* 42: 2–34.

———. 1943. Bibliography of Clinton Hart Merriam. *Journal of Mammalogy* 24: 436–57.

Gross, J. 2006. *Thomas Jefferson's Scrapbooks: Poems of Nation, Family and Romantic Love Collected by America's Third President*. New York: Steerforth.

Guthrie, J. D. 1919. *The Forest Ranger and Other Verse*. Boston: Richard D. Badger / Gorham Press.

Haeckel, E. 2000 [1869]. *The Philosophy of Ecology: From Science to Synthesis*. Eds. D. Keller and F. Golley. Athens: University of Georgia Press.

Hall, C. M. 1987. John Muir in New Zealand. *New Zealand Geographer* 43: 99–103.

Hall, E. R. 1939. Joseph Grinnell (1877–1939). *Journal of Mammalogy* 20: 409–17.

Hamilton, J. R. 1965. Alexander's Early Life. *Greece and Rome* 12: 117–24.

Hamilton, W. D. 2005. *Narrow Roads of Gene Land*. Vol. 3 of 3. *Last Words*. Ed. M. Ridley. Oxford: Oxford University Press.

Hampton, S. E., and T. A. Wheeler. 2011. Fostering the Rebirth of Natural History. *Biology Letters* (August 31, 2011), doi: 10.1098/rsbl.2011.0777.

Hartwich, C. 1882. A Botanist of the Ninth Century. *Popular Science Monthly* 20: 523–27.

Haskins, C. 1925. Arabic Science in Western Europe. *Isis* 7: 478–85.

Haskins, C. H. 1911. England and Sicily in the 12th Century. *English Historical Review* 104: 641–65.

———. 1921. Michael Scot and Frederick II. *Isis* 4: 250–75.

Haynes, G., ed. 2009. *American Megafaunal Extinctions at the End of the Pleistocene*. New York: Springer.

Heather, P. J. 1939. Some Animal Beliefs from Aristotle. *Folklore* 50: 243–58.

Henrichs, A. 1995. Graecia Capta: Roman Views of Greek Culture. *Harvard Studies in Classical Philology* 97: 243–61.

Hobbs, W. W. 1934. John Wesley Powell 1834–1902. *Scientific Monthly* 39: 519–29.

Hobson, R. 1866. *Charles Waterton: His Home Habits and Handiwork*. London: Whittaker & Co.

Holmes. A. 1913. *The Age of the Earth*. London and New York: Harper Bros.

Holmes, S. J. 1999. *The Young John Muir: An Environmental Biography*. Madison: University of Wisconsin Press.

Holt-White, R. 1901. *The Life and Letters of Gilbert White of Selborne*. Vol. 2 of 2. New York: E. P. Dutton and Co.

———. 1907. *The Letters of Gilbert White of Selborne from His Intimate Friend and Contemporary the Rev. John Mulso*. London: R. H. Porter.

Hooke, R. 2007 [1665]. *Micrographia: Or Some Physiological Descriptions of Minute Bodies*. New York: Cosimo Classics.

Hooker, J. D. 1847. *The Botany of the Antarctic Voyage of H.M. Discovery Ships* Erebus *and* Terror *in the Years 1839–1843*. London: Reeve Bros.

Hooper, S. 2003a. Making a Killing? Of Sticks and Stones and James Cook's Bones. *Anthropology Today* 19: 6–8.

———. 2003b. Cannibals Talk: A Response to Obeyesekere & Arens. *Anthropology Today* 19: 20.

Houston, S., T. Ball, and M. Houston. 2003. *Eighteenth-Century Naturalists of Hudson's Bay*. Montreal and Kingston: McGill-Queens University Press.

Humboldt, A. von. 1812. *Carte générale du royaume de la Nouvelle Espagne*. Paris: Barriere.

———. 1814. *Political Essay on the kingdom of New Spain*. 2nd ed. London:Longman & Co.

———. 1849. *Aspects of Nature in Different Lands and Different Climates*. Philadelphia: Lea and Blanchard.

———. 1852. *Personal Narrative of Travels to the Equinoctial Regions of America, during the Years 1799–1804*. Vol. 1 of 3. Trans. T. Ross. London: H. Bohn.

———. 1885. *Personal Narrative of Travels to the Equinoctial Regions of America, during the Years 1799–1804, by Alexander von Humboldt and Aimé Bonpland*. Vol. 3. Trans. T. Ross. London: George Bell and Sons.

Humboldt, A. von, and A. Bonpland. 1852. *Personal Narrative of Travels to the Equinoctial Regions of America, during the Years 1799–1804*. Vol. 2. Trans. T. Ross. London: H. Bohn.

———. 2009 [1807]. *Essay on the Geography of Plants*. Ed. S. Jackson. Trans. S. Romanowski. Chicago: University of Chicago Press.

Hussakof, L. 1916. Benjamin Franklin and Erasmus Darwin: With Some Unpublished Correspondence. *Science* 43: 773–75.

Huxley, J. 1942. *Evolution: The Modern Synthesis*. London: Allen and Unwin.

Huxley, L. 1900. *The Life and Letters of Thomas Huxley*. New York: D. Appleton and Co.

———. 1918. *Life and Letters of Sir Joseph Dalton Hooker Based on Materials Collected and Arranged by Lady Hooker*. London: John Murray.

Huxley, R. 2007. *The Great Naturalists*. London: Thames and Hudson.

Ivry, A. 2001. The Arabic Text of Aristotle's "De Anima" and Its Translator. *Oriens* 36: 59–77.

Jackson, D. D. 1962. *Letters of the Lewis and Clark Expedition, with Related Documents, 1789–1854*. Vol 1. Chicago: University of Illinois Press.

———. 1978. *Letters of the Lewis and Clark Expedition, with Related Documents, 1789–1854*. Chicago: University of Illinois Press.

James, L. 1997. *The Rise and Fall of the British Empire*. London: St. Martins.

Jardine, W. 1849. *Contributions to Ornithology 1848–1852*. London: General Books.

Jefferson, T. 1998 [1785]. *Notes on the State of Virginia*. Ed. F. Shuffelton. New York: Penguin.

Jeffrey, A. 1857. *The History and Antiquities of Roxburghshire and Adjacent Districts, from the Most Remote Period to the Present Time*. London: J. F. Hope.

Johnston, C. 1901. The Fall of Nineveh. *Journal of the American Oriental Society* 22: 20–22.

Josselyn, J. 1672. *New England's Rarities Discovered in Birds, Beasts, Fishes, Serpents and Plants of That Country*. London: G. Widdowes.

Keeney, E. B. 1992. *The Botanizers: Amateur Scientists in Nineteenth-Century America*. Chapel Hill: University of North Carolina Press.

Keller, D., and F. Golley. 2000. *The Philosophy of Ecology: From Science to Synthesis*. Athens: University of Georgia Press.

Kellogg, L. 1910. Rodent Fauna of the Late Tertiary Beds at the Virgin Valley and Thousand Creek, Nevada. *University of California Publications, Bulletin of the Department of Geology* 5: 421–37.

Keller, D. and F. Golley, eds. 2000. *The Philosophy of Ecology: From Science to Synthesis*. University of Georgia Press, Athens.

Keynes, R. 2001. *Annie's Box: Charles Darwin, His Daughter and Human Evolution*. London: Fourth Estate.

King-Hele, D. 1998. Erasmus Darwin, the Lunaticks, and Evolution. *Notes and Records of the Royal Society of London* 52: 153–80.

Kington, T. L. 1862. *History of Frederick the Second, Emperor of the Romans.* Cambridge: Macmillan.

Knight, R. L., and S. Riedel, eds. 2002. *Aldo Leopold and the Ecological Conscience.* Oxford: Oxford University Press.

Knopf, A. 1957. Measuring Geologic Time. *Scientific Monthly* 85: 225–36.

Koerner, L. 2001. *Linnaeus: Nature and Nation.* Cambridge, MA: Harvard University Press.

Kohler, R. 2002. *Landscapes and Labscapes: Exploring the Lab-Field Border in Biology.* Chicago: University of Chicago Press.

Krause, E. 1880. *Erasmus Darwin, with a Preliminary Notice by Charles Darwin.* New York: D. Appleton and Co.

Kretch, S. 2000. *The Ecological Indian: Myth and History.* New York: W. W. Norton.

Lack, D. 1957. *Evolutionary Theory and Christian Belief, the Unresolved Conflict.* London: Methuen and Co.

Lamarck, J. B. 1783–89. *Encyclopédie méthodique botanique.* 8 vols. Paris: n.p.

———. 1801. *Système des animaux sans vertèbres, ou Tableau général des classes, des ordres et des genres de ces animaux.* Paris: Musée d'Histoire Naturelle.

———. 1802. *Hydrogéologie ou recherches sur l'influence qu'ont les eaux sur la surface du globe terrestre.* Paris: n.p.

Lankester, E., ed. 1847. *Memorials of John Ray: Consisting of His Life by Dr. Derham; Biographical and Critical Notices by Sir J. E. Smith, and Cuvier and Dupetit Thouars: With His Itineraries, Etc.* London: Ray Society.

———, ed. 1848. *The Correspondence of John Ray, Consisting of Selections From the Philosophical Letters Published by Dr. Derham, and Original Letters of John Ray, in the Collection of the British Museum.* London: Ray Society.

Lankester, E. R. 1915. *Diversions of a Naturalist.* London: Methuen.

Lansdown, R. 2006. *Strangers in the South Seas: The Idea of the Pacific in Western Thought: An Anthology.* Honolulu: University of Hawaii Press.

Layard, A. H. 1867. *Nineveh and Babylon: A Narrative of a Second Expedition to Assyria during the Years 1848, 1850, and 1851.* London: John Murray.

Lear, L. 1997. *Rachel Carson: Witness for Nature.* New York: Henry Holt and Co.

Lee, S., ed. 1899. *The Dictionary of National Biography.* Vol. 62. London and New York: MacMillan.

Leopold, A. 1933. *Game Management.* New York: Charles Scribners Sons.

———. 1953. *Round River: From the Journals of Aldo Leopold.* Ed. L. Leopold. Oxford: Oxford University Press.

———. 1968. *A Sand County Almanac and Sketches Here and There.* Oxford: Oxford University Press.

Lewis, M. W. 1999. Dividing the Ocean Sea. *Geographical Review* 89: 188–214.

Lewis, M., and W. Clark. 1902 [1814]. *History of the Expedition under the Command of Captains Lewis and Clark to the Sources of the Missouri, across the Rocky Mountains, down the Columbia River to the Pacific in 1804–6.* Vol. 2 of 3. New York: New Amsterdam Books.

———. 2002 [1904]. *The Journals of Lewis and Clark.* Ed. F. Bergon. London: Penguin Classics. (Edited version of a version originally published in 1904 by Reuben Thwaites.)

Linnaeus, C. 1811. *Lachesis Lapponica, or a Tour in Lapland Now First Published from the Original Manuscript Journal of the Celebrated Linnaeus.* 2 vols. Trans. J. E. Smith. London: White and Cochrane.

Litchfield, H. 1915. *Emma Darwin: A Century of Family Letters, 1792–1896.* 2 vols. New York: D. Appleton and Co.

Lockyer, N. 1873. The Birth of Chemistry VII. *Nature* 7: 285–87.

Locy, W. A. 1921. The Earliest Printed Illustrations of Natural History. *Scientific Monthly* 13: 238–58.

Lovejoy, A. 1936. *The Great Chain of Being: A Study of the History of an Idea.* Cambridge, MA: Harvard University Press.

Lowell, J. R. 1871. *My Garden Acquaintance.* Cambridge, MA: Houghton Mifflin.

Lurie, E. 1988. *Louis Agassiz: A Life in Science.* Baltimore: Johns Hopkins University Press.

Lyell, C. 1831. *Principles of Geology, Being an Attempt to Explain the Former Changes of the Earth's Surface, by Reference to Causes Now in Operation.* 3 vols. London: John Murray.

Lyman, R. L. 2006. Late Prehistoric and Early Historic Abundance of Columbian White-Tailed Deer, Portland Basin, Washington and Oregon, USA. *Journal of Wildlife Management* 70: 278–82.

Lyman, R. L., and S. Wolverton. 2002. The Late Prehistoric–Early Historic Game Sink in the Northwestern United States. *Conservation Biology* 16: 73–85.

Lysaght, A. M. 1971. *Joseph Banks in Newfoundland and Labrador, 1766.* Berkeley and Los Angeles: University of California Press.

Lytle, M. 2007. *The Gentle Subversive: Rachel Carson,* Silent Spring, *and the Rise of the Environmental Movement.* Oxford: Oxford University Press.

Mabey, R. 2006. *Gilbert White: A Biography of the Author of* The Natural History of Selborne. London: Profile Books Ltd.

MacArthur, R. 1958. Population Ecology of Some Warblers of Northeastern Coniferous Forests. *Ecology* 39: 599–619.

Macauley, D. 1979. *Motel of the Mysteries*. New York: Graphia Press.

Macdougal, D. 2004. *Frozen Earth: The Once and Future Story of Ice Ages*. Berkeley and Los Angeles: University of California Press.

Macgillivray, W. 1834. *Lives of Eminent Zoologists, from Aristotle to Linnaeus, with Introductory Remarks on the Study of Natural History, and Occasional Observations on the Progress of Zoology*. Edinburgh: Oliver and Boyd.

Macleod, R. 2004. *The Library of Alexandria: Centre of Learning in the Ancient World*. Rev. ed. London and New York: I. B. Tauris.

Maddock, F. 2001. *Hildegard of Bingen: The Woman of Her Age*. New York: Random House.

Maplet, J. 1930 [1567]. *A Greene Forest or a Naturall Historie, Wherein May Be Seen First the Most Sovereign Virtues in All the Whole Kinde of Stones and Metals: Next of Plants, as of Herbes, Trees, and Shrubs, Lastly of Brute Beasts, Foules, Fishes, Creeping Wormes, and Serpentes, and That Alphabetically So That a Table Shall Not Neede*. London: Hesperides Press.

Marren, P. 2005. *The New Naturalists*. London: Collins.

Martin, C. 1978. *Keepers of the Game: Indian-Animal Relationships and the Fur Trade*. Berkeley and Los Angeles: University of California Press.

Martin, P. S. 1984. Prehistoric Overkill: The Global Model. In P. S. Martin and R. G. Kleins, eds., *Quaternary Extinctions: A Prehistoric Revolution*. Tucson: University of Arizona Press, 354–403.

Mater, A. G. 1911. Alexander Agassiz, 1835–1910. *Annual Report of the Board of Regents of the Smithsonian Institution for 1910*. Washington, DC: Government Printing Office, 447–72.

May, R. 1999. Unanswered Questions in Ecology. *Philosophical Transactions of the Royal Society B: Biological Sciences* 354: 1951–59.

Mayr, E. 1982. *The Growth of Biological Thought: Diversity, Evolution, and Inheritance*. Cambridge, MA: Harvard University Press.

———. 1993. *One Long Argument: Charles Darwin and the Genesis of Modern Evolutionary Thought*. Cambridge, MA: Harvard University Press.

———. 2007. *What Makes Biology Unique? Considerations on the Autonomy of a Discipline*. Cambridge: Cambridge University Press.

McCalman, I. 2009. *Darwin's Armada: Four Voyages and the Battle for the Theory of Evolution*. New York: W. W. Norton.

McCormick, R. 1884. *Voyages of Discovery in the Arctic and Antarctic Seas, and round the World: Expedition up the Wellington Channel in Search of Sir John Franklin and Her Majesty's Ships "Erebus" and "Terror" in Her Majesty's Boat "Forlorn Hope" under the Command of the Author*. London: Sampson, Low, Marston, Searle, and Rivington.

McCullough, D. 1992. *Brave Companions: Portraits in History*. New York: Simon and Schuster.

McMahon, S. 2000. John Ray (1627–1705) and the Act of Uniformity 1662. *Notes and Records of the Royal Society of London* 54: 153–78.

Meine, C. 1988. *Aldo Leopold: His Life and Work*. Madison: University of Wisconsin Press.

Merriam, C. H. 1898. Life Zones and Crop Zones of the United States. *Department of Agriculture Bulletin* 10. Washington, DC: Government Printing Office.

———. 1914. The Museum of Vertebrate Zoology of the University of California. *Science* 40: 703–04.

———. 2008 [1910]. *The Dawn of the World: Myths and Weird Tales Told by the Mewan (Miwok) Indians of California*. New York: Forgotten Books.

Merriam, C. H., and L. Steineger. 1890. Results of a Biological Survey of the San Francisco Mountain Range and the Desert of the Little Colorado, Arizona. *North American Fauna Report* 3. Washington, DC: U.S. Department of Agriculture, Division of Ornithology and Mammalogy.

Meyer, S. 1992. Aristotle, Teleology and Reduction. *Philosophical Review* 101: 791–825.

Miall, L. C. 1912. *The Early Naturalists, Their Lives and Work 1530–1789*. London: Macmillan and Co.

Middleton, W. S. 1925. John Bartram, Botanist. *Scientific Monthly* 21: 191–216.

Moore, J. 1986. Zoology of the Pacific Railroad Surveys. *American Zoology* 26: 331–41.

Moulton, G. E. 2003. *An American Epic of Discovery: The Lewis and Clark Journals*. Lincoln: University of Nebraska Press.

Muir, J. 1911. *My First Summer in the Sierra*. New York: Houghton Mifflin & Co.

———. 1913. *The Story of My Boyhood and Youth*. Boston and New York: Houghton Mifflin & Co.

———. 1916. *A Thousand Mile Walk to the Gulf*. Ed. W. F. Badé. New York: Houghton Mifflin & Co.

Nabokov, V. 2000. *Nabokov's Butterflies: Unpublished and Uncollected Writings*. Eds. B. Boyd and R. Pyle. Boston: Beacon Press.

Newbolt, H. 1929. Captain James Cook and the Sandwich Islands. *Geographic Journal* 73: 97–101.

Newman, B. 1985. Hildegard of Bingen: Visions and Validation. *Church History* 54: 163–75.

Nichols, P. 2003. *Evolution's Captain*. New York: HarperCollins.

Nicholson, H. A. 1886. *Natural History: Its Rise and Progress in Britain as Developed in the Life and Labors of the Leading Naturalists*. London and Edinburgh: W. and R. Chambers.

Numbers, R. L. 2000. "The Most Important Biblical Discovery of Our Time": William Henry Green and the Demise of Ussher's Chronology. *Church History* 69: 257–76.

Oehser, P. H. 1952. In Memoriam: Florence Merriam Bailey. *Auk* 69: 19–26.

Ogilvie, B. 2003. The Many Books of Nature: Renaissance Naturalists and Information Overload. *Journal of the History of Ideas* 64: 29–40.

Ollivander, H., and H. Thomas, eds. 2008. *Gerard's Herbal*. London: Velluminous Press.

Oppenheim, A. L. 1965. On Royal Gardens in Mesopotamia. *Journal of Near Eastern Studies* 24: 328–33.

Outram, A. K., N. A. Stear, R. Bendrey, S. Olsen, et al. 2009. The Earliest Horse Harnessing and Milking. *Science* 323: 1332–35.

Paley, W. 1813. *Natural Theology or Evidences of the Existence and Attributes of the Deity, Collected from the Appearances of Nature*. London: J. Paulder.

Park, M. 1816. *Travels in the Interior Districts of Africa Performed in the Years 1795, 1796 and 1797*. London: John Murray.

Parker King, P. 1839. *Narrative of the Surveying Voyages of His Majesty's Ships* Adventure *and* Beagle *between the Years 1826 and 1836 Describing heir Examination of the Southern Shores of South America and the* Beagle's *Circumnavigation of the Globe*. Ed. R. Fitzory. London: Henry Colburn.

Pattingill, H. R. 1901. The Brazen Head. *Timely Topics* 7: 270.

Patton, J. S. 1919. Thomas Jefferson's Contributions to Natural History. *Natural History Magazine* (April–May). http://naturalhistorymag.com/picks-from-the-past/231435/thomas-jefferson-s-contributions-to-natural-history. (Accessed July 15, 2012.)

Pedrosa, S., M. Uzun, J.-J. Arranz, B. Gutiérrez-Gil, et al. 2005. Evidence of Three Maternal Lineages in Near Eastern Sheep Supporting Multiple Domestication Events. *Proceedings of the Royal Society B: Biological Sciences* 272: 2211–17.

Penn, D. T. 2003. The Evolutionary Roots of Our Environmental Problems: Toward a Darwinian Ecology. *Quarterly Review of Biology* 78: 275–301.

Pennant, T. 1781. *History of Quadrupeds*. 2 vols. London: B. White.

———. 1793. *The Literary Life of the Late Thomas Pennant Esq. by Himself.* London: Benjamin & John White.

———. 1784. *Arctic Zoology*. London: Henry Hughs.

Perrine, F. 1926. Uncle Sam's Camel Corps. *New Mexico Historical Review* 1: 434–44.

Perry, J. 1981. *The Discovery of the Sea*. Berkeley and Los Angeles: University of California Press.

Perry, M. 1977. Saint Mark's Trophies: Legend, Superstition, and Archaeology in Renaissance Venice. *Journal of the Warburg and Courtauld Institutes* 40: 27–49.

Pimm, S. L., M. P. Moulton, and L. J. Justice. 1994. Bird Extinctions in the Central Pacific. *Philosophical Transactions of the Royal Society of London B: Biological Sciences* 347: 27–33.

Porter, B. P. 1993. Sacred Trees, Date Palms, and the Royal Persona of Ashurnasirpal II. *Journal of Near Eastern Studies* 52: 129–39.

Powell, D. 1977. The Voyage of the Plant Nursery, H.M.S. *Providence*, 1791–1793. *Economic Botany* 31: 387–41.

Raby, P. 2001. *Alfred Russel Wallace: A Life*. Princeton, NJ: Princeton University Press.

Rader, K. A., and V. E. M. Cain. 2008. From Natural History to Science: Display and the Transformation of American Museums of Science and Nature. *Museum and Society* 6, no. 2: 152–71.

Railing, C. 1979. *The Voyage of Charles Darwin*. New York: Mayflower Books.

Ramsay, W. 1896. *The Gases of the Atmosphere: The History of Their Discovery*. London: Macmillan and Co.

Raper, H., and R. Fitzroy. 1854. Hints to Travelers. *Journal of the Royal Geographic Society of London* 24: 328–58.

Raven, C. E. 1950. *John Ray: Naturalist*. 2nd ed. Cambridge: Cambridge University Press.

Raverat, G. 1953. *Period Piece: A Cambridge Childhood*. London: Faber and Faber.

Rawling, C., ed. 1979. *The Voyage of Charles Darwin*. New York: Mayflower Books.

Ray, J. 1660. *A Catalogue of Plants Growing around Cambridge*. Cambridge: Cambridge University Press.

———. 1673. *Observations, Topographical, Moral and Physiological, Made on a Journey through Part of the Low-countries, Germany, Italy, and France, with a Catalog of Plants Not Native to England, Found Growing in Those Parts, and Their Virtues. Also*

Is Added, a Brief Account of Francis Willughby, Esq., His Voyage through a Great Part of Spain. London: John Martyn.

———. 1686. *De Historia Piscium*. London: Royal Society.

———. 1686, 1693, 1704. *Historiae Plantarum*. 3 vols. London: Smith and Benjamin.

———. 1692. *Three Physico-Theological Discourses*. London: William Innys.

———. 1714 [1691]. *The Wisdom of God Manifested in the Works of the Creation in Two Parts; viz. the Heavenly Bodies, Elements, Meteors, Fossils, Vegetables, Animals (Beasts, Birds, Fishes, and Insects) More Particularly in the Body of the Earth, Its Figure, Motion, and Consistency, and in the Admirable Structure of the Bodies of Man, and Other Animals, and Also in Their Generation Etc., with Answers to Some Objections*. London: William Innys.

———. 1732. *A Compleat Collection of English Proverbs; Also the Most Celebrated Proverbs of the Scotch, Italian, French, Spanish, and Other Languages: The Whole Methodically Digested and Illustrated with Annotations, and Proper Explications*. 3rd ed. London: J. Hughs.

———. 1882 [1682]. *Methodus Plantarum Nova, Brevitatis & Perspicuitatis Causa Synoptice in Tabulis: Exhibita Cum notis Generum tim Summorum tum subalternorum Characteristicis, Observationibis nonnullis de feminibus Plantarum & Indice Copioso*. London: Faitborne & Kersey.

Reisner, M. 1993. *Cadillac Desert: The American West and Its Disappearing Water*. New York: Penguin Books.

Rich, E.E. 1954. The Hudson's Bay Company and the Treaty of Utrecht. *Cambridge Historical Journal* 11: 183–203.

Richardson, R. 1992. *American Literature and Science*. Ed. R.J. Scholnick. Lexington: University Press of Kentucky.

Riddle, J. 1984. Byzantine Commentaries on Dioscorides. *Dumbarton Oaks Papers* 38: 95–102.

Robbins, P.I. 2007. *The Travels of Peter Kalm: Finnish-Swedish Naturalist through Colonial North America, 1748–1751*. Fleischmanns, NY: Purple Mountain Press.

Rohde, E.S. 1922. *The Old English Herbals*. London: Longman's Green and Co.

Rolle, A. 1991. *John Charles Frémont: Character as Destiny*. Norman: University of Oklahoma Press.

Roosevelt, T.R. 1920. Nature Fakers. *Nature Fakers in Roosevelt's Writings: Selections from the Writings of Theodore Roosevelt*. Ed. M. Fulton. New York: MacMilllan, 258–66.

Sacks, O. 1999. *Migraine: Understanding a Common Disorder*. New York: Vintage.

Sanchez, T. 1973. *Rabbit Boss*. New York: Random House.

Sandwith, N. Y. 1925. Humboldt and Bonpland's Itinerary in Venezuela. *Bulletin of Miscellaneous Information (Royal Gardens, Kew)* 1925: 295–310.

Sarton, G. 1924. Review [of Thorndike 1923]. *Isis* 6: 74–89.

Schlesier, K. 1853. *Lives of the Brothers Humboldt, Alexander and William*. Trans. J. Bauer. New York: Harper and Bros.

Schmidly, D. J. 2005. What It Means to Be a Naturalist and the Future of Natural History at American Universities. *Journal of Mammalogy* 86: 449–56.

Schmidt-Loske, K. 2009. *Maria Sibylla Merian: Insects of Surinam*. New York: Taschen America.

Schofield, R. 1966. The Lunar Society of Birmingham: A Bicentenary Appraisal. *Notes and Records of the Royal Society of London* 21: 144–61.

Scholnick, R. J. 1992. *American Literature and Science*. Lexington: University Press of Kentucky.

Semper, K. 1881. *Animal Life as Affected by the Natural Conditions of Existence*. New York: D. Appleton & Co.

Sellers, C. C. 1980. *Mr. Peale's Museum: Charles Wilson Peale and the First Popular Museum of Natural Science and Art*. New York: W. W. Norton.

Seton, E. T. 1898. *Wild Animals I Have Known*. New York: Grosset & Dunlap.

Sheringham, J. 1902. The Literature of Angling. *British Sea Anglers Society Quarterly* 2: 33–42.

Silver, B. 1978. William Bartram's and Other Eighteenth-Century Accounts of Nature. *Journal of the History of Ideas* 39: 597–614.

Singer, C. 1958. *From Magic to Science Essays on the Scientific Twilight*. New York: Dover.

Singer, D. W. 1932. Alchemical Writings Attributed to Roger Bacon. *Speculum* 7: 80–86.

Smith, C. H., and G. Beccaloni, eds. 2008. *Natural Selection and Beyond: The Intellectual Legacy of Alfred Russel Wallace*. Oxford: Oxford University Press.

Smith, E. 1911. *The Life of Sir Joseph Banks President of the Royal Society with Some Notices of His Friends and Contemporaries*. London: Bodley Head.

Smith, G. 2002 [1875]. *Assyrian Discoveries: An Account of Exploration and Discoveries on the Site of Nineveh during 1873 and 1874*. Piscataway, NJ: Gorgias Press.

Smith, P. 2005. *Memoir and Correspondence of Sir James Edward Smith*. Vol. 1 of 2. London: General Books.

Smith, W. R. 1904. *Brief History of the Louisiana Territory*. St. Louis: St. Louis News Co.

Sprague, T. A. 1933. Plant Morphology in Albertus Magnus. *Bulletin of Miscellaneous Information (Royal Gardens, Kew)* 1933: 431–40.

Sprunt, A. 1954. *Florida Bird Life*. New York: Coward-McCann Inc.

Stafleu, F. A. 1971. Lamarck: The Birth of Biology. *Taxon* 20: 397–442.

Stanton, W. R. 1975. *The Great United States Exploring Expedition of 1838–1842*. Berkeley and Los Angeles: University of California Press.

Steadman, D. W. 1989. Extinction of Birds in Eastern Polynesia: A Review of the Record and Comparison with Other Pacific Island Groups. *Journal of Archaeology* 16: 177–205.

———. 1995. Prehistoric Extinctions of Pacific Island Birds: Biodiversity Meets Zooarchaeology. *Science* 267: 1123–31.

Stegner, W. E. 1992. *Beyond the Hundredth Meridian: John Wesley Powell and the Second Opening of the West*. New York: Penguin Books.

Stein, B. R. 2001. *On Her Own Terms: Annie Montague Alexander and the Rise of Science in the American West*. Berkeley and Los Angeles: University of California Press.

Stevens, A. 1852. Albertus Magnus. *National Magazine* 1: 309–10.

Stevenson, H. 1866. *The Birds of Norfolk with Remarks on Their Habits, Migration, and Local Distribution*. 3 vols. London: John Van Voorst.

Stilling, P. 2012. *Ecology: Global Insights and Investigations*. New York: McGraw-Hill.

Stoddard, R. H. 1859. *The Life and Travels of Alexander von Humboldt with an Account of His Discoveries and Notices of His Scientific Fellow-Labourers and Contemporaries*. London: James Blackwell & Co.

Stoever, D. H. 1794. *The Life of Sir Charles Linnaeus*. Trans. J. Trapp. London: Hobson.

Stothers, R. B. 2004. Ancient Scientific Basis of the "Great Serpent" from Historical Evidence. *Isis* 95: 220–38.

Stresemann, E. 1975. *Ornithology from Aristotle to the Present*. Cambridge, MA: Harvard University Press.

Surovell, T., and N. Waguespack. 2009. Human Prey Choice in the Late Pleistocene and Its Relation to Megafaunal Extinctions. In G. Haynes, ed., *American Megafaunal Extinctions at the End of the Pleistocene*. New York: Springer, 77–105.

Synge, M. B. 1897. *Captain James Cook's Voyages around the World*. London: Thomas Nelson and Sons.

Tansley, A. 1923. *Practical Plant Ecology*. London: Allen & Unwin.

Thiem, J. 1979. The Great Library of Alexandria Burnt: Towards the History of a Symbol. *Journal of the History of Ideas* 40: 507–26.

Thomas, N. 2003. *Discoveries: The Voyages of Capt. James Cook*. London: Penguin.

Thomas, P. D. 1996. Thomas Jefferson, Meriwether Lewis, the Corps of Discovery and the Investigation of Western Fauna. *Transactions of the Kansas Academy of Sciences* 99: 69–85.

Thompson, E.T. 1901. *Lives of the Hunted, Containing a True Account of the Doings of Five Quadrupeds & Three Birds*. New York: Charles Scribners Sons.

Thoreau, H.D. 1863 [1842]. Natural History of Massachusetts. In H.D. Thoreau, ed., *Excursions*. Boston: Ticknor and Fields, 26–46.

———. 1873 [1849]. *A Week on the Concord and Merrimack Rivers*. New and rev. ed. Boston: James Osgood and Co.

———. 1883 [1863]. *Excursions*. Boston: Houghton Mifflin & Co.

———. 1887 [1860]. *The Succession of Forest Trees & Wild Apples: With a Biographical Sketch by R.W. Emerson*. Boston: Houghton Mifflin & Co.

———. 1907. *The Writings of Henry David Thoreau: Journals*. Vol. 9: *August 16, 1856–August 7, 1857*. Ed. B. Torrey. Boston and New York: Houghton Mifflin & Co.

———. 1910 [1854]. *Walden*. Ed. R.M. Alden. New York: Longmans, Green, and Co.

———. 1993 [1854]. *Walden*. New York: Random House.

Thorndike, L. 1914. Roger Bacon and Experimental Method in the Middle Ages. *Philosophical Review* 23: 271–98.

———. 1916. The True Roger Bacon II. *American Historical Review* 21: 468–80.

———. 1922. Galen: The Man and His Times. *Scientific Monthly* 14: 83–93.

———. 1923. *A History of Magic and Experimental Science during the First Thirteen Centuries of Our Era*. 8 vols. New York: Columbia University Press.

Thorpe, T.E. 1894. *Essays in Historical Chemistry*. London: Macmillan and Co.

Tinbergen, N. 1963. On Aims and Methods of Ethology. *Zeitschrift für Tierpsychology* 20: 410–33.

Torrey, J. 1824. *A Flora of the Northern and Middle Sections of the United States: Or, A Systematic Arrangement and Description of All the Plants Hitherto Discovered in the United States North of Virginia*. New York: T. and J. Swords.

Trompf, G. 1973. The Concept of the Carolingean Renaissance. *Journal of the History of Ideas* 34: 3–26.

Trotter, S. 1903. Notes on the Ornithological Observations of Peter Kalm. *Auk* 20: 249–62.

Turner, W. 1903 [1544]. *Turner on Birds: A Short and Succinct History of the Principal Birds Noticed by Pliny and Aristotle*. Ed. A.H. Evans. Cambridge: Cambridge University Press.

Uglow, J. 2002. *The Lunar Men*. 2002. New York: Farrar, Straus and Giroux.

Van Horne, J., and N. Hoffman. 2004. *America's Curious Botanist: A Tercentennial*

Reappraisal of John Bartram (1699–1777). Memoirs of the American Philosophical Society, series 243. Philadelphia: American Philosophical Society.

Vila, R. C. Bell, R. Macniven, B. Goldman-Huertas, et al. 2011. "Phylogeny and Palaeoecology of *Polyommatus* Blue Butterflies Show Beringia Was a Climate-Regulated Gateway to the New World." *Proceedings of the Royal Society B: Biological Sciences*, doi 10:1098/rspb 2010.2213.

Voltaire, M. de. 1756. *An Essay on Universal History, the Manners, and Spirit of Nations*. Vol. 4 of 4. *From the Reign of Charlemaign to the Age of Lewis XIV*. London: General Books.

Vuilleumier, F. 2003. Neotropical Ornithology: Then and Now. *Auk* 120: 577–90.

Waguespack, N. 2005. The Organization of Male and Female Labor in Foraging Societies: Implications for Early Paleoindian Archaeology. *American Anthropologist* 107: 666–76.

———. 2007. Why We're Still Arguing about the Pleistocene Occupation of the Americas. *Evolutionary Anthropology* 16: 63–74.

Waguespack, N., and T. Surovell. 2003. Clovis Hunting Strategies, or How to Make Out on Plentiful Resources. *American Antiquity* 68: 333–52.

Walker, D.A. 1888. The Assyrian King, Asurbanipal. *Old Testament Student* 8: 57–62, 96–101.

Wallace, A.R. 1853. *Palm Trees of the Amazon and Their Uses*. London: John Van Voorst.

———. 1855. On the Law Which Has Regulated the Introduction of New Species. *Annals and Magazine of Natural History* 16: 184–96.

———. 1858. On the Tendency of Varieties to Depart Indefinitely from the Original Type. *Journal of the Proceedings of the Linnean Society* 3: 53–62.

———. 1869. *The Malay Archipelago: The Land of the Orang-Utan, and the Bird of Paradise: A Narrative of Travel with Studies of Man and Nature*. New York: Harper and Bros.

———. 1876. *The Geographical Distribution of Animals, with a Study of the Relations of Living and Extinct Faunas as Elucidating the Past Changes of the Earth's Surface*. 2 vols. New York: Harper and Bros.

———. 1880. *Island Life, or The Phenomena and Causes of Insular Faunas and Floras, Including a Revision and Attempted Solution of the Problem of Geological Climates*. London: Macmillan and Co.

———. 1889a. *Darwinism, an Exposition of the Theory of Natural Selection with Some of Its Applications*. 2nd ed. London: Macmillan and Co.

———. 1889b [1853]. *Travels on the Amazon and the Rio Negro, with an Account of the*

Native Tribes and Observations on the Climate, Geology, and Natural History of the Amazon Valley. London: Ward, Locke, and Co.

———. 1899. *The Wonderful Century, Its Successes and Failures*. New York: Dodd, Mead and Co.

———. 1905. *My Life: A Record of Events and Opinions*. Vol. 1. London: George Bell and Sons.

———. 1907. *Is Mars Habitable? A Critical Examination of Professor Percival Lowell's Book "Mars and Its Canals" with an Alternative Explanation*. London: Macmillan and Co.

———. 1908. *My Life: A Record of Events and Opinions*. Vol. 2. London: Chapman and Hall.

———. 1915. *Letters and Reminiscences*. Ed. J. Marchant. New York: Harper and Bros.

Walls, L. D. 2009. *Passage to Cosmos: Alexander von Humboldt and the Shaping of America*. Chicago: University of Chicago Press.

Walters, S. M., and E. A. Stow. 2001. *Darwin's Mentor John Stevens Henslow, 1796–1861*. Cambridge: Cambridge University Press.

Walzer, R. 1953. New Light on the Arabic Translations of Aristotle. *Oriens* 6: 91–142.

Warner, S. 1982 [1946]. *The Portrait of a Tortoise, Extracted from the Journals of Gilbert White*. London: Avon Books.

Waterfield, G. 1963. *Layard of Nineveh*. London: John Murray.

Weher, E., A. van der Werf, K. Thompson, M. Roderick, E. Garnier, and O. Eriksson. 1999. Challenging Theophrastus: A Common Core List of Plant Traits for Functional Ecology. *Journal of Vegetation Science* 10: 609–20.

Werf, E. V. 1992. Lack's Clutch Size Hypothesis: An Examination of the Evidence Using Meta-Analysis. *Ecology* 73: 1699–1705.

White, G. 1774. Account of the House Martin or Martlet, in a Letter from the Rev. Gilbert White to the Hon. Daines Barrington. *Philosophical Transactions of the Royal Society* 64: 196–201.

———. 1911 [1788]. *The Natural History and Antiquities of Selborne in the County of Southampton*. London: Macmillan and Co.

———. 1986. *The Journals of Gilbert White 1751–1773*. Vol. 1 of 3. Eds. F. Greenoak and R. Mabey. London: Century Hudson.

White, L. Jr. 1936. The Byzantinization of Sicily. *American Historical Review* 42: 1–21.

Wyhe, J. van. 2011. T*he Complete Works of Charles Darwin Online*. http://darwin-online.org.uk/EditorialIntroductions/Chancellor_Humboldt.html. (Accessed July 2 2012.)

Williams, G. C., and R. M. Nesse. 1991. The Dawn of Darwinian Medicine. *Quarterly Review of Biology* 66: 1–21.

Williams, R. M. 1994. Annie Montague Alexander: Explorer, Naturalist, Philanthropist. *Hawaiian Journal of History* 28: 113–27.

Williams-Ellis, A. 1966. *Darwin's Moon: A Biography of Alfred Russel Wallace*. London: Blackie and Sons.

Willughby, F. 1686. *Historia Piscum*. London: Royal Society of London.

Wilson, D. S. 1978. *In the Presence of Nature*. Boston: University of Massachusetts Press.

Wilson, E. O. 1994. *Naturalist*. Washington, DC: Island Press.

Winsor, M. P. 1991. *Reading the Shape of Nature: Comparative Zoology at the Agassiz Museum*. Chicago: University of Chicago Press.

Wittkower, R. 1942. Marvels of the East: A Study in the History of Monsters. *Journal of the Warburg and Courtald Institutes* 5: 159–97.

Wood, C. A., and F. M. Fyfe, eds. 1943. *The Art of Falconry by Frederick II of Hohenstaufen*. Stanford, CA: Stanford University Press.

Wood, N. 1834. *Ornithologist's Textbook*. London: John W. Parker.

Wood, W. 1634. *New England's Prospect: A True, Lively, and Experimental Description of That Part of America Commonly Called New England: Discovering the State of That Countrie Both as It Stands to Our New-Come English Planters; and the Old Native Inhabitants*. London: Thomas Cotes.

Woodcock, G. 1969. *Henry Walter Bates, Naturalist of the Amazons*. London: Faber and Faber.

Woodruff, A. W. 1965. Darwin's Health in Relation to His Voyage to South America. *British Medical Journal* 1: 745–50.

Worster, D. 1993. *The Wealth of Nature: Environmental History and the Ecological Imagination*. Oxford: Oxford University Press.

———. 2001. *A River Running West: The Life of John Wesley Powell*. Oxford: Oxford University Press.

———. 2008. *A Passion for Nature: The Life of John Muir*. Oxford: Oxford University Press.

Yoon, C. K. 2009. *Naming Nature: The Clash between Instinct and Science*. New York: W. W. Norton.

Young, C. 2002. *In the Absence of Predators: Conservation and Controversy on the Kaibab Plateau*. Omaha: University of Nebraska Press.

Young, D. A. B. 1997. Darwin's Illness and Systematic Lupus Erythematosus. *Notes and Records of the Royal Society of London* 51: 77–86.

Zeder, M. A., and B. Hesse. 2000. The Initial Domestication of Goats *(Capra hircus)* in the Zagros Mountains 10,000 Years Ago. *Science* 287: 2254–57.

INDEX